D1545456

"In *Breaking the Devil's Pact*, Jacobs and Cooperman persuasively show that the Teamsters could be freed from the tentacles of mob bosses only by an imaginative use of the civil remedies of RICO; as Congress rightly foresaw, criminal prosecutions alone were not enough."
> —G. ROBERT BLAKEY, Notre Dame Law School, principal architect of RICO

"This book is a very important addition to the already most impressive series of studies Jacobs published in the last decades on the manifold ways organized crime can get embedded in core institutions, key industries and black markets and on the huge long-term efforts it takes to liberate societies to a certain extent from such a parasitical phenomenon. For European readers the overwhelming lesson is that competent, experienced and dedicated prosecutors, police officers, and judges are an equally strategic precondition for any successful campaign against organized crime as an appropriate legal framework to contain its most damaging societal manifestations."
> —C. J. C. F. FIJNAUT, Tilburg University

"*Breaking the Devil's Pact* tells the compelling story of the government's Herculean effort to break La Cosa Nostra's stranglehold over a notorious union. It will shock and surprise you, proving once again that the truth really is stranger than fiction."
> —RANDY MASTRO, Litigation Partner, Gibson Dunn & Crutcher LLP, and former federal prosecutor

"Court-ordered reform of a private organization is more easily prescribed than implemented. *Breaking the Devil's Pact* is an intriguing account of a continuing, decades-long struggle to rid a powerful union of corrupt influences. It will certainly appeal to specialists in organized crime and labor relations. Moreover, it will be of interest well beyond a North American readership. Regulatory scholars around the world will note the very real limits to what they call 'enforced self-regulation.' Democratic theorists will recognize the challenge of voter apathy. Sociologists of organizations will see an extreme example of inertia. Political scientists will be heartened by the apolitical nature of reform efforts over four successive presidential administrations, but disappointed with the slow pace of change. Metaphorically speaking, *Breaking the Devil's Pact* is a mansion with many fascinating rooms."
> —PETER GRABOSKY, FASSA, Professor, Regulatory Institutions Network, Australian National University

Breaking the Devil's Pact

The Battle to Free the Teamsters from the Mob

James B. Jacobs and
Kerry T. Cooperman

NEW YORK UNIVERSITY PRESS
New York and London

NEW YORK UNIVERSITY PRESS
New York and London
www.nyupress.org

References to Internet websites (URLs) were accurate at the time of writing.
Neither the authors nor New York University Press is responsible for URLs
that may have expired or changed since the manuscript was prepared.

Library of Congress Cataloging-in-Publication Data
Jacobs, James B.
Breaking the devil's pact : the battle to free the Teamsters from the mob /
James B. Jacobs, Kerry T. Cooperman.
p. cm. Includes bibliographical references and index.
ISBN 978-0-8147-4308-9 (hardback) — ISBN 978-0-8147-4366-9 (ebook)
ISBN 978-0-8147-4367-6 (ebook)
1. United States. Dept. of Justice.—Trials, litigation, etc. 2. International
Brotherhood of Teamsters—Trials, litigation, etc. 3. Mafia trials—United States.
4. Racketeering—United States—History. 5. Labor unions—Corrupt practices
—United States—History. 6. Organized crime investigation—United States—
History. 7. Giuliani, Rudolph W. I. Cooperman, Kerry T.   II. Title.
KF228.U5J327 2011
345.73'0267—dc23   2011026377

Manufactured in the United States of America

10 9 8 7 6 5 4 3 2 1

To the friends who enrich my life

—JBJ

To Emily and my parents

—KTC

Contents

Acronyms and Abbreviations

ACLU   American Civil Liberties Union
AFL-CIO   American Federation of Labor–Congress of Industrial
           Organizations
AUD   Association for Union Democracy
AUSA   Assistant U.S. Attorney
BLAST   Brotherhood of Loyal Americans and Strong Teamsters
BLET   Brotherhood of Locomotive Engineers and Trainmen
BMWE   Brotherhood of Maintenance of Way Employees
CI   Chief Investigator
CIO   Congress of Industrial Organizations
DNC   Democratic National Committee
DOL   U.S. Department of Labor
DOJ   U.S. Department of Justice
EAM   Election Appeals Master
EO   Election Officer
EPC   Ethical Practices Committee
ERISA   Employee Retirement Income Security Act
FBI   Federal Bureau of Investigation
GCIU   Graphic Communications International Union
GEB   General Executive Board
IA   Independent Administrator
IBT   International Brotherhood of Teamsters
IO   Investigations Officer
IRB   Independent Review Board
LCN   Cosa Nostra
LIUNA   Laborers' International Union of America
LMRDA   Labor Management Reporting and Disclosure Act, a.k.a.
           Landrum-Griffin Act
NLRB   National Labor Relations Board
NYC   New York City

OCRS	Organized Crime and Racketeering Section of U.S. Department of Justice
PCOC	President's Commission on Organized Crime
RFK	Robert F. Kennedy
RICO	Racketeer Influenced and Corrupt Organizations Act
RISE	Respect, Integrity, Strength, and Ethics
SDNY	Southern District of New York
SEIU	Service Employees International Union
TDU	Teamsters for a Democratic Union
UMW	United Mine Workers
UPS	United Parcel Service

Preface

[United States. v. International Brotherhood of Teamsters]
flies in the face of democratic principles [and] . . . smacks of
totalitarianism.   —U.S. Senator Orrin Hatch, July 1988

[United States. v. International Brotherhood of Teamsters] is the
most significant organized-crime-[control] measure in the history
of the United States.
                    —Michael Cherkasky, IBT election officer, April 1998

I

I first heard of *United States v. International Brotherhood of Teamsters* in
the summer of 1988. Marla Alhadeff, an assistant U.S. attorney in Manhattan, called to ask if I would serve as an expert witness in a civil RICO
(Racketeer Influenced and Corrupt Organizations Act) case that U.S. Attorney Rudolph Giuliani had just filed against a slew of Cosa Nostra figures and the leaders of the International Brotherhood of Teamsters (IBT).
She sent me the RICO complaint and a box of supporting documents.
The complaint laid out a compelling story of systemic union corruption
and organized-crime racketeering over several decades. The government's
narrative of Cosa Nostra's infiltration and exploitation of the Teamsters
Union was not a revelation because, over the years, congressional hearings, criminal prosecutions, and media accounts had illuminated much of
that history.

In its scope and ambition, *U.S. v. IBT* would clearly be a seminal case.
The U.S. Department of Justice (DOJ) was simultaneously taking on the
nation's largest and most powerful union and the nation's most powerful
crime syndicate. This was also the first civil RICO lawsuit against an international union. I imagined, with trepidation, sitting on the witness stand

across from rows of defendants: nineteen Teamsters officials and twenty-six reputed mobsters.

I was both relieved and disappointed when, several months later, the parties settled, agreeing that there should be no organized-crime influence in the union and that the district court judge would appoint remedial officers to enforce a two-pronged consent decree. An investigations officer (IO) and independent administrator (IA) would investigate, "prosecute," adjudicate, and sanction IBT members' violations of the union's disciplinary rules. An election officer (EO) would supervise nationwide rank-and-file elections of IBT international officers.

I turned my attention to other research projects. However, while working on *Busting the Mob: United States v. Cosa Nostra* (1994), a contemporary history of the federal government's effort to eradicate Cosa Nostra, I encountered *U.S. v. IBT* again. Part 2 of my book consisted of five chapters, each devoted to a major organized-crime case of the 1980s. Two cases involved civil RICO lawsuits against the Teamsters Union. The first was DOJ's 1982 suit against Union City, New Jersey IBT Local 560. Controlled by powerful figures in the Genovese crime family, Local 560 was one of the most "mobbed-up" union locals in the United States. A year-long trial ended in a resounding government victory. The federal judge appointed a trustee to run Local 560 until it was purged of Cosa Nostra's presence and influence.

The second Teamsters case covered in *Busting the Mob* was *U.S. v. IBT*. Writing that chapter required a close examination of the litigation. By the time *Busting the Mob* was published, the *U.S. v. IBT* settlement had been in effect for several years. Ron Carey, an insurgent, had won an extraordinary victory for the general presidency in the first direct rank-and-file election of international officers. Moreover, the court-appointed disciplinary officers (the IA and IO) had expelled dozens of corrupt officials from the union for, among other things, being members of organized crime, associating with members of organized crime, stealing from the union, and obstructing the court-appointed officers' investigations. The remedial phase of the lawsuit seemed to be succeeding spectacularly. I could not have imagined that, a few years later, the court officers would expel General President Carey from the union or that, in 2011, they would still be on the job.

My 1999 book, *Gotham Unbound: How New York City Was Liberated from the Grip of Organized Crime*, focused on what federal prosecutors and New York City Mayor Giuliani's administration were doing to eliminate the five Cosa Nostra crime families' (Lucchese, Bonanno, Gambino, Colombo, and Genovese) entrenched position in New York City's economy, especially their control of union locals in the construction industry, garment center, cargo operations at JFK Airport, Fulton Fish Market, and Javitz Convention Center. The Cosa Nostra crime families leveraged their influence and control of unions (especially Teamsters local unions) to take over companies and set up employer cartels. However, through criminal prosecutions, civil RICO lawsuits against union locals, and innovative administrative licensing strategies (e.g., requiring a license to operate a carting company in NYC), the government had significantly weakened Cosa Nostra's grip.

In the early 2000s, I myself played a minor role in *U.S. v. IBT*. IBT General President Jim Hoffa (Jimmy Hoffa's son), who had succeeded Ron Carey, hired Edwin Stier, the former court-appointed trustee in the IBT Local 560 case, to lead an internal IBT anticorruption unit (Project RISE) that would demonstrate to DOJ and the federal judge that the *U.S. v. IBT* consent decree was no longer necessary. Stier, in turn, appointed an advisory board of organized-crime and labor-relations experts. Through service on that board, I became aware of some of the hundreds of legal battles over the court-appointed officers' authority and decisions.

The *U.S. v. IBT* remediation reached one of several critical moments in 2004, when Edwin Stier and his top assistant, former FBI official James Kossler, resigned from Project RISE, charging that General President Hoffa had reneged on his commitment to give Stier's team free rein to investigate corruption and racketeering. After the advisory board dissolved, a student coauthor and I wrote a journal article about the rise and fall of Project RISE. I then turned my attention to writing *Mobsters, Unions, and Feds: The Mafia and the American Labor Movement* (2006), a study of when, why, and how the Cosa Nostra organized-crime families became involved in labor unions, expanded their power and influence, profited from labor racketeering, and operated without significant opposition from labor officials, employers, or federal, state, and local law-enforcement agencies.

I thought I was finished writing about labor racketeering. But as the remedial phase of *U.S. v. IBT* went on and on, I realized that this case was the most important labor-union litigation since the 1950s. First, at the time the lawsuit was filed, the IBT had the largest membership of any U.S. private-sector union. Second, the IBT was indisputably the nation's most powerful union. Third, the IBT was the most written-about union. More than twenty books and scores of articles by journalists, historians, labor studies scholars, and Teamsters offer a rich, if uneven, history of a single labor union, thereby providing a window on twentieth- and twenty-first-century American labor history and American history generally. Obviously, the case warranted a major study. Thus, in 2007 and 2009, a student coauthor and I wrote two articles about the *U.S. v. IBT* remediation, one focusing on the disciplinary machinery and the other on the electoral reforms.

Because *U.S. v. IBT* was, first and foremost, meant to sever ties between Cosa Nostra and its most important economic and political power base, the IBT, this study also contributes to twentieth- and twenty-first-century organized-crime studies, especially to the history of the government's organized-crime-control strategies. *U.S. v. IBT* was groundbreaking for federal law enforcement because it stretched the legs of civil RICO farther than ever before. DOJ sought to purge Cosa Nostra's presence and influence from an international union (the United States, Canada, and Puerto Rico) with nearly seven hundred local and regional affiliates. *U.S. v. IBT* tested DOJ's ability to use civil RICO to achieve systemic organizational reform, a goal that scores of criminal prosecutions had failed to achieve. Moreover, the stakes were huge. Failure would likely dissuade DOJ attorneys from bringing future civil RICO suits against systemically corrupted organizations and might thereby encourage labor racketeering. Success would likely encourage similar lawsuits against organized crime's influence in other unions.

A close study of *U.S. v. IBT* also contributes to the history of institutional-reform litigation. Much of the extensive academic debate on the proper relationship between federal courts and state/local government agencies takes its data from constitutional litigation against public agencies, such as prisons, jails, mental hospitals, and schools. The use of litigation to reform systemically corrupted private-sector organizations has attracted little attention, except for the nascent scholarly corpus on the use of deferred prosecution agreements (requiring organizational reform in lieu of prosecution) in corporate-crime cases.

U.S. v. IBT also offers opportunity for an important case study of the potential and limits of union democracy. No other international union, let alone a union as large, geographically diffuse, and politically established as the IBT, has undergone as far-reaching a compulsory (or even voluntary) democratization. Since 1991, a court-appointed election officer, working with a sizeable staff, has thoroughly supervised five IBT international-officer elections. The consent decree's election machinery requires not only direct rank-and-file, secret-ballot election of international officers but also meticulous oversight of local-union delegate elections, campaign donations and expenditures, candidate nominations, and general-election balloting.

U.S. v. IBT also tests the efficacy of union democracy as an anticorruption prophylactic. In shaping its settlement demands, DOJ accepted union democracy proponents' argument that, in free and fair elections, the IBT rank and file would "throw the crooks out" and that the requirement that candidates for union office stand for election would, going forward, prevent mobsters and their associates from attaining positions of influence. That hypothesis led the government to insist on radical election reforms. The electoral-reform prong of the case therefore holds important lessons for the potential of both union democracy and political democracy to prevent corruption and racketeering.

II

This book presents a historical analysis of *U.S. v. IBT*, from its conception in the late 1980s through mid-2011. Chapter 1 introduces the most important participants in the litigation: the plaintiff Department of Justice and its investigative arm, the Federal Bureau of Investigation (FBI); the defendant International Brotherhood of Teamsters and that union's top officers; the defendant Cosa Nostra labor racketeers; the union reformers who participated in *U.S. v. IBT* as amici curiae; and the district court judge who presided over the case from 1988 to 2000.

Chapter 2 explains how the DOJ lawyers adapted the civil RICO law for use against entrenched corruption and racketeering in the IBT. It also explicates the 1988 settlement, which is still in effect in 2011.

Chapter 3 documents the IBT leadership's postsettlement change of heart and its resistance to the consent decree that formalized the settlement. The court-appointed officers and the federal district court judge had to withstand a legal onslaught. They issued hundreds of orders and opinions to compel the IBT's compliance.

Chapter 4 deals with the crucial 1989–1992 period, when the court-appointed investigations officer prosecuted and the independent administrator adjudicated scores of disciplinary cases against IBT officials. In three years, these officers laid down a comprehensive administrative law of IBT disciplinary violations on which, beginning in late 1992, the independent review board (IRB) continued to elaborate.

Chapter 5 focuses on the watershed 1991 election of IBT international officers—the first election supervised by the court-appointed election officer. To implement a one-man-one-vote, secret mail-ballot election for a North America–wide union with nearly 1.7 million members required, in the district court judge's words, "herculean" effort. Insurgent candidate Ron Carey's victory seemed to vindicate the amici curiae's faith in the rank and file.

Chapter 6 discusses enforcement of IBT administrative discipline during Ron Carey's administration (1992–1997). Soon after Carey took office, disciplinary authority under the consent decree shifted from the investigations officer and independent administrator to an independent review board. The IRB phase of the remediation gives the IBT a role in charging, adjudicating, and punishing disciplinary offenses, but the IRB continues to function as the front-line investigator and supervising adjudicator. Carey's own anticorruption initiatives drew praise from supporters and criticism from opponents.

If the election of Carey and the successful transfer of disciplinary authority from the IA/IO to the IRB marked high tide in DOJ's and the federal court's institutional-reform efforts, the 1996 election, covered in chapter 7, marked low tide. While Carey narrowly defeated Jim Hoffa, a post-election investigation revealed that the Carey campaign had diverted IBT funds to Carey's reelection campaign. The court-appointed officers, who previously saw Carey's victories as furthering IBT reform, declared the 1996 election null and void, disqualified Carey from the rerun election, and expelled him from the union.

Chapter 8 covers Jim Hoffa's victory in the 1998 rerun election, which almost did not occur on account of the government's and union's unwillingness to pay for the election supervision. During his campaign, Hoffa promised to persuade DOJ and the district court judge that the *U.S. v. IBT* consent decree was no longer necessary. After he became general president, Hoffa hired Edwin Stier, the former prosecutor who had served for over twelve years as the court-appointed trustee in the IBT Local 560 case, to establish "an FBI-caliber" internal IBT anticorruption unit called Project RISE. Stier hired, as his chief assistant, James Kossler, who had once headed the New York City FBI office's organized-crime investigations.

Chapter 9 describes the 2001 IBT election and the demise of Project RISE. Hoffa won a convincing reelection victory over Tom Leedham, who was strongly supported by Teamsters for a Democratic Union (TDU), a rank-and-file Teamsters organization that has vigorously opposed the reigning IBT leadership since the mid-1970s. In 2004, Stier and Kossler re-signed from Project RISE, claiming that, in response to pressure from cor-rupt Teamsters officials and mobsters in Chicago and elsewhere, Hoffa had stymied their organized-crime investigations.

Chapter 10 covers the 2006 IBT election, the IRB's ongoing disciplinary work, and the run-up to the 2011 IBT election. In December 2006, Hoffa was elected for a third time (again defeating Tom Leedham by a wide mar-gin), demonstrating that, despite fair and strictly monitored election pro-cedures, it is extremely difficult for insurgents to defeat incumbents. In the 2011 election, International Vice President Fred Gegare and New York City IBT Local 805 President Sandy Pope, endorsed by TDU, are challenging Hoffa. Now in its fourth five-year term, the IRB has a smaller caseload but continues to identify serious wrongdoing, including membership in and association with Cosa Nostra.

Chapter 11 seeks to draw lessons from the (so far) twenty-two-year his-tory of *U.S. v. IBT* and speculates about how the case will someday conclude.

James B. Jacobs
NYU School of Law

U.S. v. IBT Timeline

June 28, 1988   U.S. Attorney Rudolph Giuliani and Assistant U.S. Attorney Randy Mastro file a 113-page civil RICO complaint in federal district court in Manhattan against the International Brotherhood of Teamsters (IBT), its General Executive Board (GEB), nineteen individual IBT officers, Cosa Nostra's "Commission," and twenty-six Cosa Nostra members and associates.

March 13, 1989   The IBT and its GEB members sign a settlement with the U.S. Department of Justice (DOJ) providing for three court-appointed officers (independent administrator, investigations officer, election officer) to enforce a consent decree imposing strong disciplinary and election remedies.

June 24–27, 1991   The IBT holds its quinquennial (every five years) international convention in Orlando, Florida. Elected delegates nominate the international-officer candidates. The rank and file will vote by secret mail ballot.

December 10–13, 1991   Ron Carey, president of New York City IBT Local 804, defeats R.V. Durham and Walter Shea for IBT general president in the union's first direct rank-and-file election of international officers.

August 19, 1992   Judge David Edelstein formally approves rules for the operation of the independent review board (IRB), a triumvirate of court-appointed

	officers who, under the terms of the consent decree, replace the independent administrator and investigations officer.
July 15–19, 1996	At the IBT's Philadelphia convention, delegates nominate candidates for international office, including incumbent General President Ron Carey and challenger James P. ("Jim") Hoffa.
December 16, 1996	Carey defeats Hoffa 52 percent to 48 percent in the 1996 election for IBT general president.
August 22, 1997	Election Officer Barbara Zack Quindel announces her decision not to certify the results of the 1996 election because of the Carey campaign's use of IBT funds. She orders a rerun election for general president and for twenty-two other international officer positions.
November 17, 1997	Election Appeals Master Kenneth Conboy disqualifies Carey from the rerun election. Carey takes a leave of absence and General Secretary-Treasurer Tom Sever becomes acting general president.
July 27, 1998	Concluding that Carey knew or should have known about his campaign's illegal fundraising scheme, the IRB expels him from the IBT.
December 1998	Jim Hoffa easily wins the 1998 rerun election for IBT general president and vows to obtain termination of the *U.S. v. IBT* consent decree.
July 28, 1999	The IBT's GEB approves Project RISE, an anticorruption initiative meant to persuade DOJ and Judge Edelstein that the IBT can police itself. Hoffa appoints Edwin Stier to lead Project RISE.
August 19, 2000	Judge Edelstein dies at age ninety. *U.S. v. IBT* is reassigned to Chief Judge Loretta A. Preska.

January 2001   Ron Carey is indicted on federal perjury charges. Nine months later, a jury acquits him on all charges. Carey's lifetime expulsion from the IBT remains in effect.

November 2001   Jim Hoffa defeats Tom Leedham by a large majority in the election for IBT general president.

April 28, 2004   Project RISE ends abruptly when Edwin Stier and James Kossler resign, claiming that Hoffa is blocking their investigations and refusing to take action against corrupt IBT locals.

November 2006   Hoffa once again easily defeats Tom Leedham.

May 25, 2010   Jim Hoffa announces that he will seek reelection. International Vice President Fred Gegare announces that he will challenge Hoffa.

July 15, 2010   IBT General Secretary-Treasurer Tom Keegel, who had initially agreed to run for reelection on Hoffa's slate, unexpectedly announces his retirement. International Vice President Ken Hall replaces Keegel as Hoffa's general secretary-treasurer running mate.

October 11, 2010   New York City IBT Local 805 President Sandy Pope, endorsed by Teamsters for a Democratic Union, announces her candidacy for IBT general president.

June 27–July 1, 2011   The twenty-sixth international IBT convention is held in Las Vegas.

Principal Names

U.S. Attorneys (Southern District of New York)

Rudolph Giuliani: June 3, 1983–January 1, 1989
Benito Romano: January 1, 1989–October 16, 1989
Otto Obermaier: October 16, 1989–June 1993
Mary Jo White: June 1993–January 7, 2002
James Comey: January 7, 2002–December 15, 2003
David Kelley: December 15, 2003–September 2005
Michael Garcia: September 2005–December 1, 2008
Lev Dassin: December 1, 2008–August 13, 2009
Preet Bharara: August 13, 2009–

District Court Judges (Southern District of New York)

David N. Edelstein: presided over *U.S. v. IBT*, 1988–2000
Loretta A. Preska: presided over *U.S. v. IBT*, 2000–

IBT General Presidents

Cornelius Shea: 1903–1907
Daniel Tobin: 1907–1952
David Beck: 1952–1957
James R. Hoffa: 1957–1971
Frank Fitzsimmons: 1971–May 7, 1981
George Mock: May 7–15, 1981
Roy Williams: May 15, 1981–April 1983
Jackie Presser: April 1983–May 4, 1988
Weldon Mathis: May 5, 1988–July 18, 1988

William McCarthy: July 18, 1988–January 1991
Ron Carey: February 1991–July 27, 1998
Tom Sever: July 27, 1998–December 5, 1998
James P. Hoffa: December 1998–

Disciplinary Officers during IO/IA Phase (1989–1992)

Charles Carberry (investigations officer)
Frederick Lacey (independent administrator)

Independent Review Board (1992–Present)

Charles Carberry: IRB chief investigator, March 1992–
Frederick Lacey: IRB member appointed by DOJ, March 1992–June 2001
Harold Burke: IRB member appointed by IBT, April 1992–June 1993
William Webster: IRB member appointed by Judge Edelstein, August
    1992–
Grant Crandall: IRB member appointed by IBT, June 1993–June 2001
Benjamin Civiletti: IRB member appointed by DOJ, June 2001–
Joseph DiGenova: IRB member appointed by IBT, June 2001–

Election Officers

Michael Holland: 1991 election
Barbara Quindel: 1996 election
Michael Cherkasky: 1998 election
William Wertheimer: 2001 election
Richard Mark: 2006 and 2011 elections
Kenneth Conboy: election appeals master, 1995–

Others Key Players

Marla Alhadeff: assistant U.S. attorney working on *U.S. v. IBT*, 1988–1997
Howard Anderson: principal author of Project RISE's written history of
    the connection between organized crime and the Teamsters Union

Herman Benson: founder of Association for Union Democracy (AUD)

John Cronin, Jr.: court-appointed chief auditor of IBT, 1989–1992; IRB administrator, 1992–

Fred Gegare: IBT international vice president running for general president in the 2011 election

Peter Hoekstra: Republican representative of Michigan's 2nd congressional district

Susan Jennik: AUD executive director when *U.S. v. IBT* was filed

Tom Keegel: IBT general secretary-treasurer in Jim Hoffa's administration, 1998–2010

Karen Konigsberg: assistant U.S. attorney working on *U.S. v. IBT*, 1994–2001

James Kossler: Project RISE's lead investigator

Tom Leedham: insurgent candidate for IBT general president in 1998, 2001, and 2006

Martin Levy: independent financial auditor of the IBT, 1997–2001

Randy Mastro: assistant U.S. attorney who led team that drafted *U.S. v. IBT* complaint

Ken Paff: national organizer (and de facto head) of Teamsters for a Democratic Union

Sandy Pope: president of NYC IBT Local 805; insurgent challenger to General President Jim Hoffa in the 2011 IBT election

Andrew Schilling: assistant U.S. attorney working on *U.S. v. IBT*, November 1997–October 2007; chief of the civil division of the U.S. attorney's office (SDNY), March 2010–

Edwin Stier: court-appointed trustee of IBT Local 560; head of Project RISE

1

Introducing the Litigants
and the Judge

The leaders of the nation's largest union, the International Brotherhood of Teamsters (IBT), have been firmly under the influence of
organized crime since the 1950's. . . . [O]rganized crime influences
at least 38 of the largest [IBT] locals and joint councils in Chicago,
Cleveland, New Jersey, New York, Philadelphia, St. Louis, and other
major cities.[1]
> —President's Commission on Organized Crime, March 1986

[The impending civil RICO lawsuit against the IBT] is a groundless
attack, . . . an obviously specious attempt to interfere with the free
trade union movement . . . [and] a calculated political ploy designed
to take the pressure of numerous problems off the [Reagan] administration. . . . Organized crime has never, does not today and never
will control the international union.[2]
> —IBT official statement, June 11, 1987

The filing of *United States v. International Brotherhood of Teamsters* (*U.S. v. IBT*) in June 1988 pitted the U.S. Department of Justice (DOJ),
armed with the powerful RICO law and supported by skillful amici curiae
lawyers, against the leadership of the International Brotherhood of Teamsters (IBT), the nation's largest and strongest private-sector union, and Cosa
Nostra (LCN),* the nation's most powerful organized-crime syndicate.[3]

---

* Until the 1960s, the media usually referred to the Italian American crime families as "Mafia"
or "the mob." But wiretaps in the 1960s recorded the mobsters referring to their organization as
"Cosa Nostra" or "Our Thing." By a linguistic error, the FBI began to call it "La Cosa Nostra" (liter-
ally, "The Our Thing") and "LCN." Because it has become standard, we use the LCN acronym but
otherwise refer to Cosa Nostra without the "La."

This chapter sets the stage for this twenty-two-year (and ongoing) legal battle by introducing the plaintiff, the amici curiae, the defendants, and the judge who presided over the case for its first twelve years.

The Plaintiff: U.S. Department of Justice

U.S. Attorney Giuliani's office in the Southern District of New York (SDNY), the Federal Bureau of Investigation (FBI), and the Organized Crime and Racketeering Section (OCRS) of DOJ's headquarters (Main Justice) in Washington, D.C., jointly prepared the *U.S. v. IBT* complaint.[4]

This lawsuit launched a major battle in DOJ's decades-long war against the Cosa Nostra organized-crime families. By the end of the 1950s, due largely to the highly publicized revelations of the U.S. Senate's McClellan Committee hearings,* labor racketeering had become a salient national issue. When Robert F. Kennedy (RFK), who had served as counsel to the McClellan Committee, became U.S. attorney general in 1961, he made Italian American organized crime a top priority. (This despite lack of cooperation from FBI Director J. Edgar Hoover, who denied the existence of a national organized-crime syndicate and preferred to focus investigative resources on Communists and other "subversives.") Based on his acrimonious personal confrontations with IBT General President Jimmy Hoffa at the McClellan Committee hearings, RFK relentlessly pursued Hoffa, who began serving a prison sentence in the mid-1960s.

After J. Edgar Hoover died in 1972, the FBI reinvented itself as a modern law-enforcement agency. By the late 1970s, LCN's labor racketeering had become the FBI's and DOJ's top organized-crime-control priority.[5] The 1983–1986 work of the President's Commission on Organized Crime (PCOC) left no doubt about Cosa Nostra's firm grip on organized labor. Former IBT president Roy Williams told PCOC that "every big [IBT] local union . . . had some connection with organized crime."[6] Indeed, PCOC

---

* From 1957 to 1959, Senator John L. McClellan (R-Ark.), chairman of the Permanent Subcommittee on Investigations of the U.S. Senate Committee on Government Operations, held televised hearings on organized crime in North America, especially in the Teamsters Union. The hearings, which more than one million American households viewed, led to the criminal convictions of more than twenty people, including high-level Teamsters officers (e.g., IBT General President David Beck). The hearings cast a national spotlight on organized crime's relationship with labor unions and led to enactment of the Labor-Management Reporting and Disclosure Act of 1959 (LMRDA or Landrum-Griffin Act), which established close federal regulation of labor unions.

found strong evidence of LCN influence in thirty-eight IBT local unions and joint councils. Its March 1986 report, *The Edge: Organized Crime, Business, and Labor Unions*, urged DOJ to bring a civil RICO lawsuit against the IBT's international officers and their Cosa Nostra confederates. According to PCOC, the government's only hope for ridding the Teamsters Union of LCN's influence was a "combination of criminal prosecutions, civil action, and administrative proceedings," including a civil RICO suit and court-imposed trusteeship.[7]

U.S. Attorney Giuliani's Attack on Labor Racketeering Prior to *U.S. v. IBT*

Rudolph Giuliani served as an assistant U.S. attorney and chief of the narcotics unit in the U.S. attorney's office for SDNY in the first half of the 1970s. He was then promoted to executive U.S. attorney for that office. In 1975, DOJ brought Giuliani to Washington, D.C., to serve as associate deputy attorney general and chief of staff to the deputy attorney general. From 1977 to 1981, Giuliani worked in private law practice in NYC. In 1981, President Ronald Reagan named him associate attorney general, DOJ's third-highest position. Two years later, Reagan appointed Giuliani U.S. attorney for SDNY, headquartered in Manhattan but with jurisdiction over the Bronx and several suburban counties.

Giuliani made LCN a top priority,[8] quickly establishing himself as the nation's leading organized-crime prosecutor. One of his most important cases was the 1985 "Pizza Connection" case, *United States v. Badalamenti*,[9] which exposed a conspiracy involving U.S. and Italian organized-crime groups that used pizzerias as fronts for heroin trafficking. The trial, which lasted one and a half years and cost nearly $50 million, resulted in convictions of most of the twenty-two defendants, including Sicilian Mafia boss Gaetano Badalamenti.[10] In the 1986 "Commission" case, *United States v. Salerno*,[11] Giuliani charged leaders of four of the five NYC Cosa Nostra crime families with participating, through a pattern of racketeering activity, in the affairs of a Cosa Nostra "commission" that resolved issues and disputes among the five families. The defendants were convicted and sentenced to life in prison.

Prior to *U.S. v. IBT*, Giuliani also brought important labor-racketeering cases. In one major case, he charged union leaders and contractors who dominated NYC's poured-concrete business. IBT Local 282, which represented the drivers of the trucks that mixed and delivered concrete to construction sites, had been "mobbed up" for decades.[12] In October 1984, a federal grand jury indicted Ralph Scopo, a soldier in the Colombo crime family, president of the District Council of Cement and Concrete Workers, and president of LIUNA Local 6A (whose members poured the concrete that IBT Local 282's drivers delivered), for extorting money from construction companies. A jury convicted Scopo on all counts.[13] Two years later, Giuliani used civil RICO to place LIUNA Local 6A under a court-ordered trusteeship.[14] (Seven years later, another RICO suit resulted in a court-appointed trusteeship for IBT Local 282.)[15]

Giuliani's office brought successful civil RICO suits against other union locals, including NYC IBT Local 804 (representing drivers who haul cargo into and out of New York's JFK Airport) and Long Island City, New York IBT Local 808 (representing railway and other workers). (See fig. 1.1.) In April 1988, just a few months before filing *U.S. v. IBT*, Giuliani obtained a RICO indictment against IBT Local 804 Secretary-Treasurer John Long and IBT Local 808 Secretary-Treasurer John Mahoney. For at least a decade, according to the indictment, the defendants had conducted the affairs of their IBT locals through a pattern of bribery, kickbacks, extortion, and other offenses.[16]

Planning *U.S. v. IBT*

In January 1986, Giuliani assigned Assistant U.S. Attorney (AUSA) Randy Mastro responsibility for evaluating the possibility of bringing a successful civil RICO suit against the Teamsters Union's top leaders and their Cosa Nostra associates.[17] Four months later, Mastro and a few other AUSAs finished drafting a civil RICO complaint.[18] However, unbeknown to Giuliani, OCRS Chief David Margolis had already assembled a team in Washington, D.C., consisting of DOJ lawyers, an FBI task force ("Liberatus Squad"), and a Department of Labor (DOL) investigator (Michael Moroney), to do exactly what Mastro was doing in Manhattan.[19]

Deputy Attorney General Arnold Burns decided to keep the case in Washington, D.C.[20] (Attorney General Edwin Meese III recused himself due to his friendly relationship with IBT General President Jackie Presser.) However, seven months later, Burns transferred the case to Giuliani's office, perhaps not surprising given Giuliani's impressive track record in winning high-stakes organized-crime cases.[21] With the green light from Washington, AUSA Mastro assembled a litigation team of seven lawyers, most of whom had experience litigating prior civil RICO cases against union locals.

FIGURE 1.1
Civil RICO Cases against Labor Unions Prior to U.S. v. IBT

Name of Case	Brief Summary
United States v. Local 560, International Brotherhood of Teamsters, 550 F. Supp. 511 (D.N.J. 1982)	Year-long trial resulted in resounding victory for the government. Ed Stier was appointed trustee with authority to run the local. Thirteen years later, the union was deemed reformed and the trusteeship terminated.
United States v. Local 6A, Cement and Concrete Workers, 663 F. Supp. 192 (S.D.N.Y. 1986)	After the consent decree was signed, sixteen of the twenty-five officers of Local 6A and the District Council resigned. The consent decree called for a court-appointed trustee to run the union. The trusteeship lasted five years.
United States v. The Bonanno Organized Crime Family of La Cosa Nostra, 683 F. Supp. 1411 (E.D.N.Y. 1988)	The consent decree provided for a trustee, interim executive board, and interim board of trustees to oversee New York IBT Local 814's activities and monitor its expenditures.
United States v. Local 359, United Seafood Workers, 705 F. Supp. 894 (S.D.N.Y. 1989)	The consent decree permanently enjoined twenty-five defendants, including members of the Genovese crime family and New York Local 359 officials, from engaging in racketeering activity and from impeding competition at NYC's Fulton Fish Market. It also authorized a court-appointed administrator to monitor the market, propose regulations, and investigate violations of the injunctions. The trusteeship lasted four years.
United States v. Local 30, United Slate, Tile, and Composition Roofers, 686 F. Supp. 1139 (E.D. Pa. 1988)	The consent decree imposed a decreeship whereby a "court liaison officer" supervised the local's expenditures and contract negotiations but lacked power to remove corrupt union members. The incumbent local executive board remained in place. The decreeship lasted eleven years but achieved limited success. Four years later, the international union imposed an eighteen-month trusteeship after identifying serious financial misconduct, violence, threats of violence, and extortion at job sites.
United States v. Long & Mahoney, 697 F. Supp. 651 (S.D.N.Y. 1988)	In conjunction with the criminal prosecution, the government obtained equitable relief against NYC IBT Local 804 and NYC IBT Local 808 under RICO's civil remedies provisions.

(Margolis dispatched one member of his team to New York City to work on the case full-time.)

As rumors of an imminent civil RICO suit against the IBT began circulating, the IBT sought to mobilize political opposition. It placed ads in the *New York Times*, the *Washington Post*, and other newspapers asserting that a government takeover of the union would deal a serious blow to the U.S. labor movement.[22] Flexing its political muscle, the IBT leadership persuaded 264 members of Congress to sign a petition urging the U.S. attorney general to block Giuliani from filing the lawsuit.[23] Nevertheless, Giuliani and Mastro filed the *U.S. v. IBT* complaint in Judge David Edelstein's Manhattan federal district court on June 28, 1988.

The Amici Curiae: Teamsters for a Democratic Union and Association for Union Democracy

Teamsters for a Democratic Union

Giuliani's civil RICO litigation team found a highly knowledgeable ally in Teamsters for a Democratic Union (TDU), a left-wing faction of Teamsters rank and filers and retirees that had been battling the reigning IBT establishment since 1976.[24] TDU's goals are to democratize IBT elections, hold the IBT's leaders accountable, combat corruption and racketeering, and achieve good contracts. TDU also functions as a kind of opposition political party, taking positions on issues such as contracts, strikes, dues increases, and political endorsements. TDU recruits and endorses candidates for local IBT elections; occasionally, its endorsed candidates defeat incumbents.[25] TDU claims a membership of ten thousand, just over one half of one percent of the total IBT membership.

Throughout the late 1970s and 1980s, IBT leaders harassed, blacklisted, and red-baited TDU. Local IBT officers helped employers thwart TDU-initiated strikes and IBT General Presidents Frank Fitzsimmons and Jackie Presser frequently called TDU's members "professional agitators," "student radicals," "outsiders," and "socialist conspira[tors]."[26] IBT leaders even tried to expel from the union Pete Camarata and Al Ferdnance, two of TDU's most visible leaders.[27] The IBT's red-baiting tactics were effective in part because some TDU leaders were avowed socialists.[28] (Indeed, an editorial in TDU's newsletter acknowledged "the presence of a handful of socialist" members.)[29] Nevertheless, by the 1980s, TDU had become one of the most influential insurgent groups in the American labor movement.

The IBT's attacks against TDU became more intense in the early 1980s. With the support of IBT General President Presser, a "goon squad," called the Brotherhood of Loyal Americans and Strong Teamsters (BLAST), harassed TDUers and disrupted their events.[30] Most dramatically, in October 1983, BLAST members raided TDU's annual convention in Romulus, Michigan. They called in bomb threats, ran the TDUers out of the meeting hall, and trashed the premises.[31] Presser expressed approval: "I'm going to tell you something. We should be doing more of that. I'm going to tell you, I'm not going to let up on these people."[32] (Due to these persistent attacks, TDU keeps its members' identities confidential. Other than the three to four hundred Teamsters who attend TDU's annual convention, few TDUers publicly admit membership for fear that IBT officials and/or employers will retaliate against them.)

TDU was enthusiastic about the prospect of DOJ bringing a civil RICO suit against the IBT and its organized-crime allies. However, it opposed DOJ's rumored decision to seek the appointment of a court-appointed trustee to run the international union. Instead, TDU's "Proposal to the Justice Department," published in its newsletter, *Convoy Dispatch*, urged DOJ to make free and fair elections the centerpiece of the remedy. The proposal recommended a secret-ballot, one-member-one-vote election of all international officers; judicial supervision of international elections "in all respects"; and special *Teamster Magazine* issues with equal and free advertising space for candidates for international office. Ken Paff, the national organizer and longtime de facto head of TDU, reiterated these proposals in a letter to Assistant U.S. Attorney General Stephen Trott:

> With these kinds of remedies, blended from both the LMRDA and RICO, organized crime would be relatively powerless. There would be a chance for a serious wide open election. As we said, IBT members are no different from other American voters. They do not re-elect felons or potential felons, if they have confidence in the secrecy of the ballot.[33]

In support of TDU's thesis that free and fair elections would seriously weaken Cosa Nostra's position in the IBT, Paff cited the 1972 United Mine Workers (UMW) case. After insurgent UMW presidential candidate Joseph Yablonski and his family were murdered by hit men, DOL supervised a one-member-one-vote election of UMW's international officers. The UMW members "threw the rascals out," Paff noted, "and have peacefully and fairly voted in contested elections for top officers ever since. In the most recent election, the incumbent international president was voted out."[34]

Association for Union Democracy

The Brooklyn-based Association for Union Democracy (AUD), with the pro bono assistance of a small number of civil liberties lawyers, lobbies for and represents union members seeking to vindicate their union-democracy rights.[35] Since founding AUD in 1960, Herman Benson has published *Union Democracy in Action* and later *Union Democracy Review*, covering union members' struggles to speak freely, run for office, obtain fair union job referrals, and exercise other rights.

Unlike TDU, which functions as an IBT opposition party that takes positions on diverse IBT matters, AUD "supports the rights of all unionists, left, right, or center, [to be free] from abuse from any source, right, left, or center. [It] takes no position on questions of collective bargaining policy or national politics. . . . It will not lobby for legislation or support candidates for any office."[36] However, like TDU, AUD strongly encouraged DOJ to bring a civil RICO lawsuit against the IBT.[37] Once the lawsuit was filed, AUD sought to participate in the case as amicus curiae in order to press for making rank-and-file election of international officers the centerpiece of the remedy. However, AUD did not oppose a court-appointed trustee's taking charge of the union's operations.

TDU and AUD had an impact on *U.S. v. IBT* disproportionate to their size and power. Although these organizations' resources were minuscule compared with those of the Teamsters Union, their highly talented and energetic lawyers skillfully communicated their views to DOJ and filed strongly argued amicus briefs with Judge Edelstein. TDU and AUD played notable roles in DOJ's decision to make democratic elections, rather than trusteeship, a core feature of the complaint's requested remedy and of the consent decree. (Law Professor Michael Goldberg has observed that "TDU played a critical behind-the-scenes role in helping to shape the specifics of the consent decree.")[38] They also played leading roles in Judge Edelstein's decision to require the court-appointed election officer to supervise every facet of the IBT's elections.

The Defendants: The Teamsters Union and Cosa Nostra

The Teamsters Union

Unlike most large labor unions, which represent workers in a single craft (e.g., plumbers, electricians, bricklayers) or industry (e.g., mine workers, automobile workers), the Teamsters Union represents workers in many trades, occupations, businesses, and industries (see fig. 1.2). All told, the IBT has twenty-one trade divisions and conferences comprising geographically diverse union locals. The divisions and conferences provide information for IBT locals negotiating in the same industry or bargaining with the same employer, hold meetings to discuss shared concerns, lobby Congress,

FIGURE 1.2
Teamsters Union Membership by Industry

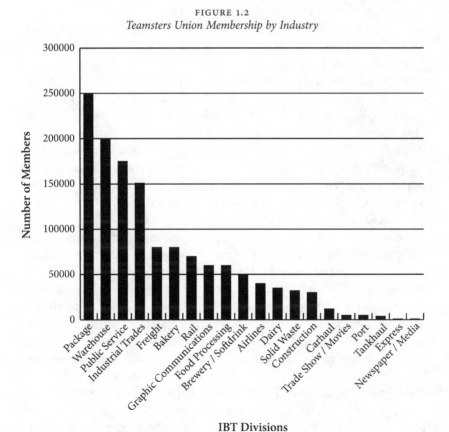

IBT Divisions

negotiate and monitor contracts, organize workers, coordinate grievance panels, and communicate with other unions.

The IBT is governed by a General Executive Board (GEB) composed of a general president, a general secretary-treasurer, seven at-large vice presidents, three eastern regional vice presidents, five central regional vice presidents, two southern regional vice presidents, three western regional vice presidents, three Canadian vice presidents, and three international trustees who monitor the union's finances. All international officers are elected to GEB positions via direct rank-and-file, secret-ballot voting following nominations by local-union delegates at quinquennial IBT conventions. Most international officers simultaneously hold leadership positions in and draw separate salaries from IBT locals and/or joint councils.[39]

Among other powers, the general president presides over the IBT conventions, supervises the union's day-to-day operations, appoints IBT staffers, imposes trusteeships on corrupt or dysfunctional locals, approves or rejects local bylaws, and imposes disciplinary sanctions (see fig. 1.3). The general president also negotiates nationwide collective-bargaining agreements (e.g., the master freight agreement) and serves as the union's national spokesperson. The general secretary-treasurer, who works closely with the general president, is the custodian of the IBT's properties, funds, and other assets.[40] The three international trustees who make up the IBT's Audit Committee are responsible for reviewing the union's books and records, submitting quarterly reports to the GEB, reviewing the work of the union's internal audit department, communicating with the union's outside auditor, and investigating complaints involving the union's finances. They may attend GEB meetings but have no voting rights.

Between IBT conventions, the GEB is the union's governing body. The IBT constitution grants the GEB all authority not expressly assigned to the general president or general secretary-treasurer. The GEB can call special conventions; adopt or amend pension, health, or welfare plans for international-union employees; approve or reject mergers of local unions; and approve or reject mergers or affiliations with other labor unions.

The general president appoints international representatives as needed to assist local unions in organizing new members, settling strikes, and launching community-service initiatives.[41] At any given time, there are between several dozen and one hundred international representatives. In addition, there are usually several dozen "personal representatives" who act on behalf of the general president, for example, by attending meetings, interviewing members, and reviewing IBT entities' books and records.[42]

FIGURE 1.3
Tenure and Criminality of IBT General Presidents

General President	Tenure	Criminal Charges
Cornelius Shea	1903–1907	Charged with conspiracy to restrain trade, commit violence, and prevent citizens from obtaining work; the first trial led to a hung jury and the second jury acquitted him (1905); sentenced to six months in prison for abandoning his wife and two children (1908); served five years in prison and two years on probation for attempted murder of his mistress (1909); acquitted for soliciting bribes in exchange for labor peace (1918); arrested, but not prosecuted, for the murder of a Chicago police officer (1922).
Daniel Tobin	1907–1952	NA
Dave Beck	1952–1957	Convicted of embezzlement (1959); convicted of federal income-tax evasion (1959).
James R. Hoffa	1957–1971	Convicted and sentenced to thirteen years in prison for jury tampering, attempted bribery, and fraud (1964).
Frank Fitzsimmons	1971–1981	Indicted on charges of extorting money from construction companies in Michigan (charges were dropped) (1953); forced to resign as an IBT Central States Pension Fund trustee on account of failure to perform his fiduciary duties by authorizing loans to LCN-controlled businesses (1976).
George Mock (interim)	May 7–15, 1981	NA
Roy Williams	1981–1983	Convicted and sentenced to fifty-five years in prison for conspiring to bribe U.S. Senator Howard Cannon (1982).
Jackie Presser	1983–1988	Forced to resign as a Central States Pension Fund trustee on account of violating his fiduciary duties by authorizing improper loans to LCN-controlled businesses (1977); charged with criminal RICO violations for embezzling union funds by paying union salaries to "ghost" employees who did no work; trial delayed for health reasons and dismissed when Presser died (1986).
Weldon Mathis (interim)	May 5, 1988– July 18, 1988	NA
William McCarthy	1988–1991	Did not face criminal charges, but Judge Edelstein found McCarthy's award of a $3.8 million printing contract to a firm owned by his son-in-law (1991) to be an act in furtherance of racketeering.
Ron Carey	1991–1998	Indicted for perjury (2001), acquitted.
Thomas Sever (interim)	July 27, 1998– Dec. 5, 1998	NA
James P. Hoffa	1998–present	NA

Rank and filers participate in the union's affairs primarily through their "locals." Over the past twenty-five years, the number of U.S. and Canadian locals that make up the Teamsters Union has fluctuated, largely on account of mergers, from approximately 450 to approximately 700. In mid-2010, there were 440 U.S. IBT locals and thirty-five Canadian IBT locals.[43] Between 2003 and 2005, the IBT absorbed 573 Brotherhood of Locomotive Engineers and Trainmen (BLET) locals, 635 Brotherhood of Maintenance of Way Employees (BMWE) locals, and 206 Graphics Communications International (GCI) locals. The largest Teamsters locals have as many as fifteen thousand members and the smallest fewer than one thousand. Locals negotiate most contracts with the employers for whom their members work; they also run "hiring halls," which assign union members to employers who require labor, and defend union members in employer disciplinary proceedings. (The international union officers negotiate national contracts with certain employer associations, e.g., freight, and multistate IBT employers, e.g., UPS.) Each local's members elect executive officers, including a president, a vice president, a recording secretary, a secretary-treasurer, and three trustees. The officers pass bylaws, hire and fire support staff, negotiate contracts, and manage the union's day-to-day affairs. Some locals' bylaws designate the president as principal officer; others designate the secretary-treasurer as principal officer.

Joint councils are intermediate-level units composed of representatives of three or more IBT locals in the same geographical area. Their executive officers, who operate pursuant to joint-council bylaws and are selected by the constituent locals' executive officers, serve as their local's representative on the joint council.[44] Joint councils coordinate organizing and strike activities, resolve locals' jurisdictional disputes, and prosecute disciplinary cases against officers and members that locals will not or cannot prosecute.

Until 1994, four regional conferences (eastern, western, southern, and central) constituted another level of IBT bureaucracy. Each conference had a small full-time staff and employed approximately twenty executive officers who received conference salaries in addition to local and joint-council salaries. In June 1994, the Carey administration's GEB abolished the area conferences on the ground that they did not accomplish enough to justify their cost.

The Teamsters Union receives about $700 million annually from members' dues. Each member pays dues equal to two and a half hours (forty-five dollars, on average) of his or her monthly wage. For the vast majority

of members, pursuant to collective bargaining agreements, dues are automatically deducted ("checked off") from their paychecks. The employers
remit the money to the members' local unions, which, in turn, keep 70 percent and pass along 22 percent to the international union, 5 percent to the
joint council, and a smaller (varying) amount to other IBT units.

Cosa Nostra

Giuliani named the Cosa Nostra organized-crime bosses as defendants
in order to define *U.S. v. IBT* as an organized-crime case. He sought an
order enjoining them from participating in or attempting to influence the
IBT's affairs. The LCN defendants had no plausible argument for participating in the union and, anyway, exerted their influence informally and
secretly. They would be able to continue doing so, personally or through
surrogates, as long as officers susceptible to promised benefits or threatened reprisals ran the union.

Cosa Nostra's infiltration of the Teamsters Union can be traced back to
the early twentieth century.[45] Beginning in the late 1920s and early 1930s,
LCN leaders in cities across the northeast and midwest gained influence
over, and sometimes operational control of, IBT locals through violence,
threatened violence, and mutually beneficial reciprocities with union leaders. By the 1940s, LCN was deeply entrenched in IBT locals across the
country. For example, Anthony Corallo, boss of the Lucchese crime family, was an officer in and allegedly embezzled tens of thousands of dollars
from IBT Local 239.[46] John Nardi, an associate in the Cleveland crime family and confederate of Bill Presser, head of Cleveland's vending-machine
rackets and father of future IBT general president Jackie Presser, served as
secretary-treasurer of IBT Vending Machine Local 410. Matthew Ianniello,
later acting boss of the Genovese crime family, controlled IBT Bus Drivers
Local 1181. John Scalish, boss of the Cleveland crime family, exerted major
influence on that city's IBT locals from the 1940s to the 1970s, as did his
successor, James Licavoli.[47]

By the 1950s, Cosa Nostra parlayed its extensive influence in IBT locals
and joint councils into influence at the union's international level. In 1955,
for example, Lucchese crime family member Johnny Dioguardi, who had
been a force in NYC IBT locals since the early 1930s, helped form several
"paper" (shell) locals, whose votes in the NYC IBT joint council swung that
council behind Jimmy Hoffa, assuring his selection as IBT general president in 1957.[48]

By the 1980s, Cosa Nostra figures controlled many key Teamsters officials at the local, joint council, and international levels. Raymond Patriarca, boss of the New England Cosa Nostra family, exerted significant influence over IBT locals in Providence and Boston.[49] Chicago crime family
("Outfit") associate Dominic Senese served as president of Chicago IBT
Local 703, and Outfit associate James Coli became secretary-treasurer of
Chicago IBT Local 727. Nick Civella, boss of the Kansas City crime family, controlled Roy Williams, who, before becoming IBT general president
in 1981, was president of Kansas City IBT Local 41, president of IBT Joint
Council 56, trustee of the IBT's Central States Pension Fund, director of the
Central Conference of Teamsters, and an IBT international vice president.
As Williams described the relationship, "To be frank, if I didn't want to get
killed, I was his boy."[50]

LCN was especially entrenched in IBT affairs in NYC and Chicago. For
example, Chicago crime family member John Glimco, Sr., was president
of Chicago IBT Local 777. Outfit member James V. Cozzo was an officer
in Chicago IBT Local 786. Chicago IBT Local 738 Principal Officer Peter
Agliata eventually resigned from the IBT after being charged with knowingly associating with Outfit members. Salvio Galiato, a member of Chicago IBT Local 714, was the nephew of Outfit underboss James Marcello.
Peter DiFronzo, a member of Chicago IBT Local 731, was a member of the
Outfit and Outfit boss John DiFronzo's (his brother) chief lieutenant.

No IBT local was more thoroughly LCN-controlled than Union City,
New Jersey Local 560, which represented over ten thousand truckers employed by approximately 425 companies.[51] For more than a quarter century, Local 560 was dominated by the Provenzano brothers (Anthony,
Nunzio, and Salvatore), organized-crime figures closely allied with and, at
least in Anthony's case, a member of NYC's Genovese crime family.[52] Anthony served as the Genovese crime family's representative in Local 560 in
the late 1940s and ascended quickly through its ranks, becoming its president in 1958 and, later, in addition, an IBT international vice president.[53]
He and his close associates ran the local by violence and intimidation, on
occasion using thugs to assault and even murder dissidents. When Anthony went to prison on a racketeering conviction, his brothers succeeded
him sequentially as IBT Local 560's president. Salvatore also served as an
IBT vice president.

Several dissidents who challenged the Provenzanos were murdered, including Walter Glockner, Local 560 Secretary-Treasurer Anthony Castellito, and Frederick Furino, who ran a trucking company that provided

nonunion labor to a firm whose employees were represented by Local 560. The Provenzano brothers treated the local's treasury as their piggy bank, funneling to themselves and their associates millions of dollars through hefty salaries, embezzlement from the union and its pension and welfare funds, "loans" to businesses that they controlled, and kickbacks from union contractors.[54]

In 1982, the U.S. attorney's office and the federal organized-crime strike force in New Jersey filed a civil RICO suit against Local 560, the first-ever civil RICO suit against a union local. According to the presiding judge, the "evil men" of the Provenzano Group had engaged in an unprecedented "orgy of criminal activity" that made Local 560 a "captive labor organization."[55] In June 1986, after a long trial and appeals process, the judge replaced the local's entire executive board with a trustee. A year later, the judge replaced that trustee with Edwin Stier, who spent the next twelve and a half years purging the local of Cosa Nostra's influence and encouraging democratic reforms.[56] (In February 1999, the government and the court determined that Local 560 was reformed and dissolved the trusteeship.)

Cosa Nostra and the IBT's General Presidents

James R. Hoffa. Jimmy Hoffa joined the IBT in 1932, at age nineteen, as an organizer for Detroit Local 299 and became the de facto head of that local in 1935.[57] He began associating with members of the Detroit underworld around 1940, seeking the mob's assistance in subduing rival unions, strong-arming employers, and intimidating Teamsters opponents.[58] (Hoffa's connections to the Detroit underworld led to relationships with mobsters in Cleveland, New York, Chicago, and other cities.)[59] He quickly forged a relationship with Paul Dorfman, a Chicago Outfit associate and former head of the Chicago local of the Waste Material Handlers Union.[60] In 1940, Hoffa became negotiating chairman of the IBT's Central States Drivers Council, a springboard for expanding his influence throughout the midwest.[61] In 1942, he formed and became the first president of the Michigan Conference of Teamsters, which quickly signed up all Michigan IBT locals.[62] Nine years later, Hoffa placed the IBT's Central States Pension and Welfare Fund (CSPF) with the Union Casualty Life Insurance Agency of Chicago, owned by Paul Dorfman's son, Allen.[63] Hoffa allowed the CSPF to be used as a kind of "mob bank" in exchange for Cosa Nostra's support of his union political ambitions. In 1952, the IBT's convention delegates elected Hoffa as an international vice president.

From 1957 to 1959, the U.S. Senate's McClellan Committee investigated union corruption, especially in the IBT. Due in large part to IBT General President Dave Beck's embarrassing performance before the Committee, Beck did not seek reelection in 1957. (Two years later, a federal jury convicted him of embezzlement and tax evasion.) To replace Beck, the GEB chose Jimmy Hoffa. The AFL-CIO then expelled the IBT from membership, largely on account of Hoffa's reputed connections with organized crime. Robert F. Kennedy, first as counsel to the McClellan Committee and then (from 1961 to 1964) as U.S. attorney general, sparred famously and publicly with Hoffa.[64] Indeed, soon after becoming attorney general, RFK created the "Get Hoffa Squad," a team of DOJ investigators and lawyers.[65]

In 1962, a federal grand jury in Nashville, Tennessee, charged Hoffa with receiving thousands of dollars in payoffs from a trucking company in exchange for Hoffa's settling a costly strike.[66] After the trial ended in a hung jury, the judge ordered a grand jury to investigate possible jury tampering. That investigation resulted in Hoffa's indictment for obstructing justice. Meanwhile, a Chicago grand jury charged Hoffa with embezzling over $1 million from the CSPF through kickbacks and improper loans to LCN-controlled hotels, casinos, and shopping centers in Las Vegas, Florida, Connecticut, and elsewhere.[67] Ultimately, a jury convicted Hoffa of both jury tampering and embezzlement. In March 1967, he began serving a thirteen-year prison term.

Frank Fitzsimmons. At Hoffa's urging, the GEB chose his executive assistant, Frank Fitzsimmons, as acting IBT general president. Prior to becoming Hoffa's right-hand man, Fitzsimmons had served as Detroit IBT Local 299 vice president, Michigan Conference of Teamsters secretary-treasurer, IBT Joint Council 43 vice president, and international vice president. Hoffa intended for Fitzsimmons to be a figurehead while he continued to direct union affairs from his prison cell. However, Fitzsimmons eventually aspired to run the IBT in fact as well as in name. After defeating a GEB attempt to oust him, he replaced several Hoffa GEB protégés with his own supporters. In 1971, delegates to the IBT's international convention elected Fitzsimmons general president.

Because Hoffa remained popular with the rank and file, Fitzsimmons had to support Hoffa's efforts to obtain parole release or a presidential pardon, but he was determined to keep Hoffa out of IBT politics. Ultimately, Fitzsimmons worked out a deal with President Richard Nixon.

Nixon would commute Hoffa's sentence in exchange for an IBT endorsement of Nixon's reelection in 1972. A condition of Hoffa's release was that
he could not participate in IBT affairs until 1980.

Once free, Hoffa began campaigning for his old position, disregarding
the prohibition on involvement in IBT affairs. He condemned Fitzsimmons as weak and corrupt, vowing that, if reelected, he would rid the
union of Cosa Nostra's influence. The LCN bosses much preferred the mal-
leable Fitzsimmons and warned Hoffa to give up his presidential ambition.
On July 30, 1975, Hoffa disappeared from the parking lot of the Machus
Red Fox Restaurant in Oakland County, Michigan (a Detroit suburb). It is
widely assumed that Cosa Nostra assassinated him.

Roy Williams. After Fitzsimmons died of lung cancer in May 1981, Roy
Williams, an IBT international vice president and trustee of the CSPF,
succeeded him as general president. Five years earlier, Fitzsimmons had
appointed Williams as director of the Central Conference of Teamsters,
which had jurisdiction over IBT locals in fourteen midwestern states.

Williams was tied to Cosa Nostra through his thirty-year relationship
with Nick Civella, boss of the Kansas City LCN family, who advanced Williams's IBT career in exchange for Williams's placing LCN's members and
friends in key union posts and supporting Civella's business interests. After
Fitzsimmons died, Civella successfully lobbied mob bosses in NYC, Chicago, and other cities to support Williams for the IBT general presidency.
The GEB named Williams interim president. In May 1981, delegates to the
IBT's convention overwhelmingly elected Williams to a full five-year term.

In 1977, Williams and Fitzsimmons were forced to resign from the CSPF
after the DOL sued them and three others for violating their fiduciary
duty. In December 1982, Williams and Allen Dorfman were convicted of
attempting to bribe Nevada Senator Howard Cannon (D-Nev.) to block
interstate trucking deregulation. A month later, Dorfman was murdered
gangland style, presumably by mobsters who wanted to keep him from
cooperating with prosecutors.[68] In April 1983, Williams resigned the IBT
presidency after a jury sentenced him to fifty-five years in prison. Hoping to
shorten his sentence, he began cooperating with government investigators,
prosecutors, and the PCOC. In 1987, testifying by videotape from a prison
hospital due to ailing health, Williams told a federal jury, "organized crime
was filtered into the Teamsters Union a long time before I came there, and
it'll be there a long time after I'm gone."[69] He added, "I was controlled by

Nick [Civella]" ever since Civella's mob associates threatened to murder his wife and children.[70] Due to poor health and cooperation with federal authorities, Williams was released from prison in September 1988. He died in April 1989.

Jackie Presser. To succeed Williams as general president, the GEB, with the Cosa Nostra bosses' approval, chose Jackie Presser, the son of William "Bill" Presser, a consummate labor racketeer who for years served as an international IBT vice president and sat on the CSPF board. In 1966, Bill set up Cleveland IBT Local 507 for Jackie to run. During the following decade, Bill, Jackie, and two colleagues, Allen and Harold Friedman, increased Local 507's membership by raiding other IBT locals. According to PCOC, Jackie's local was "infested with LCN associates and convicted felons," including John Trunzo (a former business agent convicted of coercing employers to pay for labor peace), John Felice, Jr. (an LCN associate convicted of embezzling IBT funds), and John Nardi (a "ghost" employee of Local 507, LCN bodyguard, and convicted embezzler).[71]

By 1972, Jackie was chairman of the Ohio Conference of Teamsters. He soon acceded to his father's positions as an IBT international vice president and a CSPF trustee. He also served as an FBI informant, providing information useful in prosecuting Roy Williams and other union rivals. In 1976, however, the same DOL lawsuit that forced Williams and Fitzsimmons to resign as CSPF trustees also forced Presser to resign from the CSPF, although not the GEB.[72]

In November 1980, U.S. president-elect Ronald Reagan appointed Presser as a labor adviser to his transition team. Soon after that, the media reported that DOL was investigating whether Presser had mishandled CSPF assets. The Reagan administration claimed not to have known of these allegations.[73] (By that time, the transition team had already completed its work and disbanded.)

In 1982, after it became apparent that Roy Williams would be convicted of federal crimes, midwest and east coast LCN families began negotiating over Williams's successor.[74] LCN leaders Angelo Lonardo (Cleveland crime family), Milton Rockman (Cleveland crime family), Anthony Salerno (Genovese crime family), Jackie Cerone (Chicago Outfit), and Joseph Aiuppa (Chicago Outfit) eventually threw their support behind Presser.[75] On April 21, 1983, IBT convention delegates, by acclamation, elected Presser general president.

In January 1984, General President Presser was the only leader of a large U.S. labor union to endorse President Reagan's reelection campaign. After PCOC published its 1986 report on the IBT's extensive organized-crime ties, the Reagan administration distanced itself from Presser and the IBT. (After *U.S. v. IBT* was filed in June 1988, U.S. Attorney General Meese stated that Reagan would not have accepted Presser's 1984 endorsement had he known, at the time, of the IBT's association with Cosa Nostra.)[76]

Presser launched an all-out campaign to prevent Giuliani from filing the rumored civil RICO suit.[77] He accused DOJ of acting like a totalitarian regime: "Takeovers of unions are nothing new—Communists and Fascists have been doing so for decades. However, it is a sad day in the history of the United States and the American labor movement when such tactics are employed."[78] On September 15, 1987, Presser convened a meeting of IBT local-union executive boards in Cincinnati to protest the filing of *U.S. v. IBT*. NYC IBT Local 237 President Barry Feinstein accused the government of wanting "some cop to run this union."[79] He urged the IBT "to mobilize our membership as never before, in a hurricane of protests that will shake the very foundations of the Justice Department."[80]

To build support for his campaign to prevent DOJ from filing a civil RICO suit, Presser mended fences with the AFL-CIO, North America's umbrella labor federation. Both the IBT and AFL-CIO saw advantage in realliance. Presser wanted the AFL-CIO's political support to prevent the civil RICO suit from being filed; he hoped that the labor movement's lobbying would persuade the Reagan administration to stop U.S. Attorney Giuliani.[81] The AFL-CIO found attractive the prospect of gaining the IBT's $6 million annual dues contribution and its political strength. Moreover, because AFL-CIO member unions must adhere to a "no-raiding policy," whereby one member union cannot challenge the exclusive representational status of another member union, reunification would end IBT representational challenges to AFL-CIO member unions. Further, some AFL-CIO members worried that a DOJ civil RICO suit against the IBT would pave the way for similar suits against other international unions.[82] Therefore, in October 1987, the AFL-CIO executive council unanimously voted to invite the IBT to rejoin.[83] The IBT accepted. As a result of the IBT's and other unions' aggressive lobbying, 264 members of Congress delivered a petition on December 10, 1987 to Attorney General Edwin Meese urging DOJ not to file a civil RICO lawsuit against the IBT.[84] Nevertheless, U.S. Attorney Giuliani filed the civil RICO complaint on June 28, 1988.

Judge David Edelstein

Giuliani's litigation team deliberately routed the civil RICO complaint to federal district court judge David Edelstein by asserting, in its filing documents, that *U.S. v. IBT* was related to *U.S. v. Long & Mahoney*, a pending civil RICO case against an IBT local over which Judge Edelstein was presiding. (Although cases are ordinarily assigned to judges at random in SDNY, a local court rule authorizes a plaintiff to ask a judge to preside over a newly filed case that is related to a case over which the judge is already presiding.)[85] Jed Rakoff, representing the IBT, objected to this maneuver, calling it "an attempt to steer the case to this court by a manipulation of the local rules."[86] But Judge Edelstein accepted the case.[87]

In 1988, Edelstein was seventy-eight years old, having served on the bench for thirty-seven years. He was widely considered progovernment. His most famous case up to this point was DOJ's antitrust suit against IBM. The 1956 settlement of that case authorized Judge Edelstein to enforce IBM's compliance with a consent decree, the implementation of which generated a constant flow of contentious litigation for the next forty years. In 1994, IBM's lawyers charged that Edelstein was biased in favor of the government. Ultimately, the Second Circuit Court of Appeals agreed, finding it "manifestly clear that a reasonable observer would question the judge's impartiality on the pending issue."[88] Edelstein was removed from the case. In his subsequent handling of *U.S. v. IBT*, Judge Edelstein almost always agreed with DOJ.

Conclusion and Analysis

The FBI and DOJ did not embark on *U.S. v. IBT* to make union democracy a reality in the Teamsters Union. Nor were they motivated primarily by concern about the exploitation of rank-and-file Teamsters (although Giuliani's team undoubtedly saw rhetorical advantage in stressing the violation 8ganized-crime case. Certain unions, especially the Teamsters Union, provided Cosa Nostra's crime families with money, jobs, and political influence. U.S. Attorney Giuliani adopted TDU's and AUD's election-reform recommendations because he and his colleagues came to believe that free and fair elections would bring about the ouster of corrupt union leaders and make the union more racketeer-resistant.

It is a telling commentary on U.S. politics that 264 members of Congress, without having seen the *U.S. v. IBT* complaint against the notoriously racketeer-ridden IBT, signed a petition urging that the lawsuit not be filed. Even more cynical was the petitioners' reason for opposing the lawsuit: that it would threaten the nation's free and democratic labor movement. The filing of the civil RICO suit speaks well of DOJ's political independence. Although the IBT stood virtually alone among labor unions in endorsing Ronald Reagan for president, the Reagan Justice Department filed and vigorously litigated the lawsuit.

This chapter also highlights the crucial importance of key individuals. U.S. Attorney Giuliani had the ambition, experience, leadership skills, and influence in the Department of Justice to launch the lawsuit. Importantly, Giuliani's team maneuvered *U.S. v. IBT* to Judge David Edelstein. Although legal journalist Steven Brill called that maneuver an "elaborate charade . . . that will produce anything but evenhanded, credible justice in this landmark case,"[89] it was a critical decision point in the case. Nobody can know how the case would have turned out had a different judge presided over it. We do know that Edelstein enforced the parties' settlement with absolute determination. *U.S. v. IBT* will define his almost half century as a federal judge.

Finally, the weakened states of both Cosa Nostra's and the IBT's leaderships were fortuitous for the lawsuit's success. By 1988, Cosa Nostra was reeling from the most aggressive law-enforcement attack in U.S. history. Scores of LCN leaders were in prison; many of the rest were under indictment or anticipating indictment. The IBT's leadership was in disarray. The union had not had a strong general president since Jimmy Hoffa. Fitzsimmons, Williams, and Presser all finished their presidencies in legal trouble or disgrace. William McCarthy succeeded to the general presidency after a divisive political struggle within the GEB. The civil RICO suit had already been filed when he was sworn in. McCarthy lacked the time and probably the ability (he was elderly) at that late date to carry out an effective resistance strategy.

2

The Civil RICO Complaint and Settlement

At both the international and local levels, the IBT obviously continues to suffer from the relationship with organized crime. Indeed, so pervasive has this relationship become that no single remedy is likely to restore even a measure of true union democracy and independent leadership to the IBT. Sustained commitment of governmental resources to dislodge organized crime from the IBT through a combination of criminal prosecutions, civil action, and administrative proceedings is the only approach that offers even a modest hope of success in the long run. . . . [S]ystematic use of trusteeships by the courts may be necessary to prevent organized crime from continuing to do business as usual in the IBT.[1]

—President's Commission on Organized Crime, March 1986

[W]e are very troubled by reports that the Department of Justice has chosen a broad and unprecedented enforcement strategy that must, of necessity, undermine the [IBT's] ability to perform its statutory functions as the collective bargaining representative of its members. . . . [DOJ's] imposition of trustees to administer an international union . . . is, on its face, inherently destructive of the ability of workers to represent and speak for themselves through their unions. [This] . . . establishes a precedent which strikes at the very foundation of our democracy.

—Petition to U.S. Attorney General Edwin Meese signed by 264 members of Congress, December 10, 1987

On June 28, 1988, U.S. Attorney Rudolph Giuliani and Assistant U.S. Attorney (AUSA) Randy Mastro filed a 113-page civil RICO complaint, accompanied by a 105-page memorandum of law and a 72-page attorney's declaration supporting the allegations against the International Brotherhood of Teamsters (IBT), its general executive board (GEB), one current and eighteen former GEB members, the Cosa Nostra (LCN) Commission, and twenty-six alleged LCN members and associates.[2] The complaint alleged and described the defendants' decades-long corruption of the IBT's international, regional, and local offices, often at the behest of Cosa Nostra members. The consent decree that settled the lawsuit aimed to free the union from Cosa Nostra's grip. It embodied a two-pronged remedy: court-appointed officers to enforce the settlement's and IBT's disciplinary rules and a court-appointed officer to supervise free and fair rank-and-file elections of international-union officers.

The Racketeer Influenced and Corrupt Organizations Act (RICO)

To understand the *U.S. v. IBT* lawsuit, it is necessary to understand the Racketeer Influenced and Corrupt Organizations Act. In 1968, the President's Commission on Law Enforcement and the Administration of Justice's Task Force on Organized Crime painted a picture of Cosa Nostra as a nationwide crime syndicate with massive economic and political power.[3] It warned that LCN was increasingly infiltrating the legitimate economy.[4] Several U.S. senators, notably John McClellan (D-Ark.) and Roman Hruska (R-Neb.), pressed to enhance DOJ's and the FBI's investigative powers, especially electronic eavesdropping. This led to passage of Title III of the Omnibus Crime Control and Safe Streets Act of 1968, which established a comprehensive legal regime authorizing electronic eavesdropping according to court order and strict procedures.[5] Two years later, Congress passed the Racketeer Influenced and Corrupt Organizations Act (RICO), which aimed to prevent and punish organized crime's infiltration of legitimate businesses, labor unions, and other enterprises.[6]

RICO includes criminal and civil provisions. There are four criminal offenses: (1) using funds derived from a pattern of racketeering activity or collection of an unlawful debt to obtain an interest in an enterprise; (2) obtaining an interest in an enterprise through a pattern of racketeering activity or collection of an unlawful debt; (3) conducting the affairs of an enterprise through a pattern of racketeering activity or collection of an unlawful debt; and (4) conspiring to violate 1, 2, or 3.[7]

The statute defines its key terms. An "enterprise" includes any corporation, association, or partnership. Since a union is a legal association, it qualifies as a RICO enterprise. A "racketeering act" is conduct that violates any one of a long list of federal criminal offenses or their state equivalents that Congress deemed to be characteristic conduct for organized-crime members, for example, murder, arson, extortion, fraud, bribery, theft from interstate shipments, and drug trafficking. A "pattern of racketeering activity" requires commission of at least two racketeering acts within a ten-year period. Federal prosecutors can prove those predicate racketeering acts by introducing previous convictions into evidence.

RICO also includes two civil remedies. The first civil remedy empowers victims of RICO offenses to sue their perpetrators for triple damages. This provision played no role in *U.S. v. IBT*. The second civil remedy authorizes the U.S. attorney general to seek injunctive relief to restrain ongoing RICO violations and empowers the federal district courts to use their equitable powers to prevent the defendant from committing future RICO violations.[8] Since the 1982 lawsuit against Union City, New Jersey IBT Local 560, this provision has been DOJ's primary weapon for combating labor racketeering.[9]

A civil RICO lawsuit permits the government to use the liberal discovery rules that apply in federal civil litigation. Each party can require its adversary to answer interrogatories and can depose its adversary's witnesses. Each party can also obtain from the other party books and records relevant to the dispute. The government needs to prove its case by a preponderance of evidence, rather than by criminal procedure's proof beyond a reasonable doubt burden. Because a DOJ civil RICO suit seeks "equitable" (i.e., injunctive) relief, rather than monetary damages, the defendant has no right to a jury trial.

If DOJ prevails in its civil RICO lawsuit, it can seek a remedial court order requiring the defendant to take diverse steps to purge itself of organized crime's influence. To monitor or enforce the defendant's compliance with the order, the court may appoint one or more remedial enforcement officers. (If the case was resolved by settlement, the negotiated consent decree will usually provide for the district court judge to appoint a remedial officer.) Violation of the court's remedial order constitutes contempt of court, punishable by fine or imprisonment. Depending on the terms of the remedial order, the court-appointed officers, paid for by the defendant, can remain on the job for many years, thereby providing a long-term systemic reform effort that criminal prosecution cannot achieve.

The U.S. v. IBT *Civil RICO Complaint*

The *U.S. v. IBT* complaint named five sets of defendants: (1) Cosa Nostra members and associates; (2) the Cosa Nostra Commission; (3) individual Teamsters officials; (4) the IBT's GEB; and (5) the IBT itself. The IBT, portrayed as both perpetrator and victim, was a "nominal" defendant, whose inclusion as a party defendant was necessary for purposes of fashioning an effective remedy. The complaint accused the LCN and IBT defendants of victimizing rank-and-file Teamsters through intimidation, violence, and fraud.

Cosa Nostra Defendants as RICO Violators

The complaint presented *U.S. v. IBT* as an organized-crime case.[10]

> [T]he Teamsters International Union has been a captive labor organization, which La Cosa Nostra figures have infiltrated, controlled and dominated through fear and intimidation and have exploited through fraud, embezzlement, bribery and extortion. . . . [T]his infiltration, control, domination and victimization has taken the form of multiple violations of [the RICO statute] and these violations will continue (resulting in irreparable injury to those victimized by such violations) unless and until this Court divests the defendants associated with La Cosa Nostra, those working with them and those under their control (including present and past members of the General Executive Board) of their union interests.[11]

For rhetorical effect, DOJ identified the individual LCN defendants by both their legal names and their colorful gangland nicknames, for example, Anthony "Fat Tony" Salerno (Genovese crime family underboss), Anthony "Tony Ducks" Corallo (Lucchese crime family boss), Joseph "Joe Doves" Aiuppa (Chicago Outfit boss), and Frank "Mr. B." Balistrieri (Milwaukee crime family boss). It then set out each LCN defendant's previous criminal convictions (see fig. 2.1).

In addition to twenty-six individual LCN defendants, the government named as a defendant the Cosa Nostra Commission, a kind of board of directors that the five NYC Cosa Nostra crime families used to resolve disputes and coordinate collective action.[12] This, too, was for rhetorical effect. There was no way to serve the *U.S. v. IBT* complaint on the Commission, no expectation that a Commission representative would answer the

FIGURE 2.1

Cosa Nostra Defendants in U.S. v. IBT

Defendant	Connection to Cosa Nostra	Prior Convictions
Joseph "Joey Doves" Aiuppa	Chicago Outfit boss	Convicted of unlawful possession and transportation of protected birds across state lines (1966); convicted of tax evasion and sentenced to twenty-eight years in prison for "skimming" (concealing from tax authorities) profits from Las Vegas casinos (1986).
Frank "Mr. B." Balistrieri	Milwaukee crime family boss	Convicted of tax evasion and sentenced to two years in prison (1967); convicted and sentenced to thirteen years in prison for skimming $2 million from Las Vegas casinos (1984); convicted of conspiracy and sentenced to ten years in prison (1985).
Eugene Boffa, Sr.	Bufalino crime family associate	Convicted of RICO, sentenced to twenty years in prison and forfeiture of assets worth $250,000 (1981).
John "Jackie the Lackey" Cerone	Chicago Outfit underboss	Arrested over twenty times for armed robbery, bookmaking, illegal gambling, embezzlement, and other charges; convicted and served nine months in prison for skimming $2 million from a casino (1986).
Anthony Civella	Kansas City crime family boss	Convicted of tax evasion and sentenced to five years in prison for skimming profits from Las Vegas casinos (1984); convicted and sentenced to five years in prison for selling stolen prescription drugs (1992).
Carl "Corky" Civella	Kansas City crime family boss	Convicted of tax evasion and sentenced to ten years in prison for skimming profits from Las Vegas casinos (1994).
Anthony "Tony Ducks" Corallo	Lucchese crime family boss	Arrested for grand larceny (1929); sentenced to two years in prison for paying a $35,000 bribe to an assistant U.S. attorney (1962); sentenced to four and a half years in prison for bribing the NYC Water Commissioner (1968); convicted of RICO violations and sentenced to one hundred years in prison (1986).
Carl "Toughy" DeLuna	Kansas City crime family underboss	Served twelve years in prison for skimming profits from Las Vegas casinos (1986).
Anthony "Figgy" Ficarotta	Genovese crime family member	Served five years in prison for extorting $2,000 from a company (1985).

Name	Role	Description
Christopher "Christy Tick" Furnari, Sr.	Lucchese crime family consigliere	Convicted of violating RICO for, among other predicate offenses, murdering Bonanno crime family boss Carmine Galante. Sentenced to one hundred years in prison without possibility of parole (1986).
Matthew "Matty the Horse" Ianniello	Genovese crime family acting boss from 1998 to 2005	Convicted of tax evasion and racketeering and sentenced to six years in prison (1985); sentenced to two years in prison for racketeering (2006).
Joseph "Joey the Clown" Lombardo	Chicago Outfit capo	Convicted and sentenced to fifteen years for extorting $800,000 from a construction company and for attempting to bribe U.S. Senator Howard Cannon (1983); convicted and sentenced to fourteen years for maintaining hidden interests in and skimming over $2 million from Las Vegas casinos (1986).
Gennaro "Gerry Lang" Langella	Colombo crime family underboss	Convicted and sentenced to ten years in prison for perjury and obstructing justice (1985); convicted of RICO in the "Commission" case and sentenced to sixty-five years (1987).
Angelo "The Nutcracker" LaPietra	Chicago Outfit capo	Convicted of tax evasion and sentenced to sixteen years in prison for skimming $2 million from Las Vegas casinos (1986).
Frank Manzo	Lucchese crime family capo	Convicted for loitering (1970); convicted for possession of a gambling device (1970); convicted of attempting to extort payments from trucking firms at JFK International Airport and sentenced to twelve years (1986).
Nicholas Marangello	Bonanno crime family underboss	Sentenced to eight years in prison for running a racketeering operation that controlled NYC's moving and storage industry (1987).
Joseph "Joey Messina" Massino	Bonanno crime family boss	Convicted for violating RICO, the Hobbs Act, and the Taft-Hartley Act and sentenced to ten years in prison (1986); sentenced to life in prison for committing seven murders, arson, extortion, loan sharking, illegal gambling, conspiracy, and money laundering (2004).
Carmine Persico	Colombo crime family de facto boss	Imprisoned from 1973 to 1979 for hijacking and loan sharking; convicted of RICO and sentenced to life in prison in the "Commission" case (1986).
Anthony "Tony Pro" Provenzano	Genovese crime family capo	Convicted and sentenced to four and a half years in prison for extortion (1966); convicted of racketeering and sentenced to twenty years for extorting employers (1977); convicted and sentenced to life in prison for the murder of Anthony Castellito (1978).

(continued)

FIGURE 2.1 (*continued*)
Cosa Nostra Defendants in U.S. v. IBT

Defendant	Connection to Cosa Nostra	Prior Convictions
Nunzio "Nunzi Pro" Provenzano	Genovese crime family member	Convicted and sentenced to ten years in prison for labor racketeering for attempting to extort $187,000 from four trucking companies (1981).
Philip "Rusty" Rastelli	Bonanno crime family boss	Sentenced to one year in prison for an antitrust violation and three concurrent ten-year prison sentences for extortion (1976); sentenced to twelve years in prison for extortion (1987).
Milton "Maishe" Rockman	Cleveland crime family associate	Convicted and sentenced to seven years in prison for skimming from Las Vegas casinos.
Salvatore "Tom Mix" Santoro	Lucchese crime family underboss	Convicted in the "Commission" case and sentenced to one hundred years in prison (1986).
Anthony "Fat Tony" Salerno	Genovese crime family boss	Convicted in the "Commission" case and sentenced to one hundred years in prison (1986).
Francis Sheeran	Bufalino crime family associate	Convicted and sentenced to nine years in prison for labor racketeering (1981).
John "Peanuts" Tronolone	Cleveland crime family boss	Convicted and sentenced to two years in prison for running a bookmaking operation (1975); sentenced to nine years in prison for racketeering (1989).

complaint, and no enforceable remedy against the Commission as distinct from the individual LCN defendants. Nevertheless, naming the Commission as a defendant supported DOJ's organized-crime narrative.[13]

The DOJ lawyers charged that the LCN defendants, aided and abetted by the union defendants, obtained an interest in "the Teamsters International Enterprise"* through a pattern of racketeering activity[14] that included wire fraud, blackmail, embezzlement, extortion, and murder.[15] The complaint cited the following racketeering acts, among others:

- over twenty murders, dozens of bombings, and other violent acts;
- LCN's conspiracy to use interstate transport in furtherance of embezzlement, extortion, illegal gambling, and drug trafficking;
- LCN's bribery of Teamsters officials to obtain IBT benefit-fund loans to finance casino projects in Las Vegas; and
- LCN's attempt to bribe a U.S. senator to prevent deregulation of the trucking industry, as deregulation would weaken the IBT and consequently LCN's ability, through the IBT, to influence national politics.[16]

The complaint detailed acts of violence and threats of violence against union members who challenged or even questioned corrupt IBT officials' authority or decisions, including the following examples:

- Tony Provenzano, then-president of Union City, New Jersey IBT Local 560 and a member of the Genovese crime family, hired a hit man to murder union dissident Anthony Castellito. (Years later, Provenzano was convicted for this murder.)
- Robert Rispo, a self-described "leg breaker," beat up Teamsters who objected to a labor-leasing scheme organized by defendants Eugene Boffa (an LCN associate) and Frank Sheeran (president

---

* Judge Edelstein commented that "the complaint alleges a far-flung enterprise, the Teamsters International Enterprise, comprised of the IBT, individual members of the GEB, the Commission of La Cosa Nostra and individual members of La Cosa Nostra. Before judgment can be entered against any of the defendants, the Government must prove that there was such an enterprise and that the racketeering acts committed in furtherance of such enterprise formed a pattern of racketeering." *United States v. Int'l Bhd. of Teamsters*, 708 F. Supp. 1388, 1406–07 (1989). Judge Edelstein may have misunderstood the government's pleading. The government meant to name as defendants just the IBT, not the IBT's affiliates and pension and welfare funds, though the government did mean to define the *RICO enterprise* as the IBT plus all of its affiliates and pension and welfare funds.

of Wilmington, Delaware IBT Local 326).[17] The scheme recruited nonunion workers to fill positions that, according to collective bargaining agreements, should have required membership in the IBT. Rispo admitted to many labor-racketeering crimes in his 1985 testimony before the President's Commission on Organized Crime (PCOC).

- Kansas City crime family underboss Carl DeLuna warned casino owner Allen Glick that if he resisted an IBT-financed purchase of his casino, he and his children would be killed "one by one."

According to the complaint, the LCN defendants used violence and intimidation to consolidate the union defendants' power, position, and prerogatives.

DOJ also alleged that the LCN defendants, with the aid of the IBT defendants, violated union members' right to select their union leaders. Indeed, Cosa Nostra played a key role in selecting several IBT general presidents, including Jimmy Hoffa, Frank Fitzsimmons, Roy Williams, and Jackie Presser. Once in office, those general presidents cooperated with LCN.[18] For example, Presser, three IBT international vice presidents, and several trustees ceded substantial authority over Central States Pension Fund investment decisions to Allen Dorfman, knowing that Dorfman was an associate of the Chicago LCN crime family ("the Outfit"). Moreover, Presser received from LCN associates approximately $1 million "with the intent to be influenced with respect to the Central States Pension Fund." He also provided Cosa Nostra members with "loans and other things of value in exchange for their assistance in supporting his election."[19]

Cosa Nostra's power base in the IBT paid big economic and political dividends. LCN extracted money from the union via loans (never repaid), salaries (unearned), theft, embezzlement, and service contracts with companies that LCN figures owned or controlled. LCN also used its influence in the IBT to establish and police cartels in the trucking, carting, and airfreight industries and in other business sectors in NYC and other major cities.[20] It parlayed its influence over IBT political contributions and endorsements into beneficial relationships with local, state, and national politicians.

Union Defendants as RICO Violators

The *U.S. v. IBT* complaint named as union defendants the IBT's GEB and nineteen current and former GEB members, including General President Jackie Presser and General Secretary-Treasurer Weldon Mathis. When Presser died, eleven days after *U.S. v. IBT* was filed, Mathis automatically succeeded to the presidency. A short time later, after a power struggle among the union leadership, the GEB, in a nine-to-eight vote, elected International Vice President William McCarthy to replace Mathis as IBT general president.

The complaint offered two theories to establish the IBT international officers' RICO liability. First, it asserted that the IBT defendants aided and abetted the LCN defendants' perpetration of racketeering acts by, among other things, loaning union money from the IBT's pension and welfare funds to LCN-controlled businesses; contracting with LCN-affiliated vendors; appointing LCN members and associates to union office; hiring LCN members and associates as local business agents and organizers; and arranging for LCN members and associates to obtain lucrative, sometimes no-show, jobs with IBT employers. To support these allegations, the complaint highlighted PCOC's 1986 report on labor racketeering, *The Edge: Organized Crime, Business, and Labor Unions*, which concluded, among other things, that General Presidents Hoffa and Williams were "direct instruments of organized crime" and that Presser had "associated with organized crime figures and . . . benefited from their support in his elevation to the IBT Presidency in 1983."[21]

Second, the complaint asserted that, by malfeasance and misfeasance, the IBT defendants had deprived rank-and-file members of their union democracy rights and of economic benefits that they would or could have obtained had racketeers not run their union. The lost benefits included jobs, wages, and pension and welfare benefits; the assets of IBT locals, joint councils, area conferences, and benefit funds, "including the rate of return which would otherwise be derived from the investments of such benefit funds"; economic benefits that the rank and file would have obtained but for LCN's monopolization of industries that employ or would employ Teamsters; and economic benefits that the rank and file would obtain but for the loss of leverage in collective-bargaining negotiations.[22] DOJ cited numerous examples of specific conduct that constituted "a comprehensive perversion of the democratic principles of trade unionism as guaranteed by the Landrum-Griffin Act*":[23]

- "In 1981, the Teamsters International Union officer defendants then in office elected Roy L. Williams as interim General President of the Teamsters International Union, even though at the time of the election, Williams had openly associated with various La Cosa Nostra figures."
- "In the 1980s, Roy Williams . . . appointed Jack Ancona and John Sansone to positions with the Teamsters International at the direction of Nicholas Civella, who was then the Boss of the Kansas City Family."[24]

DOJ charged that, by actively and passively cooperating with the LCN defendants, the union defendants fostered a climate of intimidation that allowed the LCN defendants to obtain an interest in the Teamsters Union and to use the union's governing machinery to deprive rank-and-file union members of their tangible and intangible (e.g., union democracy rights) property. For example, the complaint alleged that the IBT defendants "consistently failed to take action" to rid the international union, joint councils, and locals of corrupt officials, allowing those officials to remain in office after "repeatedly" failing to investigate allegations of their misconduct.[25]

> The Teamsters' General Executive Board has literally done nothing, despite its affirmative obligation under federal law and the IBT's Constitution to rid the union of corruption. . . . The inescapable conclusion from this shocking course of conduct is that the entire IBT General Executive Board has permitted La Cosa Nostra to influence and corrupt the IBT.[26]

---

* The 1959 Landrum-Griffin Act (formally the Labor Management Reporting and Disclosure Act or LMRDA) was passed in the wake of the McClellan Committee hearings to strengthen federal regulation of labor unions. It includes a bill of rights guaranteeing union members freedom of speech and assembly, the right to secret-ballot vote on dues, the right to sue the union, the right to receive copies of collective-bargaining agreements, and due process in internal union disciplinary hearings. It also requires unions to file with DOL annual reports on income, expenditures, and salaries; forbids officers from having certain conflicts of interest; and prohibits union loans exceeding $2,000 to officers and members. 29 U.S.C. §§ 401–531 (2000).

The complaint further alleged and cited specific examples of IBT defendants defrauding the membership by "improperly using their union positions to reward themselves, their relatives, and their associates."

- Joseph Trerotola, an IBT international vice president, "caused various Teamster Locals in the New York area to buy insurance from his son, Vincent Trerotola, and from insurance companies represented by Vincent Trerotola."
- Daniel Ligurotis, another IBT international vice president, "used his control over Teamsters Local 705 in Chicago, Illinois, improperly to draw approximately $330,000 in salaries from Local 705 and its Benefit Plans."[27]

Requested Remedy

U.S. Attorney Giuliani sought a preliminary injunction barring (1) LCN members and associates from participating in IBT affairs; (2) GEB members from engaging in racketeering acts, associating with LCN, or interfering with a court-liaison officer (who would review IBT appointments and expenditures and exercise the general president's and GEB's disciplinary powers); and (3) IBT officers found to be RICO violators from union membership. Giuliani also asked Judge Edelstein to appoint a trustee to conduct international-officer elections and to discharge GEB duties that "the trustee deems necessary." Finally, Giuliani asked the judge to order the LCN and IBT defendants to disgorge monies derived from their RICO violations.

On January 17, 1989, TDU's lawyers, Chicago labor lawyer Tom Geoghegan and Washington, D.C., public-interest lawyer Paul Levy, moved to intervene in *U.S. v. IBT* to "protect the rights of the innocent rank and file Teamster members."[28] American Civil Liberties Union (ACLU) lawyer Helen Hershkoff, supported by Robert Smith, a partner in a prominent NYC law firm, joined TDU in the motion. The ACLU supported TDU's preferred remedy: a government-supervised, one-Teamster-one-vote, direct election of international IBT officers.

The January–February 1989 issue of TDU's newsletter, *Convoy Dispatch*, explained TDU's position: "No Mob Control—No Government Control."

The government's attempt to combat corruption with a trusteeship is countered by IBT officials who claim there is no corruption at the top of the union. Only TDU is standing up for our union of 1.6 million hard-working men and women who have nothing to gain from corruption or trusteeship. We have everything to gain from the Right to Vote.

TDU's members were split on the desirability of a trusteeship. Some regarded "the very thought of the government taking over the Teamsters as frightening and against all constitutional principles."[29] Others concluded that corruption was so pervasive and entrenched that only a government takeover could produce systemic change.[30] In a letter published on *Convoy Dispatch*'s front page, TDU urged General President McCarthy to "[a]nnounce that the first-ever membership vote will be held for General President, General Secretary-Treasurer and 16 vice presidents by region, and invite the Justice Department, specifically Rudolph Giuliani, to monitor the election."[31] This step, TDU claimed, would resolve the RICO suit, generate a spirit of solidarity and enthusiasm among the rank and file, and demonstrate that IBT leaders are more interested in strengthening the union than protecting their own prerogatives.

Reactions to *U.S. v. IBT*

Though rumored for months, the actual filing of the *U.S. v. IBT* complaint was a huge news story. A number of high-profile politicians immediately denounced it; some charged that it was part of the Reagan administration's plan to destroy the labor movement, others that it violated a principle of American democracy. The editors of several leading newspapers, as well as many federal and state prosecutors, praised the lawsuit.

A *New York Times* editorial observed,

> If the government wins, one outcome would be a new leadership chosen by fair elections. What better cure could there be for the Teamsters' chronic and manifest illness than a stiff dose of democracy? . . . The Teamsters leadership fears losing control like the Wicked Witch of the West feared water. . . . The ideal remedy, should the Government win the racketeering lawsuit, would be Government-supervised elections by the rank and file for a new executive board and new international officers.[32]

A *Christian Science Monitor* editorial took much the same view: "The suit is not a union buster as some labor leaders claim. . . . The key to solving the Teamsters' troubles lies in one-man-one-vote elections by secret ballot for national as well as local union elections."[33] *Detroit Free Press* labor journalist James Kilpatrick stated that "to read the civil suit just brought by the Department of Justice against the Teamsters Union is to gain a horrifying glimpse into the real world of the mob. . . . This is ugly."[34]

National labor leaders expressed concern that this first-ever civil RICO suit against an international union would create bad precedent. AFL-CIO President Lane Kirkland told the *Los Angeles Times*, "It doesn't sound to me like the proper relationship between a government and a private institution in a free society."[35] John Henning, secretary-treasurer of the California Federation of Labor (formerly Under Secretary of Labor during the Kennedy and Johnson administrations), said, "If the federal government has a case against individuals, it should go to court and prove it and seek appropriate action against those individuals. . . . What the government is proposing would smear millions of union members who are in no way involved."[36]

International and regional IBT leaders denounced the civil RICO lawsuit. General President Presser said, "You know why we're first on the list [of international unions to be sued under civil RICO]? Because we're the strongest. We're the best. And we're the most militant. But we're not laying down for anybody. . . . Teamsters are not racketeers, hoodlums, gangsters and thugs. They are Mr. and Mrs. Americans."[37] IBT General Secretary-Treasurer Weldon Mathis called the suit a "vicious anti-labor attack" and a "shameful attempt to destroy a democratic union."[38] Michigan IBT Joint Council 43 President Larry Brennan said that "DOJ's plan is like a purge in Russia": "You should indict and convict each individual and not the masses. The first thing you've got to remember is that this is a democracy. We haven't had our day in court. . . . I think they may have awakened a sleeping giant."[39] IBT International Vice President Robert Holmes warned that "if they can do this to us, they could take the rest for granted. There'd be no labor movement left."[40] Virtually alone among IBT leaders, Joint Council 56 President John Couts, Jr., called the lawsuit "a good idea. It's time that the Teamsters get out from under Mafia control and give the members and officers a chance to run their union."[41]

Despite prior congressional hearings and the litany of investigations and prosecutions exposing organized-crime racketeering in the IBT, a number of national politicians (Republicans and Democrats) criticized the lawsuit. Senator Orrin Hatch (R-Utah) said, "It flies in the face of democratic principles" and "smacks of totalitarianism."[42] Congressman Jack Kemp (R-N.Y.) observed, "The United States government is not meant to be in the business of taking things over. It shouldn't take over newspapers. It shouldn't take over schools. It shouldn't take over corporations. It shouldn't take over your union."[43] Senator Paul Simon (D-Ill.) said that the suit "ought to frighten every American."[44] Reverend Jesse Jackson's spokesperson said Jackson believes "that the union belongs to the employees and that, if a problem exists in the Teamsters Union—legal or otherwise—that matter should be resolved legally. But the union should remain with the workers."[45] Congressman William Ford (D-Mich.) sarcastically suggested that "instead of the Teamsters, maybe the Reagan administration should be taken over."[46]

State and local politicians echoed these criticisms. Ohio Governor Richard Celeste called the lawsuit "just plain wrong": "The idea that the Justice Department . . . is going to come in and put its hands on the Teamsters Union makes me shudder. This union should be in the hands of the men and women who make up the Teamsters."[47] Detroit Mayor Coleman Young rhetorically asked, "If labor can be described as a criminal enterprise, what's wrong with describing a city or a state next? I think there's a danger to the freedom of the American people here."[48]

DOJ lawyers and some others defended the civil RICO suit. John Keeney, deputy assistant attorney general of DOJ's criminal division, explained that by using civil RICO rather than criminal prosecution, "we can remove not only convicted officers but also officers we can demonstrate are puppets of criminal groups."[49] James Harmon, Jr., former director of PCOC, predicted that *U.S. v. IBT* "will make it impossible for organized crime to regroup."[50] Ronald Goldstock, director of the New York State Organized Crime Task Force, pointed out that using civil RICO against labor unions controlled by Cosa Nostra

> i[s] precisely what Congress intended. What RICO does is make changes which, for example, in unions, would restore democratic processes, or in mob-dominated industries, would change the susceptibility to mob infiltration. Oftentimes, unions become captive because people maintain power through either fear of physical violence or economic reprisal.[51]

Pretrial Motions and Discovery

The IBT's Motion to Dismiss the Complaint

The IBT and several individual IBT defendants moved to dismiss the RICO complaint on grounds that (1) it violated union members' First

Amendment right to free association, (2) federal labor law preempted RICO, (3) several defendants had a statute-of-limitations defense, and (4) the complaint failed to state a viable theory and/or factual basis for relief under RICO.[52] Judge Edelstein rejected these arguments. Explaining that "it is only *lawful* association that is protected [by the First Amendment], not association for a criminal or unlawful purpose,"[53] he held that federal labor law did not preempt the RICO statute because one of RICO's primary goals was "to provide the Government with a tool to attack organized crime's alleged infiltration of legitimate enterprises, including specifically labor unions."[54] He further held that RICO's statute of limitations applies only to suits by private parties, not to DOJ actions seeking equitable remedies such as injunctions and court-appointed monitors.[55] For the same reason, Judge Edelstein denied the defendants' request for a jury trial.[56]

Judge Edelstein held that the government had sufficiently alleged a legal basis for the IBT defendants' RICO liability; that is, if the government could prove its allegations, it would satisfy its burden of demonstrating that the IBT defendants had violated RICO.

> [T]he Government is advancing a theory of collective liability based on a failure to act when there was a duty to do so. Each defendant officer is a fiduciary with respect to the Union members. They have a duty to disclose and remedy wrongdoing by the IBT. When officers engage in collective wrongdoing, courts have recognized the propriety of collective pleading.[57]

Edelstein found that the IBT's other challenges to the legal sufficiency of DOJ's complaint were "insubstantial and accordingly rejected."[58]

The IBT's Motions to Change Venue and Join IBT Locals as Defendants

The IBT defendants moved to transfer the case from Judge Edelstein's courtroom to federal court in Washington, D.C., the location of IBT headquarters ("the Marble Palace").[59] Edelstein denied that motion on the ground that Washington, D.C.'s proximity to NYC would make little difference to the convenience of any party.[60] He also rejected the IBT's motion to join as "indispensable parties" more than six hundred IBT locals, joint councils, area conferences, and benefit funds because the relief that DOJ requested would not directly affect those entities and because granting the motion would delay trial for months, if not years.[61]

DOJ's Motion for a Preliminary Injunction

Judge Edelstein decided not to grant DOJ's motion to appoint a court officer to supervise IBT expenditures, appointments, and disciplinary processes until resolution of the civil RICO suit.[62] He emphasized the need for a trial to resolve important factual and legal issues.[63] Judge Edelstein denied DOJ's motion for a preliminary injunction and ordered an expedited discovery schedule.

DOJ's Motion for Entry of Default Judgment against Certain LCN Defendants

The Cosa Nostra Commission and several individual Cosa Nostra defendants did not submit answers to the government's complaint. Consequently, Judge Edelstein authorized DOJ to enter default judgments against them. (Some Cosa Nostra defendants, acting pro se, did submit answers to the complaint. Others, including Salvatore Provenzano, Nunzio Provenzano, and Francis Sheeran, entered into consent judgments, agreeing to have no contact with the IBT.)[64] Because these defendants were enjoined from involvement in IBT affairs, any future attempt to exert influence in the IBT could be punished as contempt of court.

DOJ's Motion for Summary Judgment against Certain LCN Defendants

DOJ asked Judge Edelstein to grant summary judgment against six LCN defendants based on their prior convictions for RICO or RICO predicate offenses.[65] Judge Edelstein demurred because "the RICO claims asserted in the complaint are more far reaching than the criminal convictions of the defendants."[66] He explained that before he would enter a judgment against any defendant, DOJ had to prove that there was an "enterprise" composed of the IBT, individual GEB members, the Cosa Nostra Commission, and individual Cosa Nostra members; the alleged racketeering acts committed in furtherance of the enterprise constituted a pattern of racketeering activity; and each defendant engaged in that pattern of racketeering activity.[67]

Depositions

Because *U.S. v. IBT* was a civil action, the parties could depose each other's witnesses. The GEB members' depositions demonstrated that the named defendants and other top IBT officers had failed to adequately investigate (or to investigate at all) allegations of IBT officials' corruption and racketeering, despite 191 criminal prosecutions of and 22 civil-enforcement actions against Teamsters officials. Particularly striking was the GEB's failure to commence disciplinary investigations after the 1982 civil RICO decision against IBT Local 560, after the 1986 indictment of General President Presser on fraud charges, and after the 1986 PCOC report called the IBT the country's "most [organized-crime] controlled union."[68]

Vice President Robert Holmes, Sr., stated at his deposition that he had not asked Presser about his fraud indictment, despite the extensive negative publicity it generated for the union, because "it was none of my business. That is his problem."[69] Vice President Theodore R. Cozza claimed that he lacked both responsibility and authority to investigate criminality in "autonomous" IBT locals.[70] John H. Cleveland, another international vice president, testified that the IBT lacked the resources to investigate labor racketeering.[71] Harold Friedman, an officer of Joint Council 41 and the Ohio Conference of Teamsters, said that to have inquired into a fellow IBT officer's criminal conduct would have been "bad manners. . . . [Only] an absolute asshole would have walk[ed] up to me, whether he's a vice president or employee or anybody else and say 'hey, tell me about your case.' What the hell is it their business or anybody's?"[72]

The Settlement

Negotiations

Several individual Teamsters defendants sought to settle to avoid out-of-pocket litigation costs.[73] The GEB responded with a resolution prohibiting individual Teamsters defendants from settling separately. Judge Edelstein quickly ordered the GEB to rescind that resolution. The GEB complied. International Vice Presidents Robert Holmes, Sr., Maurice Schurr, and John Cleveland resigned from union office.[74] General Secretary-Treasurer Weldon Mathis and Vice Presidents Edward M. Lawson and Don L. West agreed not to knowingly associate with members or associates of LCN or other criminal groups.[75] The GEB denounced these individual settlements as "self-serving actions" because they "interfered with and impeded" the IBT's ability to defend against the civil RICO suit.[76]

In December 1988, IBT General Counsel James Grady requested settlement talks on behalf of the union. Giuliani and Mastro proposed a settlement in which both parties would agree that there should be no organized-crime influence in the IBT; the settlement would authorize the court to appoint a trustee with power to investigate, prosecute, and adjudicate disciplinary violations, veto union expenditures and appointments, and supervise the next five quinquennial international elections. After the GEB rejected that idea and DOJ rejected some counterproposals, negotiations stalled for several months.

Negotiations resumed less than a week before the scheduled start of trial. By then, Benito Romano had succeeded Giuliani as U.S. attorney. (Giuliani resigned in order to return to private practice and contemplate a run for NYC mayor.) Mastro, still lead negotiator, continued to insist that a settlement include three court-appointed officers, direct rank-and-file, secret-ballot elections of international officers in the next five international elections, and elimination of organized-crime influence in the union.

On March 13, the eve of trial, the remaining individual union defendants and the GEB agreed to a settlement closely tracking DOJ's terms. General President William McCarthy, the last holdout, said he was persuaded by "a chorus of [IBT] lawyers saying, 'Sign, it's the best deal you can get,'" and after his lawyer told him that ongoing litigation would cost him over one hundred thousand dollars.[77]

The Consent Decree

The parties' agreement was incorporated into a consent decree approved by Judge Edelstein. It provided that

> the union defendants acknowledge that there have been allegations, sworn testimony and judicial findings of past problems with La Cosa Nostra corruption of the IBT; and . . . the union defendants agree that there should be no criminal element or La Cosa Nostra corruption of any part of the IBT; and . . . the union defendants agree that it is imperative that the IBT, as the largest trade union in the free world, be maintained democratically, with integrity and for the sole benefit of its members and without unlawful outside influence.[78]

The consent decree enjoined all IBT members, officers, employees, and agents from committing racketeering acts, from interfering with the court-appointed officers, and from knowingly associating with any LCN members or associates, other criminal organizations, or any person enjoined from participating in IBT affairs.[79] A violation of this injunction would constitute an IBT disciplinary violation punishable by sanctions, including expulsion from the union.

The consent decree required several amendments to the IBT constitution. First, it lengthened the statute of limitations for bringing disciplinary charges from one year from the date the disciplinary violation was allegedly committed to five years from the date the disciplinary violation was discovered. Second, it permitted the IBT general president and the GEB to suspend a member facing criminal or civil charges. Third, it prescribed rules for electing convention delegates, nominating candidates for IBT office, and rank-and-file secret balloting for IBT officers. Fourth, it provided that a vacancy in the office of general president would be filled by special election rather than by GEB appointment.*

To enforce the terms of the settlement, the consent decree provided that Judge Edelstein would appoint, from the parties' list of recommendations, three officers: an independent administrator (IA), an investigations officer (IO), and an election officer (EO). These court officers would have authority to hire accountants, consultants, experts, investigators, and other personnel. The IBT would pay their salaries and expenses. After the EO "certified" the 1991 election of international officers, an independent review board (IRB) consisting of three members—one selected by DOJ, one by the IBT, and one by those two board members—would take over the IO's and IA's disciplinary enforcement duties. During the IRB phase, the IBT would play an active role in disciplinary adjudications. The IRB would continue to investigate disciplinary violations. It would also review and, if necessary, correct IBT disciplinary decisions.

---

* Previously, the GEB appointed a replacement when an international office became vacant. The previous four general presidents, and practically every international vice president for twenty years, first attained his position via a GEB appointment that was then overwhelmingly endorsed at the next IBT convention. For example, Jackie Presser was appointed as international vice president to fill the vacancy that arose when Presser's father took a permanent leave of absence. The GEB then selected Presser to be general president to fill the vacancy that arose when Roy Williams stepped down after being convicted of conspiring to bribe a U.S. senator.

Independent Administrator (IA). The consent decree empowered an independent administrator to exercise the disciplinary authority that the IBT's GEB and general president possess. This included the power to discipline corrupt IBT officers, agents, employees, and members and, when necessary, to appoint trustees to run the affairs of any local union, joint council, or area conference.[80] The IA would adjudicate disciplinary cases brought by the IO and would approve, reject, or modify the GEB's disciplinary decisions.

In the event of a conflict between the IA and IBT over union expenditures, contracts, or appointments, the consent decree provided that the IA's decision would prevail. Indeed, the IA could veto any IBT expenditure, contract, or appointment that, in the IA's view, constituted or furthered a violation of RICO or contributed to Cosa Nostra's influence over the IBT. (At the request of the general president or the GEB, the IA would have to give reasons for having vetoed an expenditure or appointment and give the general president or the GEB fourteen days to request Judge Edelstein's review.)

On May 31, 1989, Judge Edelstein appointed Frederick Lacey as IA. Lacey was well qualified for the job. From 1969 to 1971, as U.S. attorney for the District of New Jersey, he had secured convictions of numerous organized-crime figures. He then served for fourteen years as a federal district court judge (District of New Jersey). At the time of his appointment, Lacey was a partner in an NYC law firm. He quickly determined that he could not investigate corruption allegations and later adjudicate charges based on those allegations. Therefore, he separated the IA's and IO's offices. The IO would investigate and prosecute disciplinary violations. IA Lacey would preside over disciplinary hearings, decide whether the charges had been proved, and, if so, impose sanctions.[81]

Investigations Officer (IO). The consent decree authorized the IO to investigate allegations of misconduct in the international union and in IBT affiliates (i.e., local unions, joint councils, and area conferences); to bring disciplinary charges against any IBT officer, member, or employee "for the purpose and in the manner specified in the IBT Constitution"; and to institute trusteeship proceedings "for the purpose and in the manner specified in the IBT Constitution." To carry out these tasks, the IO could take lawful, reasonable, and necessary steps, including the following, to fully inform himself about the IBT's activities:

- Examining the books and records of the international union, local unions, and joint councils, upon three days' advance notice. (This included the right to hire an independent auditor.)
- Attending GEB meetings concerning the rights or duties of the IO, IA, or EO, upon advance notice to the general president.
- Taking sworn statements or sworn in-person examinations of any IBT officer, member, employee, or agent, upon ten days' advance notice.

The IO could also bring disciplinary charges against an IBT member for interfering with a disciplinary investigation.[82] Since there was no statute of limitations, the IO could bring disciplinary charges alleging misconduct that occurred years before *U.S. v. IBT* was filed.[83] For the IO position, Judge Edelstein selected Charles Carberry, who had previously served nine years as an AUSA in SDNY, including a stint as chief of that office's securities fraud unit. At the time of his appointment, Carberry was a partner in an NYC law firm.

Election Officer (EO). The consent decree provided for direct rank-and-file, secret-ballot election of international-union officers (general president, general secretary-treasurer, international vice presidents and trustees). It empowered and required the court-appointed EO to distribute election materials to the IBT membership; supervise the campaigning, nominating, and balloting processes; and certify the election results.[84] It left for future determination whether the EO's role would extend beyond the 1991 international election. DOJ would have discretion to decide whether the EO would supervise the 1996 IBT election; if it decided affirmatively, the government would have to bear the expense. After 1996, the IBT's elections would be supervised by DOL, unless both DOJ and the IBT agreed otherwise. For the EO position, Judge Edelstein selected Michael Holland, a Chicago labor lawyer who previously was general counsel to the United Mine Workers (UMW), one of very few unions that hold rank-and-file elections for international officers.

Independent Review Board (IRB). After the EO certified the 1991 election results, the IA's and IO's disciplinary authority would pass to an IRB, whose three members would serve five-year terms.[85] In the IRB phase of the remediation, the court-appointed IRB and the IBT would cooperate in processing disciplinary cases. The IRB would investigate disciplinary violations and, if warranted, recommend that the IBT bring disciplinary charges or impose a trusteeship. (The IRB would publish these recommendations in *Teamster Magazine*.) The IRB would then ensure that the IBT unit with jurisdiction over the disciplinary or trusteeship charges implemented the recommendation appropriately. If the IRB found the IBT's actions "inadequate," and the union failed to satisfactorily modify its decision, the IRB would convene a de novo hearing and render a binding judgment.

Soon after EO Holland certified the 1991 election, U.S. Attorney General William Barr nominated IA Lacey to serve on the IRB. IBT General President Ron Carey (winner of the 1991 election) nominated his campaign manager, Harold Burke, previously UMW's organizing director. When Burke and Lacey were unable to agree on a third IRB member, Judge Edelstein appointed William Webster, former federal judge, FBI director, and CIA director.

At a press conference held on the day he filed *U.S. v. IBT*, Giuliani stated that the lawsuit sought court oversight lasting "only for so long as necessary to eliminate organized crime's influence over the Teamsters, to put permanent reforms into place, and to return control of the Teamsters to the many honest working men and women of the union."[86] The consent decree does not include a time frame or sunset provision. It states only that "upon satisfactory completion and implementation of the terms and conditions of this order, this Court shall entertain a joint motion of the parties hereto for entry of judgment dismissing this action with prejudice and without costs to either party."[87] No criteria are specified for determining "satisfactory completion and implementation." In a 1993 decision, Judge Edelstein observed that "there is no timetable for the completion of the IRB's task."[88]

Paying for the Court-Appointed Officers. The consent decree required the IBT to pay the salaries and expenses of the independent administrator, investigations officer, election officer, and their staffs. The court-appointed officers would submit itemized bills every three months. If the IBT general president did not contest the bills within fourteen business days, the IBT would be obliged to pay them. After certification of the 1991 IBT election results, the IBT would be responsible for paying the IRB's costs and expenses, including communications with the IBT membership and the toll-free corruption hotline. The court would resolve disputes over compensation and expenses. (All told, the IRB's expenses have run about $3 million per year. The election officer's expenses have run about $10 million each five-year election cycle.)

Conclusion and Analysis

Referring to the Teamsters Union as a "captive labor union," and to some locals as "captive locals," the *U.S. v. IBT* complaint presented a narrative whereby Cosa Nostra figures infiltrated and exploited the Teamsters Union, with both active and passive assistance from the IBT's international officers. Rhetorically, the complaint placed the lawsuit squarely within the government's war on organized crime and portrayed the Teamsters rank and file as victims. Calling to mind civil-rights complaints that asked federal judges to enjoin constitutional deprivations suffered by prison inmates, jail detainees, mental patients, and schoolchildren,[89] the complaint charged that the LCN defendants used bribes, intimidation, and violence to violate rank and filers' rights to run for office, vote for union candidates of their choice, criticize incumbent leaders, and rely on union officers' honest services. It charged the IBT defendants with violating their fiduciary duty to serve the union and its members and with aiding the LCN defendants in looting the IBT and its pension and welfare funds.

Settlement

The settlement included electoral and disciplinary prongs. Both prongs were meant to vindicate the rights and interests of ordinary Teamsters. But rank-and-file Teamsters did not have a voice in the settlement talks. Therefore, it is worth asking whether their interests were adequately represented. DOJ claimed to be acting on behalf of the Teamsters rank and file, but its primary goal was to destroy Cosa Nostra. From the DOJ lawyers' perspective, what was good for the war on organized crime was also good for the IBT's rank and file. Certainly, there is some truth in that assertion, but it is not the whole truth. DOJ had an organizational interest in having the Teamsters Union bear the financial cost of organized-crime control. Of course, the burden has actually been borne by the membership.

The GEB defendants were obviously ill-suited to represent the rank and file in settlement talks with DOJ. According to DOJ's complaint, each of the defendants was an active or passive participant in defrauding Teamsters members of economic benefits and honest stewardship of the union. Moreover, as named defendants in the case, the GEB defendants had a conflict of interest; they would undoubtedly negotiate terms most favorable to themselves, even if not optimal for the rank and file.

Could the rank and file's interests have been more effectively represented? Jed Rakoff, the outside counsel who represented the Teamsters Union itself, was potentially well positioned to protect the interests of the rank and file. His reputation in the legal community was impeccable. However, because Rakoff was hired by Marble Palace officials, and because those officials were technically the representatives of the membership, he presumably had to act on their instructions.

TDU sought to intervene as a defendant in *U.S. v. IBT* in order to protect the rights of the rank and file, but Judge Edelstein concluded that TDU lacked standing. In any event, TDU would have been a controversial representative of the union's 1.7 million members' interests. TDU is a Teamsters faction with a specific political and policy agenda. A sizeable percentage of the rank and file has a negative opinion of TDU, not surprising given more than two decades of red-baiting and other denunciations by the IBT establishment.*

We can think of two additional possibilities. First, Judge Edelstein could have appointed representatives from IBT joint councils and/or local unions to represent the rank and file. However, this solution would also have been problematic because many local and regional IBT officers were complicit in the union leadership's exploitation of the union. Second, Judge Edelstein could have appointed an independent trustee—perhaps a highly respected union leader with no ties to the IBT—to function like a court-appointed trustee in a bankruptcy case. However, ordinary Teamsters might have viewed that kind of independent trustee as an illegitimate intruder.

The consent decree's failure to specify the IRB's tenure or DOJ's criteria for agreeing to end the case also merits comment. Historically, organizational-reform litigation has often taken on a life of its own. The court

---

* Moreover, as sociologists Lipset, Trow, and Coleman observed in their landmark study of union democracy more than half a century ago, "Ordinarily, neither rank-and-file union members nor union activists see as necessary or desirable the indefinite prolongation of a state of affairs in which one or more groups of members make it their business to be continually critical of the administration's conduct of union business." Seymour Martin Lipset, Martin Trow & James Coleman, *Union Democracy: What Makes Democracy Work in Labor Unions and Other Organizations?* New York: Anchor Books, 1956, at 271.

and its remedial agents come to see themselves as indispensable. Their responsibilities tend to expand as the complexities of organizational reform become manifest and as the parties become habituated to calling on the remedial officers to solve politically tricky problems. The court-appointed officers also have a vested financial interest in the continuation of the remediation. Over time, the constituency for ending the case often shrinks, while the constituency for continuing it expands.

3

IBT Resistance and Judge Edelstein's Resolve
July 1989–September 1992

As the Consent Decree went into effect this spring, the Government and the IBT expected to implement its reforms in a spirit of cooperation and a unity of purpose. Unfortunately, the honeymoon ended by August [1989], and the IBT and the Court Officers began sinking into a confrontational posture. . . . The day-to-day implementation of the Consent Decree became mired in a morass of accusations, venomous correspondence, applications, hearings, and ultimately, decisions by this Court, and the inevitable appeals.[1]

—Judge David Edelstein, January 17, 1990

Q: Did the IBT comply with [the consent decree's] terms and conditions?

A: That is a question I could spend the rest of the week on. They fought me at every turn.[2]

—IRB member Frederick Lacey's response to a question, in testimony before the House Subcommittee on Oversight and Investigations, July 30, 1998

The settlement in *U.S. v. IBT* by no means guaranteed eradication of Cosa Nostra's influence in the union. The union vigorously opposed the consent decree's implementation. As Judge Edelstein observed, "soon after the signing of the consent decree, the IBT waged a zealous attack on the reforms contained in the consent decree. . . . Relations between the Court Officers and the IBT began in a spirit of hoped-for cooperation and unity of purpose, but as the months passed these interactions became increasingly bitter."[3] Making matters worse, many local IBT officials and rank and filers, whom, in the court officers' and DOJ's view, the consent decree was meant to protect and empower, also opposed enforcement of the consent decree. Some Teamsters simply distrusted the "government." Others did not believe that there was organized-crime influence in their locals. Still others supported the status quo because they were the beneficiaries of corruption and racketeering.

The IBT's Counterattack

The day after signing the consent decree, General President McCarthy insisted that "the Government's case was groundless and politically motivated to embarrass the Teamsters."[4] His criticisms escalated as the IA and IO began hiring staff, launching investigations, and filing disciplinary charges. Soon, the IBT deliberatively or reflexively challenged practically all of the court-appointed officers' actions and decisions.

Attacks on the Investigations Officer's Authority and Activities

Office Space. IA Lacey asked Judge Edelstein to compel the IBT to provide IO Carberry with office space in NYC.*[5] The IBT leadership objected, pointing to language in the consent decree: "the Independent Administrator, Investigations Officer and Election Officer shall be provided with suitable office space at the IBT headquarters in Washington, D.C." and "all costs associated with the activities of these three officials (and any designee or persons hired by them) shall be paid by the IBT."[6] Despite the consent decree's explicit reference to "office space in Washington," Judge Edelstein ruled that an NYC office for IO Carberry was consistent with the consent decree's purpose and language, as well as with the signatories' intentions.[7]

Access to Records. The consent decree provided that the "Investigations Officer shall have the right . . . to examine books and records of the IBT and its affiliates."[8] The IBT argued that the union affiliates merely had to *show*

---

* The consent decree authorized only the IA, not the IO or the EO, to make "applications" to the court. The applications were numbered sequentially. Each application resulted in a court order. The IA filed over one hundred applications with Judge Edelstein from August 3, 1989 to October 10, 1992, when the IRB replaced the IA/IO.

the IO requested documents, not *provide* the IO with originals or copies. Judge Edelstein disagreed. Characterizing the IBT's position as "part of a fierce campaign to avoid the reforms that it agreed to,"[9] he ruled that the ability to obtain copies is "reasonabl[y] and necessar[il]y incident" to the IO's powers under the consent decree.[10]

Compensation and Expenses. The consent decree provided that the three court-appointed officers submit to the court itemized bills for salary and expenses every three months. The IBT general president would have fourteen days to note objections. The IBT routinely disputed the reasonableness of these expenditures and appealed them to Judge Edelstein. In order to keep the work of the court officers on track, the U.S. attorney asked Judge Edelstein to create a $100,000 operating fund against which the IA and IO could draw. The IBT strenuously objected, arguing that the consent decree did not require it, that the fund would diminish the court-appointed officers' incentive to cooperate with the union, and that the IBT had dealt fairly with the court-appointed officers' bills. Judge Edelstein adopted the U.S. attorney's proposal and admonished the union.*[11]

> After six months of these skirmishes I would now like to firmly establish that the parties must not only adhere to the letter of the Consent Decree, but must abide by its spirit as well. The spirit and intention of this Consent Decree command that its specific language be given the most reasonable possible interpretation. For this Consent Decree to continue to be viable and meaningful, the Court Officers must not be hampered in the performance of their obligatory duties.[12]

Prosecuting Disciplinary Violations. IO Carberry brought the first disciplinary charges against Harold Friedman and Anthony Hughes. Friedman was president of Cleveland IBT Local 507, president of Cleveland Bakery,

---

* Because the IBT repeatedly sought to prevent the EO from hiring staff, Judge Edelstein also approved DOJ's request to create a $150,000 fund that the EO could draw against to cover expenses and that the IBT would have to periodically replenish. After the 1991 international-officer election, Judge Edelstein combined the $150,000 EO fund with the IA/IO's $100,000 general operating fund to create a $250,000 IRB fund. The IRB had to submit expense and fee applications quarterly; if the IBT did not object within fourteen business days, or if the court overruled the objection, the IBT had to promptly reimburse the expenses. *United States v. Int'l Bhd. of Teamsters*, 829 F. Supp. 602, 604 (S.D.N.Y. 1993).

Confectionery, and Tobacco Workers International Union Local 19, president of the Ohio Conference of Teamsters, an IBT vice president, a defendant in *U.S. v. IBT*, and a signatory of the consent decree. Hughes was an IBT international representative and an IBT Local 507 officer but not a *U.S. v. IBT* defendant. Both men had been close associates of IBT General President Jackie Presser.[13] (Local 507 was Presser's home local.) Indeed, in May 1986, a federal grand jury had charged Friedman, Hughes, and Presser with embezzling Local 507 funds by paying union salaries to "ghost" (no-show) employees.[14] Despite these charges, Local 507's members reelected Friedman and Hughes president and recording secretary, respectively.

Friedman and Hughes were convicted in May 1989. The judge sentenced them to four years probation, conditioned on their not holding union office or engaging in IBT-related activities.[15] In July 1989, IO Carberry charged Friedman and Hughes with "bringing reproach upon the union" by knowingly associating with LCN figures, committing racketeering acts, and, in Friedman's case, filing a false union reporting form with DOL.[16] Hughes and Friedman mounted a strenuous defense based on § 3(d) of the IBT constitution, which stated,

> Charges against elected officers of the international union or any subordinate body shall be limited only to those activities or actions *occurring during their current term, and only to those activities and actions occurring prior to their current term which were not known generally by the membership* of the international union or the subordinate body in the case of an officer of a subordinate body.

Friedman and Hughes argued that because Local 507's members knew they had been indicted when reelecting them in 1987, the IO could not bring disciplinary charges based on the conduct charged in those indictments.[17]

The GEB then weighed in with a resolution (the "November 1, 1989 resolution") interpreting § 3(d) as making bring-reproach disciplinary charges inapplicable to allegations that IBT members knew about before a disciplinary respondent's most recent election to union office;[18] to limit bring-reproach charges to violations explicitly proscribed by the IBT constitution and committed after the consent decree took effect; and to require that the IA adhere to the GEB's interpretations of the IBT constitution.[19] This resolution would have substantially curtailed the IO's and IA's authority.

In January 1990, IA Lacey found both Friedman and Hughes culpable for bringing reproach upon the union and suspended them from their IBT officer positions for a year. Lacey rejected the November 1, 1989 resolution, stating that it "does violence" to the plain language and spirit of the IBT constitution and disrupts adjudication of pending disciplinary cases.[20] He then addressed the respondents' arguments concerning the GEB's interpretation of § 3(d). First, Lacey held that the consent decree authorized the IA to interpret the IBT constitution and to override conflicting GEB interpretations. Second, he rejected the November 1, 1989 resolution's interpretation of § 3(d) as requiring proof that local union members did not know about allegations of the respondent's misconduct when they elected respondent. To the contrary, Lacey ruled that § 3(d) burdens the disciplinary respondent with proving that, at the time of the reelection, the relevant union voters knowingly chose to ignore the respondent's illegal conduct. Third, Lacey ruled that a Teamster could be held accountable for disciplinary offenses proscribed by the consent decree but not by the IBT constitution, for example, association with LCN figures and membership in an LCN organized-crime family. Finally, Lacey rejected Hughes's argument that since he was neither a defendant in *U.S. v. IBT* nor a signatory of the consent decree, he was not subject to the consent decree's disciplinary regime. Lacey held that the civil RICO defendants who signed the consent decree represented and bound the entire IBT membership.

Judge Edelstein upheld all of Lacey's decisions. Affirming Hughes's and Friedman's one-year suspensions from union office, he pointed out that since Friedman and Hughes had vehemently denied the criminal charges, even Local 507 members who read the indictment would not have had conclusive knowledge of Friedman's and Hughes's wrongdoing.[21] Moreover, he commented sarcastically that "the Consent Decree appears to contravene the interests of only two classes of IBT members; the election oversight may imperil unfairly elected officers, and the prosecution scheme may ultimately suspend corrupt union members."[22] Judge Edelstein also affirmed the IA's authority to interpret the IBT constitution.[23]

> While the IBT argues that [the consent decree] preserves their right to interpret their constitution as they see fit, unfettered power may allow them to frustrate the implementation of the Consent Decree through "interpretations"—as done here. In order to prevent reforms from being carried out or [to] protect members from charges, the IBT could interpret existing provisions or even amend their Constitution to accomplish such

malignant aims. Such actions must be scrutinized carefully to determine their reasonableness.[24]

Judge Edelstein accused the GEB of attempting to frustrate the consent decree: "The IBT sees no moment in the important fact that the [November 1, 1989] resolution exculpates current or former GEB members from facing charges. . . . [The resolution's provisions] cannot withstand judicial scrutiny as 'reasonable,' and the Independent Administrator correctly found them [unreasonable]."[25]

In June 1990, the Second Circuit Court of Appeals upheld IA Lacey's decision to suspend Friedman and Hughes from IBT office for one year.[26] In July 1990, the Sixth Circuit Court of Appeals upheld their criminal RICO convictions.[27] Upon conviction, pursuant to the Landrum-Griffin Act, they would be barred from holding union office for thirteen years. (In 1993, IA Lacey expelled Friedman from the IBT on account of his continuing efforts to exercise control over Local 507's executive officers and for holding himself out as a leader to Local 507's members.)[28]

Attacks on the Independent Administrator's Authority and Activities

Communicating with the Rank and File. In July 1989, pursuant to the consent decree,[29] IA Lacey began reporting his disciplinary decisions in the monthly *Teamster Magazine*. Because these decisions cast the union's leadership in bad light, the GEB announced that, henceforth, it would publish *Teamster Magazine* quarterly rather than monthly. Lacey argued that such a change would impair his obligation to communicate with the rank and file.[30] Agreeing, Edelstein gave the IBT two options: continue to publish *Teamster Magazine* monthly or pay to mail monthly IA reports to the members.[31] The IBT chose the former. In a subsequent ruling, Judge Edelstein held that the IBT had to publish the IA's monthly reports in full, including each disciplinary respondent's name, local-union affiliation, and disciplinary charge.[32] He also ordered the IBT to publish in *Teamster Magazine* all court opinions and orders relating to *U.S. v. IBT*.[33]

Monitoring IBT Expenditures and Contracts. The consent decree authorized the IA to monitor the IBT's spending. To carry out this responsibility, Lacey hired as chief auditor John Cronin, previously an assistant director at the U.S. General Accounting Office (GAO). Cronin hired two full-time investigators and a full-time secretary to help him audit IBT purchases exceeding $1,000; selected out-of-work benefits; payroll expenditures exceeding $50,000; travel allowances exceeding $1,800 per month; professional fees exceeding $5,000; purchases of fixed assets over $50,000; contributions, gifts, or grants to labor-related organizations and those exceeding $10,000 to other entities; and financial assistance in excess of $25,000 to IBT affiliates.

IBT General Counsel James Grady initially resisted Cronin's monitoring. He demanded that Cronin and his staff fill out time-consuming forms identifying and justifying requests to see contracts, procurements, and travel vouchers; barred Cronin and his staff from using the IBT cafeteria and snack bar; and barred them from accessing their Marble Palace offices on weekends and on weekdays before nine a.m. and after four p.m. The IBT relented only after Lacey complained to Judge Edelstein.

When Cronin identified a proposed improper expenditure, he first wrote a letter to IBT General Secretary-Treasurer Weldon Mathis requesting cancelation or modification. If Cronin was dissatisfied with the IBT's response, he would recommend that IA Lacey veto the expenditure or publicize it in *Teamster Magazine*. (Under the consent decree, Lacey could veto only expenditures related to an act of racketeering.)

IA Lacey vetoed only two proposed IBT expenditures. First, in March 1990, the IBT proposed to extinguish a $5.3 million debt that the Western Conference of Teamsters owed to the international union. General President McCarthy explained that forgiving the debt honored a 1984 agreement between former General President Jackie Presser, General Secretary-Treasurer Weldon Mathis, and Western Conference Director Jesse Carr. However, there was neither documentation of such an agreement nor adequate justification for forgiving the loan. IA Lacey reported to Judge Edelstein,

> In this case, I found that Messrs. Presser and Carr were guilty of extorting the members' rights by virtue of their scheme to present a "loan" to the GEB for approval, while surreptitiously planning that the transaction would be converted to a "grant" at an undetermined later date. Such a scheme can only diminish the membership's confidence in the IBT leadership, promote an overwhelming sense of futility among the rank-and-file, and inevitably deprive the IBT membership of its right to a democratically run union. . . . General President McCarthy's willingness to endorse the

loan conversion by circulating a memorandum seeking the approval of the GEB, without investigating the matter and setting forth all the facts and circumstances, can only be interpreted as the same "conscious avoidance of the facts" condemned by Judge Edelstein.[34]

IA Lacey also vetoed a *Teamster Magazine* printing contract. On March 1, 1989, less than two weeks before signing the consent decree, General President McCarthy terminated the IBT's contract with *Teamster Magazine*'s printer and awarded the contract to Windsor Graphics, a company owned by his daughter and son-in-law. IA Lacey found the contracting process "seriously flawed," since the IBT had not issued bid specifications, permitted only three firms to bid, prohibited the current contractor from bidding, did not require sealed bids, and analyzed the bids imprecisely.[35] Windsor Graphics, which was run out of McCarthy's son-in-law's home, had no printing capacity, equipment, credit, contacts, or track record.[36] It billed the IBT $300,000 per month (payable in advance)[37] and subcontracted the actual printing work.

IA Lacey concluded that the Windsor Graphics contract harmed the IBT in two ways. First, the union paid unnecessarily high fees for Windsor's services; second, the union did not receive the interest it should have earned on the money advanced to Windsor.[38] He found McCarthy and IBT Communications Director F.C. Duke Zeller culpable for "extorting the rights of the members of the IBT . . . by secretly conferring advantages and benefits upon Windsor that enabled it to present what, on its face, was the lowest of three bids, but was in actuality anything but that."[39] According to Lacey, McCarthy and Zeller breached their fiduciary duties to the membership and aided and abetted the extortion of the union members' right "to democratic participation in the affairs of their union."[40] He therefore vetoed further payments to Windsor Graphics and directed the IBT to solicit new printing-contract bids. Judge Edelstein affirmed, calling the bidding process "rigged" and an "obvious ripoff of IBT funds."[41] He called the IBT's justification of its bidding process "absurd" and its argument that the Windsor Graphics contract saved the union money "sheer sophistry."[42] The Second Circuit Court of Appeals dismissed the IBT's appeal.[43]

In mid-1992, just before expiration of the IO/IA phase of the *U.S. v. IBT* remediation, IA Lacey recommended that the IBT create an inspector general's office to audit IBT expenditures, a policies and procedures manual to govern financial transactions, and a unionwide budget.[44] He argued that the absence of such controls contributed to the union's decades of corruption. (The Carey administration, 1992–1997, did not implement these recommendations. Only after Judge Edelstein approved the appointment of an independent financial auditor in late 1997 did the IBT begin to reform its financial infrastructure.)

Vetoing IBT Appointments. The consent decree authorized the IA to veto any appointment that "constitutes or furthers an act of racketeering . . . or furthers or contributes to the association directly, or indirectly, of the IBT or any of its members with LCN or elements thereof."[45] It empowered the IA to establish procedures for reviewing appointments; examining books and records; attending GEB meetings; deposing IBT officers, members, employees, and agents; and making use of an independent auditor.[46]

Lacey instituted the following appointment procedures: (1) the prospective appointee completes a questionnaire; (2) the IA forwards the questionnaire and the IBT's recommendation to the U.S. attorney; (3) the U.S. attorney forwards the information to the FBI; (4) the FBI conducts background checks for prior convictions or other disqualifying information; (5) the FBI forwards its findings to the U.S. attorney; and (6) the U.S. attorney forwards the FBI's findings to IA Lacey, who publishes a notice of the proposed appointment in *Teamster Magazine*, giving rank-and-file members an opportunity to voice objections. Based on this information, the IA could either issue a non-veto statement, allowing the appointment to become final, or request more information.[47]

By February 1992, Lacey had vetoed only one appointment—the GEB's selection of Central Conference of Teamsters Policy Committee member Jack B. Yager as an international vice president and director of the seven-hundred-thousand-member Central Conference of Teamsters. (Yager had previously served as administrative assistant to General President Roy Williams, business agent for Kansas City IBT Local 41, organizer for the Central Conference of Teamsters, and director of the union's Freight Division.) Lacey found that Yager's "silence and incomprehensible passivity" in light of General President Williams's well-publicized organized-crime ties and his vote to reelect Williams as chairman of the Central Conference of Teamsters Policy Committee aided and abetted Williams's extortion of IBT members' rights.[48] Lacey reasoned that Yager could not have worked so closely with Williams without LCN's approval. He cited FBI agents' testimony that Yager associated with prominent Cosa Nostra figures, including Nick Civella, Allen Dorfman, James Cozzo, and others in Chicago, Detroit, and Kansas City.[49] Lacey found that Yager's appointments would further the IBT's association with Cosa Nostra.[50] Judge Edelstein affirmed Lacey's decision and criticized the IBT for failing to investigate Yager's background.[51] Subsequently, McCarthy withdrew several proposed appointments when the IA expressed concerns.

Attacks on the Election Officer's Authority and Decisions

Authority to Promulgate Election Rules. On July 19, 1989, EO Michael Holland notified the IBT and DOJ that he intended to promulgate rules for conducting the 1991 international-officer election.[52] The IBT strenuously objected. According to General Counsel Grady, the consent decree's use of the word "supervise," rather than "conduct," showed that the parties intended a passive EO monitoring role, limited to distributing election-relevant information to the membership, overseeing balloting, responding to local officers' requests for advice, and certifying election results.[53] EO Holland and IA Lacey contended that the consent decree gave the EO "an active and broad mandate to intervene in and coordinate the IBT's electoral process up to and including the next general convention [in 1991]."[54] They insisted that, used as a term of art in labor law, "supervise" authorized the EO to *conduct* the IBT's 1991 election.

Once again, Judge Edelstein ruled in the court officers' favor. "Supervise," he concluded, should be interpreted according to its most expansive dictionary meaning: "to coordinate, direct, and inspect continuously and at first hand the accomplishment of; oversee with the powers of direction and decision the implementation of."[55] He added that the consent decree's reference to the 1991 election encompassed the entire electoral process, beginning with convention-delegate selection.[56]

Opposition to Direct Rank-and-File Elections. Because the consent decree formalized a settlement negotiated by the IBT international officers and DOJ, did it bind several thousand local and joint council officers who were neither *U.S. v. IBT* defendants nor consent decree signatories? A number of Teamsters officers argued that it was not binding and that the delegates at the upcoming July 1991 Teamsters convention in Buena Vista, Florida, could reject the consent decree's election reforms. They pointed to the following consent decree provision in support of this position:

> By no later than the conclusion of the IBT convention to be held in 1991, the IBT shall have formally amended the IBT constitution to incorporate

and conform with all of the terms set forth in this order by presenting said terms to the delegates for a vote. If the IBT has not formally so amended the IBT constitution by that date, the Government retains the right to seek any appropriate action, including enforcement of this order, contempt, or reopening this litigation.[57]

To head off a convention rebellion against the consent decree, U.S. Attorney (SDNY) Otto Obermaier (appointed by President George H.W. Bush in 1989) asked Judge Edelstein to enjoin the IBT from any actions inconsistent with the consent decree's provisions on the election of international officers. Judge Edelstein agreed: "[The consent decree] is fully part of the IBT constitution and the law of that union no matter what the convention delegates vote."[58] He ruled that a delegate vote on the Consent Decree would have no legal effect. "No action taken by the IBT at the convention can undercut the provisions of this Consent Decree."[59] In his strongest language yet, Judge Edelstein criticized the IBT for persistently attempting to obstruct implementation of the consent decree:

I remind the IBT that it *voluntarily* agreed to the Consent Decree and, with it, free rank and file elections. The past two years have demonstrated that the IBT had no intention of living up to its end of the agreement. The IBT has made every attempt to limit the scope and restrict the terms of the Consent Decree, and each time it has lost. But the time for challenges to the Consent Decree has now passed, and the IBT must live with the Consent Decree as written by the parties, approved by the Court, and repeatedly interpreted by this Court and the Court of Appeals. . . . I tend to be amused when I remember that the IBT by its representatives have made heroic statements from time to time to reaffirm their commitment to a union free of corruption and their dedication to free elections. How I wish that some of these statements could have been true. Time has proved, however, that these statements are empty of any meaning or purpose for the good of this important union.[60]

Pursuant to the consent decree, for the first time in IBT history, locals chose convention delegates in secret-ballot elections supervised by an independent election officer. Nevertheless, on the opening day of the convention (June 24, 1991), a large majority of the nearly two thousand delegates voted to reject the consent decree. Though legally meaningless, the vote constituted a stunning repudiation of TDU's and DOJ's insistence that, given an opportunity, rank-and-file Teamsters would enthusiastically embrace union democracy.[61]

EO Staffing. EO Holland, pointing to his responsibility to supervise an unprecedented North America–wide, rank-and-file, secret-ballot union election, asked the IBT to pay for a staff, including an executive assistant, an administrative assistant, a secretary, and a labor-economics consultant.[62] The IBT called these requested expenditures unnecessary, unwarranted, and excessive.[63] Judge Edelstein disagreed.[64] In addition, he approved Holland's request to hire a PR firm to communicate the consent decree's goals to the rank and file.[65]

IBT Locals Join the Resistance

General President McCarthy and other GEB members encouraged IBT local officers to resist enforcement of the consent decree.[66] The remedial effort would be paralyzed if local officers across the country initiated litigation. In December 1989, New Jersey IBT Joint Council 73 went to federal court in New Jersey to challenge IO Carberry's authority to examine its books and records.[67] The joint council contended that it was not bound by the consent decree because it was neither a party to *U.S. v. IBT* nor a consent decree signatory. It also argued that the IBT's general president and GEB lacked authority to delegate their disciplinary powers to court-appointed officers. New Jersey federal district court judge Harold Ackerman (who had presided over the Union City, New Jersey, Local 560 case for over a decade) transferred the case to Judge Edelstein's court in Manhattan.[68] Judge Edelstein issued a temporary restraining order barring Joint Council 73 from litigating *U.S. v. IBT* issues in any forum other than his courtroom.[69]

In December 1990, Cleveland IBT Local 507 filed a lawsuit in federal court in Ohio alleging that the IO and IA breached Local 507's "contract with the International IBT" by seeking to discipline its officers, Harold Friedman and Anthony Hughes.[70] U.S. Attorney Obermaier sought a restraining order on the ground that proliferating litigation would frustrate the consent decree. Judge Edelstein ordered the local to withdraw its lawsuit. Local 507 complied.

Leaders of five Chicago-area IBT locals also went to federal court, alleging that EO Michael Holland's plan to supervise the 1991 IBT election violated the IBT constitution.[71] They asked the judge to exempt their locals "from submitting to the strictures of the Consent Decree."[72] Judge Edelstein ordered the Chicago plaintiffs to cease and desist from taking further action in their lawsuit.[73]

Judge Edelstein's All Writs Act Opinion

After Judge Edelstein preliminarily enjoined the IBT lawsuits in Illinois, Ohio, and New Jersey, U.S. Attorney Obermaier requested a permanent All Writs Act injunction prohibiting anyone from filing any lawsuit pertaining to the *U.S. v. IBT* consent decree in any forum other than Judge Edelstein's courtroom.[74] In the past, albeit infrequently, the All Writs Act had been invoked to enjoin repeated, baseless, or vexatious litigation, and to enjoin plaintiffs from bringing parallel proceedings in different courts.*[75] In requesting an omnibus All Writs Act injunction, Obermaier argued that subordinate IBT entities were seeking to undermine the consent decree.

Judge Edelstein invited all IBT local unions (approximately seven hundred at the time), joint councils, and regional conferences to explain why he should not grant the injunction that Obermaier requested.[76] General President McCarthy urged IBT local officials to "fight this unprecedented and ill-advised attempt . . . to deprive you and your members of your legal and constitutional rights."[77] Ultimately, 282 local unions, twenty joint councils, and two state conferences submitted briefs opposing an injunction.[78]

In the most important judicial opinion in the entire *U.S. v. IBT* litigation, and probably the most sweeping All Writs Act injunction in U.S. history, Judge Edelstein prohibited anyone from bringing litigation related to the consent decree in any forum other than his court.[79] He enjoined all

---

* The All Writs Act, originally codified in the Judiciary Act of 1789, states, "The Supreme Court and all courts established by Act of Congress may issue all writs necessary or appropriate in aid of their respective jurisdictions and agreeable to the usages and principles of law." *In re Josephson*, 218 F.2d 174, 177–78 (1st Cir. 1954); 28 U.S.C. § 1651(a) (2000). Justice O'Connor once described the All Writs Act as "the last of the triad of founding documents, along with the Declaration of Independence and the Constitution itself." Sandra Day O'Connor, *The Judiciary Act of 1789 and the American Judicial Tradition*, 59 U. Cin. L. Rev. 1, 3 (1990); *see also* Dimitri Portnoi, *Resorting to Extraordinary Writs: How the All Writs Act Rises to Fill the Gaps in the Rights of Enemy Combatants*, 83 NYU L. Rev. 293 (2008). In determining whether to invoke the All Writs Act, courts consider the Anti-Injunction Act, which prohibits federal courts from issuing injunctions barring proceedings in state courts except "when necessary in aid of jurisdiction." 28 U.S.C. § 2283 (2000); *In re Baldwin-United Corporation*, 770 F.2d 328, 335 (2d Cir. 1985).

federal and state courts from exercising jurisdiction in matters relating to the case.[80] He defended this extraordinary ruling on the ground that "the recent actions by subordinate IBT entities [Joint Council 73, Local 507, and the Chicago locals] seeking independent adjudication of related matters have created an eruption of litigation unprecedented even by the warped standards practiced by the IBT in this case" and have also created a significant risk that the consent decree would be interpreted inconsistently.[81] He added that, since 1989, the "morass of accusations, venomous correspondence, applications, hearings, and decisions by this Court" demonstrate the need for a permanent All Writs Act injunction.[82] The Second Circuit Court of Appeals affirmed.[83]

Conclusion and Analysis

A period of massive resistance often accompanies the initial resolution of major institutional-reform litigation.[84] In many lawsuits attacking unconstitutional conditions and practices in public institutions, for example, government officials resisted and even tried to sabotage court-imposed remediation. This was demonstrated most dramatically in the numerous school-desegregation cases following *Brown v. Board of Education*.[85] There was similar resistance in many prison-reform and mental-hospital-reform cases.[86] Although, in some instances, such resistance succeeded in stymieing reform, more frequently, the court prevailed, often only after a change in the institution's leadership. This pattern of legal attack, institutional resistance, and consolidation of reform is evident in cases resolved by a trial and in cases resolved by a negotiated consent decree.

From August 1989 to September 1992, the IBT placed Judge Edelstein and the court-appointed officers under legal siege. In the months following issuance of the consent decree, the international union and a number of IBT locals repeatedly challenged or refused to comply with the court officers' decisions, prompting the court officers to seek judicial orders.[87] According to the U.S. House of Representative's Committee on Education and the Workforce's Subcommittee on Oversight and Investigations, from 1989 to 1992, the IBT's international, regional, and local offices spent nearly $10.5 million litigating disagreements with the court-appointed officers.[88] The relationships between the IBT and Judge Edelstein and between the IBT and the court-appointed officers were bitterly contentious. Edelstein spoke of "The Autumn of Discontent."[89] Perhaps the nadir occurred when, after Judge Edelstein issued his omnibus All Writs Act injunction, IBT Joint Council 73 filed a lawsuit challenging the IO's power to take sworn statements from IBT officers and members. The complaint charged that a previous Edelstein ruling "betrays a monumental ignorance of federal labor law." Edelstein labeled the IBT's complaint "a case study in vexatious, harassing litigation brought without any proper purpose"[90] and criticized the attorneys who filed it for "violat[ing] the most basic responsibility of a lawyer to her client and the court—to be prepared in court." He fined the lawyers $35,000 for filing a frivolous motion.[91] (The Second Circuit Court of Appeals vacated the sanction on procedural grounds.)[92]

Successfully implementing the consent decree under these contentious conditions depended on the political independence, determination, and competence of a corps of enforcers. Without a decisive and determined federal judge, a supportive court of appeals, highly competent court-appointed officers, and a sophisticated U.S. attorney's office, *U.S. v. IBT* would not have survived the IBT's legal resistance. IA Lacey consistently upheld the decisions of the IO and EO. Judge Edelstein consistently upheld the court-appointed officers' decisions. And the Second Circuit consistently upheld Judge Edelstein's decisions. Equally important was Judge Edelstein's All Writs Act injunction.[93] Without it, the consent decree's implementation would have been tied up in dozens of courts around the country, paralyzing the remedial effort.[94]

The consent decree, which the IBT signed, gave the court and its officers significant power over the union's international elections and over the operation of the union's administrative discipline. It may strike some observers as unfair that Judge Edelstein appointed the court officers, then sat in review of their decisions. We do not find this criticism persuasive. The parties could have left it to Judge Edelstein to issue and enforce all decisions himself. For efficiency, they authorized him to appoint officers to carry out the day-to-day enforcement of the consent decree. In effect, the court officers acted on the judge's behalf; technically, they issued many of their decisions as "recommendations" to the district court. It is unsurprising that Edelstein adopted nearly all their recommendations. Had he found himself in disagreement with "his" court officers, it would have been his prerogative to replace them with officers who would better carry out his will. Furthermore, the IBT always had the option, which it frequently exercised, to appeal Judge Edelstein's decisions to the Second Circuit Court of Appeals. Rank-and-file Teamsters did not rally to support DOJ's legal attack on the labor racketeers who, for decades, had intimidated them and exploited their union. Indeed, the majority of Teamsters seemed indifferent, if not opposed, to DOJ's reform effort. (We cannot resist drawing a parallel with the U.S. military's disappointment that the Iraqi population did not, en masse, celebrate the U.S. effort to bring democracy to their country.) Even Congress did not support the reform effort, as demonstrated by the petition, signed by 264 members, expressing opposition to a lawsuit that they had not yet seen.

Without the commitment and tenacity of Judge Edelstein, the court-appointed officers, and the U.S. attorney's office, *U.S. v. IBT* would likely have failed. Indeed, it may well have tracked the same path as *English v. Cunningham*, a class-action suit filed by thirteen New York Teamsters on behalf of the IBT membership in 1957. The plaintiffs asked a federal district judge to appoint a board of monitors to rout out corruption in the union's election machinery and international leadership.[95] They alleged that the IBT's international officers had rigged the 1957 Teamsters convention to elect Jimmy Hoffa, disenfranchise rank-and-file members who opposed the incumbents, and use union funds for their own benefit.[96] The settlement of the case, embodied in a consent decree, established a three-member court-appointed board of monitors to purge the union of corrupt officials and improve election procedures. That board had some initial success, but the IBT paralyzed the monitors by filing scores of legal challenges. The board dissolved in 1961, only three years after its formation. Perhaps this precedent remained part of the IBT's institutional memory a generation later as opponents of *U.S. v. IBT* sought to render the 1989 consent decree unenforceable.

4

Establishing New
Disciplinary Machinery
July 1989–September 1992

As General President of this great union, I have consistently opposed any settlement, maintaining from the outset that the Government's entire case was groundless and politically motivated to
embarrass the Teamsters. . . . While I reluctantly accept the terms of
the Consent Order, I believe it is not the vindication and exonera-
tion Teamsters deserve. The fact is this suit should never have been
filed in the first place.[1]
    —IBT General President William McCarthy, March 1989

I want you to mark and burn every word into your memory. I say
and I repeat probably ad nauseam: I will use every power of this
government, including my own power as judge, to see that this consent decree is given full force and effect and I'm determined to see
that it achieves its purpose.[2]
    —Judge David Edelstein, June 23, 1991

    Prior to *U.S. v. IBT*, the union's locals, joint councils, and GEB
rarely brought disciplinary charges against IBT officers. The disciplinary
process was used largely to punish "dissidents"; even then, disciplinary decisions and sanctions were often unrecorded, unpredictable, and unknown
to members beyond the respondent's local.[3] Disciplinary action against an
international IBT officer was unheard of. The consent decree made administrative prosecution of violations of the IBT's constitution, IBT locals' bylaws, federal criminal and labor laws, and the consent decree itself the chief
weapon for purging the union of organized crime's influence.[4]

The consent decree provided that an independent administrator (IA) and investigations officer (IO) would run the union's disciplinary process until the election officer (EO) certified that the 1991 IBT election had been conducted freely and fairly. Thereafter, a three-person independent review board (IRB) would take over the disciplinary function. Thus, from July 1989 to October 1992, IO Carberry, IA Lacey, and Judge Edelstein processed hundreds of disciplinary charges, laying down an extensive body of substantive and procedural IBT disciplinary law.[5]

Sources of IBT Disciplinary Law

IBT disciplinary law is rooted in the IBT constitution, local-union bylaws, and federal laws, as well as in the *U.S. v. IBT* consent decree. Because of its generality and adaptability, the disciplinary offense that the IO and IA found most useful was the constitutional requirement that an IBT member "conduct himself or herself at all times *in such a manner as not to bring reproach upon the union.*"[6] The IBT constitution specifically prohibits, among other conduct, embezzlement or conversion of the union's funds or property;[7] assault or provoking assault on fellow members;[8] extortion of a union member's rights;[9] disrupting or inducing others to disrupt the performance of the union's labor or contractual duties; retaliating or threatening to retaliate against a member for filing disciplinary charges (unless those charges were filed maliciously); and wrongfully retaining or destroying IBT records. However, the IO and, subsequently, the IRB always charged specific violations under the umbrella offense, "bringing reproach upon the union."

The consent decree added a few important disciplinary offenses: committing any act of racketeering activity; knowingly associating with members or associates of Cosa Nostra or any other criminal group;[10] knowingly associating with persons permanently or temporarily barred from IBT membership; and failing to cooperate with the court-appointed officers or IRB. The latter was especially useful because it enabled the IO to compel Teamsters to answer investigators' questions.

Other grounds for disciplinary charges are violations of federal labor and criminal laws, including receiving items of value from an employer;[11] loaning union money to a union member;[12] offering, receiving, or soliciting a fee, kickback, commission, gift, loan, money, or thing of value to influence the operation of an employee-benefit plan;[13] submitting false or misleading reports to DOL;[14] and using force or violence, or the threat of force or violence, to restrain, coerce, or intimidate any union member for the purpose of interfering with that member's rights under the Labor Management Reporting and Disclosure Act (LMRDA).[15] When the IO charged any of these offenses, he also added a bring-reproach-upon-the-union charge.

The Steps in a Disciplinary Case

Investigations

IO Carberry and his staff obtained investigative leads from IBT members, government agencies (e.g., the FBI), the media, legislative reports, and completed or pending criminal and civil cases. Although the IO did not have police powers (to arrest, carry a firearm, conduct searches, intercept electronic communications), the consent decree authorized him to take "all reasonable steps necessary to be fully informed on the IBT's activities."[16] It also empowered him to review the books and records of IBT entities and, with "reasonable cause," to take sworn statements of IBT members, officers, employees, and agents. Teamsters who refused to answer the IO's questions could be expelled from the union.

Adjudication

If the IO had sufficient evidence, he would serve written disciplinary charges on the respondent, who would then have thirty days to prepare a defense. Seventy-five percent of the IO's disciplinary charges settled during or soon after this thirty-day period. While, to conserve resources, the IO preferred settlement to trial, he did not bargain away charges and rarely made concessions on sanctions.[17] Some disciplinary respondents chose not to contest charges in order to avoid a formal finding of culpability or to save legal fees. If the IO and respondent reached an agreement, they submitted it to IA Lacey for approval and then to Judge Edelstein for entry as a judicial order.[18]

Judge Edelstein approved most, but not all, settlements. In 1990, for instance, IO Carberry charged Carmen Parise, former secretary-treasurer of Cleveland IBT Local 473 and former president of Ohio Joint Council 41, with bringing reproach upon the union by assaulting a Local 473 member and by refusing to answer questions about a previous assault on that same individual. Parise agreed to a tentative settlement suspending his IBT membership for three months. IA Lacey approved the sanction, but Judge Edelstein rejected it as too lenient. The Second Circuit Court of Appeals affirmed Edelstein's decision because "[t]he district court must ensure that the [settlement of the disciplinary charges] does not put the court's sanction on and power behind a decree that violates constitution, statute, or jurisprudence."[19]

Under the LMRDA, a union cannot discipline a member unless that member has been served with written specific charges, given reasonable time to prepare his defense, and afforded a full and fair disciplinary hearing.[20] Thus, if the respondent and IO failed to reach a settlement, the IA convened and presided over a hearing conducted according to rules and procedures applicable to labor arbitration hearings. Each party could present evidence, including reliable hearsay testimony, and cross-examine the other side's witnesses.[21] With the IA serving as trier of fact,[22] the IO had to prove the respondent's "culpability" by a preponderance of the evidence.

The IA did not rubber-stamp the IO's charges. For example, IA Lacey concluded that the rioting conviction of Akron, Ohio IBT Local 348's secretary-treasurer did not bring reproach upon the union. He also dismissed embezzlement charges against three NYC IBT Local 194 officers because the IO failed to prove that the respondents fraudulently intended to deprive the union of funds.[23] In another case, in which two individuals were charged with an assault that occurred in a fracas between TDUers and members of the Brotherhood of Loyal Americans and Strong Teamsters (BLAST), Lacey found the respondents not culpable because IO Carberry had not proved that they were actually involved.[24]

If Lacey found the disciplinary respondent culpable, he had discretion to determine the punishment, including reimbursement, fine, suspension (of varying duration) from union office, suspension (of varying duration) from union membership, prohibition on associating with IBT members, forfeiture of union office, and expulsion from the union.[25] He typically announced his decision in a written opinion that was subsequently published in *Teamster Magazine*.[26]

Appeals

Judge Edelstein heard appeals from the IA's disciplinary decisions. The consent decree provided that the court would use "the standard of review applicable to review of final federal agency action under the Administrative Procedure Act."[27] Under this standard, the reviewing court should affirm the hearing officer's (IA's) decision unless it was arbitrary, capricious, or an abuse of discretion.[28] If Judge Edelstein affirmed, the respondent could appeal to the Second Circuit Court of Appeals, which deferred to Edelstein's decision if it was "supportable under any reasonable standard of review" or "fell within the realm of reason."[29]

The Second Circuit Court of Appeals consistently upheld IA Lacey's sanctions. For example, IA Lacey expelled Robert C. Sansone, president of St. Louis IBT Local 682, president of Joint Council 13, president of the Missouri-Kansas Conference of Teamsters, and an international representative, for having brought reproach upon the union by willfully disregarding his fiduciary duty to investigate allegations that Anthony Parrino, the former vice president of Local 682, was a Cosa Nostra member. Although the Second Circuit considered expulsion a "drastic" sanction, it affirmed Lacey's decision because "the apparent discrepancy between the penalty imposed here and those imposed in other cases does not inexorably compel the conclusion that the Independent Administrator acted arbitrarily or capriciously."[30] In another case, when Edelstein enhanced the sanction IA Lacey had imposed on an Ohio IBT Local 100 officer for assaulting an IBT member,[31] the Second Circuit concluded that Judge Edelstein should not have modified Lacey's decision without explicitly finding that his decision was arbitrary or capricious.

The Law of Teamster Disciplinary Offenses

Although the consent decree, the Teamsters constitution, federal laws, and local-union bylaws provided a kind of code of disciplinary violations, Lacey and Edelstein had to interpret these violations in individual cases. Respondents almost always appealed IA Lacey's culpability findings to Judge Edelstein and sometimes to the Second Circuit Court of Appeals, thus generating a great deal of written precedent.

The Consent Decree's Disciplinary Offenses

Membership in Cosa Nostra. U.S. v. IBT's main purpose was to purge the IBT of LCN's influence. Toward that end, the consent decree enjoined Teamsters from membership in any organized-crime family.[32] When prosecut-

FIGURE 4.1

IBT Officers Found to Be Members of Cosa Nostra during the IA/IO Phase (1989–1992)

Name	IBT Position	LCN Affiliation	Penalty	Date
Vincent Buliaro	Vice president: Local 617	New Jersey	Resigned from IBT	1/25/91
Anthony Calagna, Sr.	President: Local 295	Lucchese (NYC)	Expelled from IBT	5/7/91
James Cozzo	Coordinator: Local 786	The Outfit (Chicago)	Expelled from IBT	7/12/90
Liborio Crapanzano	President: Local 27	Gambino (NYC)	Resigned from IBT	11/25/91
William Cutolo	President: Local 861	Colombo (NYC)	Expelled from IBT	8/20/90
Joseph Glimco, Sr.	President: Local 777	The Outfit (Chicago)	Resigned from IBT	11/30/89
Nicholas Grancio	President: Local 707	Colombo (NYC)	Resigned from IBT	8/13/91
Anthony Parrino	Vice president: Local 682	St. Louis	Resigned from IBT	6/11/91
Joseph Pecora, Sr.	Secretary-treasurer: Local 863	LaRocca crime family (Pittsburgh)	Resigned from IBT	12/28/89
Louis Rumore	Vice president: Local 812	Gambino (NYC)	Resigned from IBT	12/11/90
Dominic Senese	President: Local 703	The Outfit (Chicago)	Expelled from IBT	7/12/90
Philip Tortorici	Trustee: Local 531	Genovese (NYC)	Resigned from IBT	9/6/91
Anthony Zappi	Secretary-treasurer: Local 854	Gambino (NYC)	Expelled from IBT	5/23/91

ing a violation of this disciplinary rule, the IO introduced an FBI agent's affidavit and/or testimony to prove that the respondent was a member of an LCN crime family.[33] Figure 4.1 shows that from July 1989 to September 1992, IA Lacey disciplined thirteen Teamsters, including five local presidents, three vice presidents, and two secretary-treasurers, for being LCN members. Every case resulted in expulsion or resignation from the IBT.

IO Carberry charged NYC IBT Local 295 President Anthony Calagna, Sr., with bringing reproach upon the union by being a soldier in the Gambino crime family, refusing to answer IO Carberry's questions, and embezzling $50,000 from Local 295. At Calagna's disciplinary hearing, an FBI agent testified that the FBI believed that Calagna was a Cosa Nostra member.[34] Calagna admitted that he had met Lucchese crime family member Richard DeLuca five hundred times, had known Lucchese crime family member Salvatore Avellino for "twenty, twenty-five years," and had socialized with Gambino crime family member John Giordano.[35] Moreover, when IO Carberry asked Calagna, "[Would it be] a matter of concern to you, as a union official, that someone you know might be tied up with organized crime?" Calagna replied, "Not really. I didn't give a shit."[36]

Knowing Association with Cosa Nostra. To prove that a Teamster knowingly associated with an LCN figure, the IO had to prove that (1) the individual with whom the respondent was alleged to have associated is an LCN member or associate;[37] (2) the respondent knew or should have known that this person is an LCN figure;[38] and (3) the contact was purposeful, not incidental or fleeting.[39] As long as the contact was purposeful, it did not matter whether it occurred in a business or social context.[40] (Charges were sustained, in some cases, even if the LCN member was a family member.) The prohibited contact could have occurred many times or just once.[41] For instance, IA Lacey expelled the former vice president of Rochester, New York IBT Local 398 on the basis of the respondent's single recorded conversation with Angelo Amico, alleged boss of Rochester's organized-crime family. The respondent's admission that he had read newspaper articles that labeled Amico an LCN family boss was enough to establish knowledge.[42] Early on, Lacey established expulsion as the appropriate punishment for an IBT officer or member who knowingly associates with an organized-crime figure: "There is only one just and reasonable penalty to be imposed when a Union Officer . . . sees fit to hobnob with mob bosses and underlings—permanent debarment from the very union he has tainted."[43]

Because it was usually easier to prove knowing association with LCN figures than membership in LCN, the IO often brought only a knowing-association charge, even though the respondent was a known LCN member. Dominic Senese (Chicago IBT Local 703 president), Joseph Talerico (Chicago IBT Local 727 business agent), and James Cozzo (Chicago IBT Local 777 executive coordinator) were the first IBT members to be expelled from the union for knowingly associating with LCN figures. An FBI agent testified that Senese not only met regularly with Cosa Nostra figures but was himself an LCN member. Angelo Lonardo, a cooperating government witness who admitted to having served as acting boss of the Cleveland LCN family, testified that Senese had knowingly associated with Chicago

Outfit boss Joey Aiuppa and former Outfit underboss Jackie Cerone. Roy Williams, cooperating with federal prosecutors, confirmed Senese's association with Outfit underboss John DiFronzo. An unnamed cooperating witness linked Senese to high-ranking Outfit member Angelo LaPietra. FBI surveillance photos showed Senese meeting with Outfit boss Jackie Cerone's son. IA Lacey expelled Senese from the union. Judge Edelstein and the Second Circuit Court of Appeals affirmed.[44]

An FBI agent documented six meetings between Talerico and an LCN member in and around Las Vegas from 1981 to 1982. The agent testified that Talerico had transported to Chicago money illegally "skimmed" (i.e., hidden from tax authorities) from Las Vegas casinos. Consequently, Lacey expelled Talerico for bringing reproach upon the IBT and for knowingly associating with an LCN member. Senese and Talerico argued that because their alleged associations with LCN figures occurred before the consent decree issued, they lacked prior notice that such association constituted a disciplinary violation.[45] Judge Edelstein rejected this defense as "fanciful" because "an IBT officer plainly should know that associating with organized-crime figures would violate his oath to not bring reproach upon the union."[46]

James Cozzo faced a bringing-reproach-on-the-union charge both for being a member of the Chicago Outfit and for knowingly associating with a member of the Outfit while serving as an IBT Local 786 official. Carberry charged that Cozzo met repeatedly with high-ranking Outfit leader Joseph Lombardo. Cozzo did not respond to the IO's charges, did not appear at the IA disciplinary hearing, and did not challenge the IA's finding of culpability or expulsion order.[47]

Theodore Cozza, a named defendant in *U.S. v. IBT*, a signatory of the consent decree, an international vice president, secretary-treasurer of the Eastern Conference of Teamsters' Policy Committee, president of Pittsburgh IBT Local 211, and chairman and trustee of Local 211's pension fund, employee welfare fund, and prepaid legal services fund,[48] contested the charge that he brought reproach upon the union by knowingly associating with five members of Pittsburgh's Cosa Nostra crime family from 1970 to 1990.[49] Cozza argued that disciplining him for associating with known LCN figures violated his First Amendment right of association. Judge Edelstein rejected his argument because, by signing the consent decree, the IBT defendants (including Cozza) agreed that the IA would have power to discipline Teamsters who knowingly associate with organized-crime figures.

Other IBT officers charged with membership in or knowing association with LCN chose to resign from the union rather than go through a hearing. For example, Cirino Salerno, former president of NYC IBT Local 272, resigned in September 1990 after the IA found that he had associated with LCN members, including his brother, Anthony Salerno, underboss of the Genovese crime family and a defendant in *U.S. v. IBT*.[50] Likewise, NYC IBT Local 861 President William Cutolo resigned his union positions on the eve of a disciplinary hearing at which the IO was prepared to introduce FBI affidavits alleging that Cutolo was a leader in the Colombo crime family.[51] (Nine years later, Cutolo disappeared after a meeting with Colombo crime family boss Alphonse Persico. In 2008, federal agents found Cutolo's remains wrapped in a blue tarp beneath a field in East Farmingdale, New York.)

Knowing Association with a Barred Person. If expelled Teamsters continued to spend time at union headquarters and to meet with IBT officers and members, rank-and-file Teamsters would infer that those expelled Teamsters remained a presence in the IBT and that, eventually, the old status quo would be reestablished. Consequently, the consent decree enjoined IBT members from "knowingly associating with . . . any person otherwise enjoined from participating in union affairs."[52] (This prohibition does not apply to solely familial or incidental contacts with barred persons.)[53] This disciplinary rule, according to Judge Edelstein, was meant to "insulate honest Teamsters from people involved in organized crime and others of dubious character."[54] It gave honest Teamsters a strong incentive and justification to avoid contact with barred persons.

During the IA/IO phase of the *U.S. v. IBT* remediation (July 1989–September 1992), no Teamster was charged with this offense, probably because few Teamsters had been expelled for non-LCN reasons before 1991. However, during the IRB phase of the remediation, there have been numerous such cases.

Violation of or Failure to Enforce a Suspension Order. The consent decree prohibited suspended Teamsters from participating in union affairs. As Judge Edelstein explained,

> The suspension that is enforced only in form undermines the Consent Decree and sends the message to the membership that dishonest IBT officials are immune from the law. Moreover, the spectacle of a suspension that has

become a caricature of itself deflates the morale and dampens the zeal of those who attempt to live within the law and work within the rules.[55]

A suspended member who continues to exercise de facto control over a local union can be held in contempt of court for violating the suspension order.[56]

Suspended Cleveland IBT Local 507 President Harold Friedman continued to participate in the local's affairs by advising board members, attending board meetings, and appearing at the local's social events.[57] Finding Friedman culpable of violating the terms of his suspension, Lacey expelled him from the IBT. He warned Local 507's other executive officers that "it is the duty of all IBT officials to take every reasonable step to prevent a suspended or barred individual from violating this standard. This duty is an affirmative one; acquiescence in the face of a violation of a suspension order or a statutory debarment is a violation of that duty."[58]

Failure to Cooperate with a Disciplinary Investigation. According to the consent decree, a Teamster's unreasonable failure to cooperate fully with a disciplinary investigation or proceeding brings reproach upon the IBT.[59] Thus, a Teamster is culpable of a disciplinary violation for failing to appear for an IO interview; failing to respond to IO inquiries in a lawful, timely, and responsible manner; failing to implement the IO's or IA's decisions expeditiously; failing to inform the IA/IO of the GEB's disciplinary or trusteeship decisions; or intentionally giving misleading testimony to a court-appointed officer.[60]

IO Carberry brought ten failure-to-cooperate cases from July 1989 to September 1992. For example, he charged NYC IBT Local 295 President Anthony Calagna, Sr., with bringing reproach upon the union by refusing to answer 124 questions concerning his alleged membership in LCN and alleged embezzlement of $50,000 from that local.[61] Calagna unsuccessfully argued that the U.S. Constitution's Fifth Amendment privilege protected him from being disciplined for refusing to answer these incriminating questions.[62] The Second Circuit Court of Appeals had previously held that the Fifth Amendment privilege did not protect IBT disciplinary respondents because the U.S. Constitution does not provide protection against a private organization compelling incriminating testimony.[63]

Failure to Investigate Allegations of Corruption. In one of Lacey's first decisions as IA, he ruled that IBT officials who violate their fiduciary duty to investigate allegations of misconduct bring reproach on the union:[64] "It is imperative that not only are Union officers themselves free from the taint of corruption, but also that they do not close their eyes to the corruption around them."[65] Judge Edelstein concurred: "Each defendant officer is a fiduciary with respect to the Union members. [Each has] a duty to disclose and remedy wrongdoing." Failure to fulfill that duty constitutes "aiding and abetting the extortion of IBT members' rights to democracy and free speech."[66] The IA used failure-to-investigate charges to remove from office forty-three IBT officers who were at least passively complicit with labor racketeers. The usual sanction was expulsion from IBT office.[67]

To prove a failure-to-investigate charge, the IO first had to show that the respondent knew or should have known of the wrongdoer's misconduct.[68] The IO proved this element by media reports, criminal charges, or other information that would have put a reasonable union officer on notice.[69] For example, IA Lacey found St. Louis IBT Local 682 President Robert Sansone culpable for failing to investigate media allegations that his local's vice president was an LCN member.[70]

Second, the IO had to prove that the respondent did not reasonably investigate.[71] The IO easily satisfied that element when the respondent had done little or no investigating.[72] For example, Sansone's defense was that he asked Local 682's vice president about the LCN allegation and relied on the vice president's denial. Lacey called that "investigation" inadequate.[73] To fulfill his or her fiduciary duty, an IBT officer had to have sought investigative assistance from a law-enforcement agency, the IO's office, a private detective, or a polygraph examiner.[74]

Disciplinary Violations Established by Federal Law

The consent decree made it an IBT disciplinary violation to commit certain federal crimes, such as loaning union funds to members, filing false or misleading reports to DOL, and committing assault, extortion, or bribery. The IO focused primarily on fraud-related, fiduciary-duty-related, and corruption-related federal offenses.

Extortion and Bribery. The consent decree authorized the court-appointed officers to investigate and punish union officials' violations of the LMRDA's extortion and bribery prohibitions.[75] The most frequently charged extortions during the IO/IA phase involved respondent IBT officers forcing rank-and-file members to pay them for hiring-hall job referrals. (Union hiring halls refer members to employers pursuant to the terms of a collective-bargaining agreement.) In North Haledon, New Jersey, for example, IBT Local 11 President Robert Feeney required catering-truck drivers to pay him in order to obtain work.

The IO also brought charges against IBT officers for extorting employers by threatening labor problems. In December 1991, for example, IO Carberry charged NYC IBT Local 282 President Robert Sasso with assisting Gambino crime family members in extracting labor-peace payoffs from New York–area construction contractors.[76] Confronted with the prospect of former Gambino crime family underboss (and cooperating government witness) Salvatore Gravano testifying against him, Sasso resigned from the union hours before his disciplinary hearing.[77]

Filing False or Misleading Forms with the U.S. Department of Labor. During the IO/IA phase of the remediation, IO Carberry charged eight local officers with filing false or misleading LM-2 forms (the annual financial statements that unions must submit to DOL).[78] The most prominent of these cases involved Cleveland IBT Local 507 President Harold Friedman, whom IO Carberry charged with bringing reproach upon the union by, among other things, filing a false LM-2 on behalf of Bakery, Confectionery, and Tobacco Workers International Union Local 19, of which Friedman was also president. (Friedman's false LM-2 filing was one basis for his 1989 criminal RICO conviction.) In a similar case, IO Carberry charged International Vice President George Vitale with filing an LM-2 that improperly failed to reveal that his IBT local, rather than Vitale, had paid Vitale's FICA taxes. Lacey sustained both charges. Judge Edelstein affirmed Lacey's conclusion that a union officer breaches his fiduciary duty to the members by failing to read or review an LM-2 form before signing it.[79] After the Second Circuit Court of Appeals ruled in 1991 that this charge required proof of the respondent's fraudulent intent, Carberry used other charges to deal with financial misconduct.[80]

Prior Felony Conviction. Section 504 of the Landrum-Griffin Act prohibits an individual from holding union office for thirteen years following a felony conviction.[81] Lacey held that violating this law brings reproach upon the union.

IO Carberry charged several IBT officers with having held union office after a felony conviction. For example, he brought charges against Akron, Ohio IBT Local 348 Secretary-Treasurer Daniel Darrow for having held office after pleading no contest to second-degree riot.[82] The conflict arose between an IBT member and members of an independent dissident group called the Fraternal Association of Steel Haulers (FASH). FASH members had gone on strike at a steel plant despite their local's no-strike agreement with the employer. When other Teamsters, including Darrow, attempted to cross the picket line, a gun battle erupted; one Teamster was killed and others injured. Lacey held that the riot conviction, standing alone, without evidence that Darrow had carried a gun or engaged in violent activity, did not bring reproach upon the IBT. He distinguished Darrow's case from that of Chicago Local 727 Business Agent Joseph Talerico, whom Lacey found to have brought reproach upon the union by holding union office after being convicted of contempt for refusing to give grand jury testimony about an organized-crime scheme to skim money from a Las Vegas casino. Lacey explained that a still-in-effect 1957 AFL-CIO Executive Council statement prohibited union officers from invoking the Fifth Amendment because it creates the appearance that the union "sanctions the use of the Fifth Amendment . . . as a shield against proper scrutiny into corrupt influences in the labor movement."[83] The riot conviction in Darrow's case did not cast the same corruption shadow.

Assault. The Landrum-Griffin law provides that it is "unlawful for any person through the use . . . or threat . . . of force or violence, to restrain, coerce, or intimidate, or attempt to restrain, coerce, or intimidate any member of a labor organization for the purpose of interfering with or preventing the exercise of any right to which he is entitled under the provisions of this chapter."[84] Tracking this statute, the IBT constitution prohibits "assaulting or provoking assault on fellow members or officers . . . or any similar conduct in, or about union premises or places used to conduct union business."[85]

A disciplinary-assault charge requires proof of actual or threatened violence.[86] IO Carberry charged Pittsburgh IBT Local 249 Secretary-Treasurer William Cherilla with seriously injuring a fellow officer who was running against him in the local election. IA Lacey suspended Cherilla from the union for five years. In another case, IA Lacey suspended Cleveland, Ohio IBT Local 473 Secretary-Treasurer Carmen Parise for two years for threatening to assault a political opponent.[87]

The IBT Constitution's Disciplinary Offenses

According to the IBT constitution, it is a disciplinary offense to violate a local-union bylaw, misappropriate union funds, disclose confidential IBT information to non-Teamsters, and interfere with the IBT's contractual or legal obligations. IO Carberry most frequently brought disciplinary charges for embezzlement,[88] failure to maintain required financial controls, sham membership schemes, and other "financial misconduct."

Embezzlement. During the IO/IA phase, Carberry filed embezzlement charges against 115 respondents, virtually all of whom were IBT officers. Carberry had to prove that the respondents intended to convert union funds to personal use.[89] In one prominent embezzlement case, Carberry charged George Vitale—international vice president, secretary-treasurer of the Central States Conference of Teamsters' Policy Committee, vice president of IBT Joint Council 43, chairman of the Automobile, Petroleum, and Allied Trades Division, and president of Michigan IBT Local 283—with embezzlement, because the union had improperly paid his FICA taxes.[90] IA Lacey ruled that fraudulent intent could be inferred from a respondent's use of union property without any benefit to the union, failure to record an expenditure on the DOL's LM-2 form, and preventing other IBT officers from finding out about the unlawful benefit.[91]

In a case against two Evandale, Ohio IBT Local 100 officers, Lacey held, and Judge Edelstein affirmed, that a good-faith but erroneous belief that an expenditure provided a legitimate union benefit was not a valid defense to an embezzlement charge.[92] However, in a rare reversal, the Second Circuit Court of Appeals held that fraudulent intent is not proven if the respondent had a good-faith belief both that the funds were expended for the union's benefit and that the union had or would have authorized the expenditure.[93]

Financial Misconduct. "Financial misconduct," a charge closely resembling embezzlement, requires proof of wrongful appropriation of union property. Proof of fraudulent intent is unnecessary. The IO used this disciplinary violation to charge respondents for aiding and abetting embezzlement,[94] making unapproved expenditures,[95] giving away union property,[96] and providing union benefits to organized-crime members.[97] Punishments ranged from short suspensions[98] to lifetime bans.[99]

Insufficient Financial Controls. The court-appointed officers argued that lack of financial controls in a local or joint council provides fertile ground for corruption and organized-crime infiltration.[100] IO Carberry (and later the IRB) brought disciplinary charges against many IBT officers who failed to implement or enforce financial-monitoring procedures required by local bylaws, international-union mandates, or federal or state regulations. Specific charges included failure to keep minutes,[101] approve local bylaws,[102] and comply with audits,[103] as well as filing false or misleading financial information with IBT headquarters.[104] Frequently, the IO simultaneously filed charges against several officers. For example, Carberry charged all seven members of NYC IBT Local 831's executive board with failure to adopt bylaws[105] and charged three Long Island City, New York IBT Local 27 trustees with filing false financial statements.[106] Occasionally, rather than bringing a disciplinary charge alleging insufficient financial controls, IO Carberry would issue a "noncharge" report to a local's executive board, highlighting deficiencies in the local's financial practices and requiring prompt remedial action.

Sham Membership Schemes. The IBT constitution sets membership eligibility requirements. To knowingly extend membership to ineligible persons (who, for example, may desire membership in order to be included in the union's health-insurance plan) is a disciplinary violation.[107] For example, several officers of New York IBT Locals 917 and 868 created an "associate membership program" that permitted non-IBT employees to obtain union health-insurance coverage for ten dollars per person (to be paid by their employers).[108] IO Carberry charged that this "sham" membership scheme lined the respondents' pockets, while providing no benefit to the union or its members.[109] IA Lacey held that all seven members of both locals' executive boards had violated their fiduciary duties.[110] Sham-membership cases generally resulted in expulsion from the union.

Trusteeing Corrupted IBT Locals

The IA exercised the IBT general president's power to impose a trusteeship on a corrupted or dysfunctional local or joint council.[111] The kinds of corruption warranting trusteeship include sweetheart contracts with employers, nepotism or favoritism, dual unionism (officers maintaining membership in both the IBT and a non-IBT union), and financial misconduct.

A trusteeship is also warranted if a local union or joint council does not hold membership meetings, lacks competitive elections, has incumbent officers who are ineligible to hold union office, improperly approves salary increases, or experiences extensive embezzlement. The IBT constitution provides for imposition of a trusteeship if a local or joint council is run for the benefit of a select few rather than for the whole membership.[112] Lacey ruled that a history of organized-crime influence is a strong indicator that a local union was being run for the benefit of a select few.[113]

The consent decree authorized the IO to "institute trusteeship proceedings for the purpose and in the manner specified in the IBT constitution"[114] and authorized the IA to "discharge those duties which relate to . . . appointing temporary trustees to run the affairs" of IBT locals and joint councils.[115] The IO had to notify the IBT general president of his intent to convene a trusteeship hearing in order to give the general president the opportunity to impose a trusteeship himself. If the general president chose to impose a trusteeship, the IO and IA could review and modify that trusteeship.[116] If, within ten days, the general president took no action on an IO trusteeship recommendation, or decided against imposing a trusteeship, the IO and IA could initiate trusteeship proceeding. If a trusteeship is imposed, the general president replaces the local's or joint council's elected officers with a trustee who has authority to take charge of the local's affairs, remove any officer, appoint temporary officers, and take other actions necessary to set the IBT entity on a corruption-free course.

All told, from July 1989 to September 1992, the IA placed or approved trusteeships on nine IBT locals.[117] In early 1990, for example, IO Carberry notified General President McCarthy of his intention to institute trusteeship proceedings against Bridgeport, Connecticut IBT Local 191[118] based on evidence that its president, secretary-treasurer, and recording secretary had colluded to embezzle large sums from the local's health-insurance fund.[119] McCarthy appointed a panel of IBT officers to convene a trusteeship proceeding. That panel concluded that a trusteeship was unwarranted. McCarthy adopted its recommendation. Carberry rejected McCarthy's decision and instituted a trusteeship proceeding against Local 191. IA Lacey sustained Carberry's charges and appointed a trustee to run the local.

The most important trusteeship case of the IA/IO period concerned NYC IBT Local 295.[120] In late 1990, after finding rampant corruption within the local, Lacey expelled seven of Local 295's eight executive board members and appointed a trustee. "In my two years as Independent Administrator, I have seen few IBT Locals with the sullied reputation associated with Local 295, a reputation richly deserved, as reflected by the record in this case."[121] A year later, DOJ brought a separate civil RICO suit against the leaders of Local 295. Judge Eugene Nickerson (Eastern District of New York) concluded that, "contrary to the argument of Local 295, vestiges of its old regime are not gone. The record establishes, without significant evidentiary dispute, a consistent and extended pattern of racketeering and extortion and a sufficiently strong possibility that the corruption persists to warrant a special remedy from the court."[122] In addition, Nickerson found a court-appointed trusteeship was warranted because "[i]nstitutional practices and traditions tend to endure long after specific individuals are gone. The evidence establishes that the corruption in Local 295 was not simply in practice, but in spirit and belief."[123] He appointed a trustee to clean up the local.

Conclusion and Analysis

In just three years, 1989–1992, the IO/IA removed from the IBT more than two hundred officers, including twelve international officers, fifty local-union presidents, twenty-seven vice presidents, and forty-six secretary-treasurers. Indeed, of all the disciplinary charges filed from 1989 until 2011, approximately 25 percent were filed between 1989 and 1992. Twelve LCN members were expelled or resigned, and many LCN associates were expelled for associating with expelled or suspended IBT members. By the end of the IO/IA phase (October 1992), there had been a complete changeover of the GEB. All of the IBT defendants named in the civil RICO case had resigned or been expelled (see fig. 4.2).

The IO/IA disciplinary machinery achieved in just three years what decades of criminal prosecutions had failed to achieve, thereby proving the efficacy of RICO's civil remedy to reform a systemically corrupted organization. In the 1970s and 1980s, federal prosecutors had sent dozens of IBT racketeers to prison, but the IBT remained "a captive labor organization." LCN simply replaced the imprisoned labor racketeers with other mobbed-up operatives. By contrast, IO Carberry and IA Lacey were able to systematically purge organized-crime members, associates, and allies from dozens of IBT locals and joint councils. Most dramatically, they made it impossible for anyone with known LCN connections to serve on the GEB and very difficult for such a person to serve as an officer of an IBT local.

The IO/IA administrative disciplinary law proved to be powerful medi-

FIGURE 4.2
Fate of the Eighteen IBT Defendants in U.S. v. IBT

Name	Fate	Date
Jackie Presser	Died of cancer and heart disease	1988
Weldon Mathis	Retired	1991
Joseph Trerotola	Retired	1991
Robert Holmes, Sr.	Resigned	1989
William McCarthy	Retired	1992
Joseph Morgan	Retired	1990
Edward Lawson	Retired	1992
Arnold Weinmeister	Retired	1992
John Cleveland	Died	1989
Maurice Schurr	Retired	1988
Donald Peters	Retired	1989
Walter Shea	Defeated in first direct, rank-and-file IBT election	1991
Harold Friedman	Convicted and expelled by the IRB	1988
Jack Cox	Retired	2000
Donald West	Charged with embezzlement; found not culpable	1992
Michael Riley	Paid $40,760 to Local 986 to settle charges	1991
Theodore Cozza	Expelled from IBT	1991
Daniel Ligurotis	Expelled from IBT	1992

cine. In particular, suspending and expelling union officers for failing to act affirmatively to protect the union from corruption and racketeering set a very high standard for union officers' conduct. In effect, it equated nonfeasance with malfeasance; IBT officers were expelled from office for not aggressively opposing corruption and racketeering. The IA also expelled many officers for not cooperating with the IO's investigations.

Judge Edelstein ruled that IBT members could not assert Fifth Amendment or Fourteenth Amendment rights at the investigative or adjudicative stage of the disciplinary process because the court-appointed officers, operating under a consent decree manifesting the parties' agreement, were not state actors. This decision troubles us. We believe that when a court-appointed officer in a civil RICO case questions a potential disciplinary respondent about a corruption issue, and a federal or state prosecutor could use that individual's response against him in a subsequent criminal case, the Fifth Amendment should apply.[124] Likewise, we think that disciplinary charges should be considered state action that entitles the Teamster to Fourteenth Amendment due process protections. Of course, the IO and IA operated with a good deal of process, following the procedures generally applicable in labor arbitration proceedings; thus, Teamsters disciplinary respondents were generally afforded appropriate due process. However, they did not (and, in the ongoing IRB phase, still do not) have Fifth

Amendment protection or testimonial immunity despite the threat of forfeiture of union office.

We also think that forbidding an expelled Teamster from associating with any member of the Teamsters Union is an extreme remedy. Many of the expelled individual's friends may be union members. We recognize that our concerns would logically also apply to the disciplinary rule prohibiting Teamsters from knowingly associating with LCN figures. Admittedly, the court and court officers face such deeply entrenched corruption that a very strong remedy is necessary. Still, prohibiting ordinary Teamsters from associating with barred persons and prohibiting barred persons from associating with ordinary Teamsters comes close to (if it does not cross the line by) infringing on associational and due process rights. Certainly, this sanction should be used as a last resort.

IO Carberry's and IA Lacey's aggressive implementation of the union's new disciplinary processes demonstrated to honest Teamsters, TDU, future candidates for union office, and federal prosecutors that the IBT's old power structure was possibly doomed. Although the IO/IA phase did not completely eradicate LCN's influence in the union, it made substantial progress toward that goal and made clear that, henceforth, labor racketeering would be far more costly, risky, and inefficient than it had been for the previous five decades. In the battle between a federal court and the nation's most powerful labor union and crime syndicate, the court and court-appointed officers were unquestionably winning.

The IO and IA did not handle only organized-crime cases. The consent decree ceded to these officers the GEB's and general president's full disciplinary powers. Thus, they investigated, adjudicated, and punished many corrupt acts and schemes, whether or not organized-crime related. Arguably, this went beyond the rationale for the civil RICO suit. In retrospect, the consent decree could have limited the IO/IA's authority to organized-crime cases. However, because a respondent's organized-crime connection is often hard to prove without other Teamsters' cooperation, which the IA effectively compelled by threatening expulsion for noncooperation with an IO investigation, that limitation would have made the court officers' jobs much harder. In any event, the IO/IA quickly took the position that the broadest possible disciplinary jurisdiction was necessary because any corruption invited organized-crime infiltration. The implications of that theory could be far-reaching. For example, the theory could justify a permanent independent review board to enforce the union's disciplinary rules.

5

An Insurgent's Triumph
The IBT's 1991 Election

Welcome to the new Teamsters Union. From the day I walk in the door, the rules are going to change. We are going to clean house and never again have to apologize for being Teamsters.

　　　　　—IBT General President Ron Carey, press conference,
　　　　　　　　　　　　　　　　　　　　　　　　　December 12, 1991

Not since the thirties, when the CIO was born, has there been an event of such profound significance for U.S. labor as your [Ron Carey's] election to the presidency of the Teamsters through rank and file membership mobilization.[1]

　　　　　—Victor Reuther, cofounder of United Auto Workers,
　　　　　　　　　　　　　　　　　　Convoy Dispatch, January 1992

In negotiating the consent decree, U.S. Attorney Giuliani and his staff accepted TDU's and AUD's prediction that, given free and fair elections, Teamsters would elect candidates who opposed corruption and racketeering. Therefore, the consent decree mandated election procedures that were more democratic than those of any other U.S. labor union. First, IBT locals' rank-and-file members would elect delegates to a nominating convention.[2] Second, the convention delegates would nominate candidates for general president, general secretary-treasurer, international vice presidents, and international trustees.[3] A candidate who received 5 percent or more of the delegates' votes would earn a place on the general-election ballot. Third, IBT members would vote via secret mail-in ballots.[4] If the EO deemed the election free and fair, he or she would "certify" the result.[5] (The consent decree did not provide a definition of or criteria for certification. Judge Edelstein clarified its meaning at the end of the 1991 election cycle.)

EO Michael Holland and his staff had to face numerous, difficult policy and logistical challenges. Holland observed that "supervision of any comparable union election had never been undertaken anywhere in the world. There was no blueprint to guide us."[6] Only a handful of American unions elect their international officers via direct rank-and-file voting. (In most unions, convention delegates select the international officers.) The EO's office had to formulate election rules covering the election of convention delegates, delegates' nomination of international officers at the convention, and, for the general election, rules on voter eligibility, campaign contributions and expenditures, balloting, and the filing and resolution of election rules violation.

The 1991 Election Rules

In October 1989, in response to the IBT's argument that the consent decree authorized only passive EO monitoring (not active EO implementation) of the IBT international elections, Judge Edelstein ruled that the consent decree's use of the word "supervise" in describing the EO's powers gave the EO "the right to promulgate electoral rules and procedures for the delegate elections, nominating convention and rank and file mail balloting."[7] Accordingly, in early 1990, EO Holland proposed "Rules for the IBT International Union Delegate and Officer Election" in order (1) to "assemble in one document all the regulations affecting the nomination and election of delegates to the 1991 IBT International Convention and the nomination and election of IBT International Officers"; and (2) to "provide for fair, honest and open elections so as to permit the Election Officer to certify the election results."[8] Holland's proposed rules provided a timetable for each stage of the 1991 election, criteria for voter eligibility, procedures for nominations and balloting, regulations for campaign fundraising and expenditures, and procedures for resolving campaign protests.[9] Holland held hearings on the proposed election rules in San Francisco, Seattle, New York City, Baltimore, Chicago, Memphis, Cleveland, and Toronto. Nearly 125 Teamsters offered on-the-record comments.[10]

DOJ, supported by TDU's and AUD's amicus briefs, argued for greater EO supervision to prevent intimidation and fraud in the local-delegate elections.[11] AUD opposed allowing IBT locals to print and count delegate-election ballots, determine candidate eligibility, and conduct delegate elections.[12] "[I]n the all-pervasive lawlessness that has permeated the union, it would be foolhardy, even irresponsible, to depend upon the local union officers for safeguarding the integrity of the elections."[13] DOJ and the amici urged EO Holland and Judge Edelstein to consider, as a model for election supervision, DOL's supervision of the 1972 United Mine Workers election.*

In rebuttal, the EO, IA, and IBT (a strange alignment) argued that the locals should have primary responsibility for running their convention-delegate elections. They contended that the kind of proactive role envisioned by AUD, TDU, and DOJ would, in contravention of the consent decree, amount to "conducting" rather than "supervising" the convention-delegate elections.[14]

Judge Edelstein emphatically agreed with TDU, AUD, and DOJ. "The final election rules leave many critical election functions to the officers of local unions. This situation is unacceptable, since these same officers . . . will have great personal stakes in the election's outcome."[15] Consequently, Edelstein ordered EO Holland to amend the election rules to "provide for the Election Officer to supervise each and every portion of the election process. . . . [This] is the only way to guarantee the integrity of the elections and encourage extensive rank-and-file participation."[16] Accordingly, EO Holland amended the election rules so that the EO would have authority "to supervise all phases of the delegate and international office election process," including the authority to conduct, overturn, or rerun any phase of the election, to hear and determine protests and appeals, and to interpret, enforce, and amend the election rules.[17]

Eligibility to Vote and Run for Office

The 1991 election rules linked voter eligibility to "good standing" in the IBT. Voters had to be up-to-date on dues payments and either employed

---

* DOL's supervision of UMW's international elections resulted from the 1969 assassination of Joseph Yablonski, an insurgent candidate for UMW president. Yablonski narrowly lost the 1969 election to incumbent UMW president W.A. Boyle. Yablonski asked DOL to investigate election fraud and filed five federal suits against the UMW. Three weeks later, three hit men murdered Yablonski, his wife, and their daughter. In 1971, pursuant to the LMRDA, DOL asked a federal judge to overturn the 1969 election results. The judge granted this request and ordered DOL to "conduct" a rerun election. This time, Boyle was defeated. He was later convicted of the murders, having hired the hit men. *United States v. Int'l Bhd. of Teamsters*, 74 F. Supp. 94, 106 (S.D.N.Y. 1990) (citing *Hodgson v. United Mine Workers*, 344 F. Supp. 17 (D.D.C. 1972)).

or actively seeking employment "at the craft within the jurisdiction of the local."[18] More than 90 percent of IBT members authorize their employers to deduct union dues from their paychecks and to remit those dues directly to the union.[19] Nevertheless, problems inevitably arose. For example, only 20 percent of the 6,179 members of NYC IBT Local 732 appeared to meet the voter-eligibility criteria due to employer bankruptcies, untimely or delinquent dues postings, and turnover of union staff. However, both the IBT constitution and the LMRDA[20] state that a union member cannot be disenfranchised on account of an employer's failure to remit or report authorized dues payments.[21] Therefore, Holland ruled that a Teamster whose name appeared on the employer's most recent dues-payment list would be eligible to vote, regardless of the actual date of the employer's last dues transmittal on the member's behalf.

To be eligible to run for convention delegate or international office, a Teamster had to have been in good standing for at least twenty-four consecutive months before nomination, with no interruptions in active membership due to suspensions, expulsions, withdrawals, transfers, or failure to pay fines or assessments.[22] To nominate or second a nomination, a Teamster also had to be in good standing. Convention-delegate and international-officer candidates were permitted to form slates committed to a general presidential candidate.

The election rules provided that, prior to the 1991 convention, "accredited" slates of international-officer candidates, as well as accredited individual international-officer candidates, had the right to publish "battle pages," that is, campaign literature, in the October 1990 and February 1991 issues of *Teamster Magazine* free of charge. To achieve accreditation, presidential, secretary-treasurer, and at-large vice presidential candidates had to obtain signatures of support from 2.5 percent of the unionwide membership; regional vice presidential candidates had to obtain signatures from 2.5 percent of Teamsters in their region. Slates and candidates who achieved the 5 percent threshold of support at the convention had the right to publish campaign battle pages in *Teamster Magazine*'s October and November 1991 issues.

Electing Convention Delegates

The election rules required each local union to submit to the EO's office a plan for electing delegates and alternate delegates to the 1991 IBT convention.[23] (Holland had to determine how many convention delegates and alternate delegates each local was entitled to send to the convention.) These plans had to include specific dates for notifying the rank and file about the delegate-election process; proposed dates and times of delegate nomination meetings and elections; description of the composition and method of selecting the local-union election committees; procedures for conducting the elections; and the methods, dates, times, and places for counting ballots.[24]

Holland hired and trained twenty-three regional coordinators and field staff (mostly former DOL or National Labor Relations Board employees, labor lawyers, or retired officials from other unions) to review and, if necessary, modify the locals' delegate-election plans.[25] He followed a presumption against imposing on locals unfamiliar and complicated election procedures "unless departure from past practice afforded an enhanced and freer opportunity for participation."[26] Nevertheless, the EO required most locals to make at least a few changes.[27]

Each local had to schedule a convention-delegates-nomination meeting and then notify its members of the meeting's time and location, either by mail, publication in a union newsletter or by some other method "reasonably calculated to inform."[28] An EO staff member personally attended every local's nomination meeting, checked the eligibility of the nominators, seconders, and nominees, and resolved protests.

Candidates' Fair and Equal Access to the Electorate

The election rules required IBT entities and IBT employers to give candidates equal opportunities to communicate with the electorate. If an employer previously had allowed union members to use on-premises bulletin boards, for example, the EO required the employer to allow candidates to post campaign materials to those bulletin boards.[29] The election rules also provided that "no restrictions shall be placed upon candidates' or members' preexisting rights" to distribute leaflets or literature, conduct rallies and fundraising events, and post fliers on employer or union premises.[30]

EO Holland's assertion of authority over employers was controversial since they were neither *U.S. v. IBT* defendants nor signatories of the consent decree. This issue was resolved via litigation arising from a Ron Carey campaign allegation that an IBT employer, Yellow Freight Systems, had blatantly supported Carey's opponent, R.V. Durham, and prevented Carey's supporters from campaigning at Yellow Freight's work sites in Detroit and Chicago.[31] Yellow Freight sought to enforce its "no solicitation" rule by barring nonemployee Teamsters, including Carey campaigners, from its properties. EO Holland ruled that, with respect to Yellow Freight's Detroit site, the Carey campaign had reasonable ways to communicate with the company's Teamsters employees off the company's property; however, Holland ordered Yellow Freight to provide Carey campaigners access to its Chicago premises.[32]

Yellow Freight appealed to the IA on the grounds that the EO did not have jurisdiction over Teamsters employers and that the National Labor Relations Board (NLRB) had exclusive jurisdiction to regulate union election candidates' access to an employer's property.[33] After Lacey upheld Holland's ruling, Yellow Freight appealed to Judge Edelstein,[34] who affirmed Lacey's and Holland's decisions. He explained that the district court required jurisdiction over IBT employers in order to enforce the election-reform prong of the *U.S. v. IBT* consent decree. Edelstein also held that the NLRB did not have exclusive jurisdiction over disputes involving union candidates' access to employer property because his All Writs Act injunction prevented the NLRB from hearing disputes emanating from the consent decree.[35] Edelstein also upheld Holland's rejection of Yellow Freight's no-solicitation rule because the union incumbents' advantage could be neutralized only by allowing all candidates equal access to employers' work sites.[36] The Second Circuit Court of Appeals approved Judge Edelstein's assertion of jurisdiction over Yellow Freight pursuant to the All Writs Act, but returned the case to Edelstein to determine whether candidates had reasonable alternative means to communicate with Yellow Freight's employees.[37]

The Second Circuit Court of Appeals reaffirmed Edelstein's IBT-employer ruling in a case involving a charge that Star Market fired a member of Boston IBT Local 25 for publicly supporting Ron Carey in the 1991 election.[38] (The member's local had elected him as a convention delegate committed to Carey's slate.)[39] Holland ordered Star Market to reinstate the employee with back pay.[40] When Star Market refused to comply, the U.S. attorney asked Judge Edelstein to enforce the EO's order.[41] Edelstein held that *Yellow Freight* dictated a decision in the employee's favor.[42] The *Yellow Freight* and *Star Market* decisions established that the district court and EO have authority over IBT employers in matters concerning the *U.S. v. IBT* remediation. Employers cannot favor one IBT candidate over another and cannot retaliate against a Teamster for exercising political rights.[43]

To ensure that all Teamsters candidates would have equal access to their constituents, the 1991 election rules allowed candidates for convention delegate and international office to inspect union records in order to obtain rank and filers' names and contact information. Candidates for international office could inspect, for campaign purposes, certain collective-bargaining agreements, local unions' lists of rank and filers' work-site locations, lists of convention delegates' names and addresses, and, most important, lists containing the last known addresses of Teamsters eligible to vote. Judge Edelstein affirmed these rules,[44] explaining that candidates' full and equal access to membership lists is necessary to "foster alternative candidates," who could not reasonably compete if only incumbents had the necessary information to communicate with eligible voters.[45] Moreover, insurgent candidates needed the names and addresses in order to counteract the IBT leadership's use of *Teamster Magazine* "as a propaganda tool . . . to subvert a free and fair election by assailing the legitimacy and integrity of the Court Officers and damaging the possibility of reform."[46]

Campaign Contributions and Disclosure

The EO's campaign-finance rule tracked the consent decree and the LMRDA: "No candidate for election shall accept or use any contributions or other things of value [e.g., money, stationery, equipment, facilities, and personnel] received from any employers, representative of an employer, foundation, trust or similar entity."[47] This prohibition applies to every employer (not just IBT employers), foundation, and trust, including political action organizations, nonprofit organizations (e.g., churches and civic groups), law firms, and other professional organizations that employ staff. Candidates were also forbidden from accepting campaign contributions from any labor organizations.

The rules also sought to prevent incumbents from using union resources to benefit their campaigns.[48] A convention-delegate or international-officer candidate could not use IBT equipment, facilities, property, or personnel for campaign purposes unless the candidate fully reimbursed the union and, even then, only if all candidates had equal access (and equal prior notice of access) to those goods and services. Candidates whose campaigns received anything of value from IBT locals, joint councils, or the international union could be disqualified from the election. Because an endorsement of a candidate is a material thing of value, and thus a campaign contribution, EO Holland prohibited the leaders of IBT locals and joint councils from endorsing or soliciting endorsements for candidates.[49]

Candidates could accept contributions from non-Teamsters who were not employers, employers who were also Teamsters, and any caucus of union members or candidate's campaign organization financed exclusively by Teamsters donations.[50] Candidates could also receive money or services from employers or labor organizations (other than the IBT) to pay fees for legal or accounting services performed in assuring compliance with the election rules and to secure, defend, and clarify candidates' legal rights. The election rules placed no monetary limit on the amount that eligible contributors could donate. Moreover, any individual could volunteer his or her personal services, on his or her own free time, to any candidate as long as the individual neither received compensation for those services from an employer or labor organization nor used the supplies or services of an employer or labor organization. Because Holland believed that campaign-contribution transparency was critical to ensuring a free and fair election, he imposed reporting and disclosure requirements on international-officer candidates' campaign committees and on independent campaign committees (i.e., groups, such as TDU, composed solely of IBT members not directly affiliated with a candidate or slate, but actively supporting one or more candidates). Each candidate periodically had to report campaign contributions and expenditures exceeding one hundred dollars. Holland would monitor these reports to ensure that contributions plus debts did not exceed expenditures (and vice versa). The reports on campaign contributions and expenditures would be available for candidates to review. Holland explained that disclosure of candidates' campaign contributions and expenditures was meant to "afford information upon which [a competing candidate could] file and support a pre-election protest" and to "give candidates the opportunity to comment upon the source of their rivals' campaign contributions and expenditures as part of the political process."[51]

Election Protests and Appeals

The election rules provided a mechanism for expeditiously resolving protests alleging election-rule violations. Any IBT member, local, or other IBT entity could file an election protest with the EO's office within two days of the day the protestor became aware, or reasonably should have become aware, of the alleged violation. The EO had five days to investigate and resolve it. In some cases, Holland assigned the protest to one of twenty-three regional coordinators with responsibility for the geographical area where the protested conduct took place. In the event of an appeal, the IA had three days to conduct a hearing and two additional days to render a decision.

The Candidates for General President and Their Slates

IBT General President William McCarthy initially announced that he would seek reelection, but he abandoned his candidacy when he failed to secure the support of a large number of GEB members.[52] (Subsequently, McCarthy lost his campaign for reelection as president of Local 25. He then retired as president of Joint Council 10, which he had run for twenty years. He retired from the union soon after.) That left three principal candidates for general president: Ron Carey, R.V. Durham, and Walter Shea.[53]

Since 1967, Ron Carey (winning reelection eight times by wide margins) had been president of IBT Local 804, which represented United Parcel Service (UPS) workers in the NYC metropolitan area. In a 1979 book, *The Teamsters*, prominent legal journalist Steven Brill had extolled Carey as the best person to displace the labor racketeers who had dominated the IBT for decades.[54] Brill called Carey a "special kind of leader with immaculate integrity."[55] (Thirteen years later, labor journalist Kenneth Crowe wrote that Brill's book catapulted Carey to national recognition among the IBT rank and file.)[56]

Carey's campaign staff quickly collected enough rank-and-file members' signatures to obtain accreditation, entitling the Carey slate to publish battle pages free of charge in the October 1990 and February 1991 issues of *Teamster Magazine*.[57] TDU strongly backed Carey, advised his campaign staff, published favorable articles about him in *Convoy Dispatch*, and recruited TDUers to run for convention delegate in their locals' elections. Although Carey was not a TDU member, his agenda was compatible with TDU's positions on most issues. He accepted TDU's endorsement, but insisted throughout his campaign that TDU was just one of several organizations whose endorsement he welcomed. One Carey campaign aide noted, "The downside [of the TDU endorsement] is that for years Teamster leaders have been pounding it into the members that TDU is a bunch of complainers, dissidents, communists, and employer representatives."[58]

General presidential candidate R.V. Durham was a former North Carolina truck driver who rose through the IBT's ranks. He served as president of IBT Joint Council 9 (the Carolinas), an international vice president, an international trustee, and the first director of the Teamsters' Safety and Health Department. The majority of the GEB, including General President McCarthy, supported him and his "Unity Team" slate.[59]

The third candidate, Walter J. Shea, had a less conventional IBT career. He joined the IBT as an Eastern Conference of Teamsters research assistant and subsequently served as an international organizer, executive assistant to General Presidents Fitzsimmons, Williams, Presser, and McCarthy and ultimately as an international vice president. A few IBT leaders in the east and midwest supported Shea, but he lacked a political base in a local, joint council, or regional conference. Two weeks after Shea announced his candidacy, McCarthy, calling him "disloyal," fired him from his executive assistant position.[60]

On February 20, 1991, Jim (James P.) Hoffa, a lawyer and son of former IBT General President Jimmy (James R.) Hoffa, announced his candidacy for general president.[61] Immediately, a rank and filer in Detroit challenged Hoffa's eligibility to run for office, citing an election rule that required candidates for international office to have been "employed at the craft within the jurisdiction of the [candidate's] local" for twenty-four consecutive months prior to the month of nomination. The challenger argued that Hoffa had never worked in a Teamsters craft.[62] Hoffa argued that he satisfied the eligibility rule by working as an attorney representing IBT locals for two decades and by working, since April 1990, as an assistant to Lawrence Brennan, president of Michigan IBT Joint Council 43 and Detroit IBT Local 337.[63] EO Holland ruled Hoffa ineligible because (1) his work as a private lawyer representing Teamsters locals did not qualify as employment in a Teamsters craft; and (2) he would have worked for Brennan less than the requisite two years by the time the IBT international convention convened in June 1991.[64] Hoffa then endorsed Durham for general president.

The Convention Delegate Elections and the July 1991 Nominating Convention

EO Holland called the local-delegate election process "the most arduous component of the Election Officer's responsibilities."[65] Members of 623 local unions nominated approximately thirty-two hundred delegate candidates and fifteen hundred alternate-delegate candidates. Most delegate and alternate-delegate candidates ran on slates committed to a presidential candidate. However, contested elections occurred in fewer than half (49 percent) of the locals, actually a decline in contested elections compared to the most recent IBT local-union officer elections.

Holland had to resolve several protests.[66] He ordered rerun elections in four locals. In Rialto, California IBT Local 63, Holland ordered a rerun delegate election because the order of the slates on the printed ballots had been juxtaposed. In Grand Rapids, Michigan IBT Local 406, he ordered a rerun because after mail balloting, two winning delegates were found to be ineligible; Holland ordered a second rerun at Local 406 after finding that a candidate had improperly affixed the local's insignia to his campaign literature. In Oklahoma City IBT Local 886, Holland ordered a rerun because a delegate candidate's name was misspelled. And in Nashville, Tennessee IBT Local 480, Holland ordered a rerun because the IA ruled that a candidate had been ineligible.[67]

Holland had to resolve scores of disputes to keep on schedule the IBT international convention, held over four days in Orlando, Florida, beginning on July 21. Merely checking convention delegates' eligibility was a major challenge. Holland hired the Center for Economic Organizing to check whether delegates, alternate delegates, and nominees for international office were in good standing at the time of the convention. The Center's and EO's staffs vetted over 2,000 delegates and alternate delegates and more than 1,200 nominators. Ultimately, the EO certified the eligibility of 1,936 convention delegates and 1,030 alternate delegates from 615 locals.[68]

The convention's timetable required nominations and balloting to be conducted on the same day.[69] Floor nominations and candidate speeches took place in the morning. Immediately thereafter, the EO's staff randomly ordered the nominees' names on a draft ballot. Then the two-hour process of ballot printing commenced.[70] In late afternoon, the delegates marked their ballots in secret. Candidates who received 5 percent of delegates' votes advanced to the rank-and-file mail-ballot election to be held later in the year. Nearly seventy candidates for twenty-one international-officer positions (general president, general secretary-treasurer, sixteen vice presidents, and three international representatives) achieved the 5 percent threshold.[71] R.V. Durham received more nominating votes (1,001, or 53 percent) than Walter Shea (574, or 31 percent) and Ron Carey (289, or 15 percent) combined.

The Election Campaigns

R.V. Durham presented himself as a Teamsters leader who had already produced results, especially improving truckers' safety.* He boasted of

---

* In the chapters of this book involving IBT election campaigns, we present the candidates' claims and charges, but we do not seek to resolve their accuracy.

having successfully persuaded Congress to preempt state laws that permitted cramped truck compartments.[72] He claimed that, as director of the IBT's Safety and Health Department, he persuaded the U.S. Department of Transportation to rescind its policy of automatically canceling the licenses of truckers who had undergone heart surgery.[73] Durham called himself a reformer who supported direct rank-and-file elections and who would establish an independent ethics committee.

Durham used his *Teamster Magazine* battle pages to attack Shea and Carey. According to a Durham campaign pamphlet, "Because the Shea Team has not waged a serious campaign, their only role is as spoilers to aid Ron Carey. . . . A vote for Walter Shea is a vote for Ron Carey and TDU." Durham also attacked Shea for never having been a working Teamster or a local officer. Another Durham ad called Carey "Mr. Immunity" for allegedly cutting a deal with the government to testify against fellow Local 804 member John Long, accused of being an LCN associate. Durham sought to define Carey as TDU's candidate, hoping to gain the support of the many Teamsters who regarded TDU negatively. He also made the baseless accusation, "Scabbing on a Teamsters strike is as low as you can go. Ron Carey scabbed on a UPS strike."[74] Carey and his campaign manager, Eddie Burke, vehemently denied the scab, i.e., strike-breaking, allegation. Indeed, in October 1991, Carey filed a libel suit against Durham, his campaign manager, and ten staffers. (After winning the 1991 election, Carey withdrew the suit.)[75]

Carey published his own attack ads in *Teamster Magazine*. One battle page showed pigs feeding at a trough filled with dollar bills. The caption said, "They're feasting on your dues!" In the October issue, Carey insisted that he offered an alternative to the racketeers who had plundered the union for decades. One ad caricatured Durham arm in arm with a manacled convict and a machine-gun-toting gangster. (Durham himself had not been charged with wrongdoing, but the IO had brought charges against three vice presidential candidates on his slate, including International Vice President Michael Riley, who had allegedly concealed a $16,000 embezzlement from a Los Angeles IBT local.)[76]

Carey promised to fight corruption.[77] "The first thing we have to think about is how much money, how much bargaining strength, has been given away as a result of the corruption problem. The way to deal with it is the way I dealt with it in my own local. Take the necessary steps to get rid of the problem."[78] He vowed to reduce extravagance by, among other things, selling the IBT's fleet of jets, prohibiting multiple salaries, and reducing the size of the union's bureaucracy. In November 1991, six weeks before the mail-in-ballot deadline, the Carey campaign mailed a campaign flyer to just under half the electorate. (The campaign did not have enough money to send a pamphlet to the entire electorate.) It showed a cigar-smoking gangster wearing a Durham-slate button. The caption asked, "Guess who runs the Teamsters?" The pamphlet's flipside provided the answer: "Starting Now, You Do." The "Carey Promise" had four parts: "1. Throw out the Mafia, 2. Better Pensions, 3. Better Health Care, and 4. Stop Corruption." The flyer charged three members of Durham's slate with "corruption, kickbacks and mafia ties" and criticized Durham and his wife and son for drawing multiple IBT salaries.

Walter Shea emphasized his administrative competence over thirty years as an international organizer and executive assistant to four IBT general presidents.[79] He too promised reform. "The old guard has been shattered and destroyed. . . . I'm trying to change the direction of this union. We've been too complacent, too aloof." He promised to achieve a Teamsters minimum wage. Despite these claims and promises, Shea's campaign had little resonance with the rank and file, probably because he had never driven a truck, run a local, or negotiated a collective-bargaining agreement. As one labor reporter notes, he "skipped all of the usual rungs . . . and was promoted right to the top because of his accomplishments as an administrator and the friends he made along the way."[80] These friends, however, were not as supportive of his campaign as he had hoped. Shea failed to obtain enough signatures to become an accredited candidate.

Shea's campaign suffered a setback when, in August 1991, Chicago IBT Local 705 Secretary-Treasurer Daniel Ligurotis, Shea's running mate for general secretary-treasurer, killed his son in the basement of Local 705's headquarters.[81] Then, just a month before the general election, Joe Trerotola, Shea's most prominent vice presidential running mate and an international vice president, president of NYC IBT Joint Council 16, and chairman of the Eastern Conference of Teamsters, resigned from the union after being charged with failing to investigate LCN influence in his joint council.[82]

While Durham and Shea sought large campaign contributions from IBT local and joint council officers, Carey relied on small donations from rank and filers. From April 1990 through September 1991, the Carey campaign raised $173,000. The largest contribution was $1,000. In the same period, the Durham campaign raised over $475,000. The largest contribution was $30,000. Of the thirty-eight donors to the Durham campaign who gave at least $1,000, twenty-three were members of his slate. Their average contribution was just under $12,000. By this time, Shea had become a nonfactor in the presidential race.

The Preballoting Election Protests

The 1991 election generated fifteen hundred election protests involving, among other things, ineligibility of candidates, insufficient notification of nomination meetings, and unlawful campaign contributions. Two hundred fifty protests dealt with individuals' eligibility to participate in the delegate-nomination process. Only two protests challenged nominated candidates' eligibility. (Because postelection protests needed to be resolved only if, cumulatively, they could have affected an election result, most were not investigated or resolved.)

The Protest over Disclosing TDU's Campaign Contributors

The Durham slate brought a preelection protest demanding that TDU disclose to the EO and the candidates the names of its contributors because TDU spent its members' contributions on Carey's behalf.[83] TDU contended that "the filing and disclosure requirements of the Election Rules are directed only to nominated candidates, a category that does not include TDU," and that disclosure of its contributors' identities would subject them to retaliation, thereby threatening TDU's survival.[84] Holland ruled in Durham's favor, issuing a campaign advisory (i.e., amendment to the election rules) requiring independent committees, including TDU, to report the names of contributors of one hundred dollars or more. Holland explained that, without that requirement, candidates might be able to bypass the election rules' campaign-contribution disclosure requirement.[85]

TDU appealed to Judge Edelstein, arguing that neither the election rules nor the consent decree required disclosing its contributors and contributions.[86] Edelstein was not persuaded. However, to address TDU's concerns, he required all IBT locals to appoint sergeants at arms and directed the government to empanel a grand jury to investigate allegations of intimidation or retaliation.[87] He then criticized TDU for demanding election transparency, except for its own finances:[88]

You have gotten far more than you ever dreamed or expected. And until this happened, where were you? This union is old. You accomplished nothing. If it hadn't been for the court officers and the government that started this by bringing on the opportunity to enter into the consent decree, where would you be? . . .

I would like TDU to stand up, show some guts and start being unintimidated, and to be confrontational, if it has to, in self-defense. I am very disappointed in you and your clients. We no longer seem to be sharing the same objective and the same goals. You are now an adversary instead of an amicus. Now go to the court of appeals.[89]

The Second Circuit Court of Appeals stayed Judge Edelstein's disclosure order and, later, for the first time in the *U.S. v. IBT* litigation, reversed an Edelstein decision (and admonished Holland as well). It held that TDU was not bound by the consent decree:

[T]he interests of TDU traditionally have not coincided with those pursued by the incumbent international union leadership that negotiated the Consent Decree. . . . It follows that TDU and TRF were not adequately represented by the IBT leadership with respect to the Consent Decree, and cannot be directly bound by its provisions. . . . The Election Officer seeks, in addition, to implement his personal notions of union democracy and fair play by imposing upon nonparties to the Consent Decree filing requirements, and especially obligations of disclosure to third parties, not warranted by any applicable provision of law.[90]

In another preelection protest, the Durham campaign sought to stop the Carey campaign from accepting TDU's financial contributions and volunteer work because TDU allegedly received financial contributions from entities prohibited from making campaign donations.[91] Holland ruled that TDU could directly and indirectly support candidates as long as its election expenditures came exclusively from funds derived from persons or entities who themselves could legally contribute to candidates; TDU had to "strict[ly]" ensure that the money it received from persons ineligible to contribute to candidates' campaigns was not used to support a candidate for IBT office.[92] Durham's supporters saw this decision as further proof of Holland's pro-Carey bias.[93]

Protesting IBT Locals' Favoritism

A number of preballoting election protests involved candidates' complaints about locals' recalcitrance in disclosing their membership lists. For example, in response to a Carey campaign complaint that Chicago IBT Local 705's officers had failed to provide a list of its members' work sites, Holland ordered those officers to mail all three presidential candidates' campaign literature to its members. Likewise, he ordered Mokena, Illinois IBT Local 710 to distribute the candidates' literature at the IBT members' work sites because the local had not expeditiously provided candidates with work-site lists.

Balloting and Results

Holland chose mail balloting for the general election because, in the convention-delegate elections, mail balloting produced greater voter participation (33 percent) than in-person voting (19 percent). However, there were huge logistical challenges to conducting a mail-ballot election for such a populous and geographically dispersed union. For example, the EO needed mailing addresses for approximately 1.5 million eligible voters. Toward that end, his staff had to consult the *Teamster Magazine* mailing list, local-union executive boards, the U.S. Postal Service's national change-of-address database, and, if necessary, individuals' last known employers. In all, the EO's staff contacted 350 employers concerning eighty thousand residential addresses, eventually obtaining accurate mailing addresses for almost all eligible voters.[94]

EO Holland hired a security specialist to ensure ballot security. To prevent ballot forgery, the color of ballots for each region was not revealed until the day printing began.[95] The voters received and returned ballots by mail in nested envelopes.[96] As the first ballots arrived in Washington, D.C., they were stored in a ballot security room with twenty-four-hour security guards.[97] The candidates could designate observers to stay with the ballots and to monitor each step of the counting process.[98]

Twenty-eight percent (396,172) of eligible Teamsters cast ballots. The outcome differed radically from the outcome at the Orlando convention, where Carey had received 15 percent and Durham 53 percent of delegates' nominating votes. In the general election, Carey received 188,883 votes (48 percent), Durham 129,538 (33 percent), and Shea 71,227 (19 percent). 11,372

FIGURE 5.1

Number of IBT Locals Carried by Each Candidate, by Region,
in 1991 Election for IBT General President

Region	Carey	Durham	Shea
East	102	38	79
Central	80	77	19
South	28	23	0
West	81	38	4
Canada	5	33	1
TOTAL	296	209	103

ballots were voided on account of voter error, and 17,125 challenged ballots were never counted because, even if all were added to Durham's total, the election's outcome would have been the same. Carey defeated Durham by almost three to one in the east and by more than two to one in the west; Durham defeated Carey only in the Canadian locals. Shea showed strength in the east, where he won twice as many locals as Durham, but fewer than Carey (see fig. 5.1). Almost all the newly elected GEB members were Carey supporters. All sixteen members of Carey's slate were victorious, including Tom Sever as general secretary-treasurer and Diana Kilmury as an international vice president (the first woman ever to serve on the GEB). In Canada, where the Carey slate fielded no candidates, two members of Durham's slate were elected international vice presidents. In the east, where Carey ran only two candidates for three vice presidential slots, Philadelphia IBT Joint Council 53 President John Morris, a member of Shea's slate, was elected.

In a special postelection issue of *Convoy Dispatch*, TDU predicted that "four days in December 1991 will be recorded as a major turning point in the history of the Teamsters Union and the labor movement."[99] AUD Executive Director Susan Jennik predicted that the election would "permanently change" the union by enhancing transparency at the international level and legitimizing political discourse at the local level. Some commentators saw the election as a historic turning point for the entire U.S. labor movement. One labor journalist predicted that the IBT's successful rank-and-file election would cause "more dominoes" to fall, that is, would inspire the members of other unions to demand similar democratic elections.[100] Another labor journalist stated that "if Carey can spread his influence throughout the 615 locals in the 1.5 million-member union, he will lift the image and clout of a sagging labor movement that is desperate for a white knight. Failure will allow cynicism to recapture the Teamsters."[101] A *New York Times* editorial rhetorically asked, "Can It Be Morning in Team-sterland?" referring to the dawn of a postcorruption era.[102] The *Chicago Tribune* declared Carey's victory "an earthquake in the U.S. labor movement."[103] The *Boston Globe* called it "one of the most dramatic events in Teamster history," describing Carey as "a working-class Don Quixote, attacking corruption and entrenched union bosses few thought could be toppled from power."[104] Chris Scott, president of the AFL-CIO's North Carolina branch, mused, "In five years it is conceivable that Carey is so popular that he makes Jimmy Hoffa look like a footnote in history."[105]

Conclusion and Analysis

A successful North America–wide rank-and-file secret mail-ballot election involving 1.5 million eligible voters was an extraordinary achievement for the civil RICO suit, the judge, and the EO. Holland and his staff regulated and monitored every aspect of the election cycle, including campaign finance and expenditures, campaign conduct, nominating and voting procedures, and ballot counting and security. Holland, Edelstein, and DOJ also expeditiously resolved hundreds of protests concerning the alleged misconduct of candidates, contributors, union officials, employers, and nongovernmental organizations. Nothing like this had ever been done before. The challenge was even greater because the election reforms had been imposed on, rather than by, the membership.

The *U.S. v. IBT* consent decree embodied the view of TDU, AUD, and, ultimately, DOJ that a free and fair election of international IBT officers would contribute to purging LCN influence from the union and, thereafter, prevent LCN from regaining influence. Democratization of the international union, the government hoped, would bring about the weakening of organized crime's grip on the union. We should not accept this hypothesis as unproblematic given innumerable recent examples of corrupt incumbents and insurgents winning all sorts of elections all over the world, including in the United States. Moreover, since Cosa Nostra's influence was so entrenched at the local and regional levels of the IBT power structure, the electoral success of two dozen honest international officers would not necessarily drive LCN out of the union. Furthermore, there was no guarantee that the Teamsters rank and file, given the opportunity, would choose honest leaders. Even if they did, there was no guarantee that these leaders would remain honest. We will return to this hypothesis in later chapters.

Campaign finance was among the most important matters that had to be resolved in the run-up to the 1991 election. The DOJ lawyers who negotiated the terms of the consent decree, and perhaps even AUD and TDU, probably did not fully think through the cost of waging a North America–wide insurgent campaign. R.V. Durham began with an enormous advantage. He enjoyed the overwhelming support of some seven thousand IBT officials who not only were likely to vote but also wielded influence (via carrots and sticks) over the members of their locals. Unless the EO prevented it, these local officers could put all kinds of union resources at the disposal of the Durham campaign.

At the outset of *U.S. v. IBT*, the DOJ lawyers probably did not fully consider the logistics or cost of supervising a North America–wide rank-and-file election involving 1.5 million potential voters. Excluding the cost of the convention, which would have taken place had there been no civil RICO lawsuit, the cost of supervising and conducting the 1991 rank-and-file election amounted to more than $15 million.[106]

Holland and Edelstein were determined to create a level playing field for the general presidential candidates and their slates. In this, they may have exceeded the consent decree's requirements. A fair election does not necessarily mean an election in which all candidates have an equal chance of winning. Leveling the playing field necessarily meant helping Carey and blunting Durham's numerous advantages. For example, to assure union neutrality, the election rules forbade candidates from obtaining IBT leaders' endorsements, receiving campaign contributions from employers, and using IBT resources. Many of the EO's election rules disfavored Durham, whose relationships with IBT employers and officers, access to union resources, and fundraising ability were more extensive than Carey's. (In the 1996 election, the EO added additional rules to "level[] the playing field between incumbents and challengers."[107] The Second Circuit Court of Appeals agreed that "establishment of a somewhat level playing field is in the membership's interest.")[108] It may be an open question whether EO Holland and Judge Edelstein crossed the line of political neutrality, but they certainly skirted close to the line. There is little doubt that they hoped for a Carey victory.

It is impossible to know whether R.V. Durham would have governed the IBT in the style of Jimmy Hoffa, Frank Fitzsimmons, Roy Williams, and Jackie Presser. While Durham was a member of the Teamsters' establishment, he was not an organized-crime toady. Like Carey, Durham campaigned as a reformer. Perhaps under the new circumstances created by *U.S. v. IBT* and the court-appointed disciplinary officers, he would have set his face against corruption and racketeering. (There are such cases. For example, while the IBT reform experiment was ongoing, Mikhail Gorbachev, a former establishment figure in Soviet politics, was stunning the world with his glasnost policies.) Moreover, while Ron Carey was indisputably not part of the IBT establishment, he had served for years as head of a very large IBT local in NYC, a city where union corruption and racketeering were prevalent if not pervasive. A hard-nosed observer might have wondered whether Carey actually deserved his Mr. Clean label.

Supporters hailed Carey's stunning victory as the triumph of good over evil and of integrity over corruption. Union democracy proponents saw it as proof of the good sense and values of rank-and-file Teamsters. Still, both the disappointing number of contested delegate elections and the low general-election turnout were cause for concern. They did not indicate the democracy renaissance that the union democracy advocates had predicted. Indeed, had Shea not run or had he bowed out of the campaign, Durham would likely have won the 1991 election.

6

General President Carey and the IRB

1992–1997

The IRB will act as a constant foe of corruption and a vigilant agent of union democracy. . . . [R]egardless of a particular administration's stance toward reform, the IRB will serve as a perpetual agent of those reforms independent of the parties, vigilant in the fight against corruption, and stalwart in the promotion of union democracy.[1]   —Judge David Edelstein, August 19, 1992

I simply want to dispel the notion that the [Carey administration] is doing everything that is possible here to take care of things and clean out their own house.[2]
                    —IRB member Frederick Lacey, June 28, 1993

Ron Carey's inauguration as IBT general president in February 1992 and the IRB's assumption of disciplinary authority later that year seemed to augur well of greater cooperation between the IBT and the court-appointed officers. The IRB's chief investigator (CI) would investigate union corruption and, when appropriate, recommend disciplinary charges. If the three IRB members decided to accept the CI's recommendation, they would refer charges to the jurisdictionally appropriate IBT unit, monitor compliance, and, if necessary, take action to ensure compliance. For this phase of the consent decree to work effectively, the IBT would have to carry out its disciplinary duties in good faith.

Contrary to the expectations of the DOJ lawyers, Judge Edelstein, and the court officers, the Carey administration was frequently uncooperative.

Carey's appointee to the IRB unreasonably delayed the selection of a third IRB member. Carey's general counsel opposed DOJ's proposed rules for the IRB's operations. And Carey's staff obstructed the IRB's routine requests for compensation and reimbursements. Claiming a desire to demonstrate the IBT's independent capacity and willingness to fight corruption and racketeering, Carey appointed an Ethical Practices Committee (EPC) to investigate, charge, adjudicate, and sanction disciplinary violations. He also imposed international-union trusteeships on nearly seventy IBT locals because of alleged corruption and/or fiscal mismanagement. Carey's supporters praised these initiatives, but critics accused him of using the EPC and trusteeships to punish political rivals.

The IRB and Carey's Resistance

The EO certified the 1991 election on January 10, 1992, one month after final balloting.[3] Except for pending cases, to be completed by the IO/IA, the IRB took over disciplinary duties on October 10, 1992.*[4] AUSA Randy Mastro explained that the transition from the IO/IA to the IRB reflected the parties' intention that, whereas the IO and IA functioned as wholly independent disciplinary enforcers, the IRB would share disciplinary enforcement responsibility with the IBT. The IRB would concentrate on investigations and oversight, while the IBT would charge, adjudicate, and, where appropriate, impose sanctions.

The consent decree provided that DOJ would appoint one IRB member, the IBT would appoint another, and those two appointees would choose the third member.[5] In March 1992, DOJ appointed IA Frederick Lacey, and the IBT appointed Eddie Burke, Carey's 1991 campaign manager and then special assistant. When Lacey and Burke could not agree on the selection of a third IRB member, Judge Edelstein granted Lacey's request, over Burke's objection, to appoint former FBI and CIA director William Webster. Soon thereafter, Judge Edelstein decided that Burke was too much a part of Carey's administration to properly carry out the role of a "neutral" IRB member. Carey replaced Burke with Grant Crandall, formerly the United Mine Workers' general counsel.

---

* For clarity of exposition, the authors treat the beginning of the IRB's work as January 1, 1993.

The IRB's Disciplinary Powers: Procedures and Cases (1992–1997)

The consent decree vests the IRB with the same investigatory authority as the IBT's general president and general secretary-treasurer; empowers the IRB to hire investigative staff;[6] and requires the IRB to investigate allegations of corruption, organized-crime control or influence over any IBT entity, and failure to fully cooperate with the IRB.[7] In July 1992, before Webster's appointment, DOJ proposed comprehensive rules to govern the IRB's investigations, adjudications, enforcement of decisions, staffing, and communication with the rank and file (see fig. 6.1). Those rules authorized the IRB to investigate allegations of bribery, extortion, embezzlement, violence, aiding or abetting racketeering acts, knowing association with Cosa Nostra or persons barred from participation in IBT affairs, and failure to lawfully and timely handle disciplinary matters.[8] Judge Edelstein approved the IRB rules over the Carey's administration's objection that DOJ lacked authority to propose them. With minor modifications, the Second Circuit Court of Appeals affirmed.[9]

The consent decree and IRB rules authorize the IRB to employ a full-time chief investigator (CI) to play much the same role as the IO played under the IA/IO phase of the remediation. The IRB promptly hired IO Carberry, who, in turn, hired a staff of investigators and attorneys.[10] The CI may require sworn statements or in-person examinations of any IBT officer, member, employee, representative, or agent without having probable cause or reasonable suspicion. He also may audit and examine any IBT entity's books, records, and annual LM-2 financial reports. CI Carberry obtained additional investigative leads from legislative hearings and reports, criminal and civil litigation, media articles, more than one thousand tips per year over the hotline,[11] and referrals from the FBI, the DOL's Office of Labor Racketeering, and state and local police departments. Because the CI's staffers do not undertake physical or electronic surveillance, do not engage in undercover work, and do not have access to grand jury testimony, they rely on those agencies' investigators.

If the CI obtains sufficient evidence to warrant a disciplinary charge, he submits an investigative report to the IRB. If the IRB approves the CI's recommended disciplinary charge, it forwards a proposed charge, including the CI's investigative report, to the jurisdictionally appropriate IBT entity

FIGURE 6.1
IRB/IBT Disciplinary Roles

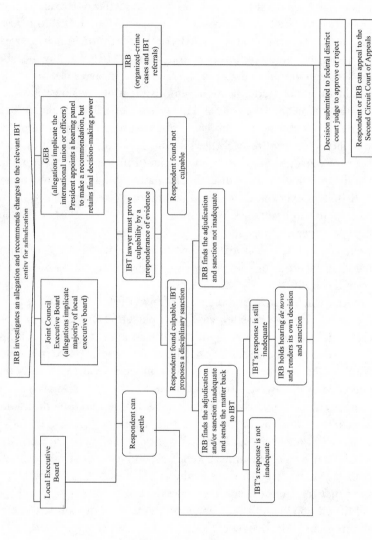

to adjudicate.* However, the IRB handles organized-crime cases from the outset because the FBI does not permit IBT lawyers to cross-examine its agents or confidential informants. The IRB also adjudicates charges involving high-ranking IBT officers.

In nearly 75 percent of disciplinary cases, the respondent and the union's "presenting attorney" negotiate a settlement that goes to the IRB and Judge Edelstein for approval.[12] If there is no settlement, the appropriate IBT entity convenes a hearing panel. An IBT member or outside attorney may represent the disciplinary respondent. The IBT's presenting attorney must prove culpability by a preponderance of the evidence.[13] If the hearing panel finds the respondent culpable, it imposes a sanction, for example, fine, restitution, prohibition against associating with Teamsters, suspension from union office or membership, or expulsion from the union.[14] The IRB then determines whether the IBT's disciplinary decision was lawful, timely, and "not inadequate." If inadequate, the IRB may request additional explanation and/or recommend a more or less severe disciplinary sanction. If the IBT's response is still inadequate, the IRB convenes a de novo disciplinary hearing and renders a binding decision.[15]

The disciplinary respondent obtains an automatic appeal when the IRB submits its decision to the district court judge as an application for a court order. The judge defers to the IRB's decision unless it is "arbitrary or capricious."[16] If the judge considers the sanction too lenient or too severe, it may remand for reconsideration.[17] Neither Judge Edelstein nor Chief Judge Preska (who took over the case in 2001 when Edelstein died) have overturned an IRB culpability decision, and they have rarely remanded a sanction for reconsideration.[18]

From January 1993, when the IRB filed its first disciplinary charge, through November 1997, when General President Carey took a leave of absence after the IRB charged him with campaign-finance violations (see

* Certain IRB disciplinary recommendations, e.g., those involving organized crime, are usually forwarded to the international union. Other IRB disciplinary recommendations, e.g., those involving financial misconduct or failure to cooperate with an IRB investigation, are usually forwarded to the relevant local union or joint council. If the recommended charges implicate the majority of a local union's executive officers, the IRB sends its recommendation to the joint council; if the recommended charges implicate a majority of executive officers on the joint council, the IRB sends its recommendation to the international union. The GEB receives disciplinary recommendations that implicate the international union or its officers, but in practice these matters are referred back to the IRB for adjudication. Occasionally, when the CI uncovers minor irregularities in an IBT entity's books or records, the IRB sends the relevant local or joint council a "noncharge report" recommending corrective action.

FIGURE 6.2

The IRB's Major Financial-Misconduct Cases (1993–1997)

Member(s)	IBT Local	IRB-Recommended Charge	Disposition
Daniel Zenga (secretary-treasurer)	Malden, MA Local 841	Embezzling the local's funds by having the local pay for his personal expenses; receiving an unauthorized salary increase	Expelled from the IBT (1993)
Steve Desanto (recording secretary)	Collingswood, NJ Local 676	Extorting payments from a member in exchange for job security	Suspended from the IBT for seven years (1993)
Donald Heim (president); Louis Esposito, Sr. (vice president); Gildo Valerio (secretary-treasurer); Richard Mall (trustee); Frank Snow (trustee)	Chicago Local 705	Embezzling from the local's treasury by improperly giving local's money to a local officer	Mall and Valerio expelled from the IBT; Heim and Esposito permanently resigned from the IBT; Cash and Snow suspended from the IBT for one year and from holding union office for five years (1993)
Rondal Owens (president)	Detroit Local 299	Expending local money without the executive board's approval	Suspended from the IBT for six months (1993)
Thomas Moskal (president)	Chicago Local 726	Embezzling from the local by receiving an unauthorized monetary bonus	Suspended from holding union office for five years (1993)
Vincent Sombrotto (president)	NYC Local 966	Embezzling from the local by providing union benefits to non-IBT locals	Expelled from the IBT (1994)
Robert Simpson (president)	Chicago Local 743	Giving away a car owned by the local	Reimbursed the local (1995)
Robert Weisenburger (president)	Minneapolis Local 320	Transferring local's assets to himself for less than actual value	Suspended from the IBT for three years (1995)
Larry Parker (president)	Orlando Local 385	Accepting money from IBT members in exchange for job referrals	Expelled from the IBT (1995)
Dennis Raymond (president)	Waterbury, CT Local 677	Giving away a union car	Suspended from the IBT for ninety days; reimbursed the local (1996)
Clarence Lark, Jr. (president)	Miami Local 390	Demanding gifts from members	Expelled from the IBT (1996)
Thomas Ryan (president)	Philadelphia Local 107	Purchasing personal items with local's funds	Suspended from the IBT for five years (1996)
Jerry Jackson (business agent)	NYC Local 813	Accepting money and Christmas gifts from an employer	Expelled from the IBT (1997)

chapter 7), the IRB recommended charges against 214 Teamsters. Forty percent of the charges alleged financial misconduct, breach of fiduciary duty, or failure to cooperate with an IRB investigation. Thirty-one Teamsters were charged with embezzlement, eight with extortion, two with bribery, and forty-five with other types of financial misconduct (see fig. 6.2).

Thirty-one charges had a direct organized-crime connection (see fig. 6.3); twelve of those alleged that the respondent associated with an LCN member, ten alleged actual membership in LCN, four charged union officials with failing to investigate an IBT member's connections to LCN, and five alleged other types of LCN-influenced racketeering. The IRB filed eight organized-crime-related charges in 1993, 1994, and 1995; two such charges in 1996; and five in 1997. The vast majority of IRB organized-crime-related 1993–1997 disciplinary recommendations involved members of IBT locals in NYC or Long Island. However, a few members of upstate New York, New Jersey, and Illinois IBT locals were also charged with organized-crime-related violations (see fig. 6.4).

FIGURE 6.3
IRB Disciplinary Charges during the Ron Carey Years (1993–1997)

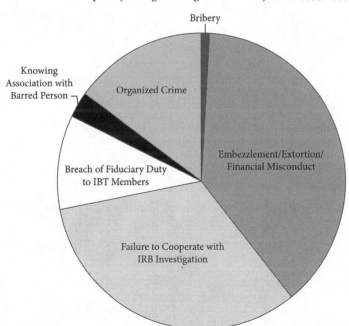

FIGURE 6.4
The IRB's Organized-Crime Cases (1993–1997)

Member(s)	IBT Local	IRB-Recommended Charge	Disposition
Frank Marsigliano (secretary-treasurer); Anthony Igneri (vice president)	Valley Stream, NY Local 854	Arranging for local to pay an LCN member's health benefits	Resigned their union positions and agreed never again to hold union office (1993)
Anthony Razza (secretary-treasurer)	Valley Stream, NY Local 851	Knowing association with Patrick Dellorusso, who allegedly ran air-freight rackets for the Lucchese crime family	Resigned from the IBT (1994)
Alan Adelstein (president); Martin Adelstein (secretary-treasurer); James Murray (vice president); Michael Giammona (recording secretary)	NYC Local 813	Failing to investigate allegations of organized-crime influence in the local[a]	Alan and Martin Adelstein suspended from IBT employment for five years; Murray and Giammona suspended from IBT employment for two years (1993)
Peter Agliata (secretary-treasurer)	Chicago Local 738	Knowing association with LCN members	Resigned from the IBT (1993)
Anthony Senter (shop steward)	NYC Local 813	Membership in the Lucchese crime family	Expelled from the IBT (1994)
Dominic Vulpis (member)	NYC Local 813	Providing employment cover for a member of the Lucchese crime family	Resigned from the IBT (1994)
Edward Garafola (member)	NYC Local 813	Membership in the Gambino crime family	Expelled from the IBT (1994)
Pasquale Sottile (member)	NYC Local 813	Providing employment cover for a member of the Gambino crime family	Expelled from the IBT (1994)
William Genoese, Sr. (secretary-treasurer)	NYC Local 732	Knowing association with LCN members	Resigned from the IBT (1994)
Angelo Paccione (member)	NYC Local 813	Knowing association with Jame Failla, a capo in the Gambino crime family	Resigned from the IBT (1995)
Michael Sciarra (member)	Union City, NJ Local 560	Membership in the Genovese crime family	Resigned from the IBT (1995)

Joseph Cammarano, Jr. (steward)	Lake Success, NY Local 282	Membership in the Bonanno crime family	Expelled from the IBT (1995)
Michael Bourgal (president); John Probeyahn (secretary-treasurer)	Lake Success, NY Local 282	Conspiring to use the local for the benefit of the Gambino crime family	Resigned their officer positions (1996)
Aniello Madonna (member)	Lake Success, NY Local 282	Knowing association with LCN figures	Resigned from the IBT (1996)

[a] Martin and Alan Adelstein were the sons of Bernard Adelstein, the former secretary-treasurer of Local 813 who assisted the Gambino, Genovese, and Lucchese crime families' control over NYC's carting industry. In its investigative report, the IRB noted that Local 813's executive officers knew about, but failed to adequately respond to, allegations that LCN had controlled Bernard Adelstein and various local members as far back as the 1950s. References to LCN control of Local 813 appeared in the McClellan Committee Reports (1957), the Report of the President's Commission on Organized Crime (1986), the Rand Report (1987), the Report of the New York State Assembly Environmental Conservation Committee on Organized Crime Involvement in the Waste Hauling Industry (1986), Steven Brill's *The Teamsters* (1978), James Jacobs's *Gotham Unbound: How New York City Was Liberated from the Grip of Organized Crime* (2001), and in many newspaper articles. Initially, New York Joint Council 16 dismissed the charges against the Local 813 officers. However, Joint Council 16's international trustee overturned the dismissal, ruling that the evidence showed that the officers knew about the allegations and did virtually nothing to investigate or address them.

The IRB's Trusteeship Powers: Procedures and Cases (1992–1997)

In addition to granting the IRB disciplinary powers, the consent decree and IRB rules authorize the IRB to recommend that the IBT general president impose international-union trusteeships on corrupted or financially mismanaged local unions and joint councils. Although neither the consent decree nor the rules provide criteria for imposing such trusteeships, the IRB's practice has been to recommend a trusteeship when a majority of the local's or joint council's executive board has been implicated in wrongdoing; the local's or joint council's officers have badly mishandled the entity's finances; the local or joint council has a long history of corruption; and/or union officers have not enforced collective bargaining contracts or have otherwise failed to act on behalf of their constituent members. The IBT almost always complies with IRB trusteeship recommendations; when it does not, the IRB itself imposes the trusteeship.

A trusteeship involves the general president replacing corrupt local or joint-council officers with a trustee. The trustee has the power to oversee, approve, reject, and make decisions regarding the local's or joint council's operations, expenditures, and disciplinary matters. Frequently, the IBT merges a trusteed local into a neighboring local. The IRB has veto power over the IBT general president's choice for trustee. (For example, in 1994, the IRB rejected Carey's selection of William F. Genoese, director of the IBT's airport division, as trustee of Queens, New York IBT Local 295, because Genoese was a close associate of the Lucchese crime family.)[19]

From September 1992 to October 1997, the IRB recommended that the IBT impose trusteeships on twenty local unions and one joint council. The IBT implemented all these recommendations. Twenty-five percent of the IRB's first-term trusteeship recommendations involved locals whose members worked for companies that mount trade shows or produce movies, businesses with long histories of labor racketeering.

One of the CI's largest investigations leading to trusteeship involved Chicago IBT Local 714. In August 1996, the IRB sent General President Carey a 120-page CI investigative report concluding that the local was being run for the benefit of Principal Officer William Hogan, Jr., President James M. Hogan, Recording Secretary Robert Hogan, and other Hogan family members and friends, rather than for the benefit of the members: "Nepotism and favoritism are prominent factors influencing entry into and work assignments in the Local's trade show/movie division which refers members to the Local's best jobs."[20] The IRB charged that the local's officers had entered into several sham collective-bargaining agreements whereby non-Teamsters received employment and benefits, and that one company, owned by a relative of the local's president, avoided making health-fund contributions on behalf of its Teamsters employees. Pursuant to the IRB's recommendation, General President Carey imposed a trusteeship on that local.[21]

The IRB recommended other trusteeships on account of local officers' financial mismanagement, associations with LCN figures, and collusion with affiliated non-IBT local unions to violate members' contract and union-democracy rights. For example, the IRB recommended that the IBT impose a trusteeship on the following locals for the following reasons:

- NYC Local 807 because that local's officers referred the most desirable union jobs to LCN members, associates, and convicted criminals rather than on the basis of seniority.
- NYC Local 240 because that local's officers allowed a former officer with LCN connections, whom a court had barred from IBT activities, to participate in the local's affairs. The local also had paid some of his personal bills.
- NYC Local 966 because that local's president allowed officers of affiliated non-IBT locals, with whom he had personal connections, to allow ineligible persons to obtain IBT benefits. The local's president also used the local's money to travel to Chicago to meet with an LCN associate.

Carey's Opposition to the IRB

Upon taking office on February 17, 1992, General President Carey promised that his victory meant "goodbye to the Mafia [and] goodbye to those who have lined their pockets at the members' expense."[22] On a number of occasions, however, Carey and his staff opposed the IRB's actions and even its existence. In an August 1992 decision, Judge Edelstein unhappily observed,

From the day the parties entered the Consent Decree, March 14, 1989, until today, the IBT has waged a zealous legal attack on the reforms contained in that agreement. . . . While the new [Ron Carey] administration has publicly disassociated itself from its predecessors' attempts to thwart reform, it has adopted its litigation strategy with respect to both the Court-Appointed Officers and the IRB.[23]

Carey's opposition to the IRB first surfaced a month after he took office. In March 1992, DOJ appointed Frederick Lacey and the IBT appointed Eddie Burke as two of the three IRB members. However, Lacey and Burke could not agree on a third IRB member. Whereas Lacey wanted someone with strong law enforcement, prosecutorial, and judicial experience, Burke wanted someone who had an understanding of labor relations and labor unions and who had overseen investigations of exactly the type that the IRB was going to be asked to investigate.[24] Presumably at Carey's direction, or at least with his approval, Burke rejected all of Lacey's recommendations. At a July 30, 1992 hearing on the impasse, Lacey told Judge Edelstein that he would attempt to find a nominee of "unchallengeable, national reputation, background and experience."[25] The next day, Lacey urged Burke to agree to William H. Webster, who had previously served as FBI director, CIA director, and federal judge. Burke objected because Webster did not have a labor background and had served on the board of directors of an IBT employer. An exasperated Judge Edelstein criticized the Carey administration for thwarting implementation of the consent decree's disciplinary prong. He told Burke, "You won't reach any agreement. Everything on this record is clear for me to conclude that you will not reach an agreement. . . . [The impasse] is hopelessly irreconcilable."[26] He then appointed Webster to the IRB.

The Carey administration strenuously objected to DOJ's proposed rules for the IRB, arguing that the consent decree did not authorize DOJ to propose those rules, that DOJ waived its right to promulgate rules by not raising the matter when the consent decree was signed, that DOJ's proposed rules would impose excessive costs on the IBT, and that the proposed rules violated federal labor law favoring the government's nonintervention in union affairs.[27] Moreover, according to the IBT's lawyers, "the democratic election of a new IBT administration dedicated to eradicating corruption obviates the need for the government's proposed rules."[28] General President Carey stated,

> The Government should acknowledge the dramatic changes in our Union and the commitment of my administration to honest trade unionism; it

should not seek to restrict our ability to manage our own affairs. . . . In less than six months, the IBT has been transformed into a labor union run by and for its members. Times have changed; this union has changed.[29]

Judge Edelstein approved the proposed rules and criticized the Carey administration's "toleration of organized crime's influence in union affairs and complacency in the face of corruption."[30] Edelstein called Carey's six-month anticorruption record "pathetic."[31]

> Rather than dedication to maintaining the union democratically, with integrity, and for the sole benefit of the membership, the International Brotherhood of Teamsters' objections to the independent review board suggest a dedication to maintaining the union autocratically, with ignominy, and for its own purposes. Despite this [Carey] administration's promise of reform, it boasts an anemic record in attempting to eradicate corruption.[32]

Carey vowed to fight "the unwarranted imposition of increased Government control over the union."[33] However, the Second Circuit affirmed Judge Edelstein's approval of DOJ's proposed IRB rules.

The Carey administration also opposed U.S. Attorney Otto Obermaier's request to compensate the three IRB members and the IRB chief investigator according to their hourly rates as lawyers up to a maximum annual remuneration of $100,000. Edelstein, in response, set a $100,000 guaranteed *minimum* salary for the IRB members and the CI:

> Given the IRB's central role in eradicating corruption in the IBT and restoring union democracy, it is essential that the IRB attract extraordinarily talented members and staff. . . . To attract such talent, IRB members and staff must be compensated at market rates based upon their usual hourly rate. . . . [A] guaranteed salary is necessary initially to attract quality individuals to these positions. . . . [A] salary floor of $100,000 will entice qualified individuals to undertake this intimidating assignment.[34]

Edelstein warned the Carey administration that the disciplinary officers' remuneration could exceed $100,000 in a matter of months if the IBT continued to pursue "needless litigation" or to mislead the IRB to pursue "frivolous investigations." (On appeal, the Second Circuit agreed with Judge Edelstein on the $100,000 guaranteed minimum annual salary, but not on compensating the IRB members and the CI at their law-firm rates because, while working for the IRB, they would not have to cover a law firm's overhead expenses.)*[35]

Carey's Ethical Practices Committee (EPC)

During the 1991 general presidential campaign, Ron Carey had promised to establish a union disciplinary apparatus that would demonstrate to DOJ and the district court that the IRB was unnecessary. Toward that end, in February 1992, at his first GEB meeting after becoming general president, Carey introduced a resolution stating that "the General President and the General Executive Board are firmly committed to ending Government supervision of the affairs of the International Brotherhood of Teamsters and substituting an effective and vigorous Ethical Practices Committee to ensure that this Union operates democratically and free from corruption at all levels."[36]

Carey appointed fifteen EPC members—five regional vice presidents, five local-union officers, and five rank-and-file members—and divided them into three-person regional hearing panels. Almost all the EPC members were Carey's political allies. He appointed Aaron Belk, an international vice president and one of his closest advisers, as the EPC's chief administrator, even though Belk had no prior investigative experience.

The EPC's purpose was to investigate allegations of corruption and serious wrongdoing that pose "imminent danger" to the union's welfare.[37] (Complaints to the EPC that did not involve imminent danger to the union would be referred to local unions or joint councils for investigation and adjudication.) The EPC invited rank-and-file Teamsters to submit complaints in writing or by phone. Belk and his small staff then had to decide whether each complaint merited investigation, that is, whether it involved potential imminent danger to the welfare of the union. (The EPC did not investigate organized-crime cases.) If Belk decided that a case should be investigated further, he assigned the case to an EPC staffer to conduct a more extensive

---

* The IRB's salaries and expenses, which the IBT pays, run approximately $3 million per year. Each IRB member is paid $100,000 per year plus $35,000 in fringe benefits. Staff investigators are paid $84,000 per year. CI Carberry bills more than $100,000 annually on account of the significant time he devotes to his investigatory work. Jones Day, the law firm at which Carberry is a partner, also bills the IBT periodically for expenses that the law firm incurs in assisting Carberry and his investigators (e.g., copying costs and court-reporter fees).

investigation. Lacking significant law-enforcement contacts, the EPC staffers mostly questioned union officers about the allegations. In some instances, they hired auditors to review locals' and joint councils' books and records. They did not hire outside investigators.

Carey delegated to Belk the general president's authority to bring disciplinary charges. If Belk decided to bring charges, he instructed the relevant regional EPC panel to convene a hearing. An IBT lawyer would present the case. Respondents were entitled to be represented by another Teamster, but not by an outside attorney. The presenting IBT lawyer and the respondent's representative could call witnesses and cross-examine opposing witnesses. The EPC panel reported its culpability finding and sanction recommendation to Carey, who rendered a decision. In some cases, Carey also used the evidence contained in EPC reports on individual disciplinary respondents as grounds to impose a trusteeship on a local or joint council. The respondent could appeal to the GEB.

One of the largest EPC investigations involved NYC IBT Local 810. Belk found that four Local 810 officials had, among other disciplinary violations, mismanaged the local's pension, health, and welfare funds; collected cash contributions from local staff members without justification; increased severance payments to local officers without membership approval; paid full-time salaries to part-time employees; and failed to hold membership meetings. Carey followed the EPC's recommendation to impose a trusteeship.[38]

Criticism of the EPC

IRB member Lacey and DOL investigator Michael Moroney criticized the EPC. Lacey observed, "This ethical practices panel is not what it seems to be: I simply want to dispel the notion that they are doing everything that is possible here to take care of things and clean out their own house."[39] Moroney called Carey's internal reform efforts "halfhearted" and occasionally obstructionist.[40] In a June 14, 1993 letter to IBT General Counsel Judy Scott, Moroney wrote, "The understanding of the corruption problem, and the will to do anything about it, is completely lacking at the International Brotherhood of Teamsters."[41]

Four years later, Rep. Peter Hoekstra (R-Mich.), chairman of the House Committee on Education and the Workforce's Subcommittee on Oversight and Investigations (1995–2000), convened hearings on the *U.S. v. IBT* remediation. CI Carberry testified that the EPC was a "political arm" of the IBT and that the CI's office limited its contact with the EPC to providing publicly available information.[42] EPC member Phillip Feaster (president of Washington, D.C., IBT Local 639) testified that, in seven of the eight disciplinary hearings that his regional panel held, the respondent was a Carey opponent.[43] Former EPC member Sam Theodus, an international vice president, told the subcommittee that he resigned his EPC position because of "totally discriminatory and retaliatory application of internal union discipline by the Carey regime."[44] In 1998, Hoekstra concluded that "IBT headquarters officials [had] used the EPC to target political adversaries."[45] He added that the EPC was not an adequate alternative to the IRB because it had failed to incorporate a code of ethics into the IBT constitution, failed to establish an educational program to ensure that rank and filers understood the required standards of ethical conduct, and used the IBT to neutralize and punish political adversaries. Hoekstra stated, "Absent the constant vigilance of an IA, IRB, or some other independent overseer, rank-and-file members have no mechanism to protect their rights. . . . To the extent the EPC was envisioned as a vehicle to end the need for government supervision, it has failed in significant respects."[46]

Carey's International-Union Trusteeships

During his tenure as general president, Carey imposed international-union trusteeships on nearly seventy IBT locals and joint councils. More than two-thirds of those trusteeships were imposed without IRB recommendations. For example, Carey trusteed the following locals:

- NYC IBT Local 272 (July 1992) because (1) several of the local's officers were indicted for receiving kickbacks from parking-lot employers in exchange for not objecting when those employers fired Teamsters and hired nonunion replacement workers and (2) infighting among the local officers interfered with their ability to represent the local's members.
- Rochelle Park, New Jersey IBT Local 11 (July 1993) because an international-union audit found that the local's president and business agent had engaged in dual unionism by transferring 115 members to an affiliated non-IBT local union without their knowledge. The audit also identified large sums of unaccounted-for money and unauthorized expenditures.

- NYC IBT Local 810 (September 1993) based on EPC charges that two local officers had mismanaged the local's pension, health, and welfare funds; required their staff members to donate to their re-election campaigns; raised their salaries without membership approval; and spent union money for personal goods and services.
- Springfield, Illinois IBT Local 916 (July 1994) because an international-union audit found that the local's officers had used union credit cards to pay for personal expenses (e.g., greens fees at golf courses) and had "double dipped" by charging meals on union credit cards while also receiving reimbursements for the same expenses. The IBT required the officers to reimburse $8,000 to the local.
- Fall River, Massachusetts IBT Local 526 (November 1994) because an international-union audit, resulting from a complaint to the EPC, found that the local had a negative net worth and that the local's officers had planned to use funds from a restricted account to reduce the local's outstanding debts.
- Chicago IBT Local 753 (November 1994) because an independent audit revealed that, in violation of federal pension laws, the local's officers had sold a building owned by the local to a local-union pension plan and used the $1.1 million proceeds to purchase new cars and to fund a 50 percent salary increase.

Carey's supporters claimed that these trusteeships demonstrated his commitment to remedying corruption and financial mismanagement. His critics charged that he used the non-IRB-recommended trusteeships to replace political enemies with his allies. Some ousted officers and rank-and-file members of trusteed locals picketed the Marble Palace, protesting Carey's removal of their elected representatives. Others went to court to challenge the existence, scope, and duration of trusteeships.[47] A few even physically resisted trustees' efforts to carry out their duties, refusing to let them in the local's offices. (Carey claimed to have hired bodyguards in response to death threats.) On occasion, even TDU questioned the propriety of Carey-imposed trusteeships.[48]

Conclusion and Analysis

The IRB

Aside from Carey's early opposition to the IRB, which Judge Edelstein swiftly quelled, the transition of disciplinary authority from the IO/IA to the IRB occurred without major difficulty. The appointments of Frederick Lacey as an IRB member and Charles Carberry as IRB chief investigator facilitated the transition. During their three years as IO and IA, respectively, they produced a comprehensive body of administrative IBT disciplinary law on which the IRB could build.

During the Carey years (February 1992–November 1997), the IRB recommended that the IBT charge 214 Teamsters with disciplinary violations. Approximately 20 percent of the respondents were charged with being members of LCN, knowingly associating with LCN members/associates, or refusing to cooperate with an investigation into LCN influence. The other 80 percent were charged with garden-variety union corruption, financial misconduct, breach of fiduciary duties, or failure to cooperate with a non-LCN-related IRB investigation. However, we should not assume that a disciplinary case involved organized crime only if a respondent was charged with an organized-crime-related offense. It is often easier to prove charges of failure to cooperate with the IRB or financial mismanagement than to prove an organized-crime link. The breach-of-fiduciary-duty and failure-to-cooperate violations often involved passive cooperation with LCN.

The DOJ lawyers believed that the *U.S. v. IBT* remediation should target ordinary corruption (i.e., corruption unrelated to LCN) because any union corruption contributes to an environment that invites LCN infiltration. This hypothesis, while plausible, is certainly not beyond question. Indeed, if confirmed, it would justify a permanent IRB.

Ironically, IBT leaders reap some benefits from the IRB. If the IRB investigates and charges disciplinary violations that the IBT would otherwise have to handle itself, the IBT leaders can avoid the political costs of disciplining powerful and/or popular IBT officials. That is an advantage for an IBT administration serious about cleaning house.

Ron Carey

It is difficult to determine to what extent Ron Carey's anticorruption efforts were bona fide. We do not know why Carey opposed the IRB, and we cannot confidently gauge the sincerity of his commitment to the EPC or to the evenhanded imposition of trusteeships. Compounding the difficulty of evaluation is the lack of agreement on how much a union president can and should do to fight corruption and racketeering. DOJ lawyers likely judge Carey by his commitment to fighting organized crime and by his cooperation with the court-appointed officers. IBT officers likely judge Carey by his willingness to respect local-union autonomy. TDU and AUD likely judge Carey by his support for democratic reforms. Rank and filers likely care most about Carey's ability to negotiate strong contracts and keep dues low.

Ron Carey's resistance to the IRB was surprising given that he would not have become IBT general president without the consent decree's mandate for rank-and-file elections of international officers. Carey was, at best, uncooperative and, at worst, subversive in negotiations with DOJ to appoint a third IRB member. His administration drew Judge Edelstein's ire when it rejected DOJ's proposal to appoint William Webster. Carey's insistence that DOJ lacked authority to issue operational rules for the IRB and his claim that the IRB was unnecessary in light of his administration's commitment to fighting corruption and racketeering seem to us disingenuous.

There is also reason to be skeptical about Carey's internal anticorruption initiatives. The EPC was seriously flawed. Its administrator had no investigative experience or expertise and, like most of the EPC members, was Carey's political ally. On at least one occasion, for political reasons, Carey apparently tried to influence an EPC regional hearing panel's disciplinary decision. It is impossible to determine how many of Carey's trusteeship decisions were motivated, wholly or substantially, by a desire to replace political adversaries with political allies. The critics certainly raised serious questions.

7

The 1996 Election Scandal

Rank and file Teamsters will watch the 1996 election with the hope
that the Union will continue to be free and democratic. They will
constantly be asking themselves whether the Union truly belongs
to them. It is not just their interests that are at stake. The American
public as a whole will benefit when this union of more than 1.4 million members is freed from the clutches of organized gangsterism.[1]
    —Judge David Edelstein, August 22, 1995

[My] investigation revealed a complex network of schemes to funnel employer and IBT funds into the Carey campaign. . . . [Thus,]
the election officer refuses to certify the [1996] election and orders a
rerun election. . . . [T]he election officer recognizes the hardship on
the candidates who just went through an expensive two-year campaign and the disruption to the institution. . . . [But] the members
cannot have confidence in their union or its leaders if they see their
choice of officers has been manipulated by outsiders.[2]
    —EO Barbara Quindel, August 21, 1997

Ron Carey could not be confident about reelection in 1996.
He had won the 1991 election largely because the IBT establishment had
split its support between R.V. Durham and Walter Shea. During his first
term, Carey was frequently reminded that he could not count on the political support of a large majority of local and regional IBT officials. More
worrisome, in 1996, he would face a challenge from James P. (Jim) Hoffa,
son of former IBT General President James R. (Jimmy) Hoffa, a Teamster
folk hero despite his Mafia ties and corruption conviction.[3]

The 1996 Candidates for General President

Ron Carey

Carey launched his reelection campaign in mid-1995. He boasted of having removed scores of corrupt union officials and trusteeing nearly seventy corrupt or financially mismanaged locals.[4] To symbolize his commitment to a less imperial central office, Carey cut his own salary from $225,000 to $150,000, sold the union's jets, canceled the Marble Palace's water-cooler contract, and fired its French chef. Stressing the importance of gender and racial diversity, his staff organized conferences on women's issues and civil rights.[5] Still, only a small minority of local and regional IBT leaders were Carey loyalists. For example, John P. Morris, president of Philadelphia IBT Local 115 and an international vice president, called the 1996 election "a case of Mr. Clean [Carey] vs. Mr. Not [Hoffa]."[6] Carl Haynes, president of NYC IBT Local 237, one of the largest Teamsters locals in the United States, stated that "if Hoffa wins, . . . we'll go back to the pre-1991 way that things were done. The cleansing of the union, which is so badly needed, will stop."[7] AFL-CIO President John Sweeney praised Carey as a "unique American" who set "standards for integrity."[8]

Although DOJ, Judge Edelstein, and most of the court officers kept their preferences private, a May 1995 *Time* magazine story disclosed a confidential letter from Frederick Lacey to Thomas Puccio, the court-appointed trustee of New York IBT Local 295, in which Lacey urged Puccio not to go public with allegations linking Carey to Cosa Nostra. Lacey warned that such charges could severely harm Carey's chances for reelection:

> During our conversation, I told you that I thought you . . . ought to have in mind what would happen if you brought Carey down in that there were "old guard" Teamsters throughout the country that were hoping that Carey would be eliminated as a candidate in 1996 so that the clock could be turned back to what it was when I first came on the scene as Independent Administrator. You indicated that you had not given any thought to that but you would keep it in mind.[9]

Both Lacey and Puccio refused to discuss the letter.

However, in a subsequent disciplinary case, an international vice president (Gene Giacumbo) facing embezzlement charges asked Lacey to recuse himself.[10] Giacumbo argued that Lacey's letter to Puccio demonstrates "clear partiality toward Carey. . . . [B]y openly aligning himself with Carey's candidacy, Lacey implicitly placed himself in opposition to individuals such as [Giacumbo] who were actively seeking Carey's ouster." Lacey refused to recuse himself and Judge Edelstein affirmed Lacey's decision.[11] The Second Circuit Court of Appeals sent the case back to Judge Edelstein because he had used the wrong standard of review to evaluate Lacey's partiality/impartiality.[12] In a concurring opinion, Judge Dennis Jacobs stated that *Time Magazine*'s disclosure of Lacey's letter was "unsettling because the letter is partisan in an election in which Lacey has no vote and should have no candidate. . . . In light of the deference that we have in the past extended to Lacey's judgment and prestige . . . [this revelation] is a depressant."[13] On remand, Judge Edelstein again supported Lacey's refusal to recuse himself.[14]

Three months after Lacey wrote the letter, the IRB released an eighty-five-page report presenting the findings of its inquiry into Carey's alleged LCN connections.[15] The report first addressed Lucchese crime family member Alfonso D'Arco's statements to the FBI that he and Carey had spoken numerous times from 1967 to 1971; that Carey was a "partner" of LCN associate and IBT official Joe Trerotola; and that when D'Arco "used to put up illegal pickets/strikes, [he] would call Carey, . . . [who] would honor the strike without even investigating [its] nature, purpose or legitimacy."[16] The IRB concluded that D'Arco was not an LCN member at the time he allegedly communicated with Carey and that D'Arco's other allegations were unsupported.[17] The IRB also investigated an allegation that, while president of NYC IBT Local 804, Carey appointed to serve as a local union trustee a person whom he knew to be a close associate of the Colombo crime family's acting boss.[18] The IRB concluded that Carey had neither appointed the trustee nor known of his LCN associations.[19] Next, the IRB addressed an allegation that, in 1975, Carey testified as a character witness for alleged Lucchese crime family member John Conti in a federal extortion case.[20] The IRB concluded that Conti was not an LCN member when Carey testified for him and that, after Conti's trial (at which Conti was acquitted), Carey had no further contact with him.[21] The IRB also concluded that Carey should not be disciplined for appointing Lucchese crime family associate William Genoese as trustee of NYC IBT Local 295 because Genoese's LCN ties were not well known at the time.[22] Finally, the IRB concluded that there was no evidence to support allegations that Carey had knowingly associated with alleged Colombo crime family associates related to his brother's wife.[23] Prominent journalist Jeffrey Goldberg observed that Lacey's earlier letter to Puccio in support of Carey should cause observers to "question the [subsequent IRB] report's credibility."[24]

Sam Theodus

Sam Theodus was an IBT international vice president and former president of a five-thousand-member Cleveland IBT local.[25] Ten years earlier, he had mounted a futile insurgency to defeat IBT General President Jackie Presser. In 1991, Theodus was elected as an international vice president on Carey's slate. However, in 1995, he split with Carey, calling his administration "vindictive" and "morally corrupt."[26] He resigned from the EPC, charging that it discriminated against Teamsters who supported Hoffa.[27] Theodus's principal campaign issues were the weakened state of IBT finances and declining IBT membership.[28] He promised that, if elected, he would create a truly independent EPC. Ultimately, he dropped his presidential candidacy in favor of a vice presidential spot on Hoffa's slate. Two years later, in hearings before the House Subcommittee on Oversight and Investigations, Theodus explained that he was "totally disillusioned, disappointed, disgusted, and dismayed" with Carey's leadership and charged the Carey administration with conducting

> a reign of terror by malicious prosecution of its detractors while they themselves [the Carey administration] engaged in various acts of corruption. . . . [The Carey administration] was singularly and compulsively obsessed with the perpetuation of its own power. Internal union politics played a part in virtually every decision made by the majority of the general executive board. It became an administration that abused all the powers of the general president and the general executive board in the areas of union disciplinary procedures, the implementation of trusteeships, the merging of local unions, and the manipulation of joint council jurisdictions, to punish its enemies and reward its supporters in virtually every opportunity that was presented.[29]

Jim Hoffa

On August 30, 1995, fifty-four-year-old Jim Hoffa formally announced his candidacy for IBT general president.[30] His five-year tenure as full-time administrative assistant to Michigan IBT Joint Council 43 President Larry Brennan made him eligible to run. His surname resonated with many rank and filers.[31] Douglas Fraser, retired president of United Auto Workers, observed, "There's an aura surrounding the Hoffa name that's still sort of magical among tuck drivers."[32] Chuck Mack, former president of California IBT Joint Council 7 and a vice presidential candidate on Hoffa's 1996 slate, added that when Hoffa Sr. was president, "we were growing and we had tremendous power vis-à-vis employers and vis-à-vis the Government. When members look back, they recall the positives. That's what Jim's running on."[33] Hoffa himself was not reluctant to invoke his father's name in aid of his candidacy: "Everywhere I go, people say, 'Without your father, I wouldn't be in the middle class. I couldn't send my kids to college.' It's because of Jimmy Hoffa that a lot of these people have good incomes."[34] One newspaper reported,

> In one of the first stops on the [1996] campaign trail for Jim Hoffa, the 54-year-old son of legendary labor boss Jimmy Hoffa, [he] received wild applause and chants of "Hoffa, Hoffa!" from the crowd. . . . Some were there to back his theme of a unified union; others were there to see the son of the man whose life inspired books, congressional investigations into the influence of crime in the union, and motion pictures, and whose disappearance has fascinated many for two decades. "I was proud just to meet him," said a construction worker with IBT Local 142 in Gary, Indiana. "Half the votes will go to him just because of the Hoffa name."[35]

Hoffa promised to reverse the deterioration of the IBT's finances.[36] (Between early 1992, when Carey took office, and late 1996, the end of Carey's first term, the IBT's treasury dropped from $152 million to $16 million.) He proposed increasing the weekly strike benefit to a $250 maximum, scaled to a member's monthly dues payment.[37] He also promised to cap officers' salaries at $150,000 and to sell the IBT's Washington, D.C., condominiums used by out-of-town IBT officials. Hoffa blasted the Carey-negotiated national master freight agreement[38] and attacked Carey for hiring administrative staff from other unions, declaring, "When I become president, I'll fire those [United] [M]ine [W]orkers and I'm putting Teamsters in those jobs."[39]

Hoffa disputed Carey's anticorruption achievements. "Whatever cleanup has happened . . . [Carey] hasn't done it. . . . The government has done it."[40]

Hoffa promised to make termination of the civil RICO suit a top priority: "It's time for the government to leave, thank you. The membership wants their union back."[41]

> I intend to sit down with the president of the United States and tell him what we've accomplished under this consent agreement. . . . If the government wants to continue to monitor our elections, fine. We can live with things like that, but we must have a timetable for when this will end. . . . The idea of the federal government running an organization like ours in a democratic society just isn't right.[42]

TDU leaders and other Carey supporters feared that a Hoffa victory would mean the end of the reform dream. They recalled Hoffa Sr.'s close associations with organized crime and fretted over Hoffa Jr.'s support from allegedly corrupt elements in the union. For instance, Hoffa had been the longtime legal counsel to George Vitale, whom the IRB had expelled from the union for embezzling more than $10,000 and attempting to appropriate a union car. Hoffa was also legal counsel to the Michigan Teamsters' health and welfare fund when the federal government compelled the fund's officers to repay $725,000 in improper expenditures. Hoffa's critics also pointed to his onetime business partnership with LCN associate Allen Dorfman.

The 1996 Election Rules

The *U.S. v. IBT* consent decree provided that if DOJ opted for a supervised 1996 election, it would have to pay for the supervision.[43] DOJ did opt for a supervised election. In early 1995, the IBT and DOJ agreed that "it is the intention of the Government and the IBT that the Election Officer function in 1996 as similarly as possible to the 1991 Election Officer."[44] Judge Edelstein appointed labor lawyer Amy Gladstein as EO. However, he removed her a few months later when he learned that she had hired her husband and law partner as the EO's legal counsel.[45] Edelstein then appointed Barbara Zack Quindel, a Milwaukee labor lawyer who, during the 1991 election, served as one of EO Holland's regional coordinators.[46] Edelstein appointed former federal judge Kenneth Conboy to be the election appeals master (EAM), who would hear appeals from EO decisions, as IA Lacey had done in the 1991 election cycle.[47] Edelstein emphasized the importance of a democratic elections process:

> It is of paramount importance that the same spirit of vigilance that vitalized the 1991 IBT election energize the 1995–96 IBT election process if the arduous and painstaking work of implementing the Consent Decree is to be preserved and built upon. It cannot be said too often that the minions of organized crime continue to haunt the IBT. These invidious enemies of union democracy continue to thrive with a perverse and persistent energy.[48]

Quindel opened an election-office headquarters in Washington, D.C., and proposed a $21.2 million election budget.[49] (Ultimately, the 1996 election cost approximately $17.5 million.) On April 24, 2005, she distributed proposed rules for the 1996 election to all IBT locals, GEB members, large IBT employers, and Teamsters who requested copies. Except for a few changes, these proposed rules were similar to the 1991 election rules.[50] One new provision, formalizing a practice Holland adopted in 1991, granted campaigners limited access to employers' parking lots.[51] Some employers objected, arguing that it violated the U.S. Supreme Court's 1992 decision in *Lechmere, Inc., v. National Labor Relations Board*, which held that the National Labor Relations Act did not authorize a nonemployee to campaign on an employer's premises.[52] Quindel countered that the consent decree provided legal authority for this rule.[53] Judge Edelstein agreed.

Persuaded that mail balloting had been successful in the 1991 convention-delegate and general elections, Quindel asked Judge Edelstein to approve rank-and-file voting by mail ballot, even though the consent decree provided that "all direct rank-and-file voting by secret ballot . . . shall be by in-person ballot box voting."[54] Judge Edelstein approved the proposed rule without addressing its apparent incompatibility with the consent decree.[55] Another proposed rule provided that the rank and file, rather than the convention delegates, would elect the three international trustees (who compose the IBT's Audit Committee). To protect IBT members against retaliation for exercising their rights under the election rules, Quindel proposed that she adjudicate postelection protests alleging retaliation, whether or not that protest's resolution would affect an election's outcome.[56] Finally, to reduce the risk of coercion or intimidation in the delegate-selection process, Quindel authorized written delegate nominations to be submitted directly to the EO's office, rather than in person to the local union's election committee.[57] Judge Edelstein approved all these proposed rules.

EO Quindel, twenty-two regional coordinators, and dozens of adjunct coordinators reviewed and sometimes modified each local's delegate-election plan. The staff monitored nominating meetings for compliance with appropriate procedures. As in the 1991 election cycle, contested elections occurred in about one-half of the locals. The EO sent a mail-in ballot to every member of every local with a contested delegate election. An EO regional representative counted the ballots in the presence of the candidates or their representatives. Ultimately, the EO certified 1,761 delegates and 748 alternate delegates from 568 IBT locals.[58] (The vast majority of delegates, once again, were IBT officeholders.)

The July 15–19, 1996 Philadelphia Convention

While General President Carey chaired the 1996 Philadelphia convention and controlled its agenda, he struggled to maintain control because Hoffa's delegates well outnumbered his. On the first day of the convention, Hoffa's supporters halted the proceedings several times.[59] They complained that Carey "was running roughshod over them, declaring the results of close voice votes as victories for his positions and turning off audience microphones to stifle debate."[60] After Carey introduced Senator Arlen Specter (D-Pa.), the delegates' shouting at Carey (who remained on the stage as Specter began his speech) "grew to a roar," causing Specter to tell the delegates, "this is a black mark on the Teamsters and a black mark on the American labor movement" before leaving the podium.[61] Carey infuriated Hoffa's delegates by rejecting their motion to prohibit voting by eighty "super-delegates" who were either appointed by joint councils or automatically selected.*[62] (Past presidents had also appointed convention super-delegates.) Carey declared the motion defeated despite some journalists' observations that the voice vote favored Hoffa's delegates.[63] The ensuing fracas triggered a call to the police, who cleared the hall.[64]

Hoffa introduced a number of proposals, including drawing $15 million from the union's treasury to increase strike benefits[65] and reinforcing

---

* Each joint council is entitled to appoint a super-delegate. GEB members, international representatives, and international trustees also enjoy super-delegate status. Super-delegates can vote on constitutional and procedural measures at IBT conventions. However, the LMRDA prohibits them from nominating candidates for international office.

the autonomy of local unions by restricting the general president's authority to impose trusteeships on locals.[66] Carey's parliamentary rulings prevented these and other Hoffa proposals from reaching floor votes. He used his control of the convention agenda to his advantage. For example, Carey proposed that candidates for international office must have been IBT local officers or have worked at least two years for Teamsters employers. That requirement would have disqualified Hoffa, who had served as an administrative assistant to a union officer, but had not himself been a union officer. (Given Hoffa's significant delegate advantage, his supporters must not have realized the significance of the vote because Carey's proposal just barely lost, 784 to 745.)[67]

Carey allocated almost a full day of the convention to debate whether the union's name, International *Brotherhood* of Teamsters, should be made gender neutral. That proposal failed by almost two to one.[68] On another day, he refused to close debate on a noncontroversial oath of office for union officers.[69] According to labor journalist Kenneth Crowe,

> Carey . . . has used his position as convention chairman to frustrate Hoffa's agenda. . . . Carey has frequently ruled opposition speakers out of order, strung out debates over procedural points and ordered time-consuming votes. Votes early in the week showed that Hoffa has a slight edge in the number of delegates, but not enough to push through his program.[70]

Labor journalist Peter Kilborn observed that Carey had "quell[ed] debate by declining to call upon Hoffa supporters who stood ready to speak."[71] When it came to the nomination balloting, Carey received fewer votes than Hoffa (775–954).[72] Clearly, he faced an uphill reelection battle.

The Election Campaigns

The candidates continued trading corruption charges after the convention. Carey's team referred to Hoffa as a "flunky of the old guard," "the same old mobbed-up, on-the-take Teamster his daddy was," and "an imposter who will bring back the weakness and corruption of the past."[73] Hoffa's campaign called Carey a "failed leader [who] resorts to power grabs out of spite and pique," a "chicken," and a "scaredy cat" for refusing to debate Hoffa.[74] It denounced Carey's campaign ads as "slimy pieces of half-truths."[75]

The acrimony resulted in Carey filing a $30 million libel suit (recalling Carey's 1991 libel suit against the Durham campaign) charging Hoffa's campaign with "false, defamatory and malicious statements and innuendo."[76] The complaint claimed that Hoffa's campaign literature falsely accused Carey of secretly holding $2 million in UPS stock (Carey admitted having inherited from his father an interest in some shares that were sold in 1992, but denied controlling them) and of improperly persuading an eighty-eight-year-old woman to bequeath him the majority of her $395,000 estate (Carey claimed that the woman, an old family friend, bequeathed the money voluntarily). Public-relations consultant and Hoffa campaign spokesman Richard Leebove called the libel suit "a political trick by Ron Carey to cover an embarrassing revelation about his financial ties to the Teamsters' largest employer."[77] Carey withdrew the libel suit soon after the 1996 election.

In early fall 1996, pursuant to an IRB recommendation, Carey imposed a trusteeship on Chicago IBT Local 714, headed by William Hogan, Jr., a powerful Hoffa ally and a vice presidential candidate on Hoffa's slate.[78] Days later, without an IRB recommendation, Carey imposed a trusteeship on Akron, Ohio IBT Local 348 on the ground that its executive board was too polarized to conduct union business.[79] Carey imposed an emergency trusteeship on Philadelphia Local 107 after an IRB investigative report found that LCN figures were influencing the local; the IRB report also objected to that local's employees receiving bonuses even though the local's finances were declining. Local 107's officers had allegedly failed to implement financial controls, misused union funds, assumed a mortgage without proper approval, and failed to hold monthly membership meetings.[80] Hoffa charged, "[Carey is] trying to steal the election by systematically eliminating key people who have the nerve and capacity to effectively oppose him."[81] A Philadelphia federal district court judge gave some credibility to Hoffa's charge, enjoining the trusteeship because Carey had not held a hearing to determine whether there was an emergency.[82] However, pursuant to Judge Edelstein's All Writs Act decision, the Philadelphia judge transferred the case to Edelstein, who vacated the injunction.[83]

Carey raised $1.8 million in campaign contributions to Hoffa $1.3 million. Carey received most of his contributions from Teamsters in the east, the south, and Canada. (He also received several large contributions from wealthy non-Teamsters.) Hoffa did best in the midwest, especially in Chicago, Detroit, and Kansas City. Fundraising in the west was more or less equal.

EO Quindel tried to schedule a presidential debate, but Carey declined, saying he was too busy.[84] Hoffa proposed that the convention delegates amend the IBT constitution to compel a presidential debate.[85] Quindel obtained an injunction from Judge Edelstein blocking this proposal on the ground that it infringed on the EO's authority.[86]

The Vote

On December 10, 1996, the EO staff began counting the mail ballots. Opening, sorting, and counting took five days. Seventy Carey and Hoffa campaign observers monitored the count.[87] Ballots from voters who were not on Quindel's eligibility list would be counted later if, cumulatively, they could affect the election's outcome. Ultimately, because most candidates' margin of victory was smaller than the number of challenged ballots, those ballots had to be counted.[88]

On December 15, Quindel proclaimed Carey the victor by fifteen thousand votes (52 percent to 48 percent).[89] His running mates were also elected, except in the central region, which elected five international vice presidential candidates on Hoffa's slate.[90] EO Quindel rejected as "completely without foundation" the Hoffa campaign's charge that more than fifteen thousand ballots had disappeared. Jere Nash, Carey's campaign manager, said, "Now is the time for the Hoffa campaign to put the force of action behind their talk of unity and to gracefully accept their defeat as the result of a fair and democratic election." Carey said, "This victory sends a message to every mob boss in America: our treasury, our pension funds will never, ever again be used by organized crime in the form of a piggy bank."[91] Ken Paff declared, "[T]he back's been broken on Mafia influence. The Mafia is losing. We're winning."[92] Hoffa called his near win an "amazing achievement": "It sends a message to Ron Carey that he should listen to the members. This union is split down the middle and will continue that way unless he reaches out to those disenchanted people who voted against him."[93]

Nullification of the 1996 Election

The 1996 election was over but not put to rest. In early December 1996, in the course of reviewing the Carey and Hoffa slates' postelection campaign contribution and expenditure reports, EO Quindel found several suspiciously large donations to Teamsters for a Corruption Free Union (TCFU), a Carey campaign fundraising committee created late in the election cycle.[94] In January 1997, after discovering more suspicious donations,[95] she initiated an investigation that revealed a sophisticated scheme to funnel IBT funds into Carey's reelection campaign by means of contribution swaps.

The "Swap" Schemes

Quindel's investigation revealed that, in early October 1996, Carey campaign manager Jere Nash asked IBT Government Affairs Director William Hamilton to arrange for the IBT to make financial contributions to various political organizations; in return, wealthy friends of those organizations would donate equal amounts to Carey's reelection campaign. Hamilton agreed. Nash also hired Martin Davis, a principal in the Washington, D.C.– based political consulting firm November Group, to help raise money for Carey's campaign. (During Carey's 1991 general presidential campaign, and throughout his first term, the November Group provided public relations and political consulting services to Nash and Hamilton.)[96] In turn, Davis recruited Michael Ansara, a principal in the Massachusetts-based telemarketing firm Share Group, to help raise funds for Carey. Ansara's wife, Barbara Arnold, contributed $95,000 to the TCFU fundraising committee. The IBT then paid the Share Group $97,000, supposedly for consulting and lobbying services.[97]

The Hoffa campaign filed a postelection protest alleging that Share Group had done little or no work to justify the IBT's $97,000 payment, that the $97,000 payment was actually a quid pro quo for Barbara Arnold's $95,000 donation to the Carey campaign, and that Share Group then reimbursed Barbara Arnold.[98] The Carey campaign denied the allegation, explaining that Arnold was "independently wealthy and donated the money [to Carey's campaign] soon after coming into an inheritance."[99] The U.S. attorney's office (SDNY) convened a grand jury to investigate whether these transactions amounted to illegal money laundering.[100]

Federal investigators focused on four other contributions that the IBT made to political organizations between mid-October and early November 1996. First, the IBT donated $475,000 to Citizen Action, a consumer-advocacy organization. Then, at the request of Michael Ansara, a Citizen Action fundraiser[101] persuaded Citizen Action supporters to donate $100,000 to Carey's campaign.[102] Second, in early November 1996, the IBT gave

$150,000 to the AFL-CIO, which then contributed a similar amount to Citizen Action, whose supporters then donated approximately $100,000 to the Carey campaign. Third, the IBT made a $175,000 contribution to Project Vote, allegedly in exchange for donations to the Carey campaign from wealthy friends of that organization. Fourth, the IBT donated $85,000 to the National Council of Senior Citizens, allegedly in exchange for similar contributions to the Carey campaign from that organization's friends.[103] These swap schemes amounted to embezzlement of IBT funds for the benefit of Carey's campaign.[104] EO Quindel also discovered that a Washington, D.C., attorney, who was also an employer, arranged for a $16,000 donation to TCFU in violation of the election rules.

Federal investigators later uncovered still another Carey-campaign money-laundering scheme exposed by the *Wall Street Journal* in August 1997 and reported by *Time Magazine* in October 1997.[105] These media reported that, in mid-1996, Martin Davis had proposed to a Democratic National Committee (DNC) fundraiser that the IBT donate $1 million to DNC's state affiliates in return for the DNC arranging for its wealthy supporters to contribute $100,000 to Carey's reelection campaign.[106] Allegedly in furtherance of this plan, the IBT donated $300,000 to Democratic Party organizations in at least thirty-five states,[107] while DNC Finance Director Richard Sullivan instructed a DNC fundraiser to deliver to the Carey campaign $100,000 that a Filipino donor had contributed to Vote Now '96, a Democratic-leaning voter-registration organization. However, because the foreign donor was an employer, and thus barred by the IBT election rules from donating to a union candidate's campaign, the fundraiser refused to consummate the deal. *Time* magazine called this "the most solid evidence yet that [Democratic] party officials actively participated in the scheme before it went bust."[108] (However, no DNC officials were charged.)

In June 1997, FBI agents arrested Martin Davis on charges of embezzling money from the IBT for the benefit of the Carey campaign.[109] The *New York Daily News* reported that Davis had said in an affidavit, "The IBT knew of the plan and wanted it done this way."[110] That same month, Ansara pled guilty to conspiracy to commit money laundering.[111] A month later, Bill Hamilton resigned his position as IBT government affairs director.[112]

The Election Officer's Decisions

On August 22, 1997, EO Quindel issued her decision not to certify the 1996 international-officer election because the "complex network of schemes to funnel . . . IBT funds into the Carey campaign . . . may have affected the outcome of the International officer election."[113] She characterized the Carey campaign's misconduct as "egregious violations by high level campaign functionaries who believed winning at all costs was more important than abiding by the 1996 Election Rules and the law." Quindel ordered a new election for general president and other GEB positions.[114] However, she did not disqualify Carey from the rerun election because of insufficient evidence that Carey himself participated in or knew of the unlawful schemes.[115] Still, Quindel noted that "important questions remain unanswered" and that Carey's denial of knowingly approving the unlawful IBT expenditures was a "surprising statement in light of their size compared to other IBT contributions in the same period."[116]

Hoffa's supporters criticized Quindel for not disqualifying Carey from the rerun election.[117] Carey's supporters attacked her for ordering a rerun election and for ignoring alleged Hoffa campaign-finance violations. EAM Kenneth Conboy directed Quindel to "thoroughly and convincingly" investigate the Carey campaign's allegations of Hoffa campaign-finance violations.[118]

On September 3, 1997, Quindel notified Judge Edelstein that she would resign after he approved the 1998 rerun-election rules.[119] In the meantime, she opened a supplemental investigation into whether Carey should be disqualified from the rerun election. Among others, Quindel interviewed Martin Davis, who by then had pled guilty to participating in the Carey campaign-finance scheme. Among other things, Davis told Quindel that, in early 1997, he proposed to the executive director of the New Party, a liberal political party in Wisconsin, a contribution-swap scheme whereby the IBT would donate money to the New Party in exchange for the New Party's finding a donor to repay some of Carey's campaign debt.[120] Quindel promptly recused herself from the supplemental investigation because she and her husband were members of the New Party.[121] Judge Edelstein appointed labor lawyer Benetta Mansfield as Quindel's interim successor and asked EAM Conboy to decide whether to disqualify Carey from the rerun election.[122]

On November 17, 1997, Conboy disqualified Carey from the rerun election, based largely on Quindel's report and on evidence provided by Ansara, Nash, Davis, and Monian Simpkins (Carey's executive assistant).[123] Conboy concluded that at least $735,000 of IBT funds had been used to obtain donations to the Carey campaign and that Carey must have played a role in at least some of the contribution swaps. Nash told investigators that

Carey had approved several swaps. For example, he said that he and Carey had discussed the possibility that Rich Trumka, the AFL-CIO's secretary-treasurer, and Andrew Stern, president of the Service Employees International Union (SEIU), would provide fundraising assistance to Carey's campaign. Nash also claimed that Carey approved the IBT's $475,000 donation to Citizen Action because it would help Martin Davis raise Carey campaign funds. Simpkins said that after Carey told her that he approved several Nash swap proposals, she signed Carey's initials to various documents to indicate his approval.

Conboy concluded that even if Carey had a plausible explanation for each illegal swap, it was highly unlikely that he was innocent in every instance. He did not find credible Carey's claim not to recall authorizing any one of the four largest IBT political contributions. Although Conboy found it troubling to "disqualify[] a previously victorious candidate, to the evident impoverishment of the democratic process," he concluded that because Carey had "tolerated and engaged in extensive rules violations in broad furtherance of his reelection campaign," the upcoming election could not be free and fair with Carey participating in it.[124]

On November 24, 1997, a week after Carey's disqualification from the rerun election, IBT General Counsel Earl Brown, Jr., signed an agreement with AUSA Karen Konigsberg providing for appointment of an accountant to audit IBT expenditures. The parties selected, and Judge Edelstein approved, Martin Levy, a certified public accountant, former FBI analyst, and expert in white-collar fraud, as independent financial auditor. Levy was authorized to

> review any expenditure or proposed expenditure of IBT funds or transfer of IBT property and to review any proposed contract entered into on behalf of the IBT (other than a collective bargaining agreement) and to veto any such expenditure, transfer or contract whenever the Independent Financial Auditor reasonably believes that such expenditures, transfer or contract would constitute or further an unlawful act or violation of the IBT Constitution or would otherwise constitute or further fraud or abuse of IBT funds or property.[125]

A Hoffa-campaign spokesperson called the appointment "an important step to protect what is left of the Teamsters treasury, which has been looted by Ron Carey," but added that it was a "sign of the failure" of government monitoring.[126] An IBT spokesperson said that the appointment of an audi-

tor "was a good idea in that it would also assure our members that everything was proper."[127] University of Michigan labor studies professor Michael Belzer noted that the IBT's "[g]iving up that kind of authority to the
government is a pretty strong admission that you don't have your house in
order."[128]

Although Levy had authority to monitor and veto disbursements from
the IBT treasury, he could not review IBT locals' expenditures or IBT pension funds' investments or, indeed, determine whether IBT expenditures
had a bona fide business purpose. In 1998, Rep. Peter Hoekstra (R-Mich.)
criticized Levy's performance:

> [Levy] is a CPA, not an auditor; he does not function as an auditor with
> regard to the IBT's finances; he does not perform any investigatory func-
> tion; he does not attempt to determine the "prudent business use" of any
> particular expenditures, and although the agreement under which he op-
> erates appears to give him veto power over IBT expenditures, he has not
> come close to exercising that authority in the approximately six months
> he's been on the job.[129]

The IBT established an internal audit committee to work with Levy on
procedures to report rules violations and to prevent union officials from
approving their own expenditures. (After four years, DOJ terminated
Levy's position, finding that the IBT had taken adequate steps to ensure the
union's financial integrity.)[130]

Hearings before the House Subcommittee on Oversight and Investigations

On August 26, 1997, Rep. Hoekstra, chairman of the House Subcommittee on Oversight and Investigations, announced his intention to convene
hearings on the invalidated 1996 election and the upcoming 1998 rerun
election. The hearings had four purposes: (1) to inform Congress of how
the federal government spent almost $20 million on the 1996 IBT election,
where that money went, and why, at the end of the day, we were left with an
election that could not be certified;[131] (2) to determine how much money a
rerun election would cost and who is going to pay for it;[132] (3) to discover
what really happened in the failed Teamsters election in 1996;[133] and (4) to
determine whether the botched 1996 election could happen again.[134]

Hoekstra's subcommittee's hearings (October 14, 1997 to October 6, 1998) sought to illuminate the 1996 campaign-finance scandal; the inaccuracy of the IBT's financial disclosures to DOL; improper justifications for Carey-administration trusteeships; the implementation of the court-appointed officers' disciplinary recommendations; the IBT's political support of the DNC; and the conduct of the election officer, the IRB, and the independent financial auditor.[135] Some congressional Democrats questioned whether Hoekstra had a political motive, perhaps to link the Democratic Party to the Carey money-laundering scandal. Rep. Patsy Mink (D-Hawaii), the ranking Democrat on Hoekstra's subcommittee, called the proposed hearings a "partisan event," pointing out that Hoekstra had called as witnesses six Hoffa supporters but only one Carey supporter.[136] Hoekstra criticized the IRB, the election officer, the independent financial auditor, DOJ, DOL, and the IBT's international officers for failing to protect taxpayers. He charged the Carey administration with failing to cooperate with the subcommittee's investigation.[137] He complained that IBT officials refused requests for interviews and requests for documents, ordered third parties (i.e., the accounting firm, the law firm, and other service providers hired by the IBT) not to provide documents, and redacted relevant information from documents that were provided. Hoekstra referred to the Carey administration as "the bad old Carey days" and called corruption in the IBT "nothing short of mind-boggling."[138]

In response to Hoekstra's complaints about Carey's stonewalling, the House of Representatives authorized the subcommittee to depose witnesses under oath pursuant to order or subpoena without the presence of committee members.[139] Consequently, the subcommittee deposed nearly two dozen witnesses, including EO Barbara Quindel, Independent Financial Auditor Martin Levy, and AFL-CIO President John Sweeney (see fig. 7.1). Several potentially valuable witnesses, including AFL-CIO Secretary-Treasurer Richard Trumka and IBT General President Ron Carey, notified the subcommittee that they would invoke their Fifth Amendment privilege not to testify.

In June 1998, eight months into the subcommittee's investigation, Hoekstra declared, "I do not see any way in which this Congress can or should ask the American people, the taxpayers, to bail out this union leadership one more time."[140] He predicted that the 1996 scandal "absolutely could happen again" because "the IBT's counterfeit leadership is still in power with its hands at the controls of the Marble Palace"; "the government's safeguards have not improved" since the 1996 election cycle; the IRB "chooses

FIGURE 7.1

Key Witnesses before the Subcommittee on Oversight and Investigations

Witness	Date	Summary of Testimony
Two rank and filers	10-14-1997	IRB failed to bring disciplinary charges against Carey supporters who assaulted them for speaking out at a local meeting.
International representative	10-14-1997	International officers threatened to fire him unless he made a financial contribution to the Carey campaign.
EO Michael Holland/ EO Barbara Quindel	10-15-1997	Described the supervision, results, and costs of the 1991 and 1996 elections. Quindel explained that the Carey campaign's illegal campaign contribution swaps did not come to light until just before the 1996 general-election balloting.
Two former international trustees	3-26-1998	Carey barred them from GEB meetings and thwarted their auditing because they had sounded warnings about the IBT's precarious financial condition.
Court-Appointed IBT Financial Auditor Martin Levy	4-29-1998	His job included neither questioning the business purpose of IBT expenditures nor auditing IBT pension funds.
EO Michael Cherkasky	4-29-1998	What his investigation of the Carey campaign's fundraising violations found.
AFL-CIO President John Sweeney	4-30-1998	Defended the AFL-CIO, especially Secretary-Treasurer Richard Trumka, against allegations of contribution swaps with the IBT.
Independent IBT Auditor Stephen Leser	6-15-1998	Not aware of a subordinate's memorandum discussing IBT expenditures for the Carey campaign.
International Vice President/ EPC Administrator Aaron Belk	6-24-1998	Did not recall that former White House Counsel Charles Ruff had performed any work for IBT's Ethical Practices Committee, contradicting Ruff's statement that the IBT hired him to advise the EPC.
Five IRB members and employees	7-20-1998	Their roles in investigating IBT corruption and organized-crime influence
EO Michael Cherkasky	9-29-1998	The timetable, funding, and oversight of the 1998 rerun election.
Mickey Kantor, former U.S. trade representative	10-6-1998	The Clinton administration's effort to pressure an IBT employer, Diamond Walnut Growers, to settle a strike with the IBT.

to take a very narrow approach to its responsibility to monitor and supervise this historically troubled Union"; DOL's financial reporting requirements for the IBT are "inadequate and do not provide meaningful information to the IBT membership"; and the DOJ-appointed independent financial auditor "has chosen to function essentially as a bookkeeper [and] is a long way from the financial junkyard dog we were led to expect by [the Department of] Justice."[141] The subcommittee further criticized the IBT for having failed to create an internal inspector general's office, a policies and procedures manual, and a budget, all three of which Frederick Lacey had previously recommended.[142]

Hoekstra admitted that placing the cost of the 1998 rerun election on the IBT was burdensome but called it preferable to burdening taxpayers: "I do not feel taxpayers should foot the bill for Teamster bosses' [i.e., Carey's] illegal conduct. I am not unmindful that by asking the IBT to pay for the re-election, I am also asking the rank and file Teamsters to pay. This is a Hobson's choice." In an obvious criticism of Carey and the liberal organizations that funneled money into his 1996 campaign, Hoekstra added, "What I would like to see is a reimbursement to the IBT from the people and organizations who caused the 1996 election to be thrown out."[143]

Ron Carey Expelled and Indicted

On November 25, 1997, a week after Carey's disqualification from the rerun election, he took an unpaid leave of absence.[144] General Secretary-Treasurer Tom Sever took over as acting general president; the international vice presidents kept their positions. A week later, Carey assured the audience at TDU's annual convention that he had been unaware of the contribution swaps: "If I had known that anything was improper, I would have stopped it dead in its tracks."[145] Carey asked the delegates to stand by him during his appeal of Conboy's decision to disqualify him from the rerun election.[146] However, Judge Edelstein and the Second Circuit Court of Appeals rejected Carey's due-process-based appeal on the ground that individuals have due process rights only against the government, not against private organizations such as the IBT (even though Carey was actually disciplined by a court-appointed officer acting pursuant to a court-approved consent decree).[147] These courts also held that Carey could be disciplined without a full and fair hearing because his disqualification was remedial, not disciplinary.[148]

On July 27, 1998, after a four-day hearing, the IRB expelled Carey from the IBT,[149] concluding that he "lied about not knowing that [improper] contributions were made" to his campaign; that he "knew of the proposed contributions and approved them"; and that his claim to have "no memory of whether he did or did not approve any of these expenditures totaling $1,458,000 was less than credible given their size and their relation to the election which Carey believed to be of vital importance."[150] Judge Edelstein affirmed the expulsion, finding it "utterly incredible that Carey had no knowledge of contributions and loans that totaled $1,485,000."[151] Edelstein added, "[T]his court remains convinced that Carey, at the very least, turned a blind eye to the improper fundraising."[152]

In August 1999, the IRB also expelled IBT Government Affairs Director William Hamilton because he "knowingly participated in the scheme in which IBT donations were made with the understanding that, in return, donations would be made to the Carey Campaign."[153] In other words, Hamilton had "knowingly used his union position to cause union donations to be made in return for contributions to the Carey campaign."[154] Judge Edelstein affirmed.[155] Three months later, a federal jury convicted Hamilton of fraud, conspiracy, embezzlement, and perjury.[156]

In January 2001, a Manhattan federal grand jury indicted Carey on five counts of violating the federal false-statement statute[157] and two counts of violating the federal perjury statute.[158] The indictment alleged that Carey had falsely denied that he and his top advisers and staffers communicated, via telephone and in writing, about monetary contributions from the IBT to certain political organizations, especially Citizen Action.[159] Carey's defense lawyer, Reid Weingarten, stated, "We will contest these charges until [Carey] is fully vindicated. His proper place in history is as a hero of the labor movement."[160]

Carey's trial began on August 27, 2001 and lasted four weeks. The prosecution's most important witnesses were Jere Nash (Carey's campaign manager), William Hamilton (the IBT's government affairs director), and Monian Simpkins (Carey's personal secretary). Nash testified that, in mid-October 2006, he urged Carey to approve a $225,000 IBT contribution to Citizen Action because it would help Martin Davis raise money for Carey's reelection campaign. Carey's lawyers called Nash a "completely dishonest, untrustworthy, greedy, manipulative, little thief" who was trying to curry favor with prosecutors in order to secure leniency for himself.[161] (Nash faced up to twenty years in prison and a $2 million fine on his fraud conviction.) Hamilton testified that, in mid-October 2006, he and Carey spoke about the second proposed ($250,000) IBT contribution to Citizen Action. Simpkins then testified that she and Carey had conferred about at least one of the IBT contributions to Citizen Action.[162]

Carey's lawyers called only two witnesses. The first was the IBT's outside counsel during the end of Carey's first term. He testified that Simpkins told him that she approved certain IBT contributions without Carey's permission. The second witness, a staffer in the general president's office, testified that Carey played no role in the contribution swaps with Citizen Action. The jury deliberated for three days. On October 12, 2001, it acquitted Carey of all charges. (The IRB-imposed lifetime ban from IBT membership remained in place.)[163]

Reactions to the Carey Scandal

It was difficult for those who had pinned their hopes for the IBT's reform on Ron Carey to accept the startling turn of events.[164] TDU praised Carey for "toppling mob rule in the Teamsters, becoming the International Union's first democratically elected General President and using his influence to change the leadership and direction of the AFL-CIO."*[165] Many critics, including local IBT officers, blamed Carey for embezzling money from the IBT treasury, committing election fraud, lying to the membership, and mishandling the union's finances. A *Washington Post* reporter wrote that Carey's negligent, or perhaps deliberate, failure to prevent his campaign staff from laundering money threatened the entire labor movement's "resurgence in both political power and public respect."[166] A *New York Times* editorial stated, "So notorious is the Teamsters' history of looting union funds for dubious purposes that Mr. Carey had a special duty to be vigilant."[167]

Conclusion and Analysis

Ron Carey's disqualification from the 1998 rerun election and his subsequent expulsion from the union marked a rare instance in which both the

---

* Ron Carey died of lung cancer at age seventy-two on December 11, 2008. His *New York Times* obituary noted his reputation for "being clean" and for "delivering at the bargaining table," as well as his insistence that he was unaware of the unlawful conduct at the heart of the campaign-finance scandal that led to his expulsion from the union. Steven Greenhouse, *Ron Carey, Who Led Teamsters Reforms, Dies at 72*, NEW YORK TIMES, Dec. 13, 2008.

electoral and disciplinary prongs of the *U.S. v. IBT* consent decree converged. (The IRB typically does not handle cases of alleged election-related misconduct; the EO has authority to adjudicate those cases.) The consent decree facilitated Carey's rise and dictated his fall. Its election machinery empowered the rank and file to vote for Carey without fear of retribution and provided the rules, oversight, investigative resources, and independent monitoring that exposed Carey's misconduct and required his punishment. In upholding Carey's disqualification, the Second Circuit Court of Appeals observed,

> We recognize the irony, indeed the poignancy, of this case in which a union leader, long pledged to internal reform, should be held accountable for corrupt practices. But the law requires no less. Union democracy, after all, is premised on fair elections. To that end, union officials such as Carey have a duty to ensure the integrity of that process and to fulfill their obligations to union members by adhering to the highest standards of governance.[168]

On the one hand, the contribution-swap scandal that led to the nullification of the 1996 election and to Carey's expulsion from the IBT places a question mark over the election-reform prong of the consent decree. That the Carey campaign embezzled and laundered well over $500,000 of Teamsters' dues money to fund Carey's reelection bid casts significant doubt on DOJ's expectation, at the outset of the case, that direct rank-and-file elections would produce an IBT leadership committed to creating a culture of accountability and integrity. Although the architects and enforcers of the consent decree were undoubtedly disappointed that a free and fair election in 1991 did not produce an incorruptible union administration, they should not have been surprised. Countless politicians, claiming to be anticorruption reformers, have been elected to public office in the United States and throughout the world, only to be exposed later as having engaged in gross corruption once in power (e.g., Rod Blagojevich in Illinois and Hamid Karzai in Afghanistan). No system of election supervision, no matter how well funded and well run, can guarantee that all candidates, once in office, will not become corrupt. As sociologists Seymour Lipset, Martin Trow, and James Coleman observed in their landmark 1956 study of union democracy, "In those cases where an entrenched oligarchy was finally dislodged, the new leaders soon reverted to the same tactics as they had denounced in the old in order to guarantee their own permanent tenure in office and reduce or eliminate opposition."[169]

DOJ's lawyers probably did not expect that *U.S. v. IBT* would eradicate all corruption. (Indeed, establishment of the IRB assumed that there would be continuing corruption that needed to be ferreted out.) Giuliani's team was primarily focused on ridding the IBT of organized crime's presence and influence. With respect to that goal, the consent decree's election-reform prong was successful; in neither 1991 nor 1996 did an organized-crime faction or known organized-crime figures compete for international-union office. Furthermore, nullification of the 1996 election was arguably an important affirmation of the effectiveness of the consent decree's election-reform prong because the monitoring process worked. The election officers uncovered corruption of the election process and removed the corrupt candidates.

The Carey-campaign swap scandal illuminates the enormous importance of money in IBT politics. While the need to amass campaign funds is a much-discussed problem in American politics and governance, its role in union and other organizational politics has drawn little attention. This is not surprising, since almost all unions choose their national leaders at conventions attended by local-union officials. That kind of selection procedure does not require campaign financing, but it also makes it practically impossible for an insurgent to win. It costs hundreds of thousands of dollars to send a single mailing to every eligible Teamster voter and tens of thousands of dollars to travel the country, barnstorming from work site to work site. Even if, in a free and fair election, union members would vote for honest candidates and against crooks, it takes a great deal of money to persuade the electorate that you are honest and that your opponent is corrupt; this is especially true when, as is almost always the case, your opponent is making the reverse argument. An insurgent candidate, whose name is not well known and who has practically no fundraising base, has almost no chance of mounting a serious challenge to an incumbent whose name and photo dominate union publications and who has extensive patronage to dispense. Although the Internet is a low-cost method for communicating with the rank and file, there is no comprehensive list of IBT members' email addresses, and many Teamsters do not use or do not regularly check email. Although candidates can post information to websites, members will not see that information unless they actively search for it.

The IBT's 1996 election makes clear that a major union's election takes place within a larger political context. The IBT and other unions are important actors in U.S. politics. The IBT seeks to influence legislation and government policy on numerous issues; politicians desire the IBT's endorsement and monetary contributions. (Over the past decade, the Teamsters Union has contributed nearly $27 million to the Democrats.) For this reason, various liberal organizations, and the DNC itself, saw advantage in engaging in contribution swaps with the Carey campaign.

Carey's fundraising scandal almost certainly would not have happened had the election rules prohibited all non-Teamsters from contributing to candidates' campaigns. Although the extant election rules prohibited certain non-Teamsters, such as employers, from donating money to Teamsters campaigns, it allowed other outsiders to contribute. Outside donors were the conduits through which the Carey campaign laundered hundreds of thousands of dollars from the IBT treasury into Carey's campaign coffers. In hindsight, the election rules' failure to prohibit campaign contributions from all non-Teamsters created a serious corruption hazard.

8

The 1998 Rerun Election and the Emerging Dominance of James P. Hoffa

The sinister forces of corruption have again found a way to hamper the IBT's progress toward a democratic union. An honest, fair and informed [rerun] election is of paramount importance as this union continues on its path to rid itself of the remains of corruption and deceit.[1]   —Judge David Edelstein, September 29, 1997

The Teamster members have spoken. This victory today is a victory for the 1.4 million members of the Teamsters Union. The Hoffa Unity Slate has won this [1998 rerun] election. . . . Despite wild and baseless charges by my political opponents, here I stand today duly elected the general president of the Teamsters Union.
                    —James P. Hoffa, remarks at the National Press Club,
                                                  December 12, 1998

The question that everybody, Members of the Committee, the U.S. Attorney, the FBI, the Department of Justice, would like to ask is are the Teamsters serious about the [Hoffa administration's] anti-corruption program [Project RISE]? Are they serious about protecting the membership from exploitation by racketeers? I am here to tell you that for 6 months I have been working full time on this project. The answer is absolutely, unqualifiedly yes. Without hesitation I can tell you that Jim Hoffa is committed to this effort without any reservation.
              —Edwin Stier, special counsel to Project RISE, testimony
         before the House Committee on Education and the Workforce,
       Subcommittee on Oversight and Investigations, March 28, 2000

On August 21, 1997, the same day EO Quindel nullified the 1996 election, she submitted a proposed rerun-election plan to Judge Edelstein. Candidates who had received 5 percent of the delegates' votes at the 1996 convention would automatically be placed on the 1998 general-election ballot. The 1996 convention delegates could also make supplemental mail-in nominations, but the 5 percent criterion was still applicable. Candidates who were members of slates in the invalidated 1996 election could not switch slates in the rerun election.

Aiming to further level the election playing field, the rules for the 1998 rerun election included campaign contribution caps. Candidates themselves could contribute no more than $5,000 to their own campaigns; other Teamsters could contribute no more than $1,000 in total to all candidates.[2] Not surprisingly, given the 1996 campaign contribution-swap schemes, the rerun election rules prohibited *all* non-Teamsters from contributing to candidates' campaigns. The rules also beefed up campaign-contribution reporting requirements. Candidates and slates would have to report all contributions, disclose the names of their vendors and contractors, and submit more frequent campaign contribution and expenditure reports to the EO's office. To limit the advantage that extensive *Teamster Magazine* coverage provides incumbents, the magazine would have to suspend regular publication eight weeks before balloting. It would also have to publish a special issue carrying, for no charge, candidates' battle pages.

After Quindel's resignation became effective at the end of September 1997, Judge Edelstein appointed Michael Cherkasky, a former NYC prosecutor and CEO of an international private investigations firm, to serve as EO for the 1998 rerun election. Edelstein acceded to Cherkasky's request that the election be put off until Cherkasky finished investigating possible Hoffa-slate 1996 campaign-finance violations.[3]

In April 1998, Cherkasky announced that the 1996 Hoffa campaign had committed several violations.[4] First, two vendors improperly contributed over $167,000 to the Hoffa campaign by grossly underbilling for their work. Second, the Hoffa campaign failed to report $44,000 in cash contributions. Third, a Hoffa-slate vice presidential candidate, Thomas O'Donnell, concealed the employment of an ex-felon. (The IRB later recommended that the IBT charge O'Donnell with filing false campaign contribution and expenditure reports. Finding the IBT's response to that recommendation inadequate, the IRB convened a de novo hearing at which it found O'Donnell culpable and imposed a nine-month suspension from the IBT.)[5] Despite these violations, Cherkasky did not disqualify Hoffa from the rerun election because his violations lacked the "hallmarks" that had resulted in Ron Carey's disqualification: personal knowledge, intentional misconduct, and abuse of official authority. Instead, he fined the Hoffa slate 10 percent of the improper contributions and barred the underbilling vendors from contracting with any IBT candidate's campaign or independent election committee.[6] Judge Edelstein called the Hoffa campaign's violations a "deliberate attempt to mislead the IBT members"[7] but affirmed Cherkasky's decision because the EO's "primary role is not to punish election misconduct, but to protect the election process from the effect of misconduct."[8] He did, however, increase the Hoffa slate's fine to $167,000, the full amount of the vendors' illegal campaign contributions.[9]

The Controversy over Financing the 1998 Rerun Election

The question of who would pay the cost of supervising the 1998 election generated heated controversy. DOJ argued that the IBT should bear the expense.[10] Objecting, the IBT insisted that the government should pay since the 1998 election would be a rerun of the 1996 election, the expense for which DOJ was responsible.[11] Judge Edelstein held that "[t]he time has come when the IBT must bear its own costs for cleansing its Augean stable. In plainer words, they made the mess. It is their job to clean it up at any price."[12] A divided Second Circuit Court of Appeals panel reversed, holding that the IBT should not have to bear the expense because it was the victim, not the perpetrator, of the Carey campaign's embezzlement and illegal campaign swaps: "If the government chooses to supervise the 1996 election, of which the rerun is conceded to be a part, the government must bear the cost."[13]

This ruling caused major uncertainty. There was no guarantee that Congress would appropriate the necessary funds. Indeed, because of the millions of taxpayer dollars wasted on the invalidated 1996 election, Congress added to the 1998 Department of Justice Appropriations Act and the 1998 Department of Labor Appropriations Act prohibitions on DOJ and DOL using funds to supervise an IBT rerun election.[14] A subsequent appropriations bill required the IBT to reimburse the government for any taxpayer money an EO might spend on supervising a 1998 election.[15] Senator Judd Gregg (R-N.H.), chairman of the Senate appropriations panel that determined DOJ's budget, rhetorically asked, "Why should the taxpayers of this country be asked to pay for the cost of overseeing a union election? It is inconceivable. It is inappropriate. It makes no sense."[16]

By the summer of 1998, with the dispute over funding the rerun election still unresolved, Cherkasky used the approximately $1 million in restitution from the three Carey-campaign defendants (Nash, Davis, and Ansara) and the November Group to cover the cost of soliciting supplemental nominations and counting the nominations' mail ballots. However, Cherkasky lacked sufficient funds to print and mail 1.4 million general-election ballots, rent office space for counting those ballots, or compensate five hundred temporary election-office employees. By the end of June, with just $750,000 remaining,[17] he asked Judge Edelstein to order either the government or the IBT to provide the necessary funds.[18]

Representative Peter Hoekstra (R-Mich.), chairman of the House Subcommittee on Oversight and Investigations, adamantly opposed using taxpayer money to supervise another IBT election. At a June 16, 1998 subcommittee hearing, he said, "I do not see any way in which this Congress can or should ask the American people, the taxpayers, to bail out this union leadership one more time."[19] Representative Patsy Mink (D-Hawaii), the ranking Democrat on Hoekstra's committee, warned, "To allow this one to go forward without any supervision is really chancing it, and the Republicans will have to bear responsibility if anything goes wrong."[20] In early August, Hoekstra and the IBT agreed to a compromise.[21] The government would give the IBT $4 million to reimburse the union for IRB-related expenses, rather than for election expenses. In turn, the IBT would contribute an equal amount to the EO's rerun-election budget.[22] This formalistic solution allowed Hoekstra to claim that Congress would not use taxpayer money to pay for supervision of the rerun election.

The IBT initially agreed to contribute between $2 million and $3 million to supervise the rerun. However, at the last minute, it reneged, pointing to the Second Circuit Court of Appeals' decision that had labeled the IBT the victim of the 1996 election debacle. An infuriated eighty-eight-year-old Judge Edelstein said that, if he could, he would hold everyone involved in contempt of court. He ordered the GEB, by September 4, 2008, to vote up or down on whether the IBT would help fund the 1998 election supervision.

On August 30, five days before Edelstein's deadline, the GEB voted to allocate $2 million to the rerun election.[23] When added to the government's $4 million contribution, Cherkasky would have $6 million to conduct an election that he estimated would cost $8.6 million. (The EOs spent between

$17 million and $20 million on each of the 1991 and 1996 elections. However, for the 1998 election, Cherkasky would not have to allocate money for delegate elections or a convention.) He started up the election machinery.

The Candidates and Their Campaigns

Both Tom Leedham, head of the IBT's 250,000-member Warehouse Division and TDU's endorsed candidate, and John Metz, head of the IBT's Public Employees Division and president of St. Louis IBT Joint Council 13, obtained the necessary number of delegates' votes to earn places on the general-election ballot. Hoffa's eligibility was guaranteed by dint of his nomination at the 1996 convention.*

Leedham claimed the reformer's mantle. He promised to carry on Carey's legacy, observing that Carey "rooted out the mob from the union," and to continue implementing the goals of the *U.S. v. IBT* consent decree.[24] "We want to carry through with the reforms, but we think reform has to come a lot faster and go a lot further."[25]

Hoffa also called himself a reformer and anticorruption candidate. However, the corruption he denounced was Ron Carey's, not LCN's. At every opportunity, he linked Leedham to the "corrupt Carey." He promised to establish an "FBI-caliber independent ethics committee" to replace the Carey administration's EPC.[26] Hoffa was, by far, the most successful fundraiser, raising twenty times more money than Leedham, who was late in entering the time-compressed 1998 rerun election and had little time to fundraise.[27] Metz raised even less money than Leedham.

Metz also stressed his anticorruption commitment. He sought to link Hoffa to the IBT's racketeering history, accusing him of associating with mobsters and corrupt Teamsters. One Metz campaign ad in *Teamster Magazine* attacked Hoffa's lack of experience as a working Teamster by

---

* Ron Carey and TDU initially endorsed general presidential candidate Ken Hall, head of the IBT's 220,000-member Small Package Division. Hall had worked closely with Ron Carey on the successful 1997 strike against UPS. However, six weeks after announcing his candidacy, citing a serious eye condition, Hall withdrew from the race. (In the 2001 and 2006 elections, Hall successfully ran as a vice presidential candidate on the Hoffa slate. In the 2011 election, Hall is running for general secretary-treasurer on Hoffa's slate.) Steven Greenhouse, *Teamsters Group Backs Reform Candidate for Union's President*, NEW YORK TIMES, Apr. 9, 1998, at A23; Kenneth C. Crowe, *Carey Backing Hall to Head Teamsters*, NEWSDAY, Apr. 6, 1998, at A22. Sam Theodus, who in 1996 had defected from Carey's slate to run as an international vice president on Hoffa's slate, also sought a place on the 1998 rerun-election ballot, but failed to obtain enough delegate-nominating votes.

depicting him as a person "Wanted for Impersonating a Union Official."[28] Metz received endorsements from several powerful east coast Teamsters leaders, including John Morris, the Pennsylvania Conference of Teamsters president and a vice presidential candidate on Metz's slate. The integrity of Metz's slate was undermined by EO Cherkasky's findings that Tom Sever, the general secretary-treasurer candidate on Metz's slate (and the IBT's acting general president following Carey's expulsion), had retaliated against several international officers who refused to endorse Metz.[29]

The 1998 Election Result

A total of 365,000 Teamsters mailed in their ballots in the rerun election. Hoffa received 55 percent of the vote, Leedham 39 percent, and Metz 6 percent.[30] In the southern region, the margin between the first- and second-place candidates was 1,003 votes out of nearly 28,000; in the western region, the margin was 5,241 out of approximately 68,000; and in Canada, Hoffa's margin of victory was 1,772 votes. It was a convincing, if not overwhelming, victory for Hoffa and his slate.

Cherkasky resolved over four hundred election protests alleging misuse of union resources, campaign-finance violations, and ineligible voters. The highest-profile election protest involved an allegation that J.D. Potter, who successfully ran for international vice president on Hoffa's slate, had contributed $10,000 (double the permissible maximum) to Hoffa's campaign. The EO and IRB confirmed this violation and also that Potter had testified falsely to conceal it. Consequently, Cherkasky refused to certify Potter's election and ordered a rerun of the rerun election for the southern region's international vice presidency. Another Hoffa supporter was elected.

Some of the media that reported the rerun election results linked Hoffa's victory to his father's notoriety. The *Chicago Tribune* stated that Jim Hoffa "owes his election as president of the International Brotherhood of Teamsters largely to the fact that he is Jimmy Hoffa's son. After all these years, the Hoffa name is still legendary in labor circles."[31] The *Baltimore Sun* commented, "Hoffa will do his surname and his union a favor by ending what his late father began. . . . To escape the public's distrust and federal oversight of his union, Mr. Hoffa must prove convincingly that the union has freed itself of all links to organized crime."[32] The *New York Times* predicted that Hoffa's victory would "make him one of the United States' most prominent and powerful union leaders."[33]

Hoffa's Anticorruption Agenda: Project RISE*

Jim Hoffa took office promising to combat corruption and racketeering: "The mob killed my father. They're never going to come back to this union."[34] He also reiterated his campaign pledge to obtain termination of the consent decree.[35] Toward that end, in July 1999, he announced the establishment of Project RISE (respect, integrity, strength, and ethics), an anticorruption initiative designed to persuade DOJ and Judge Edelstein that the IBT could and would police itself, thereby rendering the IRB unnecessary.[36]

To lead Project RISE, Hoffa appointed Edwin Stier, formerly chief of the criminal division of the U.S. attorney's office in New Jersey and subsequently director of the New Jersey Division of Criminal Justice. As the court-appointed trustee in *U.S. v. IBT Local 560*, Stier had succeeded, over the course of twelve years, in reforming one of the most organized-crime-ridden union locals in the country.[37] On July 28, 1999, the GEB formally approved Project RISE[38] and praised Stier's capacity to "assist the IBT in assuring that it is fully capable of protecting its membership and the public from exploitation of the union by organized crime and corrupt officials."[39] IBT General Counsel Patrick J. Szymanski sent a letter to the chief of the FBI's Organized Crime and Drug Operations Section stating that the IBT's leaders were "personally and irrevocably dedicated" to ridding the union of "any remaining vestiges" of organized crime.[40] Stier put his reputation behind RISE, insisting that Jim Hoffa and the other GEB members were "committed to running a clean union."[41] He called RISE "fundamentally different" from anything that any union had attempted in the past.[42] "We're trying to create a culture in which the union itself will purge all effects of organized crime."[43]

Stier pursued three strategies. First, he and Hoffa appointed a task force of local IBT officers to draft an ethics code and enforcement mechanism that would provide the legal basis and organizational machinery for investigating and adjudicating IBT disciplinary violations. He and Hoffa hoped that a credible ethics code and effective enforcement mechanism would persuade the U.S. attorney that the IRB could be phased out. Stier chose Harris Hartz, formerly a New Mexico Supreme Court judge and, before that, head of the New Mexico Organized Crime Prevention Task Force, to

---

* This section draws on James B. Jacobs & Ryan P. Alford, *The Teamsters' Rocky Road to Recovery: The Demise of Project RISE*, 9 Trends in Organized Crime 15 (2005).

chair the drafting committee.[44] Hoffa appointed twenty-two local IBT officials, balanced by geography, race, and gender, as committee members.[45] One was a prominent TDU member.

Project RISE's second prong was a comprehensive investigation of organized crime's influence in the IBT. To lead that investigation, Stier hired James Kossler, a retired FBI agent who was previously in charge of the FBI's NYC office's organized-crime-control unit. Kossler employed retired FBI agents to investigate possible organized-crime influences in every IBT local that had ever been the subject of allegations of Cosa Nostra infiltration.

Third, Stier assigned his law-firm partner, former New Jersey Deputy Attorney General Howard Anderson, to research and write a history of the IBT's relationship with Cosa Nostra. This history would, in part, aim to persuade the U.S. attorney that the forces that had previously facilitated and sustained LCN's infiltration and exploitation of the IBT were no longer operating. Finally, Stier appointed an eleven-member advisory board of professors* and former prosecutors to monitor Project RISE's initiatives and make suggestions.[46]

Some observers were skeptical of RISE. *New York Times* labor journalist Steven Greenhouse reported that "some labor relations experts question whether Mr. Hoffa might be appointing Mr. Stier less to clean up the union than to impress the Government with his plan to put in place his own anti-corruption program" in order to persuade DOJ to agree to dismantle the IRB.[47] AUD founder Herman Benson declared that "for Hoffa, the RISE program was obviously not intended to implement an anti-corruption program, but only to serve as a public relations ploy to get the government out."[48] Ron Teninty, the only TDU member on the ethics-code drafting committee, stated, "[T]he purpose of RISE is geared more toward getting the government out of our union than it is toward changing its culture and integrity."[49] Richard Hurd, a Cornell University professor of labor relations, asked (presciently, as it turned out) "whether Mr. Hoffa might someday fire Mr. Stier, the way President Richard M. Nixon once fired special prosecutor Archibald Cox, if Mr. Stier's anti-corruption mechanism targets Mr. Hoffa or his close allies."[50]

On March 28, 2000, the House Subcommittee on Oversight and Investigations held a hearing on Project RISE. IBT General President Jim Hoffa, IBT General Counsel Pat Szymanski, and Edwin Stier all vouched for its bona fides. Calling RISE "tremendously ambitious," Hoffa promised that

---

* One of this book's authors, James Jacobs, served on this advisory board.

it would keep the union free of improper outside influences. He praised Stier as "a man who was very successful in making sure that our Teamster Local 560 came out of trusteeship, [and he] is going to help us do the very same thing with regard to the International Brotherhood of Teamsters."[51] Stier told the subcommittee that he was "extraordinarily impressed by the honesty and commitment of Mr. Hoffa [and] the other officers of the International Union . . . who have contributed so much to this effort" and that he was confident RISE would be successful. Moreover, he promised to quit if he came to doubt the Hoffa administration's commitment to eradicating corruption.[52] Subcommittee Chairman Hoekstra concluded that "the new leadership in the IBT seems to be doing its part to prevent a recurrence of [organized crime in the union]."[53]

The Ethics Code and Enforcement Machinery

The ethics-code drafting committee met nine times between June 2000 and March 2001.[54] Harris Hartz did the actual drafting; the committee members debated, amended, and voted on each provision. Various RISE advisory board members attended some or all of the meetings. Each draft was sent to the IRB and to the U.S. attorney for review and comment. On its face, the code-drafting process was an impressive exercise in participatory union democracy. However, TDU's leaders suspected that, behind the scenes, high-ranking IBT officials were influencing some committee members. Support for that suspicion surfaced at the last drafting session, held in Dallas, Texas, on May 5, 2001, when the IBT's general counsel, who had not previously attended any drafting sessions or provided comments on any drafts, brought to the committee table an alternative draft of the entire ethics code. Without protest or dissent, the committee put aside months of work to examine this new proposal. When the advisory board members strenuously protested, the IBT general counsel withdrew the substitute draft.

The final draft was a twenty-thousand-word document consisting of an introductory section containing a preamble and affirmation of "Teamster core values"; a section on the basic principles underlying the code; and three substantive chapters devoted, respectively, to fiduciary duties, democratic practices, and compliance and enforcement. The preamble stated that the code's purpose was "to keep organized crime and other forms of corruption out of the union" and that violation of the code's rules constituted a disciplinary offense punishable by a range of sanctions, including expulsion from the union.[55] The code's substantive chapters set out governing procedures for IBT locals, defined IBT officers' fiduciary duties, and proscribed ethical violations.[56] Some of the code's provisions tracked federal labor law. For example, like the Taft-Hartley Act, the code prohibited sham contracts,[57] kickbacks,[58] and loans and gifts of union property.[59] Like ERISA, the code prohibited benefit-plan fraud.[60] Like the LMRDA, the code required union officers to use union money and property solely for the benefit of union members.

The code's most controversial provision granted the GEB ultimate authority to decide whether to impose discipline and, if so, to determine the sanction.[61] AUD's Herman Benson called the absence of an independent enforcement body a "fatal flaw":

> Despite its hope chest of good intentions and its endorsement of a motherhood code of morality, the program depends for enforcement on the Hoffa machine itself. Hoffa and his general executive board exercise veto power over the selection of all enforcement personnel, who can only advise and propose while Hoffa disposes; for he and his board retain the authority to ignore the findings and recommendations of the very trial bodies they have dominated.[62]

TDU dismissed the code because it "pretends to give members rights they already have in law or through our court victories"[63] and is "entirely silent" about local-union elections, "perfunctory" with respect to free speech rights, and "narrow" with respect to officers' fiduciary duties.[64] TDU added that the code fails to specify penalties for intentional, reckless, or willful misconduct and does not treat racial and gender discrimination as punishable.[65] TDU sharply criticized the absence of independent investigatory and adjudicatory machinery.[66] "The enforcement machinery is thus highly vulnerable to the coercive pressures of members who are targets of investigations . . . who hold positions of power within the Union, and may therefore retaliate against hearing panel members, investigatory staff, and ethics officers upon expiration of their terms."[67] Ron Teninty said,

> The culture of our union will not change as a result of the code. Almost all of the code, thus far, existed in one form or another prior to government intervention. . . . The majority of the [code-drafting] task-force members rejected proposals to include rules related to use of members' money for excessive and multiple salaries, pensions and perks. The same

for nepotism, elected stewards, elected bargaining committees and secret-ballot votes on mergers of local unions.[68]

General President Hoffa reneged on his promise to submit the final draft of the ethics code to the IBT membership for approval.[69] Instead, he asked the GEB to approve a code-adoption process. The GEB resolved that the proposed code should not be adopted until the IRB was terminated. At the 2001 IBT convention, the delegates approved that resolution.[70] (Stier continued to press for the code's adoption until he resigned.)

Investigating Cosa Nostra's Influence over IBT Locals and Joint Councils

James Kossler's team investigated eighty IBT locals that LCN had allegedly infiltrated or influenced at any point in the past and presented the findings in two reports, one public and the other confidential. The public report sorted the eighty locals into three categories. Category A consisted of forty-nine locals "where there is no demonstrable [current] evidence of organized crime or influence, and where present conditions suggest that infiltration by organized crime will be highly unlikely." Category B consisted of sixteen locals judged to have had no remaining organized-crime presence or influence, but which nevertheless "warrant increased vigilance because these conditions could develop into an environment hospitable to continued efforts by organized crime to gain control or influence." Category C consisted of fifteen locals "where there is demonstrable evidence of suspected organized crime control, influence, or presence, evidence of criminal conduct, or an ongoing [organized-crime-related] IBT [i.e., Project RISE] investigation."[71]

Stier believed it to be essential for Project RISE (as the IBT's disciplinary unit) to prove its capacity to conduct disciplinary investigations. Consequently, Kossler initiated investigations of several locals not already under scrutiny by the IRB, the FBI, or DOL. In 2001, he uncovered LCN activity in several locals. For example, he identified a member of Queens, New York IBT Local 295 as a Lucchese crime family soldier. Stier passed this information on to the IRB, which subsequently brought disciplinary charges that led to the individual's resignation. Kossler also identified LCN-connected pension-fund embezzlement in Miami IBT Local 390 and LCN-connected bribery of local Philadelphia government officials by IBT Local 107 officers. Additionally, he and his staff uncovered contacts between a Genovese crime family member and International Vice President Donato DeSanti (who also served as president of North Brunswick, New Jersey IBT Local 701).[72] Based on this evidence, the Hoffa administration charged DeSanti with bringing reproach upon the union.[73] DeSanti agreed to expulsion from the union.[74]

Project RISE's Report on the History of LCN Influence in the IBT

RISE's history of LCN's infiltration and exploitation of the IBT was presented in a 641-page report, *The Teamsters: Perception and Reality: An Investigative Study of Organized Crime Influence in the Union*. Its thesis was that the factors that had facilitated labor racketeering in the early years of the IBT—employees' need for "muscle" to defend against company thugs, powerful organized-crime families operating across the United States, the absence of significant law-enforcement opposition to organized crime, the decentralized organization of the union—had substantially changed. Stier and Anderson concluded that the current leaders of the union were firmly committed to opposing racketeering.

The report made no secret of its ambition to persuade DOJ and the court to terminate the consent decree:

> There are several reasons why it is important to address the reality underlying the longstanding perception that the Teamsters have been and still are controlled by organized crime. First, since the early 1980s, alleged organized crime domination of the Teamsters has been used to justify placing certain Teamster locals under government-supervised trusteeships and, beginning in 1989, subjecting the entire IBT to a government monitoring program. This report, it is hoped, will help the appropriate law enforcement agencies, as well as interested members of the public and their elected representatives, determine whether and to what extent such monitoring is currently necessary.
>
> Second, in 1999, shortly after James P. Hoffa became the president of the International Brotherhood of Teamsters, the Teamsters embarked upon Project RISE, an ambitious program of internal reform study and reform designed to root out and prevent recurrence of any racketeer infiltration of the union. Understanding the nature and history of the Teamsters' relationship with organized crime and the actual mechanisms used by racketeers to infiltrate the union is an integral part of the reform effort.

The most important reason for conducting the organized crime study and submitting this report, however, is to render an accounting to the 1.4 million Teamsters members who for more than a generation have been stereotyped by the union's organized crime legacy and by a one-sided public image that has been shaped almost entirely by outsiders. Beginning with the widely publicized McClellan Committee hearings of the late 1950s, congressional investigators, law enforcement agencies, and journalists covering Teamster-related scandals have been the chief contributors to the public record concerning Teamster involvement with organized crime.[75]

Perception and Reality emphasized the IBT's commitment to antiracketeering reforms and observed that Project RISE compared favorably with most U.S. corporations' internal compliance units.[76] It concluded that "the days of domination and significant infiltration of the Teamsters Union by organized crime are over. . . . Today's Teamsters are committed to keeping organized crime out of the union, . . . and vestiges of organized crime that remain have been identified and are under investigation."[77] Stier added that "the difference in the IBT between now and in the 1980's is absolutely dramatic; there's a 180 degree difference"[78] and that "[t]he study confirmed the vast improvement that had occurred even among the most mob-dominated locals highlighted in the government's 1988 civil RICO complaint."[79]

Perception and Reality offered four reasons for winding down the consent decree: twelve years of court-supervised enforcement of the consent decree had eliminated virtually all of the organized-crime activity that once flourished; DOJ's and the court's sustained involvement in the remediation is both costly and undemocratic; Project RISE has institutionalized the IBT's commitment to cultural change; and *U.S. v. IBT*'s final goal is to "return control of the Teamsters to the many honest men and women of the union."[80]

General President Hoffa praised the report "as showing that the Teamsters Union is winning the fight against organized crime influence": "I'm proud to say that this report shows that the Teamsters Union is clean. The mob will never again gain a foothold here."[81] Congressmen Hoekstra (R-Mich.) and Roemer (D-Ind.) called for termination of the consent decree: "It's time for the government oversight to go away. . . . I personally think significant progress has been made in terms of rooting out corruption in the Teamsters."[82]

Not everyone was persuaded. Ken Paff questioned the report's objectivity and criticized its omissions. "If you give someone [i.e., Anderson and

Stier] millions of dollars to write flattering things about you, they frequently do."[83] He noted that the report inadequately covered Hoffa Sr.'s corruption, failed to mention that the IRB had expelled Jim Hoffa's close friend and aide Michael Bane for testifying falsely about his organized-crime associations, and did not mention Hoffa's imposition of trusteeships on locals where insurgents had influence.[84] According to Paff, a culture of democracy and anticorruption was taking root in the IBT, but it was "despite the Hoffa administration, not because of it."[85]

The IRB: July 1996–July 2001

While Project RISE was striving to persuade DOJ and the court that the IRB was unnecessary, the IRB continued to investigate, prosecute, and adjudicate individual disciplinary cases and systemic corruption. By the time Hoffa took office as general president in early 1999, the IRB was midway through its second five-year term (July 1996–July 2001). During this period, the IRB recommended disciplinary charges against 188 Teamsters from fifty-five locals in forty-one U.S. and Canadian cities (see fig. 8.1).

FIGURE 8.1
IRB's Recommended Disciplinary Charges (1996–2001)

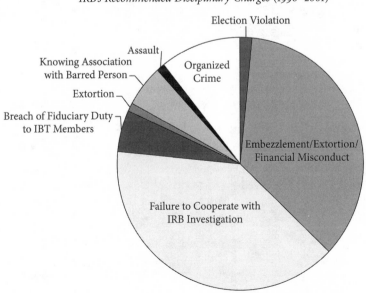

FIGURE 8.2

The IRB's Major Organized Crime Cases (1996–2001)

Member(s)	IBT Local	IRB-Recommended Charge	Disposition
Nicholas A. Nardi (Joint Council 41 president)	Cleveland Local 416	Knowing association with three Los Angeles LCN crime family members, including underboss Carmen Milano[a]	Resigned from the IBT (1998)
Peter DiFronzo (member)	Chicago Local 731	Membership in the Chicago Outfit (headed by his brother)[b]	Permanently resigned from the IBT (1998)
Vincent Fattizzi (father); Vincent Fattizzi (son); Dina Fattizzi	Valley Stream, NY Local 851	Knowing association with Anthony Razza, expelled from IBT membership on account of Lucchese crime family associations[c]	Resigned from the IBT (1999)
James Scognamiglio (steward); Richard Ciesla (member); Dennis Donahue (member); Andrew Gallina (steward)	Chicago Local 703	Knowing association with Chicago Outfit members[d]	Expelled from the IBT (2001)
Mark Houmis (member)	Pittsburgh Local 211	Refusing to answer IRB investigators' questions concerning his role in running Pittsburgh LCN family loan-sharking and gambling operations[e]	Expelled by the local's executive board (2000)
Patrick Green	Valley Stream, NY Local 295	Falsely testifying that he was not employed at a store owned by an associate of Vinnie Asaro, a Bonanno crime family capo[f]	General President Hoffa suspended Green from IBT membership for six months. After the IRB found this sanction inadequate, Hoffa increased the suspension to two years; the IRB approved (2001)[g]

[a] In the Matter of Nicholas Nardi, Affidavit and Agreement, March 31, 1998.
[b] In the Matter of Peter M. DiFronzo, Affidavit and Agreement, April 30, 1998.
[c] In the Matter of Vincent Fattizzi, Affidavit and Agreement, Nov. 11, 1999.
[d] Letters to Richard Ciesla, James Scognamiglio, Dennis Donahue, and Andrew Gallina, from IRB Administrator John Cronin, July 13, 2001.
[e] Before the executive board of Teamsters Local 211, Nov. 22, 2000.
[f] Before a panel appointed by the international union, Aug. 14, 2001.
[g] Id.

More than half of the disciplinary respondents belonged to NYC metro-area locals. The IRB rejected 25 percent of the IBT's disciplinary decisions, and, in half of those cases, the IBT failed to take adequate corrective action, thus precipitating de novo IRB disciplinary adjudications.

Organized-Crime Cases

In the IRB's second term, twenty-six respondents, including several high-ranking officials, were charged with LCN-related disciplinary violations. The IRB found two respondents to be LCN members, twelve to have knowingly associated with LCN members, and twelve to have knowingly associated with persons barred from the IBT on LCN-related charges. Seventy-five percent of the IRB's failure-to-cooperate cases also involved an organized-crime element (see fig. 8.2).

The IRB told Chief Judge Loretta Preska that it continued to observe "pervasive" influence of organized crime in certain locals.[86] For example, it reported the following disciplinary actions against Teamsters in Rahway, New Jersey IBT Local 522:

- Eleven members were charged with having LCN connections.
- The local's principal officer was expelled for knowingly associating with Lucchese crime family members, including capo Joseph DiNapoli and consigliere Steven Crea, and for hiring Lucchese family associates, including Crea's son-in-law.[87]
- The IBT expelled Crea's son-in-law, Local 522's only salaried trustee, for failing to appear for a sworn IRB examination.[88]
- Nine members were suspended, expelled, or forced to resign for failing to cooperate with IRB investigations into LCN influence.

Similarly, it reported the following disciplinary actions involving members of Youngstown, Ohio, Local 377:

- Five members were charged with LCN-related disciplinary offenses.
- Member Lawrence Garono was expelled for knowingly associating with Lenine Strollo, a member of the Pittsburgh LCN family. According to the FBI, Garono was "one of Strollo's principal associates in organized crime activities."[89]
- The IBT expelled the local's recording secretary for entering into a

FIGURE 8.3

The IRB's Disciplinary Charges against Top IBT Officials (1996–2001)

Officer	IRB-Recommended Charge	Disposition
Joseph Padellaro (international trustee)	Embezzling over $12,000 from twelve locals and two joint councils[a]	Resigned from the union (2000)
Lawrence Brennan (international representative and Detroit IBT Local 337 president)	Improperly using the local's money to promote his reelection campaign[b]	Hoffa dismissed charges against Brennan and refused to modify his decision. After a de novo hearing, the IRB found insufficient credible evidence to hold Brennan culpable (2000)[c]
J. D. Potter (Grapevine, TX IBT Local 19 principal officer)	Testifying falsely concerning the source of a contribution to Hoffa's reelection campaign[d]	Three-year suspension from IBT membership (2000)
Edward Mireles (Orange, CA IBT Local 952 secretary-treasurer and international vice president)	Establishing and implementing a practice designed to strip members who were local employees of their right to run for local office in return for their continued employment	Suspended seven years from holding IBT office; suspended four years from IBT membership (1998)
William Hogan, Jr. (president of Joint Council 25 and international representative); Dane Passo (international representative and special assistant to Hoffa)	Colluding with a labor broker to enter into a substandard contract to the detriment of Local 631 Teamsters working the Las Vegas trade show and convention industries	Expelled from IBT membership (2002)

[a] Joseph A. Padellaro, Affidavit and Agreement, April 4, 2000.
[b] *In re Charge against Larry Brennan*, Opinion and Decision of the Independent Review Board, May 31, 2001.
[c] *Id.*
[d] *In the Matter of J. D. Potter*, Affidavit and Agreement, Aug. 4, 2000.

sham collective-bargaining agreement with a company owned by Garono's wife. IRB investigators concluded that the agreement was "designed to allow Garono . . . to assist the company to gain access to union worksites."[90]

- Chief Construction Steward Anthony Antoun was expelled for knowingly associating with Garono, whom Antoun called a life-long friend.[91]
- Member Leo Connelly was expelled for knowingly associating with Strollo.[92]

Sanctioning the Top Leadership

The IRB brought disciplinary charges against high-level officials in both the Carey and Hoffa administrations. In addition to charging IBT General President Ron Carey and IBT Government Affairs Director William Hamilton, the IRB brought disciplinary charges against eleven other international officers and numerous local-union and joint-council officials (see fig. 8.3).

The IRB accused William Hogan, Jr. (head of the one-hundred-thousand-member Chicago IBT Joint Council 25, an international representative, and an officer in two Chicago locals) and Dane Passo (an international representative and a special assistant to Hoffa) of signing sweetheart deals with a labor-leasing firm (whose vice president was Hogan's brother) to pay Teamsters working at the 2001 IBT international convention wages below those that the IBT's contract with the convention required.[93] The company, allegedly in return, donated $5,100 to the James R. Hoffa Scholarship Fund.[94] AUD reported that when Las Vegas IBT Local 632 Principal Officer Tim Murphy refused to go along with this scam, Hoffa imposed an international-union trusteeship on Local 632.[95] The IRB expelled Hogan and Passo from the IBT.[96] Chief Judge Preska affirmed these sanctions.[97]

Trusteeships

During its second five-year term, the IRB recommended that the IBT impose trusteeships on fifteen locals and two joint councils in seven states. At least ten of these trusteed locals had histories of LCN influence. A number of locals, including some with organized-crime histories, were trusteed for financial misconduct or administrative abuses:

- Chicago IBT Local 714 was trusteed because the local's officers based job referrals on favoritism, knowingly associated with barred members, failed to monitor the local's finances, and had past associations with LCN figures.[98]
- East Meadow, New York IBT Local 239 was trusteed due to local officers' embezzlement from benefit funds by submitting false time sheets. The officers also issued unauthorized bonuses and failed to enforce collective-bargaining agreements.[99] The local had a long history of LCN influence.[100]
- Englewood Cliffs, New Jersey IBT Local 815 was trusteed because local officers engaged in a systematic pattern of financial mismanagement.[101] There were also careless financial practices, including signing blank checks, paying officers' salaries from accounts not subject to IBT audits, and paying trustees from the fund over which they supposedly exercised oversight.[102] In addition, Local 815 had entered into at least three sham collective-bargaining agreements.
- Indianapolis IBT Joint Council 69 was trusteed because officers diverted nearly $900,000 into a retirement plan established exclusively for their own benefit.[103] "The joint council was a nonfunctioning entity and had no need for money. It was merely a method to fund the [retirement] plan which itself was a second benefit for local officers and employees."[104]

Conclusion and Analysis

The Rerun Election

The need for a 1998 rerun election opened the door to congressional involvement in the *U.S. v. IBT* remediation. Once public money was requested, congressional oversight followed. This might have politicized and endangered the remediation. Had Congress and the IBT not reached a compromise on funding supervision of the rerun election, the election might not have occurred at all.

Congress's involvement in funding the rerun election highlights the thorny issue of how to pay for court-ordered reform of a private-sector organization. On the one hand, from the government's standpoint, it is both efficient and fair to require a corrupted organization to clean its own house.

Indeed, in signing the consent decree, the IBT agreed to bear the cost of remediation. On the other hand, the officers who signed the settlement, not the union's members, were responsible for the problems requiring remediation. These defendants would not be around to bear the costs of the remediation. Furthermore, they had a conflict of interest; concerned about their own financial liability, they had an incentive to make concessions on reforms the union would make and pay for. Thus, the IBT's members were victimized twice, first by the labor racketeers and second by millions of dollars in remediation costs.

This chapter again illuminates the critical importance of funding a nationwide campaign for IBT office. In response to the 1996 contribution-swap scandal, EO Quindel prohibited candidates for international IBT office from receiving campaign donations from non-Teamsters. However, this probably disadvantages insurgent candidates, who might be able to attract contributions from outside reformers and reform groups. The incumbent can count on donations from several thousand IBT officials. Although the imposition, in the 1998 election cycle, of a $1,000 cap on each rank and filer's contribution to candidates' campaigns dampens some of the incumbents' fundraising advantage, this does not necessarily enhance democracy. Capping voters' campaign donations in any type of election limits individuals' opportunities for political participation.

As for the 1998 election itself, while Hoffa won a clear victory, it is striking that Leedham obtained almost 40 percent of the votes, especially given Hoffa's magical name and the Leedham slate's late entrance into the race and lackluster fundraising. Unfortunately, there was no polling to reveal what influenced Teamsters voters and nonvoters. We know that only about one-quarter of eligible voters mailed back ballots. This underlines the difficulty of energizing union voters and reveals why well-organized and determined incumbents can maintain control even if they must win elections to do so.

Project RISE

Project RISE, like Carey's EPC, sought to prove to DOJ that government supervision of the union's disciplinary system was no longer necessary. By appointing Edwin Stier, a man with impeccable law-enforcement and anti-corruption credentials, to head Project RISE, Hoffa hoped to persuade both DOJ and Judge Edelstein that the IBT was willing and able to police itself.

Whether self-policing is desirable and achievable in an organization as large, politically centralized, and geographically diffuse as the IBT is an important question. The inherent risks of a self-policing IBT are that the individuals responsible for policing the union will be influenced by union officers who have authority over them and/or will use their disciplinary authority to protect their union friends and harm their union opponents. Creating a wholly internal monitoring and disciplinary apparatus that eliminates, or sufficiently mitigates, these risks seems like an impossible challenge. However, we are reminded that most organizations, public and private, essentially police themselves. Moreover, an external policing system (i.e., the IRB) also carries risks. Outside monitors may not have sufficient knowledge of and contacts within the monitored entity to effectively obtain investigative leads, evidence, and witness cooperation.

The establishment of Project RISE should count heavily in assessing Jim Hoffa's willingness to tackle corruption and racketeering in the IBT. Project RISE was much more professional, better staffed, and better funded than Carey's EPC. There is no doubt about Ed Stier's outstanding work in cleaning up IBT Local 560. Likewise, James Kossler had a sterling career in the FBI. Nevertheless, as we shall see in chapter 9, the implosion of Project RISE casts significant doubt on the bona fides of Hoffa's anticorruption and antiracketeering commitment.

9

The 2001 Election, the Demise of Project RISE, and the IRB's Third Term

In some ways, the Teamsters convention in Las Vegas at the end of June [2001] was a throwback. The huge majority of delegates voted for everything the [Hoffa] leadership proposed and against everything it opposed. As if it were a football game, they loudly cheered their team and booed their opponents.[1]
       —Randy Furst and Jim West, in *Labor Notes*, Aug. 1, 2001

General President Jim Hoffa . . . has backed away from the Teamsters' anti-corruption plan [Project RISE] in the face of pressure from a few self-interested individuals. Because the General President plays such a critical role in enforcing standards of conduct within the union, my position has now become untenable. I can no longer permit my presence in the union to act as an endorsement of his sincerity.
       —Edwin Stier, resignation letter to the GEB, April 28, 2004

The 2001 Election

The consent decree authorized DOL to supervise the 2001 IBT election. However, in February 2000, the IBT and DOJ asked Judge Edelstein to approve an agreement calling for an "election administrator" to supervise the convention-delegate elections, candidate nominations, and rank-and-file balloting.*[2] DOL's role would be limited to making recommendations. The

---

* The election "administrator" was meant to play the same role as the election "officer" in the previous three election cycles. Thus, for clarity of exposition, we will continue to refer to this election supervisor as the EO.

IBT agreed to contribute more than \$12 million to election supervision.[3] (The election ultimately cost approximately \$9 million.) Judge Edelstein reacted favorably to the joint proposal. He appointed Michigan labor lawyer William Wertheimer to serve as EO. Kenneth Conboy would continue as EAM.[4]

Edelstein approved election rules closely tracking the 1998 rules.[5] However, the campaign contribution limits were doubled so that candidates could donate \$10,000 to their own campaigns and members could donate up to \$2,000, in total, to one or more candidates. (TDU opposed these increases, arguing that they would favor Hoffa, who could count on maximum contributions from a significant percentage of IBT officials.) Virtually all convention-delegate candidates supported one of the slates of international-officer candidates. Only 30 percent of the 526 IBT locals had contested delegate elections (down from 48 percent in 1996 and 49 percent in 1998), not a sign of a politically invigorated rank and file.[6] After Judge Edelstein's death in August 2000,* Chief Judge Loretta Preska took over *U.S. v. IBT.*

The Campaigns

In the spring of 2000, Tom Leedham declared his candidacy for IBT general president. TDU enthusiastically supported him by, among other things, helping his campaign to obtain enough accreditation signatures to entitle him to free battle pages in *Teamster Magazine.* TDU published pro-Leedham articles; recruited Leedham-friendly Teamsters to run for local-delegate positions; produced pro-Leedham and anti-Hoffa campaign literature; monitored the Hoffa slate's campaign to identify potential election-rules violations; and urged TDU supporters to campaign for Leedham's slate at work sites, truck stops, and other Teamsters hubs. While Leedham did not identify himself as a TDU member (TDU keeps membership information confidential to protect its members against retaliation by IBT officials and employers), he openly welcomed its support.

---

* Judge David Edelstein died at age ninety. He had served as a federal district court judge for almost fifty years. His *New York Times* obituary, quoting U.S. Attorney Mary Jo White (SDNY), stated, "His work, in particular on the Teamsters litigation, will stand as an impressive legacy to his judicial courage and intellect." Herszenhorn, *David N. Edelstein, 90, Judge in Federal Court for 48 Years,* at B7.

Leedham recruited twenty-one candidates to join his Rank and File (R&F) Power Slate. (A full slate was twenty-six candidates.) The R&F slate received a boost in December 2000 when TDU member Dave Reynolds unseated Jon Rabine, the long-tenured president of Seattle IBT Local 763, an international vice president, a close Hoffa ally, and one of the most powerful Teamsters in the northwest. According to Ken Paff, this was the first time in IBT history that an insurgent candidate defeated an incumbent international vice president in the vice president's home local.

Leedham's campaign ads promised better contracts, better strike benefits, more rank-and-file participation in union governance, a $150,000 cap on officers' salaries, and greater accountability for pension-fund trustees. He also called for an IBT bill of rights guaranteeing Teamsters an opportunity to vote on local-union mergers and dissolutions and on the election of local business agents and stewards. Leedham condemned Hoffa for tolerating corruption and for centralizing the union at the expense of local-union autonomy and rank-and-file participation: "At every level of the union, [Hoffa's administration is] taking the members out of the process and leaving everything in the hands of officials and lawyers."[7] One Leedham campaign ad enumerated the following Hoffa failures:

1. Record Waste: More than 182 Teamster officials make more than $100,000 a year.
2. Multiple Salaries: Hoffa pays multiple salaries to 64 officials in exchange for their support in union elections.
3. Fake Reformer: Hoffa promised to limit his salary to $150,000. But when he took office, he raised it to $225,000.
4. Blind Eye to Corruption: Key Hoffa allies have been charged with embezzling funds . . . and lying about their association with organized crime. Hoffa has taken no punitive action.[8]

Leedham criticized Hoffa for failing to support rank-and-file efforts to obtain better contracts,[9] failing to support organizing drives,[10] suppressing dissidents by imposing trusteeships on locals where reformers showed strength,[11] supporting antilabor politicians,[12] and recruiting a slate of candidates without racial and gender diversity.

Leedham hammered away at Hoffa's failure to effectively confront corruption and racketeering. He reminded the electorate that, in late 2001, the IRB charged two of Hoffa's close associates, Joint Council 25 President William Hogan, Jr., and International Representative Dane Passo, with having colluded on a sweetheart contract for a labor-leasing firm and on having allowed that firm to staff the Las Vegas convention center with nonunion workers rather than Teamsters.[13] (The IBT, following the IRB's recommendations, later expelled Hogan and Passo from the union.) Leedham also highlighted the IRB's financial-misconduct charges against Detroit IBT Local 337 President Lawrence Brennan, Hoffa's mentor and former employer.[14] (However, the IRB found Brennan "not culpable.") Some Leedham supporters criticized Hoffa's decision to hold the IBT convention in Las Vegas, the physical and symbolic epicenter of the union's racketeer-ridden history.[15] In the 1970s and 1980s, organized-crime figures were a highly visible presence at the quinquennial international conventions held in Las Vegas.

Like Leedham, Hoffa called himself a prodemocracy, anticorruption reformer. He expressed support for the consent decree's election prong, promising that "[t]he Teamsters will be the standard against which all labor democracy will be measured."[16] He boasted that a *New York Times* editorial had praised Project RISE as the IBT's "most ambitious anti-corruption program in decades."[17] Tarring Leedham as a crony of the corrupt Carey administration, a Hoffa battle page in *Teamster Magazine* presented a Leedham caricature with "PHONY" printed in red letters across its chest. The accompanying text said,

> Tom Leedham was a leader and vice president in the Teamsters administration that:
>
> 1. Embezzled over $1 million of members' dues money for the purposes of getting re-elected.
> 2. Pushed the union to the edge of bankruptcy—spending nearly $1 billion in members' dues money.
> 3. Eliminated strike benefits for striking Teamsters from $200/week to $0.
> 4. Created a civil war in the Teamsters Union that made it weaker than it had ever been in history.
> 5. Gave away the right to strike in contract negotiations.*
> 6. Tried to triple the dues of Teamsters members.[18]

Another Hoffa ad criticized Leedham for failing to support Phoenix, Arizona IBT Local 104's October 2000 strike against Fred Meyer Warehouse.

---

* In 1994, Carey negotiated a national master freight agreement providing that IBT freight haulers could not strike in response to a deadlock over benefit-related grievances. Instead, such disputes would be referred to arbitration.

When Local 104's officers asked the leaders of Oregon Joint Council 37, including Leedham, to extend the strike into Oregon, where Fred Meyer Warehouse also operated, Leedham apparently decided not to sanction [the] picket line. According to Hoffa's ad, the strike captains complained that Leedham had "turned his back on the very members he now want[ed] to lead."[19] Other Hoffa ads called Leedham a scab for refusing to support Local 104's strike.

The Hoffa slate also accused Leedham of improperly accepting employer-paid travel. One Hoffa ad featured a cartoon depicting Leedham piloting a Northwest Airlines (NWA) plane with dollar bills flying out the back. The caption said, "This is Major Tom to Ground Control. . . . Can I at least keep all my frequent flyer points? (Travel illegally donated by Northwest Airlines)." The ad quotes from an EO opinion that found that Leedham and two members of his slate had traveled for free on NWA, "to support their election efforts in a manner forbidden by the rules."[20] (EO Wertheimer required Leedham to reimburse NWA for the cost of the free flights but imposed no additional sanctions because the violation was not "flagrant and knowing.")[21]

The June 2001 Las Vegas Convention

The Hoffa and Leedham slates held campaign rallies on the eve of the Las Vegas convention. Hoffa arrived at his rally in an eighteen-wheeler with horns sounding. The next day, Wertheimer ruled that Hoffa's use of the truck, owned by the Ohio Conference of Teamsters, constituted illegal use of union resources for campaign purposes. Hoffa and his delegates walked out of the convention hall when Wertheimer delivered a reprimand.[22]

Speaking to the delegates on the convention-hall floor, Hoffa called himself "the proud son of James R. Hoffa." He promised not to let "some bureaucrat in Washington or some random federal appointee" run the union. Some delegates booed when Leedham lambasted the Hoffa administration for "paying more multiple salaries than have ever been paid in the history of [the] union" and challenged Hoffa to a debate.[23] Many chanted or wore "TDU sucks" buttons.[24]

Hoffa's supporters ridiculed the delegates of IBT Local 2000, which represented NWA's flight attendants. In the lead-up to the 2001 election cycle, Local 2000's officers criticized the contracts negotiated by the Hoffa team. At the convention, delegates jeered and interrupted the Local 2000 speakers with sexist and antigay comments.[25] On one occasion, Hoffa him-self tried to calm his supporters: "Remember that what we do here, how we act, reflects on the reputation of this great union."[26]

By huge majorities, delegates voted for everything that Hoffa proposed, including removing from the IBT constitution the commitment to "rid our union of corruption."[27] Hoffa's slate insisted that pledge was now irrelevant because "corruption has been cleaned out of [the] international": "Our union today is one of the cleanest of any now on the labor scene. Organized crime has been eliminated. There are no people who have a connection with organized crime in the union today."[28] The delegates also endorsed Project RISE,[29] resolving that "the membership has clearly expressed the desire to implement the Teamsters' anti-corruption system [Project RISE] as a replacement for the Independent Review Board" and that the GEB "shall communicate to the U.S. Department of Justice the Union's deter-mination to end government oversight based on the principles of Project RISE."[30] Next, the convention delegates approved a "Self-Governance Res-olution" calling for dissolution of the consent decree.

> [T]he parties to the consent decree, the Union and the Government of the United States, have accomplished the objectives of the Consent Decree, . . . in view of the fact that the conditions that existed prior to the en-try of the Consent Decree no longer exist, there is no longer a legitimate basis for the United States Government to exercise the degree of control and influence over the internal affairs of this union as provided by the Consent Decree and . . . the Consent Decree [should] be dissolved under such terms as will protect the reforms adopted by the delegates to this Convention.[31]

The Hoffa delegates emphatically rejected Leedham's proposals to raise strike benefits and to cap officers' salaries at $150,000.[32] However, at Hoffa's urging, they added to the IBT constitution the consent decree's core elec-tion reforms: direct rank-and-file election of convention delegates and in-ternational officers.[33]

The convention delegates gave Hoffa 1,504 votes (93 percent). Leedham received just 134 votes (7 percent), enough to qualify him for the general election.[34] All twenty-five of Hoffa's running mates and fifteen of Leed-ham's running mates received enough votes to be placed on the general-election ballot. Hoffa spokesperson Richard Leebove called the convention a "huge success for the members" and dismissed TDU as "an obscure sect with very little support within the rank and file": "This appears to be a vanity campaign of Ken Paff and Tom Leedham."[35]

Entering the 2001 convention, Hoffa had already raised $700,000 in contributions.[36] Hoffa's fundraising advantage continued to grow in the months that followed. By the campaign's conclusion, he had raised $3,566,978, compared with Leedham's $340,255.[37] Much of Hoffa's money came from donations greater than $500 from local, regional, and international IBT officers. Most of Leedham's money came from small donations from rank and filers.[38]

The Presidential Debate

The 2001 election rules authorized the EO to "schedule and conduct International Officer candidate forums" and required the EO to "make every effort to schedule and conduct such forums at times and locations to insure broad participation by the membership either personally or by video or voice transmission."[39] Disappointed with low voter participation in the elections of 1991 (30.25 percent), 1996 (32.04 percent), and 1998 (28.64 percent), Wertheimer scheduled a one-hour presidential debate for September 21. He predicted that it would "energize the electorate."[40]

> The importance debate serves in self-governance cannot be overstated. Through debate, each candidate displays not only his particular ability to think critically on substantive issues, but of equal value, the candidates together demonstrate for the membership that an uninhibited, robust, wide-open exchange of views on issues important to them is not only encouraged but vital.[41]

Hoffa initially refused to debate, even though, during his 1996 campaign, he had proposed a constitutional amendment to compel presidential candidates to debate. Now that he was the incumbent and anticipated an easy victory over Leedham, he saw no advantage in debating. Wertheimer proposed to hold the debate with or without Hoffa and to mail a debate video to every Teamster. The Hoffa campaign viewed this proposal as an attempt to assist Leedham's candidacy.

> Your actions are deliberately designed to coerce Mr. Hoffa . . . into participating in the debate by threatening to spend $2 million in scarce Union funds to distribute a Leedham infomercial videotape if we refuse to

participate. . . . There is no difference, other than in amount, between this expenditure and the use of embezzled Union funds to assist the Carey slate in 1996.[42]

Ultimately, Hoffa agreed to engage in a debate at the National Press Club, where a panel of journalists would pose questions. Because the debate could energize the electorate only if widely viewed, Wertheimer committed $469,000 to produce and distribute five hundred thousand debate video-tapes. He would give the Hoffa and Leedham campaigns two hundred thousand copies each and distribute one hundred thousand copies among the 526 IBT locals. (Wertheimer originally planned to mail debate videotapes to every Teamster, but the prohibitive cost led him to abandon that idea.)

A few days before the scheduled debate, Hoffa notified Wertheimer that he could not participate due to pressing union business and that International Vice President Chuck Mack would stand in for him. At the ensuing Leedham-Mack debate, the first question posed to the debaters was whether government oversight over the IBT should cease. Mack said, "[T]here's no question it's time to end federal oversight of the Teamsters Union. That's an opinion shared by almost everybody. The government came into the Teamsters to get the mob out. The mob's gone." Leedham hedged, not wanting to endorse the Hoffa administration's anticorruption bona fides but also not wanting to embrace the IRB.

> Everyone wants the government out of the Teamsters. I believe that the best way to do it is to clean our own house and show that we can keep it clean. However, it's very difficult to say that the house is clean when, most recently, top aides [Hogan and Passo] of the Hoffa administration and Mr. Hoffa himself have been charged with some of the most egregious offenses. And as long as that kind of wrongdoing occurs, it's very difficult to say that that job has been accomplished. We have a RISE program that seems to be nothing more than a PR scheme and an opportunity for photos. RISE has held no hearings and made no charges. And yet it's held up as a reason for getting the IRB out of the union.

During the debate, Mack sought to link Leedham to "an IBT adminis-tration [the Carey administration] in which the general president was ex-pelled from the union and the government affairs director was convicted of a crime": "[T]hat Tom Leedham has not denounced those individu-als speaks volumes about the reform movement." For his part, Leedham stressed corruption in Hoffa's administration, "such as the charges against

Hoffa's former running mate Bill Hogan in Las Vegas where they tried to agree to sweetheart contracts and there were kickbacks involved. This also involved another one of his top aides Dane Passo."

In response to a question about why the Hoffa administration had, at the 2001 Teamsters convention, pushed to eliminate the IBT constitution's anticorruption commitment, Mack said, "We think that we have moved past that and have adopted a series of different constitutional changes and programs within the union that we think take us beyond the corruption path." Answering a question about whether the *U.S. v. IBT* consent decree had ever been necessary, Mack said,

> I think the consent decree was necessary and, over the years, we have seen the value of the consent decree. I think, however, that there is no question in anybody's mind that the mob is gone from the Teamsters Union. That's why the consent decree was put in place, . . . because the mob had supposedly and probably infiltrated this organization and was making decisions about . . . how the organization was run. That's been taken care of. That's been eliminated. It's now time to move on. The Hoffa administration is strongly supportive of getting the government out.

Immediately after the debate, the Hoffa campaign informed Wertheimer that it did not want and would not distribute any videotapes.

Preballoting Election Protests

EO Wertheimer and EAM Conboy resolved 549 preballoting election protests and 106 appeals. There were protests over candidates' eligibility, improper use of union resources, local officials' improper support for one candidate over another, voter intimidation, and campaign-finance violations. One preelection protest alleged that Hoffa's campaign used IBT fax machines to send out "Unity Slate Hoffagrams" in order to persuade local officers to collect accreditation signatures.[43] Wertheimer ruled that this violated the prohibition on using union resources in aid of any candidate for IBT office.[44] Consequently, he ordered Hoffa to disseminate an EO cease-and-desist order to all IBT entities. EAM Conboy affirmed because the campaigns "must maintain their headquarters, copying and fax machines, telephones and campaign mechanisms and structures in places that in no way are connected to or benefit from the resources of local unions and their memberships."[45]

The Hoffa slate filed another election protest in late 2000 alleging, among other things, that TDU had failed to disclose the names of non-Teamster contributors to its Teamster Rank and File Education and Legal Defense Foundation (TRF).[46] (Because the election rules prohibit candidates from receiving campaign contributions from non-Teamsters, TDU cannot use its TRF funds for election-related purposes.) EAM Conboy denied the Hoffa slate's request to compel TDU to release the names of its contributors to TRF, pointing to the election rule providing for

> limited disclosure to candidates from independent committee [campaign contribution and expenditure reports], but only to the extent that the identity of the contributors or their Local Unions not be revealed. With respect to contribution information reported by independent committees, only the total amount of contributions and total amount of contributors should be released to candidates.[47]

Conboy explained that the identities of both Teamster and non-Teamster contributors to independent committees, including TDU, are "not provided to any parties other than the Election Administrator and his staff."[48] He refused to distinguish TDU's election-related funds from its legal and accounting funds for purposes of disclosing contributors' identities: "Disclosure other than to the Election Administrator is barred in each instance."[49] Conboy added that his decision followed a 1992 Second Circuit Court of Appeals ruling that "TDU and TRF were not adequately represented by the IBT leadership with respect to the Consent Decree, and cannot be bound by its provisions. . . . [Thus, the EO lacked authority] as an officer of the district court . . . to compel TDU and TRF to disclose . . . the names of their supporters and associate[s]."[50]

Leedham filed a preelection protest charging that Hoffa supporters physically and psychologically intimidated delegates at the Las Vegas convention by blocking the hallway leading to the voting room.[51] At the time of that incident, Wertheimer ordered the hallway cleared, prompting a Hoffa-slate protest charging that he was biased in Leedham's favor.[52] Wertheimer recused himself from ruling on his own bias; a deputy EO sustained Leedham's protest and rejected Hoffa's. He ordered the Hoffa slate to cease and desist from voter intimidation and to mail to all Teamsters who attended the IBT convention a notice stating that the Hoffa slate "established a gauntlet . . . through which voters had to pass in order to vote."[53]

In another preelection protest, a Leedham-slate vice presidential candidate charged that the September 2000 issue of *Teamster Magazine* exhibited pro-Hoffa bias.[54] She pointed out that the magazine carried seven photographs of Hoffa, two Hoffa articles, several Hoffa quotations, and the Hoffa slate's slogan. By contrast, there was only one unidentified photograph of Leedham. Wertheimer rejected this protest, finding the magazine's reporting on Hoffa's activities reasonable because of the general president's involvement in union business.[55] Conboy affirmed.[56]

A Minneapolis IBT Local 320 preelection protest provides an excellent example of the importance of local officers' support for the incumbent. A Local 320 member complained that Hoffa's slate mailed to each Local 320 elected officer an invitation to a "gala celebration at the Minneapolis Convention Center . . . to meet [Hoffa] and hear his message of unity, pride, and strength for the Teamsters."[57] Several Local 320 officers attended the rally. Wertheimer ruled that Hoffa's mailing constituted improper solicitation of campaign contributions and that the local officers' attendance constituted improper endorsement.[58] Wertheimer required the Hoffa slate to disgorge the fruits of that fundraising event and to pay for a one-page Leedham-slate mailing to every member of Minnesota's thirteen IBT locals.[59] He also required Local 320's principal officer to include a letter stating that the gala invitation violated the election rules and that Local 320 does not endorse any candidate.[60]

The 2001 Election Results

Only 25 percent of eligible voters mailed in ballots. Hoffa's campaign attributed the low voter participation to "voter fatigue" from three general presidential elections in five years.[61] Leedham saw a deeper problem. "[T]eamster members have been locked out of participation in our union. It's not enough for Teamster leaders to ask members to vote once every five years. We have to dismantle the barriers to participation and get back to involving and mobilizing Teamster members—the real source of union power."[62]

Hoffa won 65 percent to 35 percent.[63] Leedham received 4 percent fewer votes than he received in the 1998 election. Nevertheless, in stark contrast to the minimal support (7 percent) convention delegates gave him, one in three rank-and-file voters preferred him to the incumbent general president. In the central region, Leedham received almost 40 percent of the votes.[64] In a postelection press release, Leedham said, "[W]e have succeeded in making democracy a reality in our union, not just a slogan. We gave Teamster members a choice."[65] The EO certified Hoffa's reelection on December 14, 2001.

The Demise of Project RISE *

After the election, Hoffa vowed to persuade DOJ and the district court that the IRB should be dissolved because the IBT could police itself. By early 2003, however, Ed Stier and James Kossler were increasingly frustrated by Hoffa's unwillingness to implement the RISE ethics code. Even more disturbing, they came to believe that regional IBT officers allied with the Hoffa administration were blocking RISE's investigations into LCN influence in several Chicago IBT locals and joint council.[66]

In April 2004, Stier released a report on organized crime's infiltration of several Chicago-area IBT locals.[67] Among other things, the report stated that

- John Coli, then president of Joint Council 25 and a trustee of Chicago IBT Local 727's pension and benefit funds, was the son of an Outfit member;
- the trustees of Local 727's health, pension, and welfare plan, including Coli, had received kickbacks, hired LCN associates, and contracted with LCN-controlled vendors for nearly a decade;
- Chicago IBT Local 726 officers had solicited bribes from rank and filers in exchange for job referrals;
- Chicago IBT Local 743 officers had improperly allowed Donald Peters (the former principal officer of the local and a named defendant in the 1988 civil RICO case) and Robert Simpson, Jr. (Peters's successor, whom the IRB had removed from office) to influence the local's affairs;
- an Outfit member had gained control over Chicago IBT Local 786's principal officer, subordinate officers, and major employers, and the principal officer of Local 330 regularly associated with Outfit figures.

The report further charged that, since early 2003, IBT officials with ties to the Outfit had been stonewalling RISE's investigations of LCN influence

---

* This section draws on James B. Jacobs & Ryan P. Alford, *The Teamsters' Rocky Road to Recovery: The Demise of Project RISE*, 9 TRENDS IN ORGANIZED CRIME 15 (2005).

in Chicago IBT locals. In July 2003, according to the report, Hoffa rejected Stier's recommendation to bring disciplinary charges against three Chicago Local 786 members.[68] Hoffa's executive assistant, Carlow Scalf, had allegedly vetoed corruption and racketeering charges against Chicago Locals 786 and 726. In September 2003, six informants, whom Stier called reliable, reported that the Outfit felt "its interests in Teamster matters were threatened by IBT investigative activities and ordered those activities shut down." Furthermore, in early 2004, Scalf allegedly "made repeated efforts to keep invoices for Chicago-related investigations from being paid for arbitrary reasons."[69] Soon afterward, Hoffa ordered Stier and Kossler to suspend their Chicago-area investigations. On April 1, 2004, the IBT transferred Project RISE's only full-time union staffer to another assignment.

Stier's Chicago report charged that the IBT's top leaders no longer supported Project RISE and would not "permit anti-racketeering investigations to threaten the most powerful remaining organized crime influences in the Union, which are centered in the Chicago area."[70] Moreover, "[i]f the current shutdown of IBT anti-racketeering efforts in Chicago is allowed to stand, the reason for it will be obvious to both Teamsters and outsiders: the continued influence of the Chicago Outfit and the culture of corruption that has flourished in that area for as long as the Union has."[71]

Responding for the union, General Counsel Patrick Szymanski insisted that the IBT leadership had not abandoned its commitment to fighting corruption and racketeering.[72] He called Stier's charges unfounded and self-serving[73] and ordered Stier and Kossler to discontinue their investigations.

On April 28, 2004, Ed Stier, James Kossler, nineteen of twenty RISE staffers, and the ten-member RISE advisory board resigned. In a letter to the GEB, Stier charged that General President Hoffa had paralyzed investigation into LCN influence in Chicago IBT locals, blocked investigation of kickbacks to officers of Houston, Texas IBT Local 988, and rejected RISE's recommendation to impose a trusteeship over Local 988.[74] He criticized Hoffa for failing to implement the RISE ethics code and for reneging on his public promise to identify and remove any hidden mob associates from the union. Stier asserted that there was "substantial reliable information that organized crime again threatens the union."[75] *New York Times* labor journalist Steven Greenhouse observed that Project RISE's collapse "could jeopardize the union's push to end federal oversight."[76]

IBT General Counsel Szymanski charged that Project RISE was redundant with the IRB and had become too expensive and intrusive on union autonomy. "It appears that Stier resigned because I wouldn't give him a blank check, even when the allegations he wanted to investigate were unfounded and outside [his] jurisdiction. . . . We think Ed is resigning because we're not letting him do whatever he wants to do."[77] Hoffa stated, "[T]he Teamsters Union regrets Stier's decision to resign, but rejects the reckless and false allegations he makes about our union's commitment to fighting the influence of organized crime."[78] He added that Stier resigned "because he did not want to answer legitimate questions about the credibility and significance of uncorroborated allegations he has made."[79]

On April 30, 2004, Hoffa hired Edward McDonald, former head of the federal Organized Crime Strike Force for the Eastern District of New York, to investigate Stier's allegations. A year later, McDonald presented to Hoffa a 183-page report (an abbreviated version of which was made public in July 2005) concluding that Stier's allegations were unreliable, confusing, and inconsistent. McDonald reiterated Syzmanski's explanation, i.e., that the IBT had become dissatisfied with Stier and Kossler's results given the $15 million spent on RISE. According to McDonald, "the Chicago investigations proposed by Stier Anderson were never 'shut down' in the first place"; "it is entirely unclear why [Stier and Kossler] ever accorded any weight to what the confidential sources had said and why they even repeated their allegations"; and "the IBT leadership, given its four year experience with Stier Anderson, had good reason to be dissatisfied with the firm's performance and in light of these reasons, they responded in a reasonable and responsible way to Stier Anderson's investigative proposals." Finally, McDonald asked why Stier's report, "with its inflammatory and poorly supported allegations, was ever released at all."

> We do not know what Stier Anderson's motives were when they presented their allegations and conclusions. Perhaps Stier Anderson honestly, but mistakenly, believed that the evidence that they presented in the April Report justified their explosive allegations. Perhaps they were trying to slow down discussions with the Southern District [U.S. attorney's office] with their charges and pressure the leadership into changing their minds and authorizing the investigations after all. Perhaps they acted out of spite. Or perhaps there were other reasons. Certainly, as we have demonstrated, there was no factual basis for concluding that the leadership had abandoned its commitment to reform or that Teamsters had improperly sabotaged the Stier Anderson investigations either at the direction of the Outfit or for some other reason.[80]

Stier and Kossler called McDonald's report "a one-sided, subjective, and adversarial presentation that amounts to an exercise in spin control."[81] They sought to impeach McDonald's conclusions by pointing out that McDonald never interviewed them or any RISE lawyer or investigator (other than the sole investigator who did not resign when RISE collapsed) and made no transcripts of the interviews he did conduct. These are "the hallmarks of a phony and contrived investigation," Stier later explained, calling the McDonald report an attempt "to cover up the corrupt activities of Teamsters officials that we were investigating. . . . It was a predetermined result—they intended to discredit me."[82]

The IRB Continues Its Investigations: July 2001–July 2006

RISE's collapse did not, of course, affect the IRB's investigations. In its third term (July 2001 to July 2006), the IRB recommended that the IBT bring charges against fifty-three Teamsters in twenty-four U.S. and Canadian locals (see fig. 9.1). The IRB recommended charges against nineteen

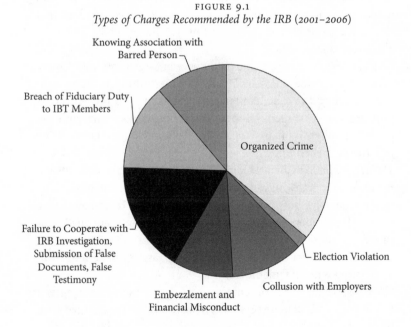

FIGURE 9.1
Types of Charges Recommended by the IRB (2001–2006)

Teamsters for knowing association with an LCN figure or refusal to testify about LCN contacts; nine for failure to cooperate with a non-LCN investigation; nine for embezzlement or other financial misconduct; six for collusion with employers; six for knowing association with a barred person; three for failing to investigate corruption; and one for improperly attempting to influence a union election. Nearly 60 percent of disciplinary respondents were members of NYC metro-area locals, and of these 22 percent were members of NYC Local 813.

Chicago Cases

In the years after RISE's demise, Stier and Kossler's allegations about organized crime's influence in Chicago locals were borne out. The IRB charged eleven members of Chicago-area IBT locals with disciplinary violations. Some were high-ranking officers:

- General President Hoffa's executive assistant, Carlow Scalf, whom Stier had identified as the Teamster most responsible for stifling RISE's investigations of LCN influence in Chicago IBT locals, agreed to a sixty-day suspension from union membership and a $69,000 fine in exchange for the IRB not recommending that the IBT charge him with submitting to the IBT false housing-allowance documents.[83]
- Chicago IBT Local 714 Principal Officer and Chicago Joint Council 25 Vice President Robert Hogan resigned from the union after the IRB alleged that he had failed to take action to prevent Local 714 Organizing Director Robert Riley from associating with expelled member William Hogan, Jr., Robert Hogan's father. (The IRB then expelled Riley.)
- The IBT expelled Chicago Joint Council 25 Vice President Joseph Bernstein for knowingly associating with expelled member William Hogan, Jr., but did not prohibit Bernstein from socializing with IBT members. The IRB found this sanction inadequate, but the IBT refused to modify it. The IRB then held a de novo hearing, expelled Bernstein from IBT membership, and forbade him from associating with IBT members.[84]
- Chicago IBT Local 705 organizer John Clancy resigned and agreed not to contact IBT members for ten years after being charged with having knowingly associated with expelled member Dane Passo.

- Finding that Chicago IBT Local 726's pension fund had entered into two ERISA-prohibited transactions totaling $125,000, the IRB barred the local's president and trustee from holding union office for three years; the local's secretary-treasurer permanently resigned his position.

The IRB also brought disciplinary charges against rank-and-file members of Chicago IBT locals:

- Local 714 members Sergio Salcedo and Donny Robles and Local 743 members Mark Jones and Cassandra Mosley were expelled for failing to appear for sworn examinations.
- Floyd Johnson, a member of Local 714, was charged with failing to cooperate with the IRB by failing to appear for a scheduled IRB deposition. He was ultimately found not culpable.

Organized-Crime Cases

More than one-third of the IRB's third-term disciplinary matters had an organized-crime connection; all but one of those respondents were expelled or resigned (see fig. 9.2). The IRB charged nineteen Teamsters with knowing association with an LCN figure or refusing to testify about LCN contacts. Several other Teamsters agreed to resign rather than face formal charges.

Sanctioning the Top Leadership

In its third term, the IRB recommended disciplinary charges against seven international officers (see fig. 9.3). One of the most serious cases involved Chuck Crawley, principal officer of Houston IBT Local 988 and an international representative. IRB investigators discovered that Crawley had asked a vendor to add $20,000 to a bid for installing telephone equipment at the local and then took a $20,000 kickback from the vendor.[85] Crawley had also instructed a local organizer to submit to the union an inflated invoice for purchases of T-shirts for members and then received a $2,500 kickback.[86] The IRB found him culpable and expelled him from the union. Chief Judge Preska and the Second Circuit affirmed. Subsequently, federal prosecutors convicted Crawley of mail fraud, embezzlement, and falsifying business records. He was sentenced to six and a half years in prison.[87]

FIGURE 9.2

Major IRB-Recommended Disciplinary Charges Involving Organized Crime (2001–2006)

Member(s)	IBT Local	IRB-Recommended Charge	Disposition
Michael Marchini (member)	NYC Local 813	Communicating with Matthew Iannello, acting boss of the Genovese crime family and principal officer of Rahway, NJ IBT Local 522	Expelled from the IBT (2001)[a]
Thomas Plino (member)	Union, NJ Local 97	Refusing to answer questions about ties to the Genovese crime family	Expelled from the IBT (2003)[b]
Robert D'Angelo (member)	NYC Local 813	Knowing association with Bonanno crime family capo Louis Restivo and Genovese crime family capo Frederico Giovanelli	Expelled from the IBT (2005)[c]
John Sperando (member)	Lake Success, NY Local 282	Knowing association with a member of organized crime	Resigned from the IBT before being formally charged (2002)
Anthony Sirabella (member)	NYC Local 813	Knowing association with an organized-crime member	Resigned from the IBT before being formally charged (2002)
Anthony Piccolo (member)	NYC Local 813	Knowing association with a member of organized crime	Resigned from the IBT before being formally charged (2003)

[a] Hearing before a panel appointed by the general president, May 13, 2002.
[b] Letter from IBT Joint Council 73 to IRB Administrator John J. Cronin, Jr., Jan. 7, 2003; letter from secretary-treasurer of IBT Local 97 to IRB Administrator John J. Cronin, Jr., Dec. 11, 2003.
[c] In re Charge against Robert D'Angelo, Opinion and Decision of the Independent Review Board, Oct. 19, 2006.

FIGURE 9.3

The IRB's Disciplinary Charges against Top IBT Officials (2002–2006)

Officer	IRB-Recommended Charge	Disposition
Edmund Burke (international representative)	Failing to take disciplinary action after a business agent in Las Vegas IBT Local 631 told Burke, the local's principal officer, that he had repeatedly communicated with barred member Dane Passo	Agreed not to hold any IBT office for two years and to terminate his membership in Local 631 (2006)[a]
Anthony Rumore (New York Joint Council 16 president)	Failing to investigate whether Barry Feinstein, an invited speaker at a Joint Council 16 event and former president of Joint Council 16, was a barred person	Suspended from the union for sixty days (2003)[b]
Anthony Rumore (New York Joint Council 16 president)	(1) Directing local employees to renovate his father's home and chauffeur his daughters to social events; (2) causing local employees to associate with a barred member; and (3) retaliating against members who refused to help pay for personal legal fees he incurred in his March 2003 disciplinary case	Expelled from the IBT (2004)[c]
John Kikes (president of Haywood, CA Local 78 and international representative)	Knowing association with a barred person	Expelled from the IBT (2005)

[a] In the Matter of Edmund Burke before the Independent Review Board, Affidavit and Agreement, July 17, 2006.
[b] United States v. Int'l Bhd. of Teamsters, 88 Civ. 4486, Application 105 of the Independent Review Board, In the Matter of Anthony Rumore, May 5, 2003.
[c] Hearing before a panel appointed by the general president, July 26, 2004.

Trusteeships

In the IRB's third term, it recommended that the IBT impose trusteeships on six locals. The union complied with all but one of those recommendations.

- The IRB recommended that the IBT trustee Cleveland, Ohio IBT
  Local 244 because "the entire local is not being run properly."[88]
  The IRB had previously charged the local's president with embezzling at least $3,000 from the union by increasing his salary 11.7
  percent in 1999 and 13.6 percent in 2000 without the local executive board's approval.[89] Hoffa placed the union under trusteeship.
- The IRB recommended that the IBT trustee Collingwood, New
  Jersey IBT Local 676 because an IRB investigation concluded that
  the local "was not being run for the benefit of the members."[90] In
  a two-page letter to the local's members, Hoffa explained that several local officers had committed "serious financial malpractices,"
  including using local-union credit cards for personal expenses
  and directing local employees to perform personal services for officers' family members.[91]
- The IRB recommended that the IBT trustee Elmsford, New York
  IBT Local 456 because President Bernard Boyle was running the
  local primarily for the benefit of his family.[92] Among other instances of favoritism and financial mismanagement, Doyle had
  paid for personal meals with a union credit card, instructed members to perform personal services at his home, and made job referrals arbitrarily.[93] Hoffa imposed an international-union trusteeship on Local 456 until the local's "ability to operate in accordance
  with applicable law and the IBT constitution is restored."[94]
- The IRB recommended that the IBT trustee Jamaica, New York
  IBT Local 522 because the local "has a long history of ties to . . . the
  Lucchese crime family.[95] Hoffa appointed a trustee in March 2003.
- The IRB recommended that the IBT trustee San Juan, Puerto Rico
  IBT Local 901. However, instead of appointing a trustee, the IBT
  trained the local's staff on proper accounting and record-keeping
  procedures. The IRB did not object to this remedy.[96]

Conclusion and Analysis

The 2001 Election

The federal prosecutors who negotiated the *U.S. v. IBT* settlement, persuaded by TDU's and AUD's arguments, hoped that free and fair rank-and-file elections would produce a corps of honest IBT officers. By the 2001 election cycle, there was no organized-crime-backed candidate or faction competing for international office. The EO did not have to exclude LCN-tainted candidates from running for office or nullify voting on account of LCN interference with the election. The relationship between the election prong of the *U.S. v. IBT* consent decree and organized-crime control had become attenuated. Of course, the guarantee of free and fair rank-and-file elections may well be necessary to prevent Cosa Nostra from influencing the selection of international officers in the future. However, the EO seemed to focus on ensuring that IBT elections were free and fair less to prevent Cosa Nostra's infiltration of the union and more to produce an exemplary election as an end in itself.

"Free and fair election" is not a self-defining term. For some union-democracy proponents (and sometimes, it seemed, for the EO), a free and fair election meant an election with a level playing field for insurgents and incumbents. Thus, the EO compelled the union to publish accredited candidates' battle pages in *Teamster Magazine*, capped members' campaign contributions, sought to mount a presidential debate, and sought to increase rank-and-file voting.

However, leveling the electoral playing field proved nearly impossible. Incumbents tend to enjoy huge advantages, especially in large constituencies, where candidates cannot make personal contact with more than a tiny percentage of voters. (On average, between 1964 and 2008, incumbent members of the House of Representatives won reelection 93 percent of the time, and incumbent U.S. senators won reelection 86 percent of the time.)[97] Name recognition, money, and patronage make a big difference. Indeed, Jim Hoffa enjoyed the support of the great majority of the nationwide corps of seven thousand local IBT officers, nearly every regional officer, and all GEB members. He raised ten times more money than Leedham, who faced an overwhelming challenge in getting his name and message to the far-flung IBT electorate. The cost of a single mailing to the more than 1.5 million union members exceeded Leedham's total campaign war chest.

Thus, Hoffa's victory surprised few. Chicago IBT Local 705 Stewards

Joe Allen and Donny Schraffenberger observed that "a Leedham victory was always a long shot" and that, because virtually every local-union officer supported Hoffa, "the full weight and resources of the union could be brought to the aid of Hoffa against Leedham."[98] Labor reporter Henry Phillips also noted that Hoffa had "all the benefits of incumbency, and the backing of a unified officialdom."[99]

The goal of *U.S. v. IBT* was to purge LCN influence from the IBT, not to make IBT elections exemplary, to increase rank-and-file voting, or to create a stable two-party system in the IBT. It would have been inappropriate for the EO to take a position on whether Tom Leedham's vision of the IBT was more democratic than Jim Hoffa's. Perhaps Leedham's leadership would have produced better processes and outcomes for the IBT, perhaps not. Without an LCN figure or faction to combat in the 2001 election, the EO's only objective should have been that the election proceed without intimidation or fraud.

The effort to level the electoral playing field frequently put the EO in the position of trying to reduce the advantages of the incumbent Hoffa administration. As EO Wertheimer commented in his final report to Chief Judge Preska, "Not once [during the election] when the interests of Hoffa and Leedham or TDU conflicted did the IBT side with Leedham or TDU. On virtually every occasion where a plausible (and at times implausible) institutional interest could be articulated in favor of Hoffa, it was."[100] Wertheimer also charged that the IBT's support for Hoffa was reflected in its attempted interference with the EO's hiring decisions:

> The parties gave themselves the right to approve election office hires. The government, while it did suggest one person, did not seek to assert this right. The IBT did and it did so after I made my hiring decisions. More troubling, in doing so, it was clear to me that it was not acting in its institutional interest, but rather in the political interest of its general president. The IBT backed off only in the face of a resignation threat. It will be important in the future to establish provisions that preserve the independence of whoever administers IBT elections.[101]

The Hoffa Administration's Anticorruption Commitment

Hoffa's Project RISE was far superior to Carey's EPC. Stier and Kossler, nationally respected and highly experienced investigators and corruption fighters, put their reputations behind the credibility of Hoffa's anticorruption commitment. As time passed, however, Hoffa's support for Project RISE proved to be conditional and strategic. He probably realized that implementing the ethics code and enforcement machinery would not result in termination of the IRB. The U.S. attorney would not agree to dissolve the IRB unless it was replaced by investigative and disciplinary machinery independent of the IBT, that is, a unit like the IRB. Unsurprisingly, the Hoffa administration would not approve that kind of independent disciplinary authority. Alternatively, a powerful Chicago faction may have pressured Hoffa to pull the plug on Project RISE.

Perhaps RISE could have survived had Stier enjoyed widespread rank-and-file support. He did not. Even TDU did not stand squarely behind him. While the Hoffa administration apparently concluded that Project RISE was too independent, TDU's leaders thought Project RISE was not independent enough. TDU's newsletter described Stier as "Hoffa's Project RISE director," "Hoffa's consultant," or the head of "a corporate law firm."[102] Stier reacted negatively, sometimes angrily, to these criticisms.[103]

Stier and Kossler's charges regarding the Hoffa administration's motives for killing Project RISE foreclosed any possibility that the U.S. attorney would agree to terminate the IRB. IBT General Counsel Szymanski stated, "You think the government's going to be anxious to go out right now and ink a deal with us? They're going to be reluctant."[104] Professor G. Robert Blakey, a member of the RISE advisory board, noted, "[W]e saw the promised land. Six months, we could have been out from under [federal oversight]. We just didn't make it."[105] Blakey's assessment seems dubious because over one-third of the IRB's third-term disciplinary cases involved LCN. In any event, as Jim Hoffa's second term and the IRB's third term concluded, the end of *U.S. v. IBT* was not in sight.

10

The 2006 Election, the IRB's Fourth Term, and the Lead-Up to the 2011 Election

On June 25 [2006] some 1,700 delegates and several hundred alternates will assemble at the Paris Hotel in Las Vegas for the 27th Convention of the Teamsters Union. The majority of these delegates will be there to rubber stamp whatever Hoffa proposes. Many see the convention as a chance to party on members' dues money. But hundreds of delegates will fight for changes to rebuild our union's power and strengthen members' rights—and history is on their side.[1]
—Teamsters for a Democratic Union, April 20, 2006

In a dramatic conclusion to the IBT's [2006] Constitutional Convention, Jim Hoffa and Tom Keegel buried their opponents for General President/Secretary-Treasurer in delegate balloting last night, winning over 94% of delegates' votes to 6% for Tom Leedham and Sandy Pope. Leedham and Pope disgraced themselves by accepting nomination, knowing they were backed by fewer than 1 of 18 delegates. The two will apparently force a $10 million general election this fall.[2]
—Hoffa campaign, June 30, 2006

The 2006 Election

As the IBT's 2006 election wound into gear, a nominating convention, followed by a nationwide rank-and-file election, no longer seemed like an experiment. The court, EO, and EAM had succeeded in routinizing free and fair international-officer elections.

The consent decree provided for DOL to supervise the 2006 election. However, as in 2001, Chief Judge Preska approved the IBT's and DOJ's joint request to appoint an "election supervisor," previously called "election officer" and "election administrator," to supervise the 2006 election.* DOL's role would be limited to making recommendations. Edelstein appointed former federal prosecutor Richard Mark as EO. (As a young AUSA in Rudolph Giuliani's office, Mark had assisted Randy Mastro in drafting the *U.S. v. IBT* complaint. In the 1998 rerun election, Mark served as EO Cherkasky's counsel.) Kenneth Conboy would continue as EAM. As in 2001, the IBT agreed to pay for the EO's election supervision, ultimately $11.5 million, perhaps because it believed that the alternative would have been even more expensive. (The consent decree did not specify who was responsible for the cost of election supervision beyond the 1996 election. However, it provided that "[n]othing herein shall preclude the United States of America or the United States Department of Labor from taking any appropriate action" in the future to enforce the *U.S. v. IBT* remediation. This provision presumably meant that the government could ask the district court to compel the IBT to pay the full cost of the election supervision.)[3]

Chief Judge Preska approved election rules virtually identical to the 2001 rules.[4] Campaign-contribution caps remained at $2,000 for IBT members and $10,000 for candidates. Contribution and expenditure reporting requirements remained unchanged. A few new election rules resulted from the merger into the IBT of three unions, representing nearly 150,000 workers. In December 2003, the 59,000-member Brotherhood of Locomotive Engineers and Trainmen (BLET), North America's oldest rail labor union, joined the IBT. This was followed by mergers of the 30,000-member Brotherhood of Maintenance of Way Employees (BMWE), a smaller rail labor union, in October 2004, and the 60,000-member Graphic Communications International Union (GCIU), representing printing and publishing workers, in January 2005. Together, BLET's and BMWE's members formed an IBT Rail Conference; GCIU's members constituted an IBT Graphic Communications Conference.[5] EO Mark issued rules authorizing the former BLET, BMWE, and GCIU members to elect 2006 IBT convention delegates and to vote in the general election.[6]

Six hundred and fourteen locals participated in the 2006 delegate-election process, but only 152 locals (25 percent) held contested elections, a slight decline from 2001.[7] A few delegate elections were highly competitive. For example, in NYC, Yanko Fuentes, a Hoffa-slate delegate candidate, sent NYC IBT Local 805's members flyers attacking Local 805 President Sandy

---

* For clarity of exposition, the authors will continue referring to this officer as the EO.

Pope, a delegate candidate and the Leedham slate's candidate for general secretary-treasurer. One Fuentes campaign ad criticized Pope for opposing IBT salaries over $100,000 while she herself drew a salary exceeding $100,000. Another ad blamed Pope for two election violations: first, in April 2006, EO Mark required Local 805 to remail delegate-election ballots because the return-ballot envelopes did not contain postage; second, in May, Mark ordered the local to rerun its delegate election because the local's election committee improperly collected returned ballots before the proper date. Fuentes accused Pope of seeking to "destroy the democratic system within our local for her own personal gain" by "sabotag[ing]" the delegate election. Mark found that Pope had properly disassociated herself from the mechanics of the delegate election and was not responsible for either violation.[8]

The 2006 Election Campaigns

With ample campaign funds, General President Hoffa was able to hire campaign staff, organize rallies, and mail campaign promos to the rank and file. He fielded a full slate of twenty-five candidates, most of them incumbents. Tom Keegel sought reelection as general secretary-treasurer. Ken Hall, the TDU-endorsed candidate for IBT general president in the 1998 rerun election, joined Hoffa's slate as a vice presidential candidate. John Coli ran for reelection as vice president on Hoffa's slate despite Stier's accusations that he played a leading role in shutting down Project RISE's Chicago investigations.

Hoffa again campaigned as an anticorruption reformer, deflecting Stier's charges and pointing to trusteeships he imposed on several corrupt locals. He claimed credit for increasing the IBT membership by 150,000 since he took office (largely attributable to the BLET, BMWE, and GCIU mergers), protecting IBT pension and welfare benefits, keeping the U.S. border closed to Mexican truckers, adding more than $60 million to the Teamster Strike Fund (from a 25 percent dues increase), and negotiating strong collective-bargaining agreements. In July 2005, he took the IBT out of the AFL-CIO, explaining that "while throwing money at politicians," the AFL-CIO had not rebated IBT dues so that the Teamsters could beef up organizing drives.[9] Hoffa then joined with Service Employees International Union (SEIU) President Andrew Stern to form a new labor coalition, Change to Win, which included the IBT, the SEIU, the Laborers' International Union of North America (LIUNA), the United Farm Workers of America, and the United Food and Commercial Workers International Union.[10]

Leedham quickly obtained enough signatures for accreditation, entitling him to free *Teamster Magazine* battle pages,[11] but fundraising was a major challenge. "We'll never match Hoffa dollar for dollar and we don't need to. Grassroots campaigns win elections with sweat and hard work, not big cash and slick PR. But our campaign will need money, and it needs seed money to get started."[12] Lacking enough money for even a single mailing to the full IBT membership, he had to rely on pressing the flesh at work sites and on *Teamster Magazine* battle pages. Leedham insisted that Hoffa had concentrated too much power in the international union at the expense of local-union autonomy. "Locals don't need . . . cookie cutter directives from Washington, D.C. and we don't need IBT staff flying in and taking over."[13] (The latter referred to Hoffa's use of personal representatives to resolve locals' and joint councils' problems.) Leedham also criticized Hoffa for increasing members' dues by 25 percent, the largest dues hike in history.

The 2006 Las Vegas Convention

Approximately seventeen hundred delegates, eight hundred alternate delegates, and several thousand guests attended the June 26–30 IBT convention in Las Vegas. Hoffa told the audience that the convention delegates would "send a loud-and-clear message to Corporate America and the last few doubters in our own ranks. Our Teamsters Union is unified, strong and ready for battle."[14] Leedham predicted that the convention would be "first and foremost a pep rally for the Hoffa administration" and a "three-ring circus."[15] He warned his delegates to anticipate taunts, heckling, and intimidation.

Hoffa's supporters jeered Leedham. Tyson Johnson, an international vice president, excoriated the Leedham slate's legal and accounting fund for accepting a $10,000 donation from the managing partner of "one of the worst union-busting law firms in America." (In *United Steelworkers of America v. Sadlowski*, 457 U.S. 102 (1982), the U.S. Supreme Court had held that although unions could prohibit nonmember financial contributions to union candidates' campaigns, unions could not prohibit nonmember financial contributions to candidates' legal and accounting funds.) Hoffa delegates chanted, "Give it back! Give it back!" They called Leedham's proposed constitutional amendments to strengthen local-union autonomy "sheer hypocrisy" in light of the Carey administration's extensive use of trusteeships. They rejected his proposals to limit union officers' compensation and to directly elect pension-fund trustees. Midconvention, Hoffa announced that his administration had reached a "historic" card-check agreement that would bring twelve thousand UPS freight employees into the IBT;* his press release called the agreement "one of the major U.S. labor-organizing victories of the past several decades."[16]

Hoffa received 1,614 convention-delegate votes (94 percent) and Leedham a meager 107 votes (6 percent), barely qualifying Leedham for the general election. Twenty-five candidates on Hoffa's slate, seventeen on Leedham's slate, and two Leedham-supported candidates running on a separate slate for eastern-region vice presidential positions achieved the 5 percent threshold. In the western region and in Canada, Leedham's vice presidential running mates did not get enough delegate votes to qualify for the general-election ballot. Hoffa demanded that the Leedham slate withdraw to save the union the millions of dollars required to run a nationwide election. On the convention's last day, the Hoffa campaign distributed a press release accusing Leedham of "exploiting" the consent decree's 5 percent rule by forcing a $10 million general election that he could not possibly win.

Postconvention Campaigning

Hoffa's battle pages in *Teamster Magazine* labeled Leedham "a front man for anti-Teamster groups" and promised not to let "Leedham and TDU weaken and divide America's strongest Union." One promo contained a Leedham caricature operating a crane with a TDU logo, an "I Love Walmart" bumper sticker, and a "TDU Wrecking Ball" swinging through a crowd of Teamsters. The caption said "'3-Time' Loser Tom Leedham spends every day tearing down our union on his TDU website." Another ad portrayed Leedham wearing a fedora and a glove with attached razor blades; the caption said "Tom 'Freddy Krueger' Leedham Keeps Coming Back to Slash and Divide the Teamsters."† Hoffa persistently sought to

---

* Card-check recognition is an agreement whereby a majority of employees in a bargaining unit sign cards stating their desire to be represented by a certain union, and the employer agrees to recognize their union status. Card-check is an alternative to achieving exclusive representational status via NLRB-supervised secret-ballot election.

† For readers not up-to-date on horror films, Freddy Krueger is the fictional serial killer in *A Nightmare on Elm Street*. He wears a fedora and a glove with razors.

link Leedham to Ron Carey. One piece of Hoffa campaign literature called Leedham "a key player in the Ron Carey Administration that stole over $1 million in dues money" and referred to the 1996 Carey campaign scandal as "Carey/Leedham mismanagement and embezzlement."

Leedham complained that, under Hoffa, truckers' pension and healthcare benefits had declined. "In the Western Fund, some members have seen cuts of up to 25%, and it's worse in other places."[17] He identified the Overnite strike as "[t]he defining failure of the Hoffa administration."*[18] In making the case for himself, Leedham claimed that, as the head of Oregon IBT Local 206, he negotiated "industry-leading contracts" with generous medical and retirement benefits. He stressed his commitment to and reputation for integrity and supporting union democracy. He promised to institute independent audits of all IBT pension and welfare funds.

Another Leedham v. Hoffa-Stand-In Debate

EO Mark, like his predecessors, sought to encourage rank and filers to vote. Toward that end, he set up a debate that would feature a panel of labor journalists posing questions to the two general presidential candidates. Hoffa again sent a stand-in, this time General Secretary-Treasurer Tom Keegel. At the event, Leedham called Hoffa "missing in action": "If he doesn't have the courage to come here and defend his own record, how will he defend [Teamsters] and their contracts?"

Keegel emphasized Leedham's TDU ties, referring to Leedham's "TDU friends," and sought to smear Leedham by association with TDU. "[He's trying] to tear down our union. . . . Him and TDU always attack, attack, attack." Keegel charged, "Tom Leedham and Ron Carey led the most corrupt administration we've had in many, many years. . . . They virtually destroyed our international union." Leedham openly welcomed TDU's support but did not confirm that he was a TDU member. As in the 2001 election, TDU worked hard to help Leedham's 2006 slate obtain accreditation and to persuade Leedham-friendly Teamsters to run for local delegate positions. TDU also produced pro-Leedham and anti-Hoffa campaign literature and scrutinized the Hoffa campaign for election-rules violations.

---

* In October 2002, after three years of dwindling participation in the Hoffa-initiated strike against Overnite Transportation, one of the largest nonunion trucking companies in the United States, Hoffa called off the strike without a new contract and few gains for the company's workers. This failure was exacerbated in May 2005 when UPS purchased Overnite, raising speculation that UPS would shift work from IBT members to Overnite's nonunionized employees.

Mark offered both campaigns twenty thousand debate DVDs. Leedham accepted; Hoffa declined. Mark then posted the debate video to the World Wide Web. However, the website was accessed only six thousand times in the thirty-five days before the 2006 election, perhaps because the quality of the Web stream was poor or perhaps because most voters were either apathetic about the race or had already made up their minds.

Preballoting Election Protests

EO Mark adjudicated 399 preballoting protests, 25 percent fewer than EO Wertheimer had adjudicated in the 2001 election cycle. This might indicate that the Hoffa and Leedham campaigns were complying more fully with the election or that the Hoffa campaign, more confident in its dominance, used less-aggressive campaign tactics.

Protests alleged, among other things, wrongful use of IBT resources, improper fundraising, voter intimidation, political retaliation, and ineligible candidates. EAM Conboy resolved eighty appeals. One preballoting protest, brought by TDU and an IBT Local 957 member, claimed that the Hoffa slate had used $2,000 of IBT funds to pay for a poll, designed by Hoffa's campaign consultant and campaign manager, asking Teamsters carhaulers how they viewed Hoffa's leadership.[19] Mark required the Hoffa slate to reimburse the union and to share the poll's results with all accredited candidates.[20]

Another preballoting protest concerned whether California IBT Local 78's officers and employees had made unlawful contributions to the Hoffa campaign.[21] During an audit of that local's campaign-finance reports, Mark's office found that, eight years before the audit, Steve Mack, Local 78's secretary-treasurer and the brother of Hoffa-slate vice presidential candidate Chuck Mack, had opened a bank account in which to deposit campaign contributions for incumbent Local 78 officers.[22] However, instead of using the money for Local 78 election campaigns, Steve Mack withdrew $14,000 to help the Jim Hoffa–Chuck Mack campaign.[23] Finding that these contributions had not been properly solicited, made, accepted, or reported,[24] Mark ordered the Hoffa-Mack campaign to reimburse Local 78 and imposed an $8,700 fine. He prohibited Local 78's officers from making any further campaign contributions in the 2006 election cycle.[25]

T.C. Bundrant, principal officer of Tennessee IBT Local 549 and a Leedham supporter, filed a protest charging that two high-level Hoffa-administration officers conspired to transfer members from his local to Local 71,

FIGURE 10.1
*Percentage of Eligible IBT Members Casting Mail-In
Ballots in IBT Elections (1991–2006)*

Year	Voter Turnout
1991	28%
1996	34%
1998	28%
2001	25%
2006	19%

which Hoffa's supporters controlled.[26] Mark vacated the transfers. Conboy affirmed, noting that the evidence "establishes both current political motivation and current political animus."[27]

A Kentucky Local 89 member and delegate candidate who supported Leedham complained that a pro-Hoffa business agent confiscated Leedham campaign literature distributed at UPS parking lots.[28] Mark ruled that this conduct violated the leafleters' right to campaign and the rank and file's right to receive campaign literature.[29] Because the business agent's conduct amounted to an illegal endorsement,[30] Mark ordered the business agent to distribute at the UPS facility a notice stating that he had violated the election rules and that Local 89 does not endorse any candidate. The EAM affirmed.[31]

The Election Results

Only 19 percent of eligible voters mailed back ballots, continuing the downward trend from 1996 (see fig. 10.1). Hoffa received 174,963 votes (65 percent) compared to 92,444 votes (35 percent) for Leedham, roughly the same margin of victory as in 2001. Hoffa's entire slate was elected. No disputed ballots had to be counted because, in total, those ballots could not change the election's outcome. Mark certified the election results on January 8, 2007.

Leedham sought to put the best spin on his defeat, pointing out that more than one-third of those who voted preferred him to Hoffa and that his slate defeated Hoffa's in seven states and eighty locals.[32] "While we did not prevail in the election, we mobilized thousands of Teamsters around a positive vision for rebuilding our union's power. Our campaign strengthened our union."[33]

The IRB: July 2006–July 2011

In the IRB's fourth five-year term (July 2006 up to November 1, 2010), it has so far recommended that the IBT file disciplinary charges against forty-nine Teamsters from twenty-two locals in twelve states and Puerto Rico.[34] Five additional respondents signed precharge settlement agreements. The IRB most frequently charged breach of fiduciary duty, embezzlement, failure to cooperate with an IRB investigation, and organized-crime membership or association (see fig. 10.2). Twenty-five percent of disciplinary respondents were members of Boston IBT Local 82, charged with offenses including favoritism and nepotism in the operation of the job-referral system, violating members' right to a fair contract-ratification process, violating local bylaws concerning financial controls, colluding with nonunion employers, and, in one case, membership in an LCN organized-crime family.

Organized-Crime Cases

More than 30 percent of the IRB's fourth-term disciplinary charges, through November 1, 2010, involved an organized-crime connection. Eight

FIGURE 10.2
Types of Charges Recommended by the IRB (2006–2010)

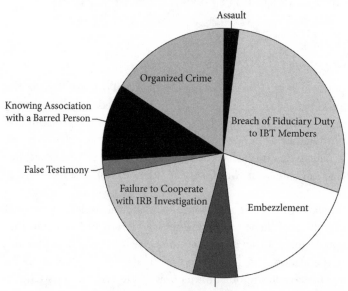

Teamsters were expelled or resigned based on charges of membership in or knowing association with an LCN members (see fig. 10.3). The IRB charged an additional seven respondents with failing to cooperate with an IRB organized-crime investigation. Four of these respondents were expelled or resigned; three respondents' cases were pending as of November 1, 2010.[35]

Sanctioning the Top Leadership

The IRB charged one international vice president and several international staffers with disciplinary violations. In 2007, pursuant to an IRB recommendation, the IBT suspended International Vice President Frank Gillen from union membership for three years and from union office for five years for testifying falsely about his association with expelled member Thomas Ryan. A few months later, International Organizer John Clancy, admitting that he met and talked with expelled member Dane Passo, resigned from the union and agreed not to seek IBT employment for ten years. International Representative William Moore agreed to a year-long suspension from IBT office and IBT employment for lying to the IRB about his association with Passo.

Several locals' principal officers or other high-ranking officers also faced disciplinary charges (see fig. 10.4). For example, the IRB continued its campaign against the Hogan family, which had dominated Chicago IBT Local 714 for decades. The IRB recommended that the IBT charge Local 714 Secretary-Treasurer Robert Hogan with failing to investigate repeated contacts between Local 714 Organizing Director Robert Riley and barred member William Hogan, Jr.[36] Following an IBT hearing, Hoffa suspended Hogan from IBT office and employment for six months. The IRB found this sanction inadequate, but General President Hoffa refused to enhance it. Consequently, in April 2008, the IRB convened a *de novo* disciplinary hearing. Before it rendered its decision, Hogan agreed to permanently resign his membership in Local 714, never to participate in Local 714's affairs, not to serve as an officer or employee of Local 727 for five years, and not to hold any IBT officer position for two years.[37] Chief Judge Preska approved the agreement.[38]

In September 2009, the IRB recommended that the IBT charge Chicago IBT Local 726 President John Falzone (and several other Local 726 officers) with breaching his fiduciary duties to the local's members by causing the local's pension fund to enter into two ERISA-prohibited transactions

FIGURE 10.3

The IRB's Charges Involving Membership in LCN and Knowing Association with LCN Members or Associates (July 2006–May 2011)

Member(s)	IBT Local	IRB-Recommended Charge	Disposition
Joseph Pirro (member)	Elmsford, NY Local 456	Knowing association with the Gambino crime family	Expelled from the IBT (2007)
Peter Innaurato (steward)	Philadelphia Local 107	Knowing association with the Philadelphia LCN family	Resigned from the IBT (2009)
Anthony Manero (member)	Lake Success, NY Local 282	Knowing association with the Gambino crime family	Resigned from the IBT (2009)
Michael Carucci (member)	Lake Success, NY Local 282	Knowing association with the Bonanno crime family	Resigned from the IBT (2009)
Vincent Federico (member)	Boston Local 82	Membership in the Patriarca crime family	Expelled from the IBT (2010)
Vincent Disario (member)	Long Island City, NY Local 1901	Membership in the Bonanno crime family	Expelled from the IBT (2010)
John Castelle (member)	Lake Success, NY Local 282	Membership in the Lucchese crime family	Expelled from the IBT (2011)
Michael Perelli (member)	Long Island City, NY Local 1901	Knowing association with the Lucchese crime family	Expelled from the IBT (2011)

FIGURE 10.4

The IRB's Charges against Top IBT Officials (July 2006–November 2011)

Officer	IRB-Recommended Charge	Disposition
Frank Gillen (international vice president)	Testifying falsely about repeated contacts with expelled member Thomas Ryan	Barred from IBT office for five years and from IBT membership for three years (2007)
Don Hahs (president of the IBT's Rail Conference and Brotherhood of Locomotive Engineers and Trainmen)	Embezzling $58,000	Suspended for one year and barred from holding IBT office or employment until 2010 (2007)
George DiPilato (Philadelphia IBT Local 502 principal officer)	Embezzling $20,000 to cover personal expenses	Suspended for five years from IBT membership and permanent resignation from local office (2007)
Ernest Sowell (Houston IBT Local 747 principal officer)	Improperly using $251,000 of his local's money	Suspended from the IBT for five years; subject to expulsion if he did not repay the $251,000 within five years (2009)
German Vazquez (San Juan, Puerto Rico IBT Local 901 principal officer)	Embezzling $55,000	Suspended from IBT office and employment until he repaid the money (2009)
Thomas Clair (Chicago IBT Local 726 principal officer)	Arranging to transfer $125,000 from the local's pension fund to the local without the fund's approval and in violation of ERISA	Resigned from the union (2009)
Richard Radek (BLET vice president)	Embezzling $6,700	Paid a fine and retired (2009)
John Falzone (president of Chicago IBT Local 726); Michael Marcatante (trustee of Chicago IBT Local 726)	Approving a $125,000 loan from the local's pension fund to the local's treasury so that the local could make up for delinquent payments to the Central States Pension Fund	Suspended for five years (2009)
Patrick Geary (president of Boston IBT Local 82)	Violating the local's bylaws concerning financial controls; violating members' rights to a fair contract-ratification process	Disciplinary case pending (2010)

FIGURE 10.5

IRB Disciplinary Charges against Teamsters Who Knowingly Associated with Barred Persons (July 2006–November 2011)

Member(s)	IBT Local	IRB-Recommended Charge	Disposition
Gary Proctor (business agent)	Pontiac, MI, Local 614	Knowing association with Michael Bane, who had been expelled from the union in 2001 for trying to thwart an IRB investigation	Expelled from the IBT (2006)
Frank Incandella (business agent)	Las Vegas Local 631	Knowing association with Dane Passo, who had been expelled in 2002 for negotiating a sweetheart contract	Expelled from the IBT (2006)
Raymond Isner (member)	Las Vegas Local 631	Knowing association with Dane Passo	Expelled from the IBT (2006)
James Jackson (member)	Detroit Local 229	Knowing association with Michael Bane	Expelled from the IBT (2007)
John Clancy (international organizer)	Chicago Local 705	Knowing association with Dane Passo	Resigned from the IBT (2007); barred for ten years from seeking employment in the IBT and from having any contact with IBT members
Michael Conway (steward)	Philadelphia Local 107	Knowing association with barred person Thomas Ryan, who had been expelled from the union in 1999 for violating the terms of his suspension	Suspended for ten years from serving as an IBT steward (2009)

totaling $125,000 and by failing to administer the pension fund properly. The IBT filed the charges; an IBT hearing panel barred Falzone from holding IBT office for three years and from serving as a fiduciary of any IBT benefit fund for five years. The IRB found these sanctions "not inadequate."

Knowingly Associating with Barred Persons

The IRB recommended that the IBT charge several Teamsters with knowingly associating with barred persons (see fig. 10.5). The IBT wrestled with how such violations should be punished.

> Cases involving a member's knowing and purposeful contact with a barred person present a number of extremely difficult considerations. Not the least of these is the fact that it is counterintuitive for a labor organization to contemplate expelling a member when, in virtually every other context, the organization is committed to retaining existing members.[39]

Ultimately, the IBT concluded that "expulsion, unfortunately, is the price one must pay for choosing to maintain his longstanding personal relationship with a barred person."[40]

Trusteeships

The IRB recommended that the IBT impose trusteeships on four locals during its fourth term:[41]

- Chicago IBT Local 714 (the Hogans' local), because the local executive board "jeopardized the local's interests," failed "to perform its duties as bargaining agent," and used its job-referral system to benefit the friends and relatives of barred members.[42] Initially, Hoffa appointed a personal representative to work with the local's officers to address the IRB's concerns. Six months later, however, Hoffa imposed a trusteeship, explaining that "additional and immediate steps must be undertaken to protect the interests of members and the integrity of Local 714."[43]
- Chicago IBT Local 726, because several local officers had engaged in financial misconduct, including skipping twelve months of mandatory pension-fund contributions, waiving a year's worth of membership dues for twenty-seven Teamsters without approval,

submitting incomplete monthly financial reports to the IBT, ignoring auditors' instructions to record severance obligations, and improperly transferring a large sum of money from the local's treasury into its pension fund.

- Philadelphia Local 502, because the local lacked adequate financial controls and operated under bylaws that the IBT had not approved.[44] Principal Officer George DiPilato had also been charged with embezzlement.

- Philadelphia IBT Local 107, because its officers were improperly using the job-referral system to refer their friends and family members for lucrative jobs in the motion-picture and trade-show industries.[45] This was Local 107's second trusteeship in fifteen years.

Looking toward the 2011 Election

The 2011 election machinery started up in November 2009. Chief Judge Preska approved the parties' agreement that EO Richard Mark and EAM Kenneth Conboy would again supervise the election.[46] Mark hired eight regional directors.[47] The IBT agreed to Mark's $11,333,500 budget.[48]

In March 2010, Mark proposed 2011 election rules that basically followed the 2006 rules. However, one new rule required that candidates either return or donate to charity unexpended campaign contributions. Another new rule required electronic, rather than hard-copy, submissions of both local-union election plans and campaign contribution and expenditure reports. Mark posted these rules to the EO's website, inviting comments from Teamsters, Teamsters employers, and outside organizations. AUD proposed an amendment that would make it easier for a candidate to qualify for the general-election ballot:

> Once the aspiring candidate produces petitions signed by 2½% of the membership [rather than 5%] he/she by virtue of those petitions [should be] guaranteed a place on the ballot. . . . The danger in the Teamsters union is that international elections will become, as they were before the consent decree, a travesty of democracy. If 30,000 or 40,000 Teamsters who have openly declared their support for a candidate by signing a petition discover that their choice is denied even a place on the ballot, how can they take such an election seriously? How can they be expected to do it again

in a subsequent election? Faith in the very process of democracy is undermined. Cynicism leads to apathy. Apathy reopens the door to corruption.[49]

TDU proposed that the election rules require a general presidential debate, that stand-ins not be permitted to participate, and that a DVD copy of the debate be mailed to every Teamster. Neither AUD's nor TDU's proposals were accepted. In April 2010, Chief Judge Preska approved the EO's proposed rules.[50] On May 25, 2010, Jim Hoffa and Tom Keegel announced that they would seek reelection as general president and general secretary-treasurer.[51] That same day, Fred Gegare—an international vice president, former president of Green Bay, Wisconsin IBT Local 75, and director of the IBT's Dairy Conference and Food Processing Division—announced that he would challenge Hoffa. He criticized Hoffa for surrounding himself with "the wrong people," "forgetting the membership," and thwarting local-union autonomy.[52] Gegare subsequently recruited eight running mates, two of whom currently serve on the GEB.[53] Gegare's campaign website states that "[t]he Teamsters Union has been headed by Tony Soprano wannabes for too long" and that Hoffa "hasn't eliminated the need for the Independent Review Board."[54]

On July 15, 2010, General Secretary-Treasurer Keegel announced that he had changed his mind and would retire in 2012. In a letter to the GEB, he implicitly criticized Hoffa by observing that "continuing down the same road as the IBT has traveled for the last few years will not lead us out of our present difficulties or help us avoid problems yet to come."[55] International Vice President Ken Hall replaced Keegel on Hoffa's full slate of twenty-eight candidates, most of whom obtained enough rank and filers' signatures to achieve accreditation, entitling them to free battle pages in *Teamster Magazine* and on the IBT's website.

On October 10, 2010, Sandy Pope—the president of twelve-hundred-member NYC IBT Local 804 and a former truck driver, warehouse worker, steelhauler, and international representative—launched her candidacy for general president. In the 2006 election, as Leedham's general secretary-treasurer running mate, Pope received more votes than anyone else on that slate. TDU's steering committee immediately endorsed Pope, who explained that, as general president, her main priorities would be to protect members' jobs, to obtain better contracts, and to grow the union's health and pension funds.[56] In a *Labor Notes* interview the day after she announced her candidacy, Pope predicted that Hoffa and Gegare would split the support of the Teamsters establishment, as R.V. Durham and Walter

Shea had done in 1991.[57] Pope has not formed a slate or recruited running mates, but she easily obtained enough members' signatures to become an accredited candidate. (Gegare failed to achieve accreditation, an ominous sign for his campaign.)

As of mid-April 2011, EO Mark has decided 224 election protests, and EAM Conboy has decided thirty-five appeals. The protests have involved, among other things, improper use of union or employer resources for campaign purposes, failure to report campaign contributions and expenditures properly, and ineligibility of convention-delegate candidates. The Gegare campaign filed the most important election protest, accusing General President Hoffa and three incumbent vice presidents of offering bribes (union jobs and benefits) to three Teamsters leaders if they would support the Hoffa slate.[58] In effect, this accusation charged Hoffa and his colleagues with attempting to use union funds to further their campaigns (a variation of the embezzlement-of-Teamsters-funds charge that led to Carey's downfall in 1998.) After a six-month investigation, EO Mark concluded that Hall had offered IBT Joint Council 94 President Fred Zuckerman (Gegare's vice presidential running mate) a new job with higher pay and an additional pension if he dropped his bid for a GEB position. He also found that International Trustees Frank Gallegos and Henry Perry (a Gegare running mate) were offered jobs as full-time international representatives if they agreed to resign from the GEB and support Hoffa. Zuckerman, Gallegos, and Perry rejected these enticements.

Mark observed that the bribe proposals reflected "a culture, or mind-set where elected union officials do not clearly distinguish between their fiduciary responsibilities to the union and their separate political objectives of achieving election."[59] However, he ruled that the proposals did not violate the election rules because "there are no improperly solicited or dispensed funds to return, there is no adverse employment action to undo, and there was no use of a resource that could be balanced by an order for equal access."[60] Mark explained that if the proposed bribes "had advanced to concrete action, serious consequences would quite likely follow," but that the respondents "were saved from serious consequences . . . because their proposals were rejected by those to whom they were offered."[61]

EAM Conboy reversed, explaining that the job offers "represent exactly the type of misconduct that the Election Supervisor was charged with remedying."[62] Conboy concluded that the offers themselves constituted an improper use of union resources for election purposes and, more generally, threatened the integrity of the election process. On remand, Mark ordered the Hoffa campaign (1) to cease and desist from attempting to use union resources for political activity and (2) to mail a notice to all IBT locals describing the attempted bribery and the cease-and-desist order, to publish that notice in *Teamster Magazine*, and to post the notice on the IBT's website for the duration of the election cycle. Conboy affirmed that sanction.

Conclusion and Analysis

The 2006 Election

The 2006 IBT election, again supervised by an independent monitor operating in the shadow of the federal court, was free and fair by any reasonable standard. Although the candidates sharply criticized each other, the campaigning was peaceful and lawful and the convention mostly orderly. The IBT provided adequate funding. In resolving election protests, Mark drew on precedents established in hundreds of prior election-protest rulings. The IBT has accomplished what no other international union has ever done, running a nationwide rank-and-file election according to fair and enforceable rules covering convention-delegate elections, convention procedures and nominations, campaign contributions and expenditures, campaign conduct, general-election balloting, and election protests.

Nevertheless, some critics (e.g., TDU and AUD) still find the IBT elections unfair because the incumbents continue to enjoy big advantages.[63] In their view, fairness would require a completely level playing field on which incumbents enjoyed little, if any, advantage. But it seems to us that the test of whether an election is free and fair cannot be whether challengers and incumbents have equal chances of winning. As Lipset, Trow, and Coleman pointed out fifty years ago in their seminal study of union democracy, "The nature of large-scale organizations is such as to give the incumbent officials overwhelming power as compared with that of the opposition."[64]

The IBT general president has practically universal name recognition; through IBT publications, such as *Teamster Magazine*, he can shape the opinions and perceptions of the rank and file. The general president has immense patronage at his disposal because he controls the hiring, firing, salaries, and fringe benefits of union employees, including executive assistants, representatives, auditors, and organizers. He appoints local and international officers to paid positions on various union committees and can make or break union careers. Consequently, the incumbent general president can count on the support of most of the more than seven thousand IBT officeholders.

It is difficult for an insurgent candidate to raise sufficient funds to mount a competitive nationwide campaign. Because of the 5 percent rule, it is not even guaranteed that an insurgent candidate will make it to the general election. In 2006, some of Leedham's vice presidential running mates did not receive enough votes at the nominating convention to earn places on the general-election ballot. Had just fifteen fewer convention delegates voted for Tom Leedham, there would have been no general election for IBT president.*

The IRB

In the second half of the IRB's fourth five-year term, there was a slight surge in the number of IRB disciplinary recommendations. The IRB recommended charges against more disciplinary respondents (nineteen) in 2010 than in any year since 2000. Still, the IRB has recommended far fewer disciplinary charges per year in its fourth term than the disciplinary officers brought or recommended in the first decade of the *U.S. v. IBT* remediation. In the IA/IO phase of the consent decree (July 1989–October 1992), the IO brought charges against seventy-five Teamsters per year. In the IRB's first five-year term (October 1992–July 1997), it recommended charges against forty-three Teamsters per year. In its second five-year term (July 1997–July 2001), it recommended charges against thirty-seven per year. In its third five-year term, it recommended charges against eleven per year. And in its fourth five-year term, up to November 1, 2010, it recommended charges against approximately ten per year. This trend may reflect a declining amount of corruption, better concealed corruption, or a shift in the IRB's investigative priorities. We think the latter is most likely.

Despite the overall decline in the number of disciplinary recommendations, the IRB continues to identify serious wrongdoing, including organized-crime influence. Although there is no evidence that Cosa Nos-

---

* AUD's Herman Benson has called the 5 percent rule a "dangerous flaw" in the IBT election process, urging its replacement with a rule that entitles a candidate who obtains 2.5 percent of members' supporting signatures to a place on the general-election ballot. Disagreeing, former AUD Executive Director Susan Jennik supports the 5 percent rule, noting that a candidate who cannot muster the support of this small fraction of delegates has no realistic chance of winning the general election. Herman Benson, *Teamster Convention Reveals Fatal Flaw in Election Rules*, UNION DEMOCRACY REVIEW, July–Aug. 2006, at 7; interview with Susan Jennik, Jan. 21, 2010.

tra continues to influence the union's selection of international officers or the operation of its pension and welfare funds, its influence clearly has not been eradicated. So far in the IRB's fourth term, at least fifteen Teamsters (30 percent of all disciplinary respondents) have been charged with LCN-related disciplinary offenses.

The IRB will never purge the IBT, a 1.3-million-member union spread across North America, of all run-of-the-mill corruption. The signatories of the consent decree (especially the union defendants) almost certainly did not have that goal in mind. DOJ brought the *U.S. v. IBT* civil RICO complaint because of organized-crime infiltration and exploitation, not because of ordinary corruption. Thus, the IRB's past accomplishments and future mission should not be measured by the number of "ordinary corruption" cases investigated, prosecuted, and punished. Instead, the performance of and the need for the IRB should be gauged by the amount of organized-crime influence in the union and the IRB's success in investigating and eliminating it. Admittedly, it will not be easy to determine when LCN's influence has been eliminated. That the IRB, in 2010 alone, charged three Teamsters with being members of three different Cosa Nostra organized-crime families (Patriarca, Bonanno, and Lucchese) clearly demonstrates that success has not yet been achieved.

The 2011 Election

The 2011 IBT election is shaping up to be the most competitive election for general president since the 1996 battle between incumbent Ron Carey and challenger Jim Hoffa. As in the 1991 election, the IBT leadership, including the GEB members, regional officers, and local officers, are not squarely behind one candidate. Most Teamsters officers will probably support Jim Hoffa, either because they are in his administration or because they depend on his goodwill and largesse. Nevertheless, some officers have already thrown their support behind International Vice President Fred Gegare; several have joined his slate. If Hoffa and Gegare split the support of the union's leadership and, in turn, of the rank and file, Sandy Pope has a better chance than any insurgent candidate since Ron Carey.*

---

* On June 30, 2011, the convention delegates gave sufficient votes to nominate all three general presidential candidates for the general-election ballot: Hoffa (1326); Gegare (141); and Pope (137).

11

Lessons, Reflections, and Speculations

Racketeering is the cancer that almost destroyed the American trade-union movement.[1]

—David Dubinsky, *A Life with Labor*, 1977

We got our money from gambling, but our real power, our real strength, came from the unions. With the unions behind us, we could shut down . . . the country.[2]

—Vincent Cafaro, lieutenant, Genovese crime family,
April 1988

Regardless of unionism's strength, politics, or workplace locale . . . accusations of corruption, bossism, and union bureaucracy are deployed . . . to discredit the unions, both those that are tarnished by such malfeasance and those that are squeaky clean. . . . [Due to this] demonization . . . the unions are now highly regulated institutions, far more so than almost any other voluntary institution in American society. . . . But all that has not stopped those who still tag the unions as a fount of corruption, payoffs, and barely veiled coercion.[3]

—Nelson Lichtenstein, in the *Chronicle of Higher Education*,
January 17, 2010

Politics

U.S. v. IBT, a government lawsuit that charged the nation's largest and most powerful private-sector union with being racketeer ridden, has to be placed in political context. This lawsuit would be impossible in most countries, especially where there is a "Labor" political party. That *U.S. v. IBT* was politically possible in 1988 confirms what all well-informed American political and labor observers know: the private-sector labor movement has weakened dramatically since the mid-twentieth century. Indeed, the Teamsters Union experienced a 35 percent membership decline from 1976 (2 million members) to 2010 (1.3 million members). Nevertheless, nearly one in five private-sector union members is a Teamster. The IBT also continues to wield considerable political clout; in 2010, it ranked twenty-first among all political contributors in the United States, ahead of Goldman Sachs, Microsoft, and Walmart.

DOJ attracted a barrage of criticism for filing *U.S. v. IBT*. Many labor leaders, politicians, and celebrities, among others, damned the lawsuit as an attack on a free and democratic labor movement. We find such criticism highly cynical. The close relationship between organized crime and the Teamsters Union had been common knowledge at least since the Senate's 1957–59 McClellan Committee hearings. Indeed, in 1957, the AFL-CIO expelled the IBT from the labor federation on account of corruption and racketeering. Scores of criminal prosecutions over the next three decades confirmed and illuminated organized crime's influence in the union. In the mid-1980s, the President's Commission on Organized Crime (PCOC) reported that the IBT was the most racketeer-ridden union in the United States. The IBT's leaders had done nothing to resist Cosa Nostra's influence. To the contrary, they (some actively and some passively) collaborated with LCN to exploit the union and its rank and file. It is a depressing comment on the state of American politics that, despite this notorious record, 264 members of Congress signed a petition, in 1988, denouncing DOJ's anticipated civil RICO lawsuit against the IBT as an attack on a democratic labor movement.

Given the labor movement's close relationship with the Democratic Party, the government probably would not have brought *U.S. v. IBT* when the Democrats controlled the White House. Indeed, the lawsuit's opponents claimed that it demonstrated the Reagan administration's intent to destroy the labor movement. (President Reagan had previously drawn labor's enmity for breaking the Professional Air Traffic Controllers Organization strike in the first year of his first presidential term.)

Ironically, the IBT, practically alone among labor unions, had endorsed Reagan's presidential candidacy in 1980. President Reagan delivered a taped address to the 1981 IBT international convention, thanking the union for supporting his campaign and effusively praising the union, including General President Roy Williams and former General President Frank

Fitzsimmons. "I hope to be in team with the Teamsters," Reagan said.[4] The IBT endorsed Reagan again in 1984 and George H.W. Bush's presidential candidacy in 1988. That Reagan's DOJ filed *U.S. v. IBT* in 1988 therefore shocked some labor-movement pundits and, of course, most Teamsters.

By the mid-1980s, the FBI's and DOJ's organized-crime-control program had achieved unstoppable momentum. Cosa Nostra was the FBI's number-one crime target; major prosecutions were taking place all over the country. Still, the 1986 President's Commission on Organized Crime criticized the Reagan administration for not aggressively moving against organized crime's power base in labor unions, especially the Teamsters. Given the momentum of the attack on LCN and the well-known long-term relationship between the IBT and LCN, White House political operatives probably could not have stopped *U.S. v. IBT*, even if they had wanted to do so, without risking a scandal. While we do not argue that federal law enforcement is completely apolitical (especially in light of the U.S. attorneys' scandal during George W. Bush's administration),* we view *U.S. v. IBT* as good evidence of a substantially apolitical federal law-enforcement establishment. That DOJ has sustained the remedial phase of *U.S. v. IBT*, without interruption or diminution of vigor, under Presidents George H.W. Bush, Bill Clinton, George W. Bush, and Barack Obama, supports this conclusion.

Other than 264 congresspersons' petition to Attorney General Meese, the only significant political involvement in *U.S. v. IBT* was Rep. Peter Hoekstra's hearings, from October 1997 to October 1998, on the invalidated 1996 IBT election and on the fairness, competency, and expense of the court-appointed officers.[5] We cannot discern Hoekstra's motives in convening the House Subcommittee on Oversight and Investigations hearings, which led to legislation that denied public funds for monitoring the 1998 rerun election. The propriety of using taxpayer money to supervise a union election, especially a rerun election, is not a surprising concern for a fiscal conservative such as Hoekstra. However, the organization and tenor of the hearings suggest that protecting the taxpayers was probably not his only motive. Given the IBT's influence in Hoekstra's Detroit congressional district and his relationship with Jim Hoffa, it is likely that he also meant to demonstrate and generate support for Hoffa, including Hoffa's ambition to

---

* Fortunately, the powerful negative reaction to the political firings of nine U.S. attorneys in 2007, and subsequent resignations of nine DOJ officials, including the U.S. attorney general, suggests that the firings were the exception that proves the rule. *See* Bruce A. Green & Fred Zacharias, *The U.S. Attorneys Scandal and the Allocation of Prosecutorial Power*, 69 OHIO ST. L.J. 187 (2008).

bring about termination of the consent decree. Undoubtedly, Hoekstra also welcomed the opportunity to embarrass the Democratic Party, some of its liberal supporters, and the AFL-CIO by illuminating their roles in the 1996 campaign-contribution-swap scandal.

Civil RICO

Congress enacted RICO in 1970 to combat Cosa Nostra's infiltration of the legitimate economy, explicitly including labor unions.[6] However, it took almost a decade for federal prosecutors to become comfortable using the complex new statute. Although federal prosecutors brought scores of successful RICO and other criminal prosecutions against LCN members and associates between 1970 and 1985, PCOC charged that LCN's power in the legitimate economy remained strong. When LCN members or associates went to prison, the LCN crime families promoted others to take their places. Corrupted unions remained corrupted. PCOC strongly recommended that DOJ bring a civil RICO suit against the Teamsters Union. Indeed, it called such a suit the only hope for breaking LCN's hold on the union.

Starting with the civil RICO lawsuit against Union City, New Jersey IBT Local 560, jointly brought by the New Jersey U.S. attorney and the federal organized-crime strike force in 1982, civil RICO proved to be an ideal weapon for attacking systemic labor racketeering. In many cases, the FBI and DOJ did not need to launch a new investigation. They could draft a strong civil RICO complaint based on organized-crime figures' and union officials' previous criminal convictions. DOJ lawyers named the union itself as a nominal defendant in *U.S. v. IBT* for purposes of shaping the remedy. In other words, to prevent the defendant mobsters and union officials from continuing to commit RICO offenses, it was necessary to reform the union's operations, especially its disciplinary enforcement machinery and election procedures. The biggest advantage of using civil RICO to combat organized crime's exploitation of a labor union is the opportunity to obtain a court-appointed and court-supervised remedial team for as long as is necessary to purge the union of organized crime's influence.

Since 1982, DOJ has filed more than twenty civil RICO suits against racketeer-ridden labor unions.[7] All of these suits have resulted in favorable outcomes for the government, including court-appointed trustees or monitors. However, not all of the trusteeships and monitorships have succeeded.

Civil RICO is not a panacea. Achieving reform has been much more difficult than winning a judgment. Unfortunately, after more than twenty-five years, there is no government-sponsored research or best practices on civil RICO trusteeships. Still, it is clear that for a civil RICO lawsuit against a racketeer-ridden union to achieve its goals, there must be a strong consent decree and a team of government lawyers ready, willing, and able to go to court, time and again, to make the defendants abide by its terms. Moreover, the reform effort will fail unless the presiding judge is willing and able to enforce both the letter and the spirit of the decree. However, even that, though necessary, is not sufficient. There must be a highly determined and competent court-appointed monitor with ample authority and resources to enforce the decree. Some monitorships have failed because the consent decree did not give the monitor sufficient investigative or adjudicative authority or adequate resources. Others have failed because the monitors, perhaps distracted by other work, did not devote the necessary time and energy to the task. In still other cases, the monitors were just not savvy enough or tough enough to stand up to the racketeers and their lawyers.

The *U.S. v. IBT* remediation has been fortunate, since the beginning, in having determined and competent enforcers. The U.S. attorney's office for SDNY has always enjoyed an outstanding reputation for being apolitical and highly competent. At the time it brought *U.S. v. IBT*, U.S. Attorney Giuliani's office had already successfully prosecuted some of the most ambitious organized-crime cases in U.S. history. It also had considerable experience litigating civil RICO cases against labor racketeers.

Giuliani's team predicted correctly that Judge David Edelstein would be a good choice to handle the first civil RICO suit against the leadership of an international union. From the outset, Edelstein took ownership of the case. He issued decisions expeditiously and emphatically, demonstrating time and again his intent to use all available judicial authority to cleanse the IBT of organized-crime influence. His determination was best exhibited in his breathtakingly ambitious nationwide All Writs Act injunction, which ordered that all litigation relating to the *U.S. v. IBT* consent decree be brought only in his courtroom. Without this ruling, the whole remedial effort would have been stymied.

Judge Edelstein required the IBT to provide ample funding for the court officers and their staffs. His appointments to these positions proved to be brilliant. It is hard to imagine three enforcement officers more competent than Charles Carberry, Frederick Lacey, and Michael Holland. As

IO, IA, and EO, they relentlessly pressed the remediation forward, at times overcoming intense IBT opposition. They were also able to draw on the assistance of the FBI and DOJ. When one of Holland's successors as EO faltered, Edelstein replaced her immediately. The rest of Edelstein's EO appointments performed extremely well.

The Consent Decree

To be successful, civil RICO institutional-reform litigation requires a strong remedial order or, in the case of a settlement, a strong consent decree. A strong consent decree depends, of course, on a strong government case, the government's ability to prevail at trial if necessary, and well-conceived and well-drafted remedial provisions.

DOJ had a strong case against the IBT based on decades of publicly available information documenting LCN's extensive influence in the Marble Palace, many IBT locals and joint councils, and the Central States Pension Fund. The biggest challenge for DOJ was to decide what remedy would provide the best chance of achieving organizational reform. In some of the civil RICO lawsuits against union locals (e.g., the IBT Local 560 case), a court-appointed officer substituted for the union's executive authority. In those cases, the court-appointed officer actually ran the union, including its collective-bargaining negotiations and grievance handling. This probably would not have been feasible in the case of an international union. Even if feasible, it would not have been desirable because the reform effort would have bogged down in the massive responsibilities of day-to-day administration. Giuliani's team wisely decided to focus on taking control of and using the union's disciplinary apparatus to attack corrupt union officials and their mobster allies. The principal reform strategy would be expelling those union officials who had cooperated with LCN, actively or passively. Toward that end, the federal lawyers won a crucial victory in making resignation the price of settlement for incumbent GEB officers. In addition, the consent decree created an investigative and prosecutorial unit and process that functioned like an administrative criminal justice system just for the Teamsters Union. Whether the decision to reform the IBT's system for selecting international officers was as wise as the decision to use the disciplinary machinery to purge corrupt officers is a question we explore later.

The Consent Decree's Disciplinary Prong

From July 26, 1989, through November 1, 2010, the IO and IRB brought or recommended disciplinary charges against 668 Teamsters who belonged to 138 different IBT locals located in 78 cities in 21 U.S. states, Washington, D.C., Canada, and Puerto Rico. More than a third (230) of these cases were brought in the first three years of the twenty-two-year (and counting) remediation (see fig. 11.1). The disciplinary respondents included 212 rank and filers, 102 local presidents, 102 local secretary-treasurers, 48 local vice presidents, 38 local recording secretaries, 18 business agents, and two dozen international officers, including one IBT general president (Ron Carey). These impressive numbers actually understate the extent of the remediation because several mobbed-up IBT locals—for example, Union City, New Jersey Local 560 and Long Island City, New York Local 808— were subject to separate civil RICO lawsuits that resulted in independent court-appointed trustees who carried out their own discipline. In addition, an unknown number of IBT officers and rank and filers resigned or retired from the IBT because they anticipated being charged.

More than half of all disciplinary respondents (336) were members of New York locals, especially NYC Local 813, Lake Success Local 282, and Valley Stream Local 295; these three locals account for over one hundred disciplinary respondents. Moreover, as figure 11.2 shows, nearly 40 percent of all disciplinary respondents belonged to just fifteen racketeer-ridden or mobbed-up locals. Over half of the disciplinary respondents (374), including fifty-three local presidents, more than a dozen international officers, and one general president (Carey), have been expelled or agreed to resign.

Figure 11.3 shows the distribution of disciplinary charges. By far the most common disciplinary charges (40 percent) involved misappropriation of union funds. One-quarter of all disciplinary respondents (about 160) faced embezzlement charges. Eighty-nine others were charged with other financial-misconduct violations, including extortion, bribery, making illegal loans to union officers, violating bylaws governing financial controls, improperly influencing pension-fund investments, providing union benefits to non-Teamsters or LCN figures, sham collective-bargaining agreements, and spending union money without approval. About one-fifth of disciplinary cases (120) explicitly involved organized crime. Twenty-five Teamsters were expelled from the IBT for being members of a Cosa Nostra crime family; sixty-one were expelled for knowingly associating with Cosa Nostra figures; and approximately three dozen were expelled or suspended

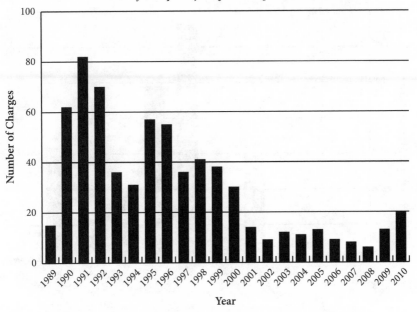

FIGURE 11.1
Number of Disciplinary Respondents per Year (1989–2010)

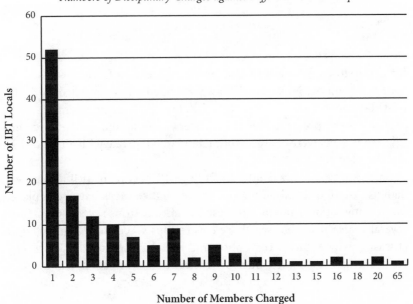

FIGURE 11.2
Numbers of Disciplinary Charges against Different Individuals per Local

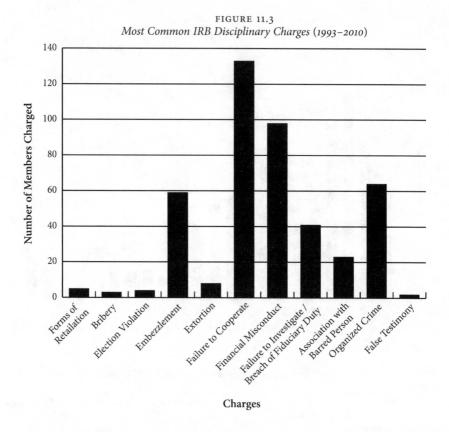

FIGURE 11.3
Most Common IRB Disciplinary Charges (1993–2010)

for failing to cooperate with IRB investigations into Cosa Nostra's influence in the union. Nineteen IBT local presidents were expelled for LCN-related disciplinary violations; of the IO's first thirty-eight organized-crime cases, all the respondents were IBT officers. Another one-fifth of disciplinary respondents were charged with failing to cooperate with an IO or IRB investigation.

Since July 1989, pursuant to direct IA or IRB action or IRB recommendations, fifty-four local unions and three joint councils have been placed under international-union trusteeships, lasting from several months to several years. In some cases, those trusteeships successfully eliminated, or at least greatly reduced, corruption and racketeering. In other cases, corrupt practices reappeared after the trusteeship's termination, and the local had to be retrusteed (e.g., Philadelphia IBT Local 107).

The sum total of this administrative disciplinary enforcement is extraordinary. There has never been private-sector organizational reform on this scale; the administrative infrastructure of the IBT has significantly changed. Much space has opened up for new leadership, and investigations, adjudications.

The Consent Decree's Election Prong

The *U.S. v. IBT* consent decree is the only civil RICO consent decree involving an international union that included a remedial-election-reform prong.*[8] The DOJ lawyers who negotiated the settlement accepted AUD's and TDU's thesis that free and fair rank-and-file elections would lead to the removal of LCN-influenced officers and would prevent corrupt individuals from attaining union office. This thesis conceals two assumptions: first, that rank and filers know, or will find out, which candidates for international office are controlled or influenced by LCN; second, that accurately informed rank and filers will vote against corrupt candidates. Both assumptions should be questioned.

How is the ordinary Teamster to know which candidates for international-union office are influenced or controlled by organized-crime figures or are otherwise corrupt? Many candidates boast of their own integrity and call their opponents corrupt. Every IBT general presidential candidate since 1991 has claimed to be honest, reform-minded, and hostile to organized crime; invariably, they accuse their opponents of being the opposite. Charges and countercharges fly back and forth. There is no judge to decide who is telling the truth. The ordinary Teamster has likely never met the general presidential or vice presidential candidates; even if he or she had, it probably would not improve his or her capacity to make an informed opinion about their commitment to rooting out corruption.

Moreover, most Teamsters, like most rank and filers in other unions, pay little attention to union politics, including the campaigns of candidates for international office. Political apathy is the rule. Since the *U.S. v. IBT* settlement decreed elections for convention delegates, more than 50 percent

---

* There have been only four civil RICO suits against international unions. In addition to *U.S. v. IBT*, DOJ obtained consent decrees in suits against the Hotel and Restaurant Workers International Union and the Laborers' International Union of America (LIUNA). DOJ's civil RICO complaint against the International Longshoremen's Association was dismissed and then amended and refiled; as of May 2011, it is still pending.

of all convention-delegate elections have gone uncontested. Moreover, 75 percent of Teamsters have not bothered to cast mail-in ballots for general president and other international officers.

The minority who did vote likely based their opinions of the candidates on their friends' and local-union officers' opinions and on information contained in *Teamster Magazine* and in candidates' campaign literature. Unlike elections for local, state, and federal office, there are no independent "good government" organizations or media sources that provide information or opinions about IBT international-union officers. Indeed, it would be very difficult for a "neutral" reporter to competently investigate a candidate's integrity or anticorruption commitment. Even if such a reporter could do so, it is unlikely that he or she could persuade readers that his or her reporting is reliable and unbiased. TDU, of course, purports to be a reliable truth-telling organization, but it is hardly seen as neutral. TDU functions like an opposition party or faction, relentlessly criticizing IBT officialdom and endorsing insurgent candidates.

Even if the rank and file could determine which candidates are honest and which corrupt, the second assumption—that knowledgeable Teamsters will vote for the honest candidates—is not necessarily true. During the drafting stage of the *U.S. v. IBT* complaint, TDU insisted that Teamsters, like other Americans, would not vote for racketeers. Unfortunately, however, many Americans have and do vote for corrupt candidates. In federal, state, and local elections for legislative and executive offices, voters frequently reelect candidates who are tainted by corruption allegations and scandals. They overwhelmingly reelect incumbents, despite allegations of misconduct, and they are little influenced by the opinions of "good government" organizations. (On average, incumbent members of the House of Representatives win election more than 90 percent of the time, and incumbent U.S. senators win reelection more than 85 percent of the time.) Even criminal charges may not prevent reelection.[9] Moreover, even if a majority of voters rejects a corrupt incumbent, there is no assurance that the incumbent's successor is or will remain honest.* IBT rank

---

* World and U.S. history are filled with examples of self-professed reformers who turn out to be corrupt officeholders. For example, Rod Blagojevich, who was removed as governor of Illinois and later convicted of a federal crime based on his alleged attempt to "sell" a vacant U.S. Senate seat, based his successful 2002 Illinois gubernatorial campaign largely on an anticorruption platform. Upon announcing his candidacy, he proclaimed that "a governor must be willing to take on the special interests, not carry their water. . . . It means shaking up a system that serves itself instead of the people." Joanna Lin, *He Campaigned as a Reformer*, Los Angeles Times, Dec. 10, 2008.

and filers, with or without accurate information, might prefer the devil they know to the devil they do not know. ("He may be a crook, but he's our crook.") They may themselves be dependent on corrupt officers for special benefits. They may fear retaliation if they vote against the incumbent (even though convention-delegate and international-officer balloting is anonymous).

Some mob-connected IBT officials have been charismatic and personally popular. Jimmy Hoffa, Sr.'s name remains hugely popular among rank-and-file Teamsters even though he was convicted of union-related corruption. After Ed Stier became trustee of IBT Local 560 and oversaw a free and fair election, the members chose the Provenzano brothers' nephew as the local's principal officer. Of course, Ron Carey was voted into the IBT general presidency as an anticorruption reformer and proved to be corrupt himself. (Indeed, even after the IRB found that Carey had embezzled money from the union via his campaign's contribution-swap scheme, many Teamsters, including some who professed to be greatly concerned about corruption, continued to praise him.)

Lessons for Union Democracy

Fifty years ago, in a classic study of the Typographical Workers Union, Lipset, Trow, and Coleman found that

> [a]pathy of the members is the normal state of affairs. There are good reasons for this. Most union members, like other people, must spend most of their time at work or with their families. Their remaining free time is usually taken up by their friends, commercial entertainment and other personally rewarding recreational activities.[10]

The authors applied Robert Michels's "iron law of oligopoly" to union governance:

> In few areas of political life is the discrepancy between the formal juridical guarantees of democratic procedure and the actual practice of oligarchic rule so marked as in private or voluntary organizations such as trade unions. . . . In fact, as many observers have noted, almost all such organizations are characterized internally by the rule of a one-party oligarchy. That is, one group, which controls the administration, usually retains power

indefinitely, rarely faces organized opposition, and when faced with such opposition often resorts to undemocratic procedures to eliminate it.[11]

When "reformers" win office, according to Lipset, Trow, and Coleman, they often resort to their predecessors' corrupt tactics to hold on to the reins of power.[12]

The architects of the *U.S. v. IBT* consent decree would have been well advised to consider Lipset, Trow, and Coleman's observations before committing themselves to rank-and-file elections as an antidote to corruption and racketeering. While the IBT's elections have been, for the most part, free and fair, they continue to disappoint those who believe that a politically energized rank and file will elect insurgents. During the twenty-two-year remedial phase of *U.S. v. IBT*, the union has become steadily more centralized. Like practically all unions, it functions as a one-party organization. Indeed, the 2011 international-officer election is the first election in which the overwhelming majority (twenty out of twenty-eight) of candidates will automatically be installed as GEB members without a rank-and-file vote; Sandy Pope currently has no running mates and Fred Gegare has only eight running mates. While TDU is well entrenched as an opposition faction, it plays no role in union governance. TDU-endorsed candidates hold office in few locals, but the 35 percent of Teamsters who have voted for the TDU-backed slate have no role in union governance. We are reminded of the observations of Clyde Summers, the most prominent academic champion of union democracy:

> If our goal is ideal democracy, and we will accept nothing less, then we, indeed, must be pessimistic. Elected union leaders will continue to dominate the political structure and seek to create a monolithic bureaucracy which eliminates or immobilizes organized opposition in the name of efficiency and loyalty. The law cannot and does not mandate a two-party system, and there is no reason to hope that such a system will emerge. Unions will continue to be one-party states.[13]

An important lesson of *U.S. v. IBT* is that it is a mistake to equate union democracy with democratic elections. Union democracy, like democracy itself, involves more than just free and fair elections. Democracy includes respect for free speech, equal treatment, due process, minority interests, local autonomy, and opportunities for rank-and-file participation.

Lessons for Court-Supervised Institutional Reform

This case study should inform the extensive academic and political debate about the role and competence of courts in bringing about organizational change. To date, almost all of the data for this debate have been drawn from constitutional challenges to conditions and practices in public institutions and agencies such as schools, jails, prisons, and mental hospitals. Critics of court-ordered institutional reform object to courts imposing administrative burdens and monetary costs on state and local agencies.[14] They complain that courts frequently fail to anticipate the unintended negative consequences of their reform interventions. Proponents argue that when the legislative and executive branches of government are unable or unwilling to address unconstitutional conditions in public institutions, politically insulated (by life tenure) federal judges have no alternative but to step in. By and large, according to these proponents, federal-court interventions have been successful. *U.S. v. IBT* provides an opportunity for legal scholars and political scientists to examine the potential and limits of court-supervised institutional reform in the private sector, where the wrongdoers are not state or local officials but union officials and organized-crime figures.

Critics oppose "the government" "taking over" or "running" a labor union because it is "undemocratic" and destructive of workers' right to organize and pursue their interests collectively. We disagree. There was certainly nothing democratic about IBT governance in the decades prior to *U.S. v. IBT*. Certainly, the IBT is far more democratic now than it was prior to the lawsuit. Union members today can speak their minds, run for office, vote, and criticize their leaders without fear of physical retribution and/or blacklisting.

Furthermore, we do not view the consent decree in *U.S. v. IBT* as a government or court takeover of the IBT. (In the 2001 IBT general presidential debate, both candidates referred to getting "the government" out of the union.) Unlike some of the civil RICO lawsuits against local unions, the court-appointed officers in *U.S. v. IBT* have no authority over collective bargaining, contract administration, strikes, organizing, lobbying, grievance handling, and day-to-day union administration. The election remedy, though sweeping, affects only the election of IBT international officers, not the election of local or joint-council officers. It establishes no new offices and imposes no new executive responsibilities, except that GEB officers must not ignore corruption.

That court-appointed officers operate the union's disciplinary system is undoubtedly an intrusion into union self-governance. However, this is the raison d'être of the civil RICO suit, that is, that the heavily corrupted union leadership systematically victimized the rank and file and the union as an entity. If removing corrupt Teamsters officials administratively is undue interference with a democratic labor movement, then so is sending corrupt union officials to prison.

Still, the undesirability of excessive government or court regulation of labor unions should be a basic principle guiding the design, imposition, and operation of civil RICO litigation against labor unions. DOJ did not file *U.S. v. IBT* to see the union run better or more fairly, or even to eliminate run-of-the-mill corruption. The lawsuit aimed to deny Cosa Nostra an important economic and political power base. When Cosa Nostra's influence in the union has been eradicated, the consent decree should end.

Who Pays?

The *U.S. v. IBT* remediation has been expensive.* From issuance of the consent decree in March 1989 through December 2010, well over $100 million has been spent to supervise elections and investigate disciplinary violations. The IBT has covered almost all of this expense, including $3 million per year to operate the IRB and at least $10 million every five years to supervise the elections. U.S. taxpayers have also picked up some of the tab, including $20 million for supervision of the 1996 and 1998 elections and the U.S. attorney's (SDNY) office's litigation expenses.

In assessing the remediation's cost to the IBT, however, observers should note that, without the IRB, the union would have had to expend resources on an internal disciplinary enforcement unit. Of course, a cost-conscious union, on its own initiative, probably would not have spent as much as the IO/IA and IRB have spent. However, the union probably would not have spent enough to mount an effective anticorruption effort. The court-appointed disciplinary officers, through investigations and deterrence, have likely saved the union a great deal of money by reducing theft, fraud, and other misappropriation of union funds. Further, had there been no election

---

* Days before the 2011 IBT convention, general presidential candidate Fred Gegare and others filed a (legally meritless but perhaps politically salient) lawsuit against Hoffa and DOJ demanding the consent decree's dissolution and stating that its implementation has already cost the IBT $147 million. *See* http://www.fred2011.org/docs/Complaint%5B1%5D.pdf.

officer, a properly functioning IBT would still have had to cover the cost of international conventions, each of which costs millions of dollars. Moreover, direct rank-and-file elections have probably saved the union money by improving international officers' accountability. Ultimately, the IBT has received substantial benefits for its *U.S. v. IBT* expenditures, including the near elimination of LCN's influence and four (not counting 1996) free and fair international elections.

Still, the question remains: who should pay for enforcement of the consent decree? On the one hand, it makes sense to require the IBT to pay the cost of remediating the systemic corruption that its leaders had long tolerated and, in some cases, actively furthered. On the other hand, the IBT's rank and filers, not its corrupt leaders, ultimately pay the cleanup bill via their monthly dues. The rank and filers are doubly victimized, first by the labor racketeers and second by having to bear the cost of remediating labor racketeering.

Is it fair to require rank-and-file Teamsters to pay the cost of eliminating the corrupt union officers who exploited and intimidated them? We cannot answer that question without considering the fairness and desirability of the alternative: requiring taxpayers to pick up the tab. If the government had to cover the remediation cost, the whole effort would have been politicized and thereby jeopardized. A few resolute members of Congress would have been able to shut down the whole remedial effort by refusing to support it (or refusing to support it adequately). Faced with that prospect, we believe that requiring the corrupted organization to pay for the remediation is not only the better alternative but also the only alternative.

The *U.S. v. IBT* remediation has generated many financial disputes, for example, the remuneration of the court-appointed officers, the IO's request for an NYC office, the size of the court officers' staffs, the extent of election regulation and monitoring, the IA's need to hire a public-relations firm, and the EO's decision to produce and distribute debate videos. We are in no position to second-guess each expenditure; however, we recognize that some of these expenditures would be difficult to defend (e.g., paying court officers Wall Street lawyer–level fees).

The Challenge of Evaluation

There is no existing methodology for determining whether *U.S. v. IBT* has achieved its goals and, if so, at what cost. Assessing the accomplishments of

U.S. v. IBT on some kind of "success index" would require identifying the goals against which the accomplishments of the lawsuit should be measured. The DOJ lawyers who drafted the *U.S. v. IBT* complaint, as well as the AUD and TDU leaders who sought to influence the lawsuit, undoubtedly had different goals and timetables in their minds. Indeed, all or some might not have fully thought through their ultimate ambitions for the lawsuit. Perhaps some DOJ lawyers hoped to deliver a mortal wound to Cosa Nostra by denying the crime syndicate one of its most important power bases. However, had those lawyers been asked what would constitute success, they might have been more modest. It is unlikely that all seven DOJ attorneys who worked on the complaint-drafting team had the same expectation about how much impact *U.S. v. IBT* would have on Cosa Nostra and how long it would take to achieve that impact. Some may have believed that the lawsuit would quickly eradicate certain LCN families, others that the lawsuit could claim success if it merely contributed (substantially? modestly? nontrivially?) to weakening one or two LCN families. The leaders of AUD, TDU, and probably some DOJ attorneys hoped that the civil RICO suit would jump-start a vibrant democracy in the IBT. But it is unlikely that they had a clear sense of how much democracy would have to occur in order to constitute success. Some, but not all, probably saw the sine qua non of success as TDU's capturing the IBT general presidency and the GEB.

In the two decades since the filing of *U.S. v. IBT*, LCN's size, resources, power, and influence have significantly diminished. By 2011, some LCN crime families have virtually ceased to exist. Some criminologists question whether Cosa Nostra will survive much longer.[15] It is impossible to say how much the whole corpus of civil RICO labor-racketeering lawsuits, much less *U.S. v. IBT* by itself, has contributed to organized crime's decline. Evaluation is complicated by the fact that, from 1980 to 2011, hundreds of criminal prosecutions removed LCN leaders, members, and associates from the streets.[16] It is impossible to disentangle the impact of these criminal prosecutions from the impact of the twenty-plus civil RICO lawsuits against organized-crime-infiltrated unions.

Evaluation of the disciplinary prong of the *U.S. v. IBT* consent decree requires analysis of the extent to which LCN's influence in the IBT has diminished. Until well into the 1980s, Cosa Nostra counted on the Teamsters Union (the international office and dozens of locals and joint councils) to provide LCN members and associates with money, jobs, and political influence. Here, there is good news. Practically all Teamsters officials known or suspected of belonging to Cosa Nostra, as members or associates, have been expelled from the IBT. Most IBT officials who publicly associated with Cosa Nostra members have also been expelled, as have scores of officers who turned a blind eye to organized crime's influence.

Of course, the civil RICO suit could not be considered successful if LCN has continued to exert influence through intermediaries. It is impossible to prove that this has not happened, but we believe it has not (at least not to any meaningful degree). The IRB has been aggressive in bringing disciplinary charges against IBT officials who continue to associate with barred members, thereby making intercourse between LCN members and IBT members risky. Although the IRB continues to identify Teamsters who are members or associates of LCN, the Teamsters Union is no longer a political or economic power base for LCN. Moreover, Cosa Nostra's leaders no longer influence, much less dictate, the selection of IBT leaders at the local, regional, or international level; businesses associated with Cosa Nostra no longer receive "loans" from the IBT's pension and welfare funds; and far fewer Cosa Nostra associates and friends obtain no-show jobs with the union or with Teamsters employers.

An End in Sight?

The *U.S. v. IBT* consent decree provides for the termination of the decree upon the petition of both parties and the approval of the judge.[17] Since the IBT has desired the consent decree's end from the day it went into effect, how much longer the consent decree will continue depends on DOJ, first and foremost on the U.S. attorney for SDNY (in 2011, Preet Bharara). We can expect the U.S. attorney to be highly risk-averse in deciding whether it is time to end the consent decree. If, after termination of the lawsuit, LCN were to reassert its influence in the IBT, two decades of remedial accomplishments would be undermined, possibly nullified. Premature termination of the consent decree would be an embarrassment for the incumbent U.S. attorney and for the U.S. attorney general. By contrast, maintaining the consent decree is a low-risk and low-cost decision. At this point, the lawsuit does not make big demands on the resources of the U.S. attorney's office; most of the remedial work, both disciplinary and election related, is handled by the court-appointed officers, whose salaries and expenses the union pays.

It is practically inconceivable that the U.S. attorney would agree to terminate the lawsuit in the face of the IRB's opposition or perhaps without the IRB's affirmative recommendation. Without such a recommendation, the U.S. attorney would be susceptible to severe criticism in the event that LCN racketeering reemerged. For its part, the IRB has little incentive to declare its work complete. First, the IRB members and staff have a financial interest in continuing their employment. Second, after so many years of engagement, the CI, IRB members, and staffers have every reason to believe in the importance of their work and that premature termination of the consent decree might undo more than two decades of remediation. This is even truer if the IRB defines its job as prosecuting and preventing all corruption on the theory that any corruption contributes to an organizational environment conducive to LCN infiltration and exploitation.

Almost certainly, a cautious U.S. attorney would not agree to terminate the IRB without the IBT having established an effective disciplinary unit and process independent of the IBT's general president and GEB. A further complication is that, during the IRB phase of the *U.S. v. IBT* remediation, the IBT does not prosecute LCN-related disciplinary violations because the FBI does not permit its agents to testify before IBT disciplinary hearing panels. Thus, the IRB itself adjudicates all LCN-related disciplinary charges. How would such cases be handled if the IRB dissolved? It is inconceivable that the U.S. attorney would agree to terminate the *U.S. v. IBT* consent decree without assurance that a viable mechanism for handling organized-crime-related disciplinary matters would replace the IRB. Any acceptable IBT replacement for the IRB would require a secure budget and a boss whom the IBT leadership could not remove. Because these would be difficult pills to swallow, the IBT leaders might prefer to live with the IRB, which it can continue to blame for disciplinary decisions that would be politically costly if made by IBT leaders on their own.

Since the IBT adopted the consent decree's election prong into the union's constitution in 2001, is it now a permanent feature of IBT governance? This is not an easy question to answer. On the one hand, union constitutions change; delegates to the IBT's quinquennial international conventions can, and often do, amend the constitution. On the other hand, General President Hoffa has been a consistent supporter (at least publicly) of a nominating convention followed by a rank-and-file election. However, a future administration might take the position that, after more than twenty years under the civil RICO consent decree, the IBT should be free to change the way it selects international officers, especially because reverting to a national convention alone would save millions of dollars. Perhaps in exchange for agreeing to terminate the consent decree, DOJ would seek an IBT commitment to hold independently supervised rank-and-file elections for several more election cycles. But enforcement of such a promise would present a problem.

The Hoffa administration could retreat less drastically, but perhaps equally effectively, from the current regime of rank-and-file elections by raising the percentage of convention-delegate votes that a candidate needs to qualify for the general international-officer election. The incumbent administration could argue that a candidate who receives only 5 percent of the convention delegates' nominating votes is not a serious contender for international office and should not be able to trigger a multimillion-dollar election. If the threshold number of convention-delegate votes were raised to 10 percent, there is a strong possibility that no general presidential challenger, and probably no member of the challenger's slate, would qualify for the general election. In that case, the convention delegates would, in effect, select the general president, secretary-treasurer, and GEB officials.

In constitutional litigation over jails, prisons, schools, and other institutions, it has often proved difficult and controversial to terminate the consent decree. There have been efforts in Congress, so far unsuccessful, to make it easier to terminate consent decrees. For example, in March 2005, Senator Lamar Alexander (R-Tenn.) introduced a bill (Federal Consent Decree Fairness Act) that sought to authorize state and local governments to ask the relevant federal court to terminate a consent decree upon the earlier of (1) the passage of four years from the date the consent decree took effect, or (2) the expiration of the term of office of the highest elected state or local government official authorizing the consent decree.[18] This bill never reached a Senate or House vote.

The U.S. Supreme Court has also weighed in on the issue of terminating consent decrees in public-sector litigation. In a 2009 decision, *Horne v. Flores*, the U.S. Supreme Court explained that a consent decree providing for federal-court supervision of an agreement to provide adequate funding for in-school English-language instruction must end when violations of federal law cease, even if the consent decree's stated goals remain unachieved.[19] Expressing concerns that federalism principles may be infringed, that government officials might use consent decrees to circumvent political constraints, that some consent decrees persist after circumstances have changed, and that there is a "risk of collusion between advocacy groups and executive officials who want to bind the hands of future policymakers," the Supreme Court explained that courts must take a "flexible approach" to . . . motions addressing such decrees. . . . A flexible approach allows courts to ensure that "responsibility for discharging the State's obligations is returned promptly to the State and its officials" when the circumstances warrant. . . . In applying this flexible approach, courts must remain attentive to the fact that "federal-court decrees exceed appropriate limits if they are aimed at eliminating a condition that does not violate federal law or does not flow from such a violation."[20]

Both the proposed Consent Decree Fairness Act and the *Horne* decision are directed at federal-court remediation of state and local institutions charged with violating federal constitutional and/or statutory law. To our knowledge, there has not been any discussion of whether and, if so, how concern about excessive federal-court involvement in organizational reform applies to civil RICO litigation against private organizations, such as labor unions. While federalism is not at issue in *U.S. v. IBT*, as it was in *Horne*, there are similar issues of (1) a reform decree taking on a life of its own, and (2) binding an organization's governance many years after the original defendants have left the scene. At a minimum, after twenty-two years, it would make sense for the court now to assert its own authority to end the consent decree, even over DOJ's objection, *if it finds that the threat of ongoing RICO violations is no longer present.*

Of course, even if Chief Judge Preska had the authority without a DOJ motion to modify the consent decree's provision on termination, it would be difficult for her to determine if the threat of future RICO violations remains. Those who favor ending the consent decree cannot prove the negative—that there is no organized-crime influence in the IBT. There will always be a good reason to extend the consent decree a little longer.

Acknowledgments

Many people, some of them participants in the events examined in this book, have generously assisted us in establishing an accurate historical record of this most remarkable litigation. The book could not have been written without their cooperation.

Over the years, several NYU law students made important contributions to the research leading up to this book. The chapter on *U.S. v. IBT* in *Busting the Mob: United States v. Cosa Nostra* (NYU Press, 1994) was prepared with the assistance of Christopher Panarella and Jay Worthington III. A few years later, Coleen Friel and Robert Radick, my coauthors on *Gotham Unbound: How New York City Was Liberated from the Grip of Organized Crime* (NYU Press, 1998), did a good deal of work on labor racketeering generally, including on the Teamsters Union. In 2005, Ryan Alford and I coauthored an article titled "The Teamsters' Rocky Road to Recovery: The Demise of Project RISE." More recently, Dimitri Portnoi and I published two law review articles, one on *U.S. v. IBT*'s disciplinary prong and the other on its election-reform prong. Kerry Cooperman, a Criminal Justice Center fellow, worked full-time on the book from October 1, 2009, until we delivered the manuscript on November 8, 2010. He is, in every respect, the coauthor of this volume. I am ever appreciative to Dean Richard Revesz, who provides constant support and encouragement and who made Kerry's fellowship possible. Thanks, too, to the D'Agostino-Greenberg Faculty Research Fund. Finally, during the past year, we received valuable research assistance from Elizabeth Dondlinger, Daniel Friedman, and Shira Peleg.

James B. Jacobs
NYU School of Law

Notes

NOTES TO CHAPTER 1

1. President's Commission on Organized Crime, *The Edge: Organized Crime, Business, and Labor Unions*, Washington, D.C.: U.S. Government Printing Office, 1986 [hereinafter *The Edge*], at 89.

2. Leslie M. Werner, *U.S. Seeks Control of Teamsters Union*, NEW YORK TIMES, June 11, 1987, *available at* http://www.nytimes.com/1987/06/11/us/us-seeks-control -of-teamster-union.html; Robert L. Jackson & Ronald J. Ostrow, *Teamsters Assail Justice Dept. Suit, Deny Mafia Controls Union, Call Action "Political Ploy,"* LOS ANGELES TIMES, June 11, 1987, available at http://articles.latimes.com/1987-06-11/ news/mn-6525_1.

3. DOJ comprises its Washington, D.C., headquarters ("Main Justice") plus ninety-three U.S. attorney offices, one in each federal judicial district. The U.S. attorneys, like the U.S. attorney general, are appointed by the president and confirmed by the Senate.

4. OCRS must approve U.S. attorneys' offices' RICO cases. U.S. Attorney's Manual, § 9-110.320.

5. *See, e.g.,* James B. Jacobs, *Mobsters, Unions, and Feds: The Mafia and the American Labor Movement*, New York: NYU Press, 2006 [hereinafter *Mobsters, Unions, and Feds*], at 2.

6. *The Edge*, at 89.

7. *Id.* at 138.

8. Peter Stoler, Walter Calling, Roberto Suro & Barry Kalb, *The Sicilian Connection*, TIME, Oct. 15, 1984.

9. *United States v. Badalamenti*, 887 F.2d 1141 (2d Cir. 1989), *cert. denied*, 110 S. Ct. 1138 (1990).

10. James B. Jacobs, Christopher Panarella & Jay Worthington III, *Busting the Mob: United States v. Cosa Nostra*, New York: NYU Press, 1994 [hereinafter *Busting the Mob*], at ch. 4.

11. *United States v. Salerno*, 868 F.2d 524 (2d Cir. 1989).

12. John O'Rourke, president of the local from 1931 to 1965, was a close associate of Johnny Dioguardi and Anthony Corallo of the Lucchese family; John Cody, president of the local from 1976 to 1984, was controlled by the Gambino family;

and Robert Sasso, who succeeded Cody, was also an associate of the Gambino family. In 1982, Cody was convicted of racketeering and labor bribery. Years later, Sasso pled guilty to racketeering. Ronald Goldstock, Martin Marcus, Thomas D. Thacher II & James B. Jacobs, *Corruption and Racketeering in the New York City Construction Industry: Final Report to Governor Mario M. Cuomo from the New York State Organized Crime Task Force*, New York: NYU Press, 1990.

13. *United States v. Scopo*, 861 F.2d 339, 341 (2d Cir. 1988).

14. *United States v. Local 6A*, 832 F. Supp. 674 (S.D.N.Y. 1993).

15. James B. Jacobs, Coleen Friel & Robert Radick, *Gotham Unbound: How New York City Was Liberated from the Grip of Organized Crime*, New York: NYU Press, 1999 [hereinafter *Gotham Unbound*], at 215.

16. *United States v. Long*, 697 F. Supp. 651 (S.D.N.Y. 1988).

17. Kenneth C. Crowe, *Collision: How the Rank and File Took Back the Teamsters*, New York: Scribner, 1993 [hereinafter *Collision*], at 13–22.

18. *Id.* at 20–21.

19. *Id.*

20. *Id.* at 22.

21. *Id.* at 67.

22. Henry Weinstein & Ronald Ostrow, *Teamsters Rally Forces to Battle U.S. Takeover*, Los Angeles Times, Sept. 10, 1987.

23. Letter to Attorney General Meese from 264 members of Congress, Dec. 10, 1987; *see also Busting the Mob*, at 182–83.

24. *See generally* Michael J. Goldberg, *Teamster Reformers: Their Union, Their Jobs, Their Movement*, 72 J. Transportation Law, Logistics & Policy 13 (2005).

25. In 1977, for example, four TDU-endorsed candidates won elections in Green Bay, Wisconsin IBT Local 75. In 1978, TDUer Jack Farrell became president of Oklahoma IBT Local 886. In 1979, TDU's entire seven-person slate was elected to lead Spokane, Washington IBT Local 690. In 1980, TDU member Jerry Bliss defeated incumbent candidate Bobby Holmes, Jr., the son of Detroit IBT Local 337's president, to become secretary-treasurer of that local. Dan La Botz, *Rank and File Rebellion*, New York: Verso, 1990 [hereinafter *Rank and File Rebellion*], at 159.

26. *Id.* at ch. 13.

27. *Id.* at 189. In March 1977, Detroit IBT Local 299 expelled Camarata and Ferdnance, concluding that they had interfered with the union's contractual obligations by supporting a carhauler strike. But TDU obtained a temporary restraining order in federal court reinstating them. Eventually, after TDU organized rallies and distributed leaflets in opposition to the expulsions, Local 299 dropped the charges against Ferdnance, and Michigan Joint Council 43 reversed the expulsion of Camarata.

28. *Id.* at 186–88.

29. *Id.* at 188.

30. *The Edge*, at 114.

31. *Id.*

32. Transcript, Meeting of IBT Joint Council 41, Oct. 31, 1983, Cleveland, Ohio (subpoenaed by the PCOC); *see also* James Neff, *Mobbed Up: Jackie Presser's High-Wire Life in the Teamsters, the Mafia, and the FBI*, New York: Atlantic Monthly Press, 1989 [hereinafter *Mobbed Up*], at 383–86.

33. Letter from Kenneth Paff, National Organizer, Teamsters for a Democratic Union, to Stephen Trott, Assistant Attorney General, May 4, 1987 (obtained from TDU; on file with author).

34. CONVOY DISPATCH, June–July 1987.

35. According to its website, AUD is a "national, pro-labor, non-profit organization dedicated to advancing the principles and practices of democratic trade unionism in the North American labor movement." http://www.uniondemocracy .org/.

36. Herman Benson, *Rebels, Reformers, and Racketeers: How Insurgents Transformed the Labor Movement*, New York: 1st Books, 2004.

37. Interview with Herman Benson, Nov. 10, 2009.

38. *See generally* Goldberg, *Teamster Reformers*, at 18.

39. IBT, "Teamsters Structure," http://www.teamster.org/content/teamsters -structure.

40. IBT Constitution, Art. 7, § 1.

41. Telephone conversation with IBT historian Karin Jones, Apr. 6, 2010.

42. IBT Constitution, Art. 6, § 1(f).

43. IBT, "Facts," http://www.teamster.org/content/fast-facts.

44. IBT, "Teamsters Structure," http://www.teamster.org/content/teamsters -structure.

45. Stier, Anderson & Malone, LLC, *The Teamsters: Perception and Reality: An Investigative Study of Organized Crime Influence in the Union*, Washington, D.C.: IBT, 2001 [hereinafter *Perception and Reality*]; Mitchel P. Roth, *Organized Crime*, Boston: Allyn & Bacon, 2009.

46. *Mobsters, Unions, and Feds*, at 28.

47. *United States v. Licavoli*, 725 F.2d 1040 (6th Cir. 1984).

48. Dioguardi was later charged with conspiring to hire a thug to throw acid in the face of journalist Victor Riesel, who wrote articles exposing corruption and racketeering in the IBT. Charges against Dioguardi were dropped when the government's cooperating witnesses recanted their pretrial statements implicating Dioguardi and claimed that they did not know who ordered the Riesel attack. Bill Becker, *Key Dio Witness Refuses to Talk*, NEW YORK TIMES, May 21, 1957; Edward Ranzal, *Dio Case Dropped from Court Docket*, NEW YORK TIMES, May 28, 1957.

49. Other LCN figures exerted racketeering influence in other unions. Anthony Anastasio, a labor racketeer in the Genovese crime family, was business manager

and vice president of ILA Local 1814. Tony Accardo, the boss of the Chicago Outfit, controlled Hollywood's movie-industry unions. Joseph Aiuppa, a later boss of the Chicago Outfit, controlled LIUNA's locals in Chicago and St. Louis.

50. *Busting the Mob*, at 191 (quoting Roy Williams's deposition).

51. *United States v. Local 560*, 581 F. Supp. 279 (D.N.J. 1984); *see also* James B. Jacobs & David Santore, *The Liberation of IBT Local 560*, 37 CRIM. L. BULLETIN 125 (Mar.–Apr. 2001).

52. Anthony was a business agent (1948–1958), president (1958–1966), and secretary-treasurer (1975–1978) of Local 560. Salvatore's Local 560 positions included business agent (1959–1961), trustee (1961–1965, 1966), president (1966–1975, 1981–1984), and vice president (1975–1981). Nunzio served as business agent (1963–1966, 1970–1973), clerk (1969–1970), secretary-treasurer (1973–1975), and president (1975–1981).

53. *Perception and Reality*, at 210.

54. *Local 560*, 581 F. Supp. at 304.

55. *Id.* at 282–83.

56. House Committee on Education and the Workforce, Subcommittee on Oversight and Investigations, *Lessons Learned from the Teamsters Local 560 Trusteeship: Hearing before the Subcommittee on Oversight and Investigations*, 106th Cong., 1st sess., June 30, 1999.

57. Arthur A. Sloane, *Hoffa*, Cambridge: MIT Press, 1991 [hereinafter *Hoffa*], at 10, 36.

58. *Id.* at 32 (noting that Hoffa began meeting with Detroit mobsters in 1941).

59. *Id.* at 33.

60. Thaddeus Russell, *Out of the Jungle: Jimmy Hoffa and the Remaking of the American Working Class*, New York: Knopf, 2001 [hereinafter *Out of the Jungle*], at 174–75.

61. *Id.* at 97.

62. *Hoffa*, at 36.

63. *Out of the Jungle*, at 174. Indeed, in February 1978, DOL filed a civil suit against seventeen former trustees and two officials of the CSPF, claiming that, over a seventeen-year period, the CSPF improperly loaned over $500 million to mob-controlled hotels and casinos in Las Vegas. In September 1982, DOL and the CSPF entered into a consent decree whereby an independent special counsel and a new court-approved fiduciary would "assure that the fund's [$5 billion] assets are managed for the sole benefit of the plan's participants and beneficiaries." As of January 1, 2011, the consent decree remains in effect. U.S. General Accounting Office, *Dep't of Labor's Oversight of the Mgm't of the Teamsters' Central States Pension and Health and Welfare Funds*, report to the Permanent Subcommittee on Investigations, Commission on Government Affairs, U.S. Senate, July 18, 1985. For a detailed discussion of Paul Dorfman's relationship with Jimmy Hoffa, see Gus Russo,

Supermob: How Sidney Korshak and His Criminal Associates Became America's Hidden Power Brokers, New York: Bloomsbury, 2006, at ch. 8.

64. *See* Arthur M. Schlesinger, *Robert Kennedy and His Times*, Boston: Mariner Books, 1978.

65. *Id.* at 279–80.

66. Walter Sheridan, *The Fall and Rise of Jimmy Hoffa*, New York: Saturday Review Press, 1972, at ch. 8.

67. *Id.* at ch. 11.

68. *Dorfman Slain in Parking Lot*, MILWAUKEE JOURNAL, Jan. 21, 1983.

69. Arnold H. Lubasch, *Ex-Teamster Chief Tells Jury Mafia Controls Union Leaders*, NEW YORK TIMES, June 2, 1987.

70. *Id.*

71. *The Edge*, at 105.

72. Robert A. Dobkin, *U.S. Sues to Recover Pension Fund Losses in Teamster Plan*, ASSOCIATED PRESS, Feb. 1, 1978.

73. Edward Pound, *Union Dissidents and 2 in Congress Assail Teamster in Reagan Group*, NEW YORK TIMES, Dec. 17, 1980; Robert Parry, *Reagan Unaware Appointee Had Reputed Crime Links*, ASSOCIATED PRESS, Dec. 16, 1980.

74. Arnold H. Lubasch, *Mob Figures Chose Teamsters' Chief, Government Says*, NEW YORK TIMES, Nov. 25, 1986; George Lardner, Jr., *Mob Backed Presser, Trial Told*, WASHINGTON POST, Nov. 27, 1985.

75. William Serrin, *Jackie Presser's Secret Lives Detailed in Government Files*, NEW YORK TIMES, Mar. 27, 1989; John Doyle, *Mob Boss Accused of Rigging Presser's Election as Teamsters Head*, ASSOCIATED PRESS, Nov. 24, 1986.

76. Kenneth R. Wallentine, *A Leash upon Labor: RICO Trusteeships on Labor Unions*, 7 HOFSTRA LAB. L.J. 341 (1990) (quoting 134 CONG. REC. S8663 (1988) (Statement of Senator Hatch)); Lawrence Zuckerman, Raji Samghabadi & Elaine Shannon, *Breaking a Devil's Pact*, TIME, July 11, 1988, *available at* http://www.time .com/time/magazine/article/0,9171,967865,00.html.

77. Ronald J. Ostrow & Robert L. Jackson, *U.S. Suit, Citing Crime Link, Will Seek Teamster Takeover*, WASHINGTON POST, June 10, 1987, at A1.

78. *Collision*, at 67 (quoting F.C. "Duke" Zeller).

79. *Id.* at 71 (quoting Barry Feinstein).

80. *Id.*

81. Matt Yancey, *AFL-CIO Welcomes Teamsters: Union Returns to Federation under Threat of U.S. Lawsuit*, NEW YORK TIMES, Oct. 27, 1987, at A5, *available at* http://www.laborers.org/AP_Teamo_AFL_10-25_87.html.

82. *Mobbed Up*, at 420–21.

83. Yancey, *AFL-CIO Welcomes Teamsters*.

84. Letter to Attorney General Meese from 264 members of Congress, Dec. 10, 1987; *see also Busting the Mob*, at 182–83.

85. According to the local rule, "Cases are related if they present common questions of law or fact, or arise from the same source or substantially similar transactions, happenings, events, or relationships, or if for any other reason they would entail substantial duplication of labor if assigned to different judges." In *U.S. v. Long & Mahoney*, which Giuliani's office had transferred to Judge Edelstein three weeks before filing *U.S. v. IBT*, Giuliani's office brought civil RICO claims against IBT Locals 804 and 808 after concluding that their secretary-treasurers had administered the locals via bribery, extortion, and other offenses for at least a decade. The *U.S. v. IBT* complaint stated, "In both this case and in *U.S. v. Long . . .* the United States has brought suit under the civil provisions of RICO to remedy corruption within the IBT. This case deals with corruption at the international level, while *U.S. v. Long* deals with corruption at the local level [IBT Locals 804 and 808]." Complaint, *United States v. Int'l Bhd. of Teamsters*, No. 88 Civ. 4486, at 6.

86. *Collision*, at 90.

87. Steven Brill, *When the Government Goes Judge Shopping*, Am. Law., Nov. 1988.

88. *In re International Business Machines Corp.*, 45 F.3d 641, 644 (2d. Cir. 1995).

89. Brill, *When the Government Goes Judge Shopping*.

NOTES TO CHAPTER 2

1. President's Commission on Organized Crime, *The Edge: Organized Crime, Business, and Labor Unions*, Washington, D.C.: U.S. Government Printing Office, 1986 [hereinafter *The Edge*], at 138.

2. Complaint, *United States v. Int'l Bhd. of Teamsters*, No. 88 Civ. 4486 [hereinafter Complaint], at ¶¶ 4–52.

3. Task Force on Organized Crime, *Task Force Report: Organized Crime: Annotations and Consultants' Papers*, Washington, D.C.: U.S. Government Printing Office, 1967.

4. *Id.* The task force concluded that organized crime's power and activities were increasing. Rep. Dante B. Fascell, Chairman, House Committee on Government Operations, Subcommittee on Legal and Monetary Affairs, *The Federal Effort against Organized Crime: Part 1*, 90th Cong., 1st sess., Apr. 5, 1967.

5. 18 U.S.C. §§ 2510–20 (2000).

6. 18 U.S.C. §§ 1961–65 (2000); *see also* Gerald E. Lynch, *RICO: The Crime of Being a Criminal, Parts I & II*, 87 Colum. L. Rev. 661 (1987); Gerald E. Lynch, *RICO: The Crime of Being a Criminal, Parts III and IV*, 87 Colum. L. Rev. 920 (1987); G. Robert Blakey, *RICO: The Genesis of an Idea*, 9 Trends in Organized Crime 8 (2006); Gregory P. Joseph, *Civil RICO: A Definitive Guide* (2d ed.), Chicago: ABA, 2000; Douglas E. Abrams, *The Law of Civil RICO*, Boston: Little, Brown, 1991;

Frank J. Marine & Patrice M. Mulkern, *Civil RICO: A Manual for Federal Attorneys*, Washington, D.C.: U.S. Department of Justice, 2007.

7. Under § 1961(1) of the RICO law, "racketeering activity" means (A) any act or threat involving murder, kidnapping, gambling, arson, robbery, bribery, extortion, dealing in obscene matter, or dealing in a controlled substance or listed chemical, which is chargeable under state law and punishable by imprisonment for more than one year; (B) any act indictable under the bribery, counterfeiting, felony theft, embezzlement, extortion, fraud, gambling, unlawful procurement of nationalization, obscenity, obstruction of justice, tampering, retaliation, false passport, forgery, peonage, trafficking, robbery, interference with commerce, unlawful welfare-fund payments, money laundering, murder for hire, sexual exploitation, copyright infringement, or weapons provisions of Title 18; (C) any act indictable under Title 29's provisions restricting payments and loans to labor organizations and prohibiting embezzlement from union funds; (D) any offense involving Title 11 fraud, fraud in the sale of securities, or the felonious manufacture, importation, receiving, concealment, buying, selling, or otherwise dealing in a controlled substance or listed chemical punishable under any federal law; (E) any act indictable under the Currency and Foreign Transactions Reporting Act; (F) any act indictable under the Immigration and Nationality Act; or (G) any act indictable under any provision listed in § 2332b(g)(5)(B) of the statute.

8. 18 U.S.C. § 1965 (2000); *see also* Gerald A. Toner, *New Ways of Thinking about Old Crimes*, 16 J. FINANCIAL CRIME 41 (2009).

9. James B. Jacobs, Eileen Cunningham & Kimberly Friday, *The RICO Trusteeships after 20 Years: A Progress Report*, 19 LABOR LAWYER 419 (2004).

10. Complaint, at 1–2.

11. *Id.*

12. *Id.* at 5.

13. James B. Jacobs, Christopher Panarella & Jay Worthington III, *Busting the Mob: United States v. Cosa Nostra*, New York: NYU Press, 1994 [hereinafter *Busting the Mob*], at ch. 3.

14. Complaint, at 104–15.

15. *Id.; see also* James B. Jacobs & Ellen Peters, *Labor Racketeering: The Mafia and the Unions*, in 30 CRIME AND JUSTICE: A REVIEW OF RESEARCH 229 (Michael Tonry ed.), Chicago: University of Chicago Press, 2003.

16. Complaint, Exhibit AQ.

17. Frank Sheeran, like Anthony Provenzano, is a good example of an individual who held positions in both Cosa Nostra and the IBT. Although Sheeran was Irish and, therefore, ineligible for full Cosa Nostra membership, he was a powerful associate of the Bufalino (northwestern Pennsylvania) organized-crime family. *See* Sheeran's posthumously published autobiography, transcribed by Charles Brandt, *"I Heard You Paint Houses": Frank "The Irishman" Sheeran and the Inside Story of*

the Mafia, the Teamsters, and the Last Ride of Jimmy Hoffa, Hanover, N.H.: Steer-forth, 2004.

18. Bob Drogin, *Mafia Leader Indicted over Presser Link*, Los Angeles Times, Nov. 25, 1986.

19. James Neff, *Mobbed Up: Jackie Presser's High-Wire Life in the Teamsters, the Mafia, and the FBI*, New York: Atlantic Monthly Press, 1989.

20. *See United States v. Salerno*, 85 CR 139 (S.D.N.Y. 1985). For example, in the 1986 "Commission case," Giuliani's office proved that control of NYC's District Council of Cement and Concrete Workers Unions enabled LCN to establish a car-tel so that NYC contractors had to pay an "organized-crime tax" for each cubic yard of poured concrete. LCN also ran a highly lucrative waste-hauling cartel in NYC. *Busting the Mob*, at 84.

21. *The Edge*, at 89–90.

22. Complaint, at 76–83.

23. *See generally id.*; *see also* 29 U.S.C. § 431 et seq. (2000).

24. Complaint, at 67–68, 73.

25. *Id.* at 58.

26. *See* Government's Memorandum of Law in Support of Its Motion for Pre-liminary Relief, *United States v. Int'l Bhd. of Teamsters*, 708 F. Supp. 1388 (S.D.N.Y. 1989) (No. 88 Civ. 4486) (June 28, 1988).

27. Complaint, at 73, 75.

28. TDU Motion to Intervene as Defendant.

29. Convoy Dispatch, Aug.–Sept. 1988, at 2.

30. *Id.*

31. *Id.*

32. Editorial, *The Right Medicine for the Teamsters*, New York Times, Sept. 4, 1988, at E14.

33. Editorial, *Democracy for the Teamsters*, Christian Science Monitor, July 11, 1988.

34. James J. Kilpatrick, *Justice Can't Abide a Brick in the Face*, Detroit Free Press, July 8, 1988.

35. Henry Weinstein, *U.S. Move against Teamsters Jolts Labor*, Los Angeles Times, June 14, 1987.

36. David Alcott, *Area Teamsters Denounce U.S. Plan to Oust Leaders*, Oak-land Tribune, June 12, 1987.

37. Jon Pepper, *Teamsters Press Fight to Halt U.S. Takeover*, Detroit News, Apr. 16, 1987.

38. *U.S. Government Files Suit to Oust Top Teamster Bosses*, Reuters, June 29, 1988.

39. Pepper, *Teamsters Press Fight to Halt U.S. Takeover*.

40. *Id.*

41. Marquis Shepherd, *Backing Federal Suit, Local Teamsters Chief Says Mob Rules Union*, KANSAS CITY TIMES, June 16, 1987.

42. *See* Kenneth Wallentine, *A Leash upon Labor: RICO Trusteeships on Labor Unions*, 7 HOFSTRA LAB. L.J. 341 (1990) (quoting 134 CONG. REC. S8663 (1988) (Statement of Senator Hatch)); Lawrence Zuckerman, Raji Samghabadi & Elaine Shannon, *Breaking a Devil's Pact*, TIME, July 11, 1988, *available at* http://www.time .com/time/magazine/article/0,9171,967865,00.html.

43. Pepper, *Teamsters Press Fight to Halt U.S. Takeover.*

44. *Id.*

45. Robert L. Jackson & Ronald J. Ostrow, *Presidential Hopefuls Rally behind Teamsters*, LOS ANGELES TIMES, September 5, 1987.

46. Margaret Trimer, *Teamsters Stage Rally against Takeover Plan*, DETROIT FREE PRESS, Nov. 9, 1987.

47. *Reagan Uninvolved in Union Takeover Talk, Presser Says*, CLEVELAND PLAIN DEALER, Aug. 4, 1987.

48. *Teamsters Takeover Plan "A Disgrace," Young Says*, DETROIT NEWS, June 1987.

49. Eric Freedman, *Union Takeovers Fuel Crime Fighting Debate*, DETROIT NEWS, Sept. 14, 1987.

50. John Schwartz, *Breaking the Teamsters: U.S. Officials Want to Oust All the Top Bosses*, NEWSWEEK, June 22, 1987.

51. Freedman, *Union Takeovers Fuel Crime Fighting Debate.*

52. *Int'l Bhd. of Teamsters*, 708 F. Supp. at 1392.

53. *Id.* at 1393 (emphasis in the original).

54. *Id.* at 1395.

55. *Id.* at 1402.

56. *Id.* at 1408.

57. *Id.* at 1401.

58. *Id.* at 1402.

59. *Id.* at 1404.

60. *Id.* Judge Edelstein doubted the sincerity of the IBT's concern for the convenience of the government's witnesses. "In so far as these witnesses are employees of the plaintiff, this point merits no discussion." *Id.*

61. *Id.*

62. Order Denying Preliminary Relief, *United States v. Int'l Bhd. of Teamsters*, No. 88 Civ. 4486 (S.D.N.Y.) (July 7, 1988).

63. *Id.* at 4.

64. *Int'l Bhd. of Teamsters*, 708 F. Supp. at 1405 n.8 and n.9. Anthony Provenzano died soon after *U.S. v. IBT* was filed.

65. *Id.* at 1405.

66. *Id.* at 1406.

67. *Id.* at 1406–07.

68. *The Edge*, at 89.

69. *United States v. Int'l Bhd. of Teamsters*, No. 88 Civ. 4486, Deposition of Robert Holmes, Sr., at 156–57.

70. Stier, Anderson & Malone, LLC, *The Teamsters: Perception and Reality: An Investigative Study of Organized Crime Influence in the Union*, Washington, D.C.: IBT, 2001 [hereinafter *Perception and Reality*], at 299.

71. *United States v. Int'l Bhd. of Teamsters*, No. 88 Civ. 4486, Deposition of Harold Friedman, at 111.

72. *Id.* at 163–64.

73. *Perceptions and Reality*, at 300; *Collision*, at 95–97.

74. Henry Weinstein & Ronald J. Ostrow, *Ex-Teamsters Officials Endorse Reforms*, LOS ANGELES TIMES, Feb. 2, 1989, at A18.

75. Henry Weinstein, *Teamsters Split Despite Suit Accord: No. 2 Hits Settlement with U.S. by Union Leaders*, LOS ANGELES TIMES, Apr. 4, 1989, at A4; Henry Weinstein, *3 More Teamsters Board Members Reach Settlements in Federal Racketeering Case*, LOS ANGELES TIMES, Mar. 8, 1989.

76. Henry Weinstein, *Teamsters, Justice Department Plan Final Effort to Settle Suit*, LOS ANGELES TIMES, Mar. 11, 1989.

77. *Collision*, at 103.

78. *United States v. Int'l Bhd. of Teamsters*, 88 Civ. 4486 (DNE) (Mar. 14, 1989).

79. Consent Decree, *United States v. Int'l Bhd. of Teamsters*, No. 88 Civ. 4486 (S.D.N.Y.) (Mar. 14, 1989) [hereinafter Consent Decree], at 6.

80. *Id.* at ¶ 3.

81. Summary Report of the Independent Administrator, *United States v. Int'l Bhd. of Teamsters*, No. 88 Civ. 4486 (S.D.N.Y.) (Feb. 29, 1992), at 166 (citing Consent Decree at 13).

82. Consent Decree, at ¶ 12.

83. *Id.* at 4; *Int'l Bhd. of Teamsters*, 725 F. Supp. at 167.

84. Consent Decree, at ¶ 12(d).

85. *Id.* at ¶ 12.

86. United States Attorney's Office for the Southern District of New York, *Outline of Civil Complaint*, press release, June 28, 1988.

87. Consent Decree, at 2; Andrew B. Dean, *An Offer the Teamsters Couldn't Refuse: The 1989 Consent Decree Establishing Federal Oversight and Ending Mechanisms*, 100 COLUM. L. REV. 2157 (2000).

88. *Int'l Bhd. of Teamsters*, 803 F. Supp. at 780.

89. Steve J. Martin & Sheldon Ekland-Olson, *Texas Prisons: The Walls Came Tumbling Down*, Austin: Texas Monthly Press, 1987; David J. Rothman & Sheila M. Rothman, *The Willowbrook Wars: Bringing the Mentally Disabled into the Community*, New Brunswick, N.J.: Transaction, 2005; James B. Jacobs, *Individual Rights and Institutional Authority: Prisons, Mental Hospitals, Schools, and Military: Cases and Materials*, Indianapolis: Bobbs-Merrill, 1979; Margo Schlanger & G. Shay, *Pre-*

serving the Rule of Law in America's Jails and Prisons: The Case for Amending the Prison Litigation Reform Act, 1 U. PA. J. CONST. L. 139 (2008).

NOTES TO CHAPTER 3

1. *United States v. Int'l Bhd. of Teamsters*, 728 F. Supp. 1032, 1045 (S.D.N.Y. 1990).

2. House Committee on Education and the Workforce, Subcommittee on Oversight and Investigations, *The Internal [sic] Review Board: Hearing before the Subcommittee on Oversight and Investigations*, 105th Cong., 2d sess., July 30, 1998, 12.

3. *United States v. Int'l Bhd. of Teamsters*, 803 F. Supp. 761, 777 (S.D.N.Y. 1992); *Int'l Bhd. of Teamsters*, 728 F. Supp. at 1042.

4. *Id.*

5. Application I of Independent Administrator.

6. Consent Decree, *United States v. Int'l Bhd. of Teamsters*, No. 88 Civ. 4486 (S.D.N.Y.) (Mar. 14, 1989) [hereinafter Consent Decree].

7. *Int'l Bhd. of Teamsters*, 803 F. Supp. at 769–70. Even after Judge Edelstein issued this order, however, the IBT continued to obstruct Carberry's efforts to obtain a New York office. It took a second hearing before the IBT finally approved a lease.

8. Consent Decree, at 11–12.

9. *Int'l Bhd. of Teamsters*, 803 F. Supp. at 769.

10. *Id.* at 772.

11. *United States v. Int'l Bhd. of Teamsters*, 723 F. Supp. 203, 210 (S.D.N.Y. 1989), aff'd, 931 F.2d 177 (2d Cir. 1991).

12. *Int'l Bhd. of Teamsters*, 723 F. Supp. at 210–11.

13. *See generally* James Neff, *Mobbed Up: Jackie Presser's High-Wire Life in the Teamsters, the Mafia, and the FBI*, New York: Atlantic Monthly Press, 1989.

14. *United States v. Friedman et al.*, Cr. 86-114 (N.D. Ohio) (White, J.); *United States v. Int'l Bhd. of Teamsters*, 743 F. Supp. 155, 157 (S.D.N.Y. 1990), aff'd, 905 F.2d 610 (2d Cir. 1990). On May 16, 1986, a federal grand jury returned an indictment charging Friedman and Hughes with (1) violating the RICO statute, 18 U.S.C. § 1962(c) (1988); (2) RICO conspiracy, 18 U.S.C. § 1962(d) (1988 & Supp. 1993); and (3) embezzling union funds, 29 U.S.C. § 501(c) (1988). Friedman was also charged with filing false reports with the Secretary of Labor, 29 U.S.C. § 439(b) (1988).

15. *United States v. Friedman*, 107 F.R.D. 736 (N.D. Ohio 1985).

16. *Int'l Bhd. of Teamsters*, 743 F. Supp. at 157–58. Article II, Section 2(a) of the IBT constitution required each Teamster "to conduct himself or herself at all times in such a manner as not to bring reproach upon the Union." Article XIX, Section 6(b)(2) made the violation of this provision a specific basis for union disciplinary action.

17. *Int'l Bhd. of Teamsters*, 725 F. Supp. at 165; *Int'l Bhd. of Teamsters*, 905 F.2d at 618.

18. Resolution of the IBT General Executive Board, Nov. 1, 1989.

19. *Int'l Bhd. of Teamsters*, 743 F. Supp. at 162–63. The IBT constitution provides that each member "pledges his honor . . . to conduct himself or herself in such a manner as not to bring reproach upon the union." "Bringing reproach" is the most general and widely used disciplinary offense. The November 1, 1989, resolution called the "bring reproach" language "so vague and indefinite that it does not sufficiently inform trade union members and officers of the specific conduct which it covers." *Id.* at 160; General Executive Board Resolution, at §1(a) (Nov. 1, 1989).

20. *Int'l Bhd. of Teamsters*, 743 F. Supp. at 160–61.

21. *Investigations Officer v. Friedman and Hughes*, Decision of the Independent Administrator (Jan. 11, 1990), at 24–41, *aff'd, United States v. Int'l Bhd. of Teamsters*, 743 F. Supp. 155 (S.D.N.Y. 1990); *Int'l Bhd. of Teamsters*, 725 F. Supp. at 165.

22. *Int'l Bhd. of Teamsters*, 743 F. Supp. at 169.

23. *Int'l Bhd. of Teamsters*, 725 F. Supp. at 162. Paragraph F.12.(A) of the consent decree expressly vests the IA with disciplinary power equal to that of the IBT's general president.

24. *Int'l Bhd. of Teamsters*, 743 F. Supp. at 163; *United States v. Int'l Bhd. of Teamsters* (*In re Application VII by the Independent Administrator*), 88 Civ. 4486 (DNE) (Mar. 13, 1990).

25. *Int'l Bhd. of Teamsters*, 743 F. Supp. at 164.

26. *Int'l Bhd. of Teamsters*, 735 F. Supp. at 506.

27. *United States v. Friedman*, 908 F.2d 974 (6th Cir. 1990).

28. *Investigations Officer v. Gerald Yontek, et al.*, Decision of the Independent Administrator, June 21, 1993.

29. Consent Decree, at ¶ F.12(E).

30. Application VI of Independent Administrator; *see also Int'l Bhd. of Teamsters*, 803 F. Supp. at 772 (adjudicating this dispute).

31. The court issued its order on November 16, 1989, apparently without a published opinion. The order is discussed in a subsequent opinion, 803 F. Supp. at 772. The IBT appealed Judge Edelstein's decision, but the Second Circuit dismissed the appeal on December 13, 1989.

32. *Id.* at 173; *United States v. Int'l Bhd. of Teamsters*, 735 F. Supp. 502, 503–06 (S.D.N.Y. 1990).

33. Summary Report of the Independent Administrator, *United States v. Int'l Bhd. of Teamsters*, No. 88 Civ. 4486 (S.D.N.Y.) (Feb. 29, 1992) [hereinafter Summary Report], at 172–73.

34. *Id.* at 85.

35. *United States v. Int'l Bhd. of Teamsters*, 765 F. Supp. 1206, 1209 (S.D.N.Y. 1991).

36. *Id.* at 1211.

37. The IBT agreed to advance Windsor Graphics a monthly sum of one month's paper costs for Windsor Graphics to keep on account. From May 5, 1989,

to November 2, 1989, the IBT deposited over $1.3 million in this account. At any given time, the amount on deposit with Windsor Graphics ranged from $140,000 to $247,000.

38. Summary Report, at 99. Lacey noted the "increased costs involved in Windsor's unwarranted label mark-ups and color separation charges." *Id.*

39. *Id.* at 85.

40. *Id.* at 99.

41. *Int'l Bhd. of Teamsters*, 765 F. Supp. at 1211.

42. Summary Report, at 99.

43. *United States v. Int'l Bhd. of Teamsters*, Nos. 91-6160, 91-6182, 1991 WL 346072 (2d Cir. Sept. 17, 1991).

44. Laborers for Justice, "V. Special Investigations of the Subcommittee," http://www.thelaborers.net/teamsters/investigation_of_the_teamsters.htm.

45. Consent Decree, at ¶ F.12.(B)(iii).

46. Summary Report, at 131.

47. *Id.* at 132–33. In investigating Jack B. Yager, Lacey took the depositions of fifteen members of the GEB, including General President McCarthy. *United States v. Int'l Bhd. of Teamsters*, 761 F. Supp. 315, 316 (S.D.N.Y. 1991).

48. *Int'l Bhd. of Teamsters*, 761 F. Supp. at 317–18.

49. *Id.* at 318, 320.

50. *Id.* at 318.

51. *Id.* at 321.

52. Affidavit in Support of Application II of the Independent Administrator, *United States v. Int'l Bhd. of Teamsters*, No. 88 Civ. 4486 (S.D.N.Y. Sept. 29, 1989) [hereinafter IA Affidavit], at 2.

53. *Int'l Bhd. of Teamsters*, 723 F. Supp. at 205; *see also* IA Affidavit, ¶ 7.

54. *Int'l Bhd. of Teamsters*, 723 F. Supp. at 206.

55. *Id.* Judge Edelstein also agreed with Lacey and Holland that, in this context, the term "supervise" was a term of art that "should incorporate the connotations connected to its use in the labor law field." *Id.*

56. *Id.* at 207.

57. Consent Decree, at 9(b).

58. *Int'l Bhd. of Teamsters*, 764 F. Supp. at 792.

59. *Id.* at 794. Judge Edelstein explained that "the Government in no way intended to give the convention delegates 'veto' power over the entire Consent Decree or any portion of it. Nor does the language of the Consent Decree, its purpose or history provide for such power." *Id.* at 792.

60. *Id.* at 794–95.

61. *Id.*

62. *Int'l Bhd. of Teamsters*, 723 F. Supp. at 208.

63. *Id.* Holland requested $81,000 per year plus benefits for the executive assistant; $39,000 per year plus benefits for the administrative assistant; a range of

$26,000 to $32,000 per year plus benefits for the secretary; and $75 per hour for the professional labor-economics consultant. *Id.*

64. *Id.* at 208–09; *see also Int'l Bhd. of Teamsters*, 803 F. Supp. at 770.

65. *Int'l Bhd. of Teamsters*, 742 F. Supp. at 106.

66. Stier, Anderson & Malone, LLC, *The Teamsters: Perception and Reality: An Investigative Study of Organized Crime Influence in the Union*, Washington D.C.: International Brotherhood of Teamsters, 2001 [hereinafter *Perception and Reality*], at 305.

67. *Joint Council 73 v. Int'l Bhd. of Teamsters* (*Joint Council 73 II*), 741 F. Supp. 491, 492 (S.D.N.Y. 1990).

68. *Id.*

69. *Id.*

70. *United States v. Int'l Bhd. of Teamsters*, 728 F. Supp. 1032, 1037–38 (S.D.N.Y. 1990).

71. *Investigations Officer v. Friedman & Hughes*, Decision of the Independent Administrator, at 9–11 (Jan. 22, 1990), *aff'd*, 743 F. Supp. at 155. The plaintiffs included Chauffeurs, Teamsters & Helpers, Lake County, Illinois, Local 301, and Robert Barnes, its president; Truck Drivers, Oil Drivers, Filling Station & Platform Workers, Local 705, and Donald Heim, its president; State & Municipal Teamsters, Chauffeurs & Helpers, Local 726, and C.S. Spranzo, its secretary-treasurer; Bakery Cracker, Pie, Yeast Wagon Drivers & Miscellaneous Workers, Local 734, and Robert N. Meidel, its president; and Miscellaneous Warehousemen, Airline, Automotive Parts, Service, Tire & Rental, Chemical & Petroleum, Ice, Paper & Related Chemical & Production Employees Union, Local 781, and Joseph Bernstein, its president.

72. *Int'l Bhd. of Teamsters*, 728 F. Supp. at 1037–38.

73. *Id.*

74. *Id.* at 1036.

75. *Id.* at 1043; *see also Safir v. United States Lines, Inc.*, 792 F.2d 19, 23–24 (2d Cir.1986); *United States v. New York Telephone*, 434 U.S. 159, 172 (1977).

76. *Int'l Bhd. of Teamsters*, 728 F. Supp. at 1039.

77. Kenneth C. Crowe, *Collision: How the Rank and File Took Back the Teamsters*, New York: Scribner, 1993 [hereinafter *Collision*], at 121.

78. *Int'l Bhd. of Teamsters*, 728 F. Supp. at 1040.

79. *United States v. Int'l Bhd. of Teamsters* (*Joint Council 73 III*), 134 F.R.D. 50, 58–59 (S.D.N.Y. 1991).

80. *Int'l Bhd. of Teamsters*, 728 F. Supp. at 1046–49.

81. In 1996, Judge Edelstein extended the reach of his All Writs Act opinion to a Canadian employer who refused to comply with an EO order relating to IBT candidate access to the employer's parking lot. Edelstein held that the employer had the necessary minimum contacts with the United States to establish personal jurisdiction because its actions in Canada had an effect in the United States. Spe-

cifically, the company's actions in Canada could hinder the EO's ability to supervise the election in the United States, thereby compromising the goal of a fair, free, and democratic 1996 IBT election, as well as endangering the consent decree's goal of eradicating organized crime from the IBT. *United States v. Int'l Bhd. of Teamsters* (*Labbat's*), 945 F. Supp. 609, 612 (S.D.N.Y. 1996).

82. *Int'l Bhd. of Teamsters*, 728 F. Supp. at 1045.

83. *United States v. Int'l Bhd. of Teamsters*, 907 F.2d 277, 280–81 (2nd Cir. 1990).

84. For a critical analysis of courts' capacity to bring about social reform, see Gerald N. Rosenberg, *The Hollow Hope: Can Courts Bring About Social Change?* Chicago: University of Chicago Press, 1991.

85. *See generally* Bert Brandenberg, *Brown v. Board of Education and Attacks on the Courts: Fifty Years Ago, Fifty Years Later*, 37 WTR BRIEF 66 (2008); Gabriel J. Chin, Roger Hartley, Kevin Bates, Rona Nichols, Ira Shiflett & Salmon Shomade, *Still on the Books: Jim Crow and Segregation Laws Fifty Years after Brown v. Board of Education*, 2006 MICH. ST. L. REV. 457 (2006); Eugene C. Patterson, *Progress through Political Sacrifice: Southern Politicians' Response to Brown v. Board of Education*, 34 STETSON L. REV. 465 (2005); Kevin M. Kruse, *The Paradox of Massive Resistance: Political Conformity and Chaos in the Aftermath of Brown v. Board of Education*, 48 ST. LOUIS U. L.J. 1009 (2004).

86. *See generally* Steve J. Martin & Sheldon Ekland-Olson, *Texas Prisons: The Walls Came Tumbling Down*, Austin: Texas Monthly Press, 1987; David J. Rothman & Sheila M. Rothman. *The Willowbrook Wars: Bringing the Mentally Disabled into the Community*, New Brunswick, N.J.: Transaction, 2005; Susan Sturm, *Resolving the Remedial Dilemma: Strategies of Judicial Intervention in Prisons*, 138 U. PA. L. REV. 805 (1990); Margo Schlanger, *Civil Rights Injunctions Over Time: A Case Study of Jail and Prison Court Orders*, 81 NYU L. REV. 550 (2006); Margo Schlanger, *Inmate Litigation*, 116 HARV. L. REV. 1555 (2003).

87. *Int'l Bhd. of Teamsters*, 728 F. Supp. at 1040–42.

88. House Committee on Education and the Workforce, Subcommittee on Oversight and Investigations, *The Internal [sic] Review Board: Hearing before the Subcommittee on Oversight and Investigations*, 105th Cong., 2d sess., July 30, 1998.

89. *Int'l Bhd. of Teamsters*, 728 F. Supp. at 1040.

90. *Joint Council 73 III*, 134 F.R.D. at 61.

91. *Id.* at 64.

92. *United States v. Int'l Bhd. of Teamsters*, 948 F.2d 1338, 1340, 1347 (2d Cir. 1991) (holding that Judge Edelstein had not adequately explained how the union attorneys' conduct justified Rule 11 sanctions under the Federal Rules of Civil Procedure).

93. *Int'l Bhd. of Teamsters*, 728 F. Supp. at 1044.

94. *Id.*

95. *English v. Cunningham*, 269 F.2d 517 (D.C. Cir. 1959); Michael J. Goldberg,

The Teamsters Board of Monitors: An Experiment in Union Reform Litigation, 30 LABOR HISTORY 563 (1989); Michael J. Goldberg, *Cleaning Labor's House: Institutional Reform Litigation in the Labor Movement*, DUKE L.J. 903 (1989).

96. *Cunningham*, 269 F.2d at 519.

NOTES TO CHAPTER 4

1. IBT, press release, Mar. 13, 1989, 1; *see also* Stier, Anderson & Malone, LLC, *The Teamsters: Perception and Reality: An Investigative Study of Organized Crime Influence in the Union*, Washington D.C.: IBT, 2001 [hereinafter *Perception and Reality*], at 304.

2. Frank Swoboda, *The Teamsters' New Face: Judge Leads Army of Federal Monitors to Union Convention to Keep Reforms on Track*, WASHINGTON POST, Jun. 23, 1991, at H1.

3. James B. Jacobs & Dimitri D. Portnoi, *Administrative Criminal Law and Procedure in the Teamsters Union: What Has Been Achieved after (Nearly) Twenty Years*, 28 BERKELEY J. EMP. & LAB. L. 429, 459 (2007) [hereinafter Jacobs & Portnoi].

4. *United States v. Int'l Bhd. of Teamsters*, 775 F. Supp. 90, 94 (S.D.N.Y. 1991).

5. *Id.*

6. IBT Constitution, at Art. II, § 2(a).

7. *Id.* at Art. XIX, § 7(b)(3) ("Breaching a fiduciary obligation owed to any labor organization by any act of embezzlement or conversion of union's funds or property.").

8. *Id.* at Art. XIX, § 7(b)(6) ("Disruption of Union meetings, or assaulting or provoking assault on fellow members or officers, . . . or any similar conduct in, or about union premises or places used to conduct union business.").

9. *Id.* at Art. XIX, § 7(b)(10) ("Retaliating or threatening to retaliate against any member for exercising his rights under this Constitution or applicable law including the right to speak, vote, seek election to office, support the candidate or one's choice, or participate in the affairs of the Union.").

10. The consent decree stated that "knowingly associating" should have "the same meaning as that term has in the context of comparable federal proceedings or federal rules and regulations." Consent Decree, *United States v. Int'l Bhd. of Teamsters*, No. 88 Civ. 4486 (S.D.N.Y.) (Mar. 14, 1989) [hereinafter Consent Decree], at 7.

11. 29 U.S.C. § 186 (2000); IBT Constitution, at Art. XIX, § 7(b)(13).

12. 29 U.S.C. § 503(a) (2000) ("No labor organization shall make directly or indirectly any loan or loans to any officer or employee of such organization which results in a total indebtedness on the part of such officer or employee to the labor organization in excess of $2,000.").

13. 18 U.S.C. § 1954 (2000); *United States v. Int'l Bhd. of Teamsters (Perrucci)*, 965 F. Supp. 493, 500–01 (S.D.N.Y. 1997) (quoting 18 U.S.C. § 1954 (1994)).

14. 29 U.S.C. § 431(b) (2000).

15. 29 U.S.C. § 530 (2000). Not all violations of federal law constitute disciplinary violations. For example, IO Carberry did not prosecute strike-related misconduct, drug possession, domestic violence, or sexual harassment. Interview with Charles Carberry, Jan. 12, 2010.

16. Consent Decree, "Access to Information," at ¶ 1.

17. Interview with Charles M. Carberry, Jan. 12, 2010.

18. *United States v. Int'l Bhd. of Teamsters*, 970 F.2d 1132 (2d Cir. 1992).

19. *Id.* at 1137.

20. 29 U.S.C. § 411(a)(5) (2000).

21. *Investigations Officer v. Senese*, Decision of the Independent Administrator, at 23 (July 12, 1990), *aff'd, United States v. Int'l Bhd. of Teamsters*, 745 F. Supp. 908, 914–15 (S.D.N.Y. 1990), *aff'd*, 941 F.2d 1292, 1297–98 (2d Cir. 1991). Despite the IBT's objections, Judge Edelstein and the Second Circuit Court of Appeals affirmed IA Lacey's conclusion that hearsay evidence was admissible if reliable. Indicia of reliability include "the opportunity to cross-examine the declarant, the detail contained in written reports, corroboration among independent hearsay reports, and the preparation of reports according to an established routine." *United States v. Int'l Bhd. of Teamsters*, 978 F.2d 68, 72 (2d Cir. 1992). Kansas City IBT Local 41 employee Nicholas A. DiGirlamo, whom IA Lacey expelled for knowingly associating with four LCN members, unsuccessfully argued that hearsay should not be admissible at a disciplinary hearing. *United States v. Int'l Bhd. of Teamsters (DiGirlamo)*, 19 F.3d 816, 823 (2d Cir. 1994). Likewise, Chicago IBT Local 703 President Dominic Senese and Chicago IBT Local 727 Business Agent Joseph Talerico, whom IA Lacey expelled for knowingly associating with LCN members, vigorously, but unsuccessfully, contested IA Lacey's decision to allow the introduction of hearsay evidence at their disciplinary hearings. *Int'l Bhd. of Teamsters*, 745 F. Supp. at 914.

22. *United States v. Int'l Bhd. of Teamsters*, 754 F. Supp. 333, 337 (S.D.N.Y.1990).

23. *Investigations Officer v. Catenaro, Leary, and Baker*, Decision of the Independent Administrator (May 6, 1991).

24. *Investigations Officer v. Bernard and Hands*, Decision of the Independent Administrator (May 22, 1990).

25. *United States v. Int'l Bhd. of Teamsters*, 838 F. Supp. 800, 815 (S.D.N.Y. 1993), *aff'd*, 33 F.3d 50 (2d Cir. 1994).

26. IRB website, www.irbcases.org.

27. *Int'l Bhd. of Teamsters*, 838 F. Supp. at 819–20.

28. The reviewing court could reverse IA decisions that were (1) arbitrary, capricious, an abuse of discretion, or otherwise discordant with law; (2) contrary to constitutional right, power, privilege, or immunity; (3) in excess of statutory jurisdiction, authority, or limitations or short of statutory right; (4) in violation of procedures required by law; (5) unsupported by substantial evidence; or (6) unwarranted by facts that were subject to trial de novo by the reviewing court. 5 U.S.C. § 706 (2000).

29. *United States v. Int'l Bhd. of Teamsters*, 981 F.2d 1362, 1368 (2d Cir.1992).

30. *Id.*

31. *United States v. Int'l Bhd. of Teamsters*, 978 F.2d 68, 70, 73–74 (2d Cir. 1992).

32. Consent Decree, at 6.

33. *See, e.g., Investigations Officer v. Salerno*, Decision of the Independent Administrator, at 9–10 (Aug. 20, 1990), *aff'd, Int'l Bhd. of Teamsters* (*Salerno*), 745 F. Supp. 189 (S.D.N.Y. 1990) ("Thus, given DeVecchio's extensive background and experience, I accept him as an expert knowledgeable in investigation and structure of organized crime in New York.").

34. *United States v. Int'l Bhd. of Teamsters*, 88 Civ. 4486, 1991 WL 161084, *2 (S.D.N.Y. Aug. 14, 1991).

35. *Id.*

36. *Id.* at *3.

37. *See, e.g., Salerno*, Decision of the Independent Administrator, at 23–24; *Investigations Officers v. Cozza*, Decision of the Independent Administrator, at 10–15 (Jan. 4, 1991).

38. Summary Report of the Independent Administrator, *United States v. Int'l Bhd. of Teamsters*, No. 88 Civ. 4486 (S.D.N.Y.) (Feb. 29, 1992) [hereinafter Summary Report], at 20.

39. *Senese*, Decision of the Independent Administrator, at 35.

40. *E.g., Investigations Officer v. Kosey*, Decision of the Independent Administrator (Apr. 22, 1992), *aff'd, United States v. Int'l Bhd. of Teamsters* (*Kosey*), 88 Civ. 4486 (DNE), Slip Op. (S.D.N.Y. May 18, 1992) ("Respondent would have us excuse his inaction because Glimco was his father-in-law and taking any step against him might have given rise to domestic problems. The implications of such a specious proposition are limitless. The mere placing of a family member on the Executive Board could then confer an immunity of sorts and excuse the violation of one's fiduciary responsibility."); *Salerno*, Decision of the Independent Administrator, at 11 (sustaining charges against Cirino Salerno for associating with his brother, Anthony Salerno, the Genovese family underboss). *DiGirlamo*, 19 F.3d at 822 (quoting *United States v. Albanese*, 554 F.2d 543, 546 & n.6 (2d Cir. 1977)).

41. *Senese*, Decision of the Independent Administrator, at 36–37.

42. *Investigations Officer v. Misuraca*, Decision of the Independent Administrator, at 18 (Mar. 6, 1991), *aff'd, United States v. Int'l Bhd. of Teamsters* (*Misuraca*), 88 Civ. 4486, 1991 U.S. Dist. LEXIS 9666 (S.D.N.Y. July 16, 1991).

43. *Investigations Officer v. Cozza*, Decision of the Independent Administrator (Jan. 4, 1991), *aff'd, United States v. Int'l Bhd. of Teamsters*, 764 F. Supp. 797 (S.D.N.Y. 1991), *aff'd*, 956 F.2d 1161 (2d Cir. 1992); *United States v. Int'l Bhd. of Teamsters*, 745 F. Supp. 908 (S.D.N.Y. 1990), *aff'd*, 941 F.2d 1292 (2d Cir. 1991).

44. *Int'l Bhd. of Teamsters*, 745 F. Supp. at 908.

45. *Id.* at 919 n.2.

46. *Id.* at 913–14.

47. *Id.*

48. *Int'l Bhd. of Teamsters*, 764 F. Supp. at 799.

49. These Pittsburgh Cosa Nostra members included John S. LaRocca, Gabriel "Kelly" Mannerino, Michael Genovese, Joseph "JoJo" Pecora, and Joseph Sica.

50. *Salerno*, Decision of the Independent Administrator, at 11 (sustaining charges).

51. *Salerno & Cutolo*, Decision of the Independent Administrator, at 33.

52. Consent Decree, at 6; *see United States v. Int'l Bhd. of Teamsters*, 22 F. Supp. 2d 135, 144–45 (S.D.N.Y. 1998).

53. *Id.* at 145 ("Paragraph E(10) [of the consent decree] provides no exceptions based on the stated reasons for the permanent bar.").

54. *Id.*

55. *Int'l Bhd. of Teamsters*, 838 F. Supp. at 809.

56. *Id.* at 811 ("As Machiavelli explained several centuries ago, power may be wielded in subtle, deceptive, and devious ways.").

57. *Id.* at 800.

58. *Investigations Officer v. Friedman*, Decision of the Independent Administrator, at 23 (June 21, 1993).

59. Consent Decree, at § F(12)(C).

60. *United States v. Int'l Bhd. of Teamsters*, 803 F. Supp. 761 (S.D.N.Y. 1992).

61. *United States v. Int'l Bhd. of Teamsters*, 88 Civ. 4486, 1991 WL 161084, *1 (S.D.N.Y. Aug. 14, 1991).

62. *Id.* at *3.

63. *Id.*

64. *Investigations Officer v. Sansone*, Decision of the Independent Administrator, at 1–3 (Mar. 30, 1992).

65. Summary Report, at 25.

66. *United States v. Int'l Bhd. of Teamsters (Motion to Dismiss)*, 708 F. Supp. 1388, 1401 (S.D.N.Y. 1989); *United States v. Int'l Bhd. of Teamsters (Yager Veto)*, 761 F. Supp. 315, 319 (S.D.N.Y. 1991).

67. *Int'l Bhd. of Teamsters*, 803 F. Supp. at 742 (barred permanently from IBT); *Int'l Bhd. of Teamsters*, 981 F.2d at 1368 ("permanently barred . . . from (1) ever holding any IBT officership in the future; (2) any employment with Local 682, Joint Council 13, the Missouri-Kansas Conference of Teamsters, or the International; and (3) any employment with any IBT-affiliated entity without prior approval of the Independent Administrator"); *Int'l Bhd. of Teamsters*, 803 F. Supp. at 753 (permanently barred from IBT office; required to obtain IA/IRB position before taking other IBT employment; permanently barred from employment with Local 727); *United States v. Int'l Bhd. of Teamsters (Bertino and Raimondi)*, 829 F. Supp. 608, 610 (1993) (barred from holding IBT office or receiving any IBT compensation for two years).

68. *See, e.g., Int'l Bhd. of Teamsters*, 981 F.2d at 1368–69.

69. *Id.*; *Investigations Officer v. Coli*, Decision of the Independent Administrator, at 5 (May 15, 1992), *aff'd*, *United States v. Int'l Bhd. of Teamsters* (*Coli*), 803 F. Supp. 748, 750 (S.D.N.Y. 1992) (finding James Coli's awareness that Joseph Talerico had been twice incarcerated and had invoked his Fifth Amendment privilege under government questioning constituted evidence that Coli should have been on notice that an investigation was necessary).

70. *Int'l Bhd. of Teamsters*, 981 F.2d at 1365–66.

71. *See, e.g., id.* at 1368–69.

72. *See, e.g., Investigations Officer v. Calagna*, Decision of the Independent Administrator, at 21–22 (June 14, 1991), *aff'd*, *United States v. Int'l Bhd. of Teamsters* (*Calagna*), 138 F.R.D. 50 (S.D.N.Y. Jul. 30, 1991) ("Against this sordid background, there appears to be little, if anything, that any of the Respondents or other members of the [Local 295] Executive Board have ever done to cleanse the Local's reputation.").

73. *Coli*, Decision of the Independent Administrator, at 15 ("At a minimum, Coli should have retrieved the Nevada court records.").

74. *Calagna*, Decision of the Independent Administrator, at 25 ("While expensive, it would have cost the Local far less than the $150,000 in legal fees the Executive Board has agreed to pay Calagna's attorney, and the massive salary increase and 'severance' benefits the board voted to give Calagna.").

75. Consent Decree, at 19.

76. *See* Selwyn Raab, *Linked to Mafia, Union Chief Quits*, NEW YORK TIMES, Apr. 16, 1992, *available at* http://www.nytimes.com/1992/04/16/nyregion/linked-to-mafia-union-chief-quits.html?pagewanted=all.

77. *Id.*

78. Every labor union must submit LM-2s (Labor Organization Annual Reports) to the DOL's Office of Labor Management Standards. The LM-2s provide each affiliate's assets, liabilities, receipts, disbursements, investments, loans, and salaries. Filing an improper LM-2 form is a disciplinary offense under the IBT constitution and a crime under the LMRDA. 29 C.F.R. § 403 (2000).

79. *Int'l Bhd. of Teamsters*, 775 F. Supp. at 100.

80. Summary Report, at XX (quoting *United States v. Int'l Bhd. of Teamsters* (*Nunes*), 962 F.2d 4 (2d Cir. Mar. 27, 1992) (Table, No. 91-6300), *aff'g* 141 L.R.R.M. 2483 (S.D.N.Y. Nov. 8, 1991), *aff'g Investigations Officer v. Nunes*, Decision of the Independent Administrator (Sept. 6, 1991)).

81. 29 U.S.C. § 504 (2000).

82. *Investigations Officer v. Daniel Darrow*, Decision of the Independent Administrator, at 1–3 (Oct. 2, 1991).

83. This decision was based in part on the AFL-CIO Executive Council Statement on the Use of the Fifth Amendment in Investigations of Racketeering, Jan. 28, 1957, condemning the use of Fifth Amendment protection by a union officer on the ground that it may create the appearance that the union "sanctions the use of the

Fifth Amendment . . . as a shield against proper scrutiny into corrupt influences in the labor movement." *Investigations Officer v. Senese, Talerico, and Cozzo*, Decision of the Independent Administrator, at 30 (July 12, 1990).

84. 29 U.S.C. § 530 (2000).

85. IBT Constitution, at Article XIX, § 7(b)(6).

86. *See Investigations Officer v. Parise*, Decision of the Independent Administrator, at 3–5 (July 29, 1991), *aff'd, United States v. Int'l Bhd. of Teamsters (Parise)*, 777 F. Supp. 1133 (S.D.N.Y. 1991), *aff'd*, 970 F.2d 1132 (2d Cir. 1992).

87. *Parise*, Decision of the Independent Administrator, at 14–16.

88. The IBT constitution forbids "[b]reaching a fiduciary duty owed to any labor organization by any act of embezzlement or conversion of union's funds or property." IBT Constitution, at Art. XIX, § 7(b)(3). This provision tracks the LMRDA. 29 U.S.C. § 501(c) (2000) states, "Any person who embezzles, steals, or unlawfully and willfully abstracts or converts to his own use, or the use of another, any of the moneys, funds, securities, property, or other assets of a labor organization of which he is an officer, or by which he is employed, directly or indirectly, shall be fined not more than $10,000 or imprisoned for not more than five years, or both."

89. *Investigations Officer v. Vitale*, Decision of the Independent Administrator, at 10 (Dec. 18, 1990), *aff'd, Int'l Bhd. of Teamsters (Vitale)*, 775 F. Supp. at 90, *aff'd in part, rev'd in part*, No-91-6154, Slip Op. (2d Cir. Oct. 31, 1991) (quoting *United States v. Welch*, 728 F.2d 1113, 1118 (8th Cir. 1989) ("Nevertheless, under any test union officials violate Section 501(c) only when they possess fraudulent intent to deprive the union of its funds.")).

90. *Vitale*, Decision of the Independent Administrator, at 12–14.

91. *Id.* at 14–15 ("[Vitale's] intent is evidenced from the proposed timing of the . . . purchase and the direct prohibition of the proposed transfer in the bylaws.").

92. *Int'l Bhd. of Teamsters*, 978 F.2d at 72.

93. *Id.*

94. *See, e.g.*, letter from Ron Carey, General President, Int'l Bhd. of Teamsters, to Frank Pischera, former president, IBT Local 240 (notifying Pischera that charges of aiding embezzlement against him had been sustained for signing local-union checks to pay for Warren Selvaggi's use of the local's calling card after Selvaggi was removed from the union pursuant to a court order).

95. *See, e.g., In the Matter of Article XIX*, Charges against Scott Dennison, Decision of General President Ronald Carey, Intern'l Bhd. of Teamsters (Jul. 22, 1996) (sustaining charges against Local 186 Secretary-Treasurer Scott Dennison for the unauthorized expenditure of $1,300 to attend a TDU conference).

96. *See, e.g., Application XX of the Independent Review Board, United States v. Int'l Bhd. of Teamsters (Raymond)*, No. 88 Civ. 4486 (S.D.N.Y. Jun. 29, 1995) (requesting approval of an agreement with the Local 677 executive board settling charges of transferring title to union-owned cars to a retiring officer).

97. *See, e.g., Application V of the Independent Review Board, United States v. Int'l Bhd. of Teamsters (Ruane)*, No. 88 Civ. 4486 (S.D.N.Y. Feb. 3, 1994) (requesting approval of the IRB's finding of culpability against Local 854 President Maureen Ruane for paying the benefits of former officer Frank Dapolito, identified as an LCN member).

98. *See, e.g.,* Opinion of the Independent Review Board in the Matter of the Hearing of Maureen Ruane (Feb. 3, 1994) (suspending Ruane for six months from performing her duties as president of Local 854).

99. Decision in the Matter of Article XIX Charges against Theodore J. Brovarski and Theodore M. Brovarski (July 2, 1996) (banning Theodore J. Brovarski from the IBT permanently).

100. Independent Review Board's Five-Year Report (1992–1997) to Honorable David N. Edelstein, United States District Judge, *United States v. Int'l Bhd. of Teamsters*, No. 88 Civ. 4486, at 1 (S.D.N.Y. Nov. 6, 1997) [hereinafter First Five-Year Report].

101. *See, e.g.,* Decision of the Executive Board of Joint Council 10 in the Matter of Daniel Zenga, Andy Bellemare, and William Schomburg, at 2 (Jan. 12, 1993) (charging Recording Secretary William Schomburg with failure to keep minutes and charging Secretary-Treasurer Daniel Zenga with allowing Schomburg to fail to keep minutes).

102. *See, e.g., id.* at 3–4 (charging Local 831 President Andrew Bellemare and Secretary-Treasurer Zenga for failing to submit appropriate bylaws for approval).

103. IBT Constitution, at Art. X, § 10(c) ("Any officer of a subordinate body refusing to turn over the books, bills, vouchers, or records to the delegated officer shall be subject to discipline under the provisions of Article XIX, and shall be liable to expulsion by the General Executive Board."); IBT Constitution, at Art. X, § 10(d) ("If the representative delegated to audit the books discovers any dishonesty or incompetency in the officers which warrants him to notify the General President and General Secretary-Treasurer, he shall do so and they shall take whatever action they deem advisable.").

104. *See, e.g., Investigations Officer v. Burke*, Decision of the Independent Administrator, at 24–25 (Oct. 1, 1992) ("Article X, Section 10 of the IBT Constitution authorizes the General Secretary-Treasurer to audit the books of Local Unions. The Article makes interference with the authority of the General Secretary-Treasurer a basis for discipline under Article XIX.").

105. *Application XLVII by the Independent Administrator, United States v. Int'l Bhd. of Teamsters (Alongi)*, No. 88 Civ. 4486 (S.D.N.Y. Aug. 5, 1991).

106. Affidavit & Agreement, *United States v. Int'l Bhd. of Teamsters (Congemi)*, No. 88 Civ. 4486 (S.D.N.Y. May 21, 1992).

107. IBT Constitution, at Art. II, § 2(a) ("Any person shall be eligible to membership in this organization upon compliance with the requirements of this Constitution and the rulings of the General Executive Board.").

108. *Int'l Bhd. of Teamsters*, 817 F. Supp. at 342–43.

109. *Id.*

110. *See, e.g., Int'l Bhd. of Teamsters*, Decision of the Independent Administrator, at 8–12.

111. "If the general president believes that any of the officers of a Local Union . . . are dishonest or incompetent, or that such organization is not being conducted in accordance with the Constitution and laws of the International Union or for the benefit of the membership, or is being conducted in such a manner as to jeopardize the interests of the International Union or its subordinate bodies, or if the General President believes that such action is necessary for the purpose of correcting corruption or financial malpractice, assuring the performance of collective bargaining agreements or other duties of a bargaining representative, restoring democratic procedures or preventing any action which is disruptive of, or interferes with the performance of obligations of other members or Local Unions under collective bargaining agreements, or otherwise carrying out legitimate objects of the subordinate body, he may appoint a temporary Trustee to take charge and control of the affairs of such Local Union or other subordinate body." IBT Constitution, at Art. VI, § 5(a).

112. Trusteeship Recommendation Concerning Local 714, at 1 ("[T]he Local is being run for the benefit of its principal officer William Hogan, Jr., President James M. Hogan, Recording Secretary Robert Hogan and their family and friends.").

113. Of the seventeen entities placed in trusteeship in the IRB's second term, 1996–2001, ten had a history of organized-crime influence. Second Five-Year Report, at 13.

114. Consent Decree, at (F)(12)(A)(i).

115. *Id.* at 8.

116. *Id.*

117. *Int'l Bhd. of Teamsters*, 803 F. Supp. at 808; Summary Report, at 147–52.

118. *Int'l Bhd. of Teamsters*, 754 F. Supp. at 347.

119. *Id.* at 335.

120. *See* James B. Jacobs, *Mobsters, Unions, and Feds: The Mafia and the American Labor Movement*, New York: NYU Press, 2006, at 58–63.

121. *Investigations Officer v. Anthony Calagna, Sr., Michael Urso-Pernice, Robert W. Reinhardt, Anthony Calagna, Jr., Salvatore E. Cataldo, Ralph Delsardo, and John Moran, Jr.*, Decision of the Independent Administrator, at 24 (June 14, 1991).

122. *United States v. Local 295, Int'l Bhd. of Teamsters*, 784 F. Supp. 15, 18 (E.D.N.Y. 1992).

123. *Id.* at 19.

124. *See Garrity v. New Jersey*, 385 U.S. 493 (1967); *Lefkowitz v. Turley*, 414 U.S. 70 (1973); *Jackson v. Metro Edison Co.*, 419 U.S. 345 (1974); Akhil R. Amar & Renee B. Lettow, *Fifth Amendment First Principles: The Self-Incrimination Clause*, 93 Mich. L. Rev. 857 (1995).

NOTES TO CHAPTER 5

1. Victor Reuther, *Carey Slate Sweeps!* CONVOY DISPATCH, *Special Post-Election Issue,* Jan. 1992, at 1.

2. Consent Decree, *United States v. Int'l Bhd. of Teamsters,* No. 88 Civ. 4486 (S.D.N.Y.) (Mar. 14, 1989) [hereinafter Consent Decree], at 13–15.

3. *Id.* at 13–14.

4. *Id.* at 15.

5. Michael H. Holland, *The Cookbook: How the Election Officer Supervised the 1991 Teamster Election,* July 1992 [hereinafter *The Cookbook*], at 107–11.

6. *Id.* at i.

7. *United States v. Int'l Bhd. of Teamsters,* 723 F. Supp. 203, 207 (S.D.N.Y. 1989), *aff'd,* 931 F.2d 177 (2d Cir. 1991).

8. Rules for the IBT International Union Delegate and Officer Election, Michael H. Holland, Election Officer, Aug. 1, 1990 [hereinafter 1991 Election Rules], Preamble.

9. *The Cookbook,* ch.1, at 1.

10. *United States v. Int'l Bhd. of Teamsters (Election Rules Order),* 742 F. Supp. 94, 98 n.1 (S.D.N.Y. 1990).

11. *Id.*

12. 1991 Election Rules, Art. II, § 2.

13. Kenneth C. Crowe, *Collision: How the Rank and File Took Back the Teamsters,* New York: Scribner, 1993 [hereinafter *Collision*], at 126.

14. *Election Rules Order,* 742 F. Supp. at 106.

15. *Id.*

16. *Id.*

17. 1991 Election Rules, Article I.

18. *Id.,* Art. VI(1).

19. *The Cookbook,* ch. 4, at 5–6.

20. 29 U.S.C. §§ 401–531 (2000).

21. *The Cookbook,* ch. 4, at 7–8.

22. 1991 Election Rules, Art. VI(1).

23. *The Cookbook,* ch. 2, at 8.

24. 1991 Election Rules, Art. II(2).

25. *Election Rules Order,* 742 F. Supp. at 104.

26. *The Cookbook,* ch. 2, at 12.

27. *Id.,* ch. 2, at 7–8.

28. *Id.*

29. *Id.,* ch. 6, at 29–30.

30. 1991 Election Rules, VIII(10).

31. *United States v. Int'l Bhd. of Teamsters (Yellow Freight II),* 948 F.2d 98 (2d Cir. 1991); *see also The Cookbook,* ch. 1, at 17–19.

32. *Yellow Freight II*, 948 F.2d at 100–01.

33. *Id.* at 101–02.

34. *United States v. Int'l Bhd. of Teamsters (Yellow Freight I)*, 88 Civ. 4486, 1991 WL 51065, at *1 (S.D.N.Y. Apr. 3, 1991).

35. *Id.* at *3–4.

36. *Id.* at *3.

37. *Int'l Bhd. of Teamsters*, 948 F.2d at 99–100. Three months after the Second Circuit's decision on the Yellow Freight matter, the U.S. Supreme Court decided in *Lechmere, Inc., v. National Labor Relations Board* that the National Labor Relations Act did not authorize a nonemployee to campaign on an employer's premises. 502 U.S. 527, 541 (1992). This did not overrule the Second Circuit's *Yellow Freight* decision, which was based on the terms of the *U.S. v. IBT* consent decree.

38. *United States v. Int'l Bhd. of Teamsters (Star Market)*, 776 F. Supp. 144, 147, 154–55 (S.D.N.Y. 1991).

39. *Id.*

40. *Id.*

41. *Id.* at 148–49.

42. *Id.* at 150. Star Market argued before the Second Circuit Court of Appeals that the EO's and IA's hearings violated due process and contravened an existing arbitration agreement. *United States v. Int'l Bhd. of Teamsters*, 954 F.2d 801, 804 (2d Cir. 1992).

43. *Int'l Bhd. of Teamsters*, 776 F. Supp. at 154.

44. *Election Rules Order*, 742 F. Supp. at 98–106.

45. *Id.* at 102.

46. *Id.*

47. 1991 Election Rules, Art. X(1).

48. *Id.*, Art. X(1)(3).

49. *The Cookbook*, ch. 15, at 5.

50. 1991 Election Rules, Art. X, § 1(b); *The Cookbook*, ch. 15, at 2–3.

51. *The Cookbook*, ch. 15, at 4.

52. *Teamster Chief Won't Seek Reelection in '91*, NEW YORK TIMES, Oct. 11, 1990.

53. *The Cookbook*, ch. 3, at 65. There were also three minor candidates for general president: (1) Lou Riga (secretary-treasurer of San Jose, California, Local 576); (2) William Genoese (director of New York airline employees Local 732); and (3) James P. Hoffa (son of Jimmy Hoffa). None of them made it onto the ballot, either because they did not obtain the requisite 5 percent at the nominating convention or, in Hoffa's case, because he could not satisfy the requirement of twenty-four consecutive months of membership in good standing.

54. *See* Steven Brill, *The Teamsters*, New York: Simon and Schuster, 1978, ch. 5.

55. *Id.* at 160.

56. *See generally Collision*.

57. *Id.* at 176.

58. *Id.* at 144–45, 180.

59. *Id.* at 153–54.

60. *Id.* at 161.

61. *Id.* at 168.

62. *Id.*

63. *Id.*

64. *Id.*

65. *The Cookbook*, ch. 2, at 1.

66. *Id.*, ch. 2, at 48–49.

67. *Id.*, ch. 2, at 52.

68. *Id.*, ch. 2, at 16, 18–25.

69. *Id.*, ch. 3, at 15–17.

70. *Id.*, ch. 3, at 6, 16.

71. *Id.*, ch. 3, at 2.

72. *Collision*, at 158.

73. *Id.*

74. Teamster Magazine, Oct. 1991.

75. Peter T. Kilborn, *Carey Takes the Wheel*, New York Times, June 21, 1992, at 7.

76. James D. Jacobs & Dimitri D. Portnoi, *Administrative Criminal Law and Procedure in the Teamsters Union: What Has Been Achieved after (Nearly) Twenty Years*, 28 Berkeley J. Emp. & Lab. L. 429, 471 n.273 (2007).

77. *Collision*, at 133.

78. *Id.* at 142.

79. *Id.* at 160.

80. *Id.*

81. Ligurotis was charged with second-degree murder but was later acquitted. Lorraine Forte, *Teamsters Leader Daniel Ligurotis, Sr.*, Chicago Sun-Times, Dec. 10, 1999. In October 1992, IA Lacey expelled Ligurotis from the union for embezzling money from Local 705. *Investigations Officer v. Daniel C. Ligurotis*, Decision of the Independent Administrator, Oct. 27, 1992. For an in-depth analysis of rank-and-file efforts to eliminate corruption in Local 705, see Robert Bruno, *Reforming the Chicago Teamsters: The Local 705 Story*, DeKalb: Northern Illinois University Press, 2003.

82. In 1986, Trerotola hosted a lavish party for thousands of union delegates in honor of newly elected General President Jackie Presser in Caesars Palace, Las Vegas, paid for by the Eastern Conference of Teamsters. As *New York Times* labor journalist Bruce Lambert described the scene, "The high point came as [Trerotola] and Jackie Presser, the Teamsters president, were borne into the room reclining on an imperial chariot wheeled by men wearing the costumes of Roman soldiers while martial music played and the loudspeaker proclaimed 'Hail, Caesar!'" Bruce

Lambert, *Joseph Trerotola, Unionist, 82; Led Teamsters Unit for 26 Years*, NEW YORK TIMES, May 30, 1992.

83. *The Cookbook*, ch. 15, at 13; Election Officer Case No. P-249-LU283-MGN, *aff'd*, 91-Elec.App.-158.

84. *United States v. Int'l Bhd. of Teamsters*, 968 F.2d 1506, 1510 (2d Cir. 1992).

85. *Id.* at 1508; *Collision*, at 245.

86. *The Cookbook*, ch. 15, at 16; *Collision*, at 246.

87. *Int'l Bhd. of Teamsters*, 968 F.2d at 1510.

88. *Collision*, at 246.

89. *Id.* at 246–49.

90. *Int'l Bhd. of Teamsters*, 968 F.2d at 1511–12.

91. *The Cookbook*, ch. 6, at 15–16.

92. *Id.*, ch. 6, at 16.

93. *Id.*, ch. 6, at 17. However, the decision also provided precedent for allowing the Teamsters National Black Caucus and the Teamsters Hispanic Caucus to contribute to Durham's campaign. The Teamsters National Black Caucus was formed at the 1971 IBT international convention in Miami to improve the representation of African American Teamsters in local, regional, and national leadership positions. At that time, there were no African Americans on the GEB. IBT, "Teamsters National Black Caucus," http://www.teamster.org/content/teamsters-national-black-caucus. The Teamsters Hispanic Caucus was formed to assist and promote the interests of Hispanic Teamsters on the local, state, and national levels by, among other things, (1) awarding educational scholarship to community youth, (2) contributing to charitable organizations that serve the communities of the membership, and (3) conducting community-improvement and community-education programs. IBT, "Teamsters Hispanic Caucus—Bylaws," http://www.teamster.org/content/teamsters-hispanic-caucus-bylaws-0.

94. *The Cookbook*, ch. 4, at 24.

95. *Id.*, ch. 4, at 15–16.

96. *Id.*, ch. 4, at 93.

97. *Id.*, ch. 4, at 46.

98. The counting process called for the ballots to pass through work stations. At station 1, staff checked voter eligibility. At station 2, a slitter machine opened the ballot-reply envelope. At station 3, a ballot counter removed the envelope containing the sealed ballot from the outer envelope. Any marking on this envelope that disclosed the voter's identity voided the ballot. At station 4, another slitter machine opened the ballot. At station 5, count workers extracted the ballots and determined whether the optical scanning machine could read the ballots. If a ballot was torn, crumpled, or incorrectly filled out (e.g., bubbles were not completely filled in), count workers "remade" the ballot by copying the information from the voter's ballot to a clean ballot. This procedure generated the most disputes because it required

discerning the voter's intent. At station 6, after all ballots from members of an IBT local were processed, an optical scanning machine tabulated the ballots.

99. CONVOY DISPATCH, *Special Post-Election Issue*, Jan. 1992, at 1.

100. Jim Woodward, *Will More Dominoes Fall? What the Teamster Election Means for the Labor Movement*, LABOR NOTES, Jan. 1992, at 15.

101. Bob Baker, *Reforms Pose Tough Task for Teamsters Winner Carey*, LOS ANGELES TIMES, Dec. 14, 1991, at 18.

102. Jonathan Tasini, *Can It Be Morning in Teamsterland?* NEW YORK TIMES, Dec. 13, 1991, at A39.

103. Stephen Franklin, *Reformer Declares Teamsters Victory*, CHICAGO TRIBUNE, Dec. 13, 1991, at C1.

104. Bruce D. Butterfield, *Teamster Chief Rides Reform Wave*, BOSTON GLOBE, Dec. 13, 1991, at 73.

105. *Collision*, at 258.

106. *The Cookbook*, ch. 16, at 3.

107. *United States v. Int'l Bhd. of Teamsters*, 896 F. Supp. 1349, 1365 (S.D.N.Y. 1995).

108. *United States v. Int'l Bhd. of Teamsters*, 86 F.3d 271, 275 (2d. Cir. 1996).

NOTES TO CHAPTER 6

1. *United States v. Int'l Bhd. of Teamsters*, 803 F. Supp. 761, 781 (S.D.N.Y. 1992).

2. Jeff Gert, *Despite Change, Reform Is Slow in the Teamsters*, NEW YORK TIMES, June 28, 1993.

3. *United States v. Int'l Bhd. of Teamsters*, 88 Civ. 4486, 1992 U.S. Dist. LEXIS 15016, at *3 (S.D.N.Y. Oct. 6, 1992).

4. The consent decree extended the IA's authority beyond the October 10, 1992, deadline in order (1) to "resolve to completion and decide all charges" filed by the IO on or before October 10, 1992, or (2) to refer those charges to the IRB. Consent Decree, *United States v. Int'l Bhd. of Teamsters*, No. 88 Civ. 4486 (S.D.N.Y.) (Mar. 14, 1989) [hereinafter Consent Decree], at G(m); *United States v. Int'l Bhd. of Teamsters*, 88 Civ. 4486, 1992 U.S. Dist. LEXIS 15016, at *3 (S.D.N.Y. Oct. 6, 1992).

5. *United States v. Int'l Bhd. of Teamsters*, 12 F.3d 360, 362 (2d Cir. 1993).

6. Consent Decree, at § G(a), G(b).

7. *Id.* at § G(a).

8. *United States v. Int'l Bhd. of Teamsters*, 829 F. Supp. 602, 605 (S.D.N.Y. 1993).

9. On remand, Judge Edelstein approved the rules as modified in accordance with the Second Circuit's decision. *Id.* The Second Circuit required four modifications to the IRB rules. First, the full three-person board must make decisions and issue opinions; second, the IRB members' compensation would be based on their usual billing rate *minus* that portion of their hourly rate attributable to law-office overhead; third, the IRB need only report its activities in *Teamster Magazine* when

"necessary to facilitate [the IRB's] investigations and ensure the proper implementation of its decisions"; fourth, absent compelling circumstances, IRB members should make applications to the district court as an entity, not individually. *Int'l Bhd. of Teamsters*, 829 F. Supp. 602.

10. Telephone interview with Charles M. Carberry.

11. *See* IRB Hearings (Statement of Charles M. Carberry, Chief IRB Investigator) ("We have allegations that come in from members or from other people, sometimes anonymously, sometimes with information that we follow up on.").

12. *See, e.g.,* letter from John Jackson, President, Local 676, to Ind. Review Bd. (Jul. 7, 1993), *available at* http://www.irbcases.org/pdfs/122_irb.pdf.

13. IBT Constitution, Art. XIX, § 1(e).

14. *Int'l Bhd. of Teamsters*, 829 F. Supp. at 606. *See, e.g.,* Johnnie Brown, Int'l Tr., Joint Council 16, Decision of the Int'l Tr. of Joint Council 16 on the Referral from the Indep. Review Bd. of Charges against Local 813 Officers Martin Adelstein, Alan Adelstein, James Murray, and Michael Giammona (Aug. 2, 1993).

15. Rules and Procedures for Operation of the Independent Review Board for the International Brotherhood of Teamsters [hereinafter IRB Rules], at G(i), G(g).

16. *United States v. Int'l Bhd. of Teamsters*, 978 F.2d 68, 73 (2d Cir. 1992); *United States v. Int'l Bhd. of Teamsters* (*DiGirlamo*), 120 F.3d 340, 346 (2d Cir. 1994) ("[T]he Consent Decree contains 'an extremely deferential standard of review' of decisions of the IRB by the district court.").

17. *United States v. Int'l Bhd. of Teamsters* (*Giacumbo III*), 170 F.3d 136, 145 (2d Cir. 1999), *vacating and remanding* No. 88 Civ. 4486 (S.D.N.Y. Jul. 28, 1997).

18. The district court modified an EO's decision on sanctions, finding that the ruling had inappropriately departed from the election rules. *United States v. Int'l Bhd. of Teamsters* (*Carey Slate Protest*), 9 F. Supp. 2d 354, 362 (S.D.N.Y. 1998), *aff'd*, 168 F.3d 645 (2d Cir. 1999).

19. Just before Carey took office, DOJ filed a civil RICO suit against Local 295, claiming that LCN figures had drained the local's treasury and extorted millions of dollars from air-freight companies. District court Judge Eugene Nickerson approved a trusteeship for Local 295. Carey later called his appointment of Genoese an honest mistake that had "come back to haunt" him. Judge Nickerson appointed Thomas Puccio, a former federal prosecutor, as trustee of Local 295. Gert, *Despite Change, Reform Is Slow in the Teamsters.*

20. Memorandum from the IRB to General President Carey Re Trusteeship Recommendation Concerning Local 714, Aug. 5, 1996.

21. *Teamster Chief Takes Over Chicago Local*, NEW YORK TIMES, Aug. 10, 1996.

22. Peter T. Kilborn, *Teamsters' New Chief Vows to Put Members First*, NEW YORK TIMES, Dec. 13, 1991.

23. *Int'l Bhd. of Teamsters*, 803 F. Supp. at 777.

24. *Int'l Bhd. of Teamsters*, 9 F. Supp. 2d at 363.

25. *Id.*

26. Transcript of Aug. 4, 1992, hearing before Judge David Edelstein, at 26–27.

27. *Int'l Bhd. of Teamsters*, 803 F. Supp. at 780; *Int'l Bhd. of Teamsters*, 998 F.2d 1101, 1106 (2d Cir. 1993).

28. *Int'l Bhd. of Teamsters*, 803 F. Supp. at 777.

29. *Id.* at 786–87.

30. *Id.* at 786, 788.

31. *Id.*

32. *Id.* at 788.

33. *Id.*

34. *Id.* at 799.

35. *Int'l Bhd. of Teamsters*, 998 F.2d at 1109.

36. House Committee on Education and the Workforce, Subcommittee on Oversight and Investigations, *Report on the Financial, Operating, and Political Affairs of the International Brotherhood of Teamsters*, 106th Cong., 1999, at 16.

37. Teamster Magazine, Jan.–Feb. 1993.

38. *Int'l Bhd. of Teamsters v. Local Union 810*, 19 F.3d 786 (2d Cir. 1994). Carey obtained an order from Judge Edelstein enjoining Local 810 from resisting the trusteeship. The Second Circuit affirmed Judge Edelstein's injunction.

39. *Id.*

40. Gert, *Despite Change, Reform Is Slow in the Teamsters*.

41. *Id.*

42. House Committee on Education and the Workforce, Subcommittee on Oversight and Investigations, *Report on the Financial, Operating, and Political Affairs of the International Brotherhood of Teamsters*, at 90.

43. *Id.*

44. House Committee on Education and the Workforce, Subcommittee on Oversight and Investigations, *Financial Affairs of International Brotherhood of Teamsters: Hearing before the Subcommittee on Oversight and Investigations*, written statement of Sam Theodus, 105th Cong., 2d sess., Mar. 26, 1998.

45. *Id.* For instance, in July 1994, after an NLRB administrative law judge ruled that Worcester, Massachusetts IBT Local 170 Secretary-Treasurer Ernest Tusino had operated an illegal hiring hall, Belk charged Tusino with "bringing reproach upon the union." The EPC panel recommended that Carey dismiss the charges. However, Carey rejected the recommendation and suspended Tusino from IBT membership for three months and from IBT office for two years. The subcommittee reported that "numerous witnesses attribute the action taken against Mr. Tusino to his outspoken opposition to Mr. Carey." One EPC member reported that IBT General Counsel Judy Scott telephoned Tusino's hearing panel to give her opinion on the case. A Northeastern University law professor testified that Scott told him that the case was "politically charged." *Tusino v. Int'l Bhd. of Teamsters*, 38 Fed. Appx. 91 (2d Cir. 2002); House Committee on Education and the Workforce,

Subcommittee on Oversight and Investigations, *Report on the Financial, Operating, and Political Affairs of the International Brotherhood of Teamsters*, at 90–92.

46. House Committee on Education and the Workforce, Subcommittee on Oversight and Investigations, *Report on the Financial, Operating, and Political Affairs of the International Brotherhood of Teamsters*, at 90.

47. Steven Greenhouse, *Teamsters Chief, Despite Victory, Is Remaining Defiant*, NEW YORK TIMES, Dec. 16, 1996.

48. Interviews with Ken Paff.

NOTES TO CHAPTER 7

1. *United States v. Int'l Bhd. of Teamsters*, 896 F. Supp. 1349, 1353–55 (S.D.N.Y. 1995)

2. *In re Cheatem, et al.*, Post-27-EOH, Aug. 21, 1997, at 2.

3. Steven Greenhouse, *Once Again, the Hoffa Name Rouses the Teamsters' Union*, NEW YORK TIMES, Nov. 17, 1996.

4. Dave Hage, *Battle over Teamsters Is Fight Worth Watching: Future of Organized Labor Affects All Americans*, STAR TRIBUNE, Feb. 11, 1996.

5. *Id.*

6. Peter T. Kilborn, *Teamsters Chief Expects Convention Challenges*, NEW YORK TIMES, July 15, 1996. In November 1999, General President Jim Hoffa stripped Morris of his officer positions because of "a pattern of erratic behavior." Joseph R. Daughen, *Hoffa Removes Philadelphia-Area Teamsters Leader*, KNIGHT RIDDER TRIBUNE BUSINESS NEWS, Nov. 17, 1999.

7. Steven Greenhouse, *Bitter Battle for Teamsters' Leadership in New York*, NEW YORK TIMES, Dec. 3, 1996.

8. Steven Greenhouse, *Teamster Counterrevolution: Why It Nearly Won Election*, NEW YORK TIMES, Dec. 22, 1996.

9. Richard Behar, *A Teamster Tempest*, TIME, May 15, 1995.

10. *United States v. Int'l Bhd. of Teamsters*, 170 F.3d 136, 146 (2d Cir. 1999).

11. *Id.*

12. *Id.* at 146–47.

13. *Id.* at 147–48 (Jacobs, J., concurring).

14. *United States v. Int'l Bhd. of Teamsters*, No. 88 CIV. 4486, 1999 WL 169635, at *4 (S.D.N.Y. Mar. 26, 1999).

15. Independent Review Board, Report of Investigation of General President Ronald Carey, July 11, 1994, at 1.

16. *Id.* at 2.

17. *Id.* at 22.

18. *Id.* at 23.

19. *Id.* at 31.

20. *Id.* at 31–32.

21. *Id.* at 34.

22. *Id.* at 40.

23. *Id.* at 47. In October 1997, labor reporter Richard Behar published a lengthy *Fortune* magazine exposé reiterating many of the LCN-related allegations against Carey. Richard Behar, *The Trouble with the Teflon Teamster: The Feds and the Press Overlooked the Dark Side of Ron Carey*, FORTUNE, Oct. 27, 1997.

24. Jeffrey Goldberg, *Cash and Carey: More Trouble with the Teamsters*, NEW REPUBLIC, Aug. 11, 1997.

25. Sandra Livingston, *Theodus Will Challenge Carey in Teamster Race*, CLEV. PLAIN DEALER, Jan. 3, 1995, at 1C.

26. Sandra Livingston, *Theodus to Run on Hoffa Ticket*, CLEV. PLAIN DEALER, Mar. 5, 1996, at 1C; Livingston, *Theodus Will Challenge Carey in Teamster Race.*

27. House Committee on Education and the Workforce, Subcommittee on Oversight and Investigation, *Written Statement by Aaron Belk: Hearing before the Subcommittee on Oversight and Investigation*, 105th Cong., 2d sess., July 24, 1998.

28. Sandra Livingston, *"A First-Class Hanging": Teamsters Gripe about Hearing on Conferences*, CLEV. PLAIN DEALER, May 28, 1994, at 1C.

29. House Committee on Education and the Workforce, Subcommittee on Oversight and Investigations, *Financial Affairs of International Brotherhood of Teamsters: Hearing before the Subcommittee on Oversight and Investigations*, 105th Cong., 2d sess., Mar. 26, 1998.

30. Don Lee, *James Hoffa to Run for Teamsters Post*, LOS ANGELES TIMES, Aug. 31, 1995, *available at* http://articles.latimes.com/1995-08-31/news/mn-40812_1_james-r-hoffa; Tom Robbins, *In the Name of the Father: Hoffa's Son Is Going for the Brass Ring, the Teamsters Presidency*, NEW YORK DAILY NEWS, June 4, 1995, at 14; *see* Charles Brandt, *"I Heard You Paint Houses": Frank "The Irishman" Sheeran and the Inside Story of the Mafia, the Teamsters, and the Last Ride of Jimmy Hoffa*, Hanover, N.H.: Steerforth, 2004; Lester Velie, *Desperate Bargain: Why Jimmy Hoffa Had to Die*, New York: Reader's Digest Press, 1977.

31. Greenhouse, *Teamster Counterrevolution.*

32. *Vote Renews Jimmy Hoffa's Mystique*, CHICAGO SUN-TIMES, Dec. 7, 1998.

33. Peter T. Kilborn, *Teamsters Chief Expects Convention Challenges*, NEW YORK TIMES, July 15, 1996.

34. Greenhouse, *Once Again, the Hoffa Name Rouses the Teamsters Union.*

35. Larry Bretts, INDIANA POST-TRIBUNE, Sept. 10, 1995.

36. John O'Brien, *Hoffa Son Vows Power to Union*, CHICAGO TRIBUNE, June 14, 1996, at 4.

37. John D. Schulz, *Teamsters Kick Off Feisty Election; Carey Claims Lead over "Junior" Hoffa*, TRAFFIC WORLD, July 15, 1996, at 22.

38. John D. Schulz, *Hoffa Preparing '96 Challenge to Carey*, TRAFFIC WORLD, Jan. 23, 1995, at 14.

39. Randolph Heaster, *Teamsters Hear Message from Hoffa*, KAN. CITY STAR, June 10, 1996, at B1.

40. Schulz, *Hoffa Preparing '96 Challenge to Carey*, at 14.

41. *Id.*

42. Mike Dooley, *Hoffa Says Graft Tops Problems in Union*, FORT WAYNE (IND.) NEWS SENTINEL, May 18, 1996, at 8A.

43. Consent Decree, *United States v. Int'l Bhd. of Teamsters*, No. 88 Civ. 4486 (S.D.N.Y.) (Mar. 14, 1989), at 16.

44. Philip Dine, *Running Teamsters Election Full-Time Job for This U.S. Appointee*, ST. LOUIS POST-DISPATCH, Feb. 24, 1995, at 1C.

45. *Id.*

46. *Labor Lawyer from Milwaukee to Oversee '96 Teamsters Vote*, J. COM., June 1, 1995, at 3B.

47. *Federal Judge Appoints a New Overseer for Teamsters' Election*, NEW YORK TIMES, Sept. 30, 1997, at A26.

48. *Int'l Bhd. of Teamsters*, 896 F. Supp. at 1353–54.

49. Memorandum of Law in Support of Election Officer Application XIII ("EO Br."), at 2. DOJ contributed $322,953 for IBT election supervision in fiscal year 1994, $1,708,407 in fiscal year 1995, and $6 million in fiscal year 1996. DOL contributed $5.6 million for IBT election supervision in fiscal year 1996 and $3.8 million in fiscal year 1997. *United States v. Int'l Bhd. of Teamsters*, 989 F. Supp. 468, 471 (S.D.N.Y. 1997).

50. *Int'l Bhd. of Teamsters*, 896 F. Supp. at 1355.

51. Rules for the IBT International Union Delegate and Officer Election [hereinafter 1996 Election Rules], Art. VIII, Sec. 11(d).

52. 502 U.S. 527, 538 (1992).

53. *1996 Election Rules Decision*, 896 F. Supp. at 1365. The presumption could be rebutted by showing that "access to that particular employer's employee parking lot is neither necessary nor appropriate to meaningful exercise of democratic rights." Judged Edelstein later ruled that these rules applied to Canadian as well as U.S. employers. *United States v. Int'l Bhd. of Teamsters*, 945 F. Supp. 609 (S.D.N.Y. 1996) (finding Labatt's Brewing Co. in Toronto subject to the election rules promulgated pursuant to the consent decree.)

54. *United States v. Int'l Bhd. of Teamsters (Consent Order Modification)*, 159 F.R.D. 437, 440 (S.D.N.Y. 1995).

55. *Id.* at 438–40.

56. *Int'l Bhd. of Teamsters*, 896 F. Supp. at 1360–61.

57. *Int'l Bhd. of Teamsters*, 159 F.R.D. at 438–39.

58. House Committee on Education and the Workforce, Subcommittee on Oversight and Investigations, *1996 Teamster Elections: Barbara Zack Quindel: Hearing before the Subcommittee on Oversight and Investigations*, 105th Cong., 1st sess., Oct. 15, 1997.

59. Jeffrey Brodeur, *Boos Mark Teamsters Convention*, St. Paul Pioneer Press, July 16, 1996, at 8D.

60. Frank Swoboda, *Angry Hoffa Backers Force Recess at Teamsters' Meeting*, Washington Post, July 16, 1996.

61. *Id.*

62. Peter T. Kilborn, *Delegate Battle Delays Teamsters Meeting*, New York Times, July 16, 1996, at A12.

63. Merrill Goozner, *Teamsters Open with Shouting Match*, Chicago Tribune, July 16, 1996, at 1.

64. *Uproar Halts Teamsters Convention*, St. Louis Post-Dispatch, July 16, 1996, at 5A.

65. Kenneth C. Crowe, *Teamsters President Ties Rivals in Red Tape*, Newsday, July 18, 1996, at A51.

66. Peter T. Kilborn, *Teamster Chief Outmaneuvers Foes at Meeting*, New York Times, July 19, 1996, at A10.

67. Peter Szekely, *Teamsters Leader Cuts Off Challenge: Carey Abruptly Ends Convention Dominated by Hoffa*, Akron Beacon J., July 20, 1996, at D1.

68. Peter T. Kilborn, *Cause for Sibling Rivalry at Teamsters*, New York Times, July 17, 1996, at A16; Peter T. Kilborn, *In New Rebuff to Leader, Teamsters Vote to Remain a Brotherhood*, New York Times, July 18, 1996, at D23.

69. Chris Isidore, *Gridlock Grips Teamster Meeting*, J. Com., July 18, 1996, at 1B.

70. Kenneth C. Crowe, *Collision: How the Rank and File Took Back the Teamsters*, New York: Scribner, 1993 [hereinafter *Collision*], at 168.

71. Kilborn, *Delegate Battle Delays Teamster Meeting*.

72. Glenn Burkins, *Teamsters Chief Carey Loses Straw Poll of Delegates to Rival Candidate Hoffa*, Wall St. J., July 19, 1996, at A14.

73. Peter T. Kilborn, *Teamsters Chief Expects Convention Challenges*, New York Times, July 15, 1996.

74. *Id.*

75. *Id.*

76. *Teamsters' President Sues Rival, Charging Campaign Libels Him*, New York Times, Oct. 1, 1996.

77. *Id.*

78. *Teamster Chief Takes over Chicago Local*, New York Times, Aug. 10, 1996, at 12.

79. Janet Moore, *Carey-Hoffa Race Divides Akron Local: Teamsters' 1.4 Million Members Will Vote by Mail in November*, Akron Beacon J., Aug. 13, 1996, at C6.

80. *Local 107 v. Int'l Bhd. of Teamsters*, 935 F. Supp. 599, 600–01 (E.D. Pa. 1996).

81. *Hoffa Says Trusteeships Politically Motivated*, J. Com., Aug. 16, 1996, at 4B (quoting James P. Hoffa's statement about his opponent).

82. *Int'l Bhd. of Teamsters*, 935 F. Supp. at 604.

83. *United States v. Int'l Bhd. of Teamsters (In re IBT's Application to Enjoin*

Plaintiffs in Int'l Bhd. of Teamsters Local Union 107), 939 F. Supp. 280, 287 (S.D.N.Y. 1996).

84. John D. Schulz, *No Carey-Hoffa Debate*, TRAFFIC WORLD, July 15, 1996, at 8.

85. *United States v. Int'l Bhd. of Teamsters (Hoffa Debates)*, 939 F. Supp. 226, 227 (S.D.N.Y. 1996).

86. Schulz, *No Carey-Hoffa Debate*, at 8; *see also Hoffa Debates*, 939 F. Supp. at 233.

87. Philip Dine, *After Long, Interesting Race, Teamsters Union Re-elects President*, ST. LOUIS POST-DISPATCH, Dec. 20, 1996, *available at* 1996 WLNR 4593256.

88. *Id.*

89. John D. Schulz, *Teamster Election Validated: Election Officer Discounts Hoffa Claims Contesting Carey's Margin of Victory*, TRAFFIC WORLD, Jan. 13, 1997, at 26.

90. *In re Cheatem, et al.*, Post-27-EOH, Aug. 21, 1997, at 115.

91. Steven Greenhouse, *With a Clear Lead, Teamsters President Is Claiming Victory*, NEW YORK TIMES, Dec. 15, 1996.

92. Greenhouse, *Teamster Counterrevolution*.

92. Greenhouse, *With a Clear Lead*.

94. *In re Cheatem, et al.*, Post-27-EOH, Aug. 21, 1997.

95. Email from Barbara Quindel to the author, Aug. 19, 2010.

96. Decision of Kenneth Conboy to Disqualify IBT President Ron Carey (Nov. 17, 1997), at 1–2, *available at* http://www.spa.ucla.edu/ps/pdf/W00/PSM232/PDF/ Carey.PDF [hereinafter Conboy Decision]. Early in the 1991 election cycle, Eddie Burke, Carey's campaign director, hired the November Group to help the Carey campaign fundraise, strategize, and increase voter turnout. Soon after Carey took office in February 1992, he hired Jere Nash (who previously led the transition team of Governor Ray Mabus (D-Miss.) and later served as a consultant to the 1996 Clinton-Gore campaign) to oversee his transition into the general presidency. Throughout Carey's first term, Nash and Hamilton relied heavily on the November Group to lobby local, state, and federal legislators and policymakers. From 1992 to 1996, the November Group billed the IBT $650,000 for its services. Jim Larkin, *The Teamsters: What Went Wrong? The Campaign Money Scandal of Teamster President Ron Carey*, IN THESE TIMES, Dec. 14, 1997, http://laborers.com/ITT_12-14 -97.html.

97. *Id.*

98. Conboy Decision, at 1–2. It was also alleged that Share Group had overcharged the union $26,000 for phone banking. Edward Barnes, *Donorgate in the Teamsters*, TIME, Mar. 24, 1997, at 66.

99. Steven Greenhouse, *U.S. Investigates Campaign Gift to Teamster Chief*, NEW YORK TIMES, Mar. 27, 1997.

100. Bernard J. Wolfson, *Justice Eyes Carey Gift: Teamster Election $$ under Fire*, BOSTON HERALD, Mar. 8, 1997, at 14.

101. Citizen Action was a consumer-advocacy group formed in 1979 and headquartered in Cleveland, Ohio. It worked closely with Ralph Nader's Public Interest Research Groups. At its peak, Citizen Action had nearly 1.5 million members. It dissolved in 1997 in the wake of Carey's campaign-finance scandal. DiscoverTheNetworks.org, "Citizen Action(CA)," http://www.discoverthenetworks .org/groupProfile.asp?grpid=7284.

102. Kenneth C. Crowe, *Court to Rule on Teamster Info*, NEWSDAY, June 11, 1997, at A19.

103. Laborers for Justice, "V. Special Investigations of the Subcommittee," http://www.thelaborers.net/teamsters/investigation_of_the_teamsters.htm.

104. Kevin Galvin, *Feds Probe Citizen Action's Alleged Ploy to Fund Teamster Elections*, AMADOR (CALIF.) LEDGER DISPATCH, June 10, 1997, at A5.

105. Steven Greenhouse, *3 Teamster Aides Make Guilty Pleas and Hint at Plot*, NEW YORK TIMES, Sept. 19, 1997, at A1.

106. The *Wall Street Journal* reported that a top DNC official wrote a memorandum in mid-1996 calling for the IBT's political action committee to donate nearly $1 million to DNC affiliates. In return, according to a note written by Davis, the DNC made a "commitment" to help the IBT. Glenn R. Simpson, *Teamsters' Election Funding Is Subject to Federal Inquiry*, WALL STREET JOURNAL, A1, Aug. 8, 1997.

107. Steven Greenhouse, *Ex-Teamster Official Guilty in Campaign Finance Case*, NEW YORK TIMES, Nov. 20, 1999.

108. Michael Weisskopf, Michael Duffy & Edward Barnes, *A New Witness to the Teamster Cash-Swap Plan*, TIME, Oct. 13, 1997.

109. Greg B. Smith, *Teamster Boss Aide Faces Embezzle Case*, NEW YORK DAILY NEWS, June 7, 1997, at 10.

110. *Id.*

111. Kevin Galvin, *Probe Ties Illegal Aid to Top Teamster Liberal Consumer Group Allegedly*, NEWARK STAR-LEDGER, June 10, 1997, at 69.

112. Chris Isidore, *Teamsters' Hamilton Steps Down amid Probe*, J. COM., July 31, 1997, at A15; Kevin Galvin, *Calling Probe a "Circus," Teamsters' Top Lobbyist Quits*, ASSOCIATED PRESS, July 30, 1997.

113. *In re Cheatem, et al.*, P-32-IBT-EOH, Aug. 21, 1997, at 1–2.

114. *Id.* at 2. *Feds Order New Teamsters Election*, CNN, Aug. 22, 1997, *available at* http://www.cnn.com/ALLPOLITICS/1997/08/22/teamsters/; House Committee on Education and the Workforce, Subcommittee on Oversight and Investigations, *Statement of Michael G. Cherkasky: Hearing Before the Subcommittee on Oversight and Investigations*, 106th Cong., 1st sess., Apr. 29, 1999.

115. *In re Cheatem, et al.*, P-32-IBT-EOH, Aug. 21, 1997, at 114.

116. *Id.* at 119.

117. Stephen Labaton, *Teamsters Election Monitor Is Reported Planning to Quit*, NEW YORK TIMES, Aug. 30, 1997, at 8.

118. *United States v. Int'l Bhd. of Teamsters (Carey Slate Protest)*, 9 F. Supp. 2d 354, 356 (S.D.N.Y. 1998), *aff'd*, 168 F.3d 645 (2d Cir. 1999).

119. Chris Isidore, *Resignation Could Delay Rerun of Teamster Vote*, J. COM., Sept. 25, 1997, at 16A.

120. Steven Greenhouse, *Teamster Chief Claims Aides Betrayed Him*, NEW YORK TIMES, Sept. 24, 1997.

121. *Id.*

122. *United States v. Int'l Bhd. of Teamsters (Rerun Election Plan)*, 981 F. Supp. 222, 232 (S.D.N.Y. 1997).

123. Conboy Decision, at 5.

124. *Id.* at 32. The only prior time a Teamster had been disqualified from standing for election was in a Covina, California IBT Local 63 case. Michael H. Holland, *The Cookbook: How the Election Officer Supervised the 1991 Teamster Election*, July 1992, ch. 6, at 26–28. However, in that case, Holland disqualified delegates to the national convention, not a candidate for international-union office. Conboy Decision, at 29.

125. Kevin Galvin, *Teamsters Chief Takes Unpaid Leave: By Stepping Aside, Carey Clears Way for Hoffa Challenger*, ASSOCIATED PRESS, Nov. 25, 1997; Laborers for Justice, "V. Special Investigations of the Subcommittee."

126. *Id.*

127. *Id.*

128. *Id.*

129. House Committee on Education and the Workforce, Subcommittee on Oversight and Investigations, *Opening Statement of Chairman Peter Hoekstra: Hearing before the Subcommittee on Oversight and Investigations*, 105th Cong., 2d sess., May 19, 1998.

130. Steven Greenhouse, *U.S. Officials Ending Monitoring of Teamsters' Finances*, NEW YORK TIMES, Jan. 11, 2002, *available at* http://www.nytimes.com/2002/01/11/us/us-officials-ending-monitoring-of-teamsters-finances.html?pagewanted=1.

131. House Committee on Education and the Workforce, Subcommittee on Oversight and Investigations, *Opening Statement of Chairman Peter Hoekstra: Hearing before the Subcommittee on Oversight and Investigations*, 105th Cong., 2d sess., June 16, 1998.

132. House Committee on Education and the Workforce, Subcommittee on Oversight and Investigations, *Statement of Chairman Pete Hoekstra: Second Hearing on the Invalidated 1996 Teamsters Election*, 105th Cong., 1st sess., Oct. 15, 1997.

133. *Id.*

134. *Id.*

135. *Id.*

136. *Id.*

137. *Id.*

138. Richard Sisk, *Union Rebels Rap Carey*, NEW YORK DAILY NEWS, Oct. 15, 1997.

139. House Committee on Education and the Workforce, Subcommittee on Oversight and Investigations, *Statement of Chairman Pete Hoekstra: Second Hearing on the Invalidated 1996 Teamsters Election*, 105th Cong., 1st sess., Oct. 15, 1997.

140. *Id.*

141. House Committee on Education and the Workforce, Subcommittee on Oversight and Investigations, *Opening Statement of Chairman Peter Hoekstra: Hearing before the Subcommittee on Oversight and Investigations*, 105th Cong., 2d sess., June 16, 1998.

142. Laborers for Justice, "V. Special Investigations of the Subcommittee."

143. House Committee on Education and the Workforce, Subcommittee on Oversight and Investigations, *Opening Statement of Chairman Peter Hoekstra: Hearing before the Subcommittee on Oversight and Investigations*, 105th Cong., 2d sess., May 19, 1998.

144. Kevin Galvin, *Teamsters Chief Takes Unpaid Leave: By Stepping Aside, Carey Clears Way for Hoffa Challenger*, ASSOCIATED PRESS, Nov. 25, 1997.

145. John Russell, *Ron Carey Vows to Fight to the End*, AKRON BEACON J., Nov. 23, 1997, at B1.

146. *Id.*

147. *United States v. Int'l Bhd. of Teamsters (Carey Disqualification)*, 988 F. Supp. 759, 770 (S.D.N.Y. 1997), *aff'd*, 156 F.3d 354 (2d Cir. 1998).

148. LMRDA Section 101(a)(5) provides that "[n]o member of any labor organization may be fined, suspended, expelled, or otherwise disciplined . . . by such organization or by any officer thereof unless such member has been (A) served with written specific charges; (B) given a reasonable time to prepare his defense; [and] (C) afforded a full and fair hearing." Carey argued that his expulsion constituted "discipline" and that, accordingly, the EAM could not disqualify him from the rerun election without convening a hearing.

149. *United States v. Int'l Bhd. of Teamsters*, 88 Civ. 4486, Opinion and Order, Aug. 27, 1999.

150. *Id.* at 24.

151. *Id.*

152. *Id.*

153. *Id.* at 34.

154. *Id.*

155. *Id.*

156. Greenhouse, *Ex-Teamster Official Guilty in Campaign Finance Case.*

157. 18 U.S.C. § 1001 provides, "Whoever, in any matter, within the jurisdiction of the executive, legislative, or judicial branch of the government of the United States, knowingly and willfully makes any materially false, fictitious or fraudulent statement or representation, is guilty of a crime."

158. 18 U.S.C. § 1623 provides, "Whoever, under oath in any proceeding, before any court or grand jury of the United States, knowingly makes any false material declaration, is guilty of a crime."

159. *Ex-Teamster Chief Carey Indicted in Funds Probe*, CHICAGO TRIBUNE, Jan. 26, 2001, at 3; Robert Gearty, *Ex-Teamsters Boss Goes on Trial*, NEW YORK DAILY NEWS, Aug. 27, 2001, at 17.

160. Steven Greenhouse, *Ex-President of Teamsters Is Charged with Lying*, NEW YORK TIMES, Jan. 26, 2001.

161. Trial transcript, at 2241, lines 4–6.

162. Other witnesses testifying for the government were Aaron Belk (Carey's executive assistant), Angelo Manso (office manager for the Carey campaign), Hal Manchow (cofounder of the November Group), Kimberly McCaffrey (FBI special agent), Susan Davis (lawyer who represented Carey's election committee), and Robert Muehlenkamp (Carey's assistant and IBT organizing director).

163. Nancy Cleeland, *Ex-Teamster Leader Carey Acquitted*, LOS ANGELES TIMES, Oct. 13, 2001, at A18.

164. *See* Kevin Galvin, *Carey's Downfall Seen as a Blow to Labor Reform*, AMADOR (CALIF.) LEDGER DISPATCH, Nov. 25, 1997, at A14.

165. TDU, "Ron Carey: Visionary Teamster Leader Dies at 72," http://www.tdu.org/node/2619.

166. Frank Swoboda, *Teamsters' Carey Disqualified from Running in New Election*, WASHINGTON POST, Nov. 18, 1997.

167. *Ron Carey's Sad Fall*, NEW YORK TIMES, Nov. 18, 1997.

168. *United States v. Int'l Bhd. of Teamsters*, 247 F.3d 370, 397 (2d. Cir. 2001).

169. Seymour Martin Lipset, Martin Trow & James Coleman, *Union Democracy: What Makes Democracy Work in Labor Unions and Other Organizations?* New York: Anchor Books, 1956, at 6.

NOTES TO CHAPTER 8

1. *United States v. Int'l Bhd. of Teamsters*, 981 F. Supp. 222, 226 (S.D.N.Y. 1997).

2. *Id.* at 229–30.

3. Quindel had declined to act on Carey's protest. Conboy ordered her to conduct a full investigation. *United States v. Int'l Bhd. of Teamsters* (*Carey Slate Protest*), 9 F. Supp. 2d 354, 356 (S.D.N.Y. 1998).

4. *Id.*

5. *In re Thomas R. O'Donnell*, Opinion and Decision of the Independent Review Board, Apr. 2, 2001.

6. *In re: Election Office Case No. Carey Slate*, PR-035-EOH (Post-47-EOH).

7. *Carey Slate Protest*, 9 F. Supp. 2d at 360.

8. *Id.*

9. The Second Circuit Court of Appeals affirmed the decision not to disqualify

Hoffa. *United States v. Int'l Bhd. of Teamsters* (*Carey Slate Protest I*), 159 F.3d 757, 759 (2d Cir. 1998). In another decision, the Second Circuit Court of Appeals affirmed Judge Edelstein's increase of the Hoffa campaign's fine. *United States v. Int'l Bhd. of Teamsters* (*Carey Slate Protest II*), 168 F.3d 645, 648 (2d Cir. 1999). The fine would be used to help finance the rerun election. Kenneth C. Crowe, *Hoffa Fined to Help Fund Election*, NEWSDAY, June 24, 1998, at A51.

   10. *United States v. Int'l Bhd. of Teamsters* (*Rerun Funding I*), 989 F. Supp. 468, 472 (S.D.N.Y. 1997), *rev'd*, 141 F.3d 405 (2d Cir. 1998).

   11. *Id.* at 474.

   12. *Id.* at 478.

   13. *Int'l Bhd. of Teamsters*, 141 F.3d at 409.

   14. *Int'l Bhd. of Teamsters*, 989 F. Supp. at 471–72. DOJ's and DOL's 1998 appropriations acts contained identical language: "None of the funds made available in this Act may be used to pay the expense of an election officer appointed by a court to oversee an election of any officer or trustee for the [IBT]."

   15. David Hosansky, *Tackling Teamsters Ties*, J. COM., Sept. 18, 1997, at 6A.

   16. Kevin Galvin, *Teamsters Vote Supervision May End*, ASSOCIATED PRESS, July 22, 1998.

   17. *Teamster Monitor Seeking Funds*, CLEV. PLAIN DEALER, June 26, 1998, at 3C.

   18. Steven Greenhouse, *Money Dispute May Obstruct Teamster Vote, Monitor Says*, NEW YORK TIMES, June 26, 1998.

   19. House Committee on Education and the Workforce, Subcommittee on Oversight and Investigations, *Opening Statement of Chairman Pete Hoekstra: Hearing before the Subcommittee on Oversight and Investigations*, 105th Cong., 2d sess., June 16, 1998.

   20. Galvin, *Teamsters Vote Supervision May End*.

   21. Phillip Dine, *GOP Offers to Help Fund, Oversee Teamsters Vote*, ST. LOUIS POST-DISPATCH, Aug. 5, 1998, at A11.

   22. *United States v. Int'l Bhd. of Teamsters* (*Rerun Election Plan III*), 22 F. Supp. 2d 131, 133 (S.D.N.Y. 1998).

   23. Ellen Simon, *Teamsters Ante Up for Vote*, NEWARK STAR-LEDGER, Sept. 1, 1998, at 19.

   24. Gail Kinsey Hill, *Tom Leedham's Unlikely Journey*, OREGONIAN, July 26, 1998, at B1; Philip Dine, *Third Man in Teamsters Stresses His Credentials*, ST. LOUIS POST-DISPATCH, July 19, 1998, at B4.

   25. *Id.*

   26. Ellen Simon, *Campaign for Change*, NEWARK STAR-LEDGER, July 28, 1998, at 19.

   27. John D. Schulz, *Hoffa-Leedham Rematch*, TRAFFIC WORLD, June 12, 2000, at 21.

   28. Philip Dine, *Attack Dogs May Chew on Hoffa's Lead*, ST. LOUIS POST-DISPATCH, Aug. 7, 1998, at C2.

29. Kevin Galvin, *Teamster Chief Told to End Retaliation*, NEWARK STAR-LEDGER, Aug. 17, 1998, at 4.

30. *Hoffa Vows Revival*, CINCINNATI-KY. POST, Dec. 8, 1998, at C6.

31. *Ushering in a New Era of Hoffa and the Teamsters*, CHICAGO TRIBUNE, Dec. 8, 1998.

32. *Redeeming the Hoffa Name*, BALTIMORE SUN, Dec. 13, 1998.

33. *On Second Try, Hoffa Is Elected President of Teamsters Union*, NEW YORK TIMES, Dec. 6, 1998; *Hoffa Seeking Decisive Victory in Teamsters Election: Union Prepares to Vote after Feverish Campaign*, NEW YORK TIMES, Nov. 1, 1998.

34. Janet L. Fix, *Hoffa Vows No Ties to Mob for Union*, PHILA. INQUIRER, Dec. 7, 1998, at A06.

35. *See* Janet L. Fix, *Hoffa Says He Can Handle Array of Teamsters' Problems*, PHILA. INQUIRER, Dec. 8, 1998, at A08.

36. James P. Hoffa, Comments on Fourth Day of 2001 IBT Convention, Morning Session.

37. James B. Jacobs & David N. Santore, *The Liberation of IBT Local 560*, 37 CRIMINAL LAW BULLETIN 125 (2001).

38. Before Stier resigned, Project RISE documents were posted on the Web. However, much of this information can still be accessed by using the Internet Archive's "Wayback Machine" feature. *See, e.g.,* Project RISE: Basic Principles of the Plan, at http://web.archive.org/web/20021122224101/http://www.teamsters.org/rise/principl.htm; Origin of the Plan, at http://web.archive.org/web/20021122212257/www.teamsters.org/rise/origin.htm; Project RISE: Phase 1, at http://web.archive.org/web/20021122215110/www.teamsters.org/rise/phase_1.htm; and Project RISE Press Releases, at http://web.archive.org/web/20021122224623/www.teamsters.org/rise/press.asp.

39. Retainer letter for Stier, Anderson & Malone LLC, June 8, 1999.

40. Letter from Pat Szymanski to Chief of the FBI's Organized Crime and Drug Operations Section, Feb. 2000 (obtained from TDU).

41. IBT, *Hoffa Announces Anti-Mob Initiative*, press release, July 29, 1999, *available at* http://web.archive.org/web/20021203145839/www.teamster.org/99Hoffa/072999_antiplan.html.

42. Andrew W. Singer, *Teamsters Revving Up for a Nonstop Ethics Journey*, ETHIKOS, Mar.–Apr. 2000, *available at* http://www.singerpubs.com/ethikos/html/teamsters.html.

43. *Id.*

44. IBT, *Teamsters Name New Mexico Appellate Judge to Anti-corruption Program*, press release, Sept. 23, 1999, *available at* http://web.archive.org/web/20021122224623/www.teamsters.org/rise/press.asp.

45. IBT, *Task Force Members*, *available at* http://web.archive.org/web/20021122225457/www.teamsters.org/rise/taskforc.htm.

46. Stier, Anderson & Malone, LLC, *The Teamsters: Perception and Reality: An*

Investigative Study of Organized Crime Influences in the Union, Washington, D.C.: IBT, 2001 [hereinafter *Perception and Reality*]. A summary of the report is available at Laborers for Justice, *Project RISE Summary*, http://www.thelaborers.net/teamsters/project_rise_summary.htm.

47. Steven Greenhouse, *Hoffa Chooses Leader for Reform Effort*, New York Times, July 7, 1999.

48. Herman Benson, *A Double Miscalculation Ended RISE*, 151 Union Democracy Review, June–July 2004, *available at* http://www.uniondemocracy.com/UDR/65-Fall%20of%20RISE%20in%20IBT.htm.

49. Ron Teninty, letter to The Nation, Sept. 7, 2000, *available at* http://www.thenation.com/article/discreet-charm-hoffa-jr.

50. Greenhouse, *Hoffa Chooses Leader for Reform Effort*.

51. *Id.*

52. *Id.*

53. House Committee on Education and the Workforce, Subcommittee on Oversight and Investigations, *The International Brotherhood of Teamsters One Year after the Election of James P. Hoffa: Hearing before the Subcommittee on Oversight and Investigations*, 106th Cong., 2d sess., Mar. 28, 2000.

54. Interview with Robert C. Stewart, Mar. 27, 2005.

55. Ethics Code, Second Published Draft [hereinafter Code of Conduct], Introduction to § 1. This version speaks explicitly of the need to keep organized crime out of the IBT.

56. Code of Conduct, Chapter II, § 1(a).

57. *Id.*, Chapter I, § 5(b)(i).

58. *Id.*, Chapter I, § 1 (a)(ii)(C).

59. *Id.*, Chapter I, § 4(a).

60. 29 U.S.C. § 1001 et seq. (2000).

61. Barry Eidlin, *Is Teamster "Code of Conduct" Just Window-Dressing? Reformers Criticize Hoffa's Anti-corruption Program*, Labor Notes, May 2000.

62. Herman Benson, letter to The Nation, Sept. 7, 2000, *available at* http://www.thenation.com/doc/20000918/letter.

63. Letter from Ken Paff to Project RISE Special Counsels Ed Stier and Harris Hartz, Apr. 28, 2000 (obtained from TDU).

64. TDU, Appendix, *Comments by Teamsters for a Democratic Union on the "RISE" Code of Conduct*, Apr. 7, 2003.

65. *Id.*

66. *Id.*; Ethics Code, ch. I, § 1.B.1, at 3.

67. TDU, Appendix, *Comments by Teamsters for a Democratic Union on the "RISE" Code of Conduct*, Apr. 7, 2003.

68. Ron Teninty, letter to The Nation.

69. Project RISE Phase 2, Code Approval and Kick-Off, *available at* http://web.archive.org/web/20021128202410/www.teamsters.org/rise/phase_2.htm.

70. IBT, *Teamsters Reaffirm Support of Anti-corruption Effort*, press release.

71. Project RISE Report on Cosa Nostra's influence over IBT locals and joint councils.

72. Jacobs & Santore, *The Liberation of IBT Local 560*.

73. Steven Greenhouse, *Teamsters Accuse Top Union Official of Scheming with Organized Crime*, NEW YORK TIMES, Jan. 25, 2003.

74. *DeSanti Cops a Plea*, 210 CONVOY DISPATCH, June–July 2003.

75. *See generally Perception and Reality*.

76. Laborers for Justice, *Project RISE Summary*, at 19–20, 23–24.

77. IBT, *Organized Crime Study*, "Proof of Our Promise," Oct. 4, 2002, http://www.teamster.org/content/organized-crime-study-%E2%80%98proof-our-promise%E2%80%99.

78. Steven Greenhouse, *Teamsters Have Cleaner Union, Study Finds*, NEW YORK TIMES, Oct. 3, 2002, at A20, *available at* http://www.nytimes.com/2002/10/03/us/teamsters-have-cleaner-union-study-finds.html?n=Top/Reference/Times%20Topics/Subjects/O/Organized%20Crime.

79. IBT, *Organized Crime Study*, "Proof of Our Promise."

80. United States Attorney's Office for the Southern District of New York, *Outline of Civil Complaint*, press release, June 28, 1988.

81. Comments of President Hoffa at press conference held at the National Press Club on the subject of the release of *Perception and Reality*, Oct. 3, 2002, *available at* http://web.archive.org/web/20021203104156/www.teamster.org/hoffa/percepandreality.htm; *Teamsters Winning Fight against Organized Crime: New Study Shows Union No Longer Dominated by Organized Crime: Hoffa Commits Union to Being "Forever Vigilant,"* PR NEWSWIRE, Oct. 3, 2002, *available at* http://www.thefreelibrary.com/Teamsters+Winning+Fight+Against+Organized+Crime%3B+New+Study+Shows...-a092426372.

82. *Id.*

83. *Teamsters Now Corruption-Free?* ASSOCIATED PRESS, Oct. 6, 2002. The Associated Press reported that the IBT was to pay Stier's firm between $2 million and $3 million for the report.

84. Ken Paff, *Where Do Hoffa's Tactics Fit in a Mob-Free Teamsters Union?* COUNTERPUNCH, Oct. 12, 2002, http://www.counterpunch.org/paff1012.html.

85. *Id.*

86. *United States v. Int'l Bhd. of Teamsters*, 88 Civ. 4486, Independent Review Board's Report for the Period 1996–2001 to Honorable Loretta A. Preska, July 12, 2001, at 7.

87. *In re John Ferrara*, Opinion and Decision of the Independent Review Board, Apr. 14, 1999.

88. *United States v. Int'l Bhd. of Teamsters*, 88 Civ. 4486, Independent Review Board's Report for the Period 1996–2001 to Honorable Loretta A. Preska, July 12, 2001, at 7.

89. *In re Lawrence Garono*, Opinion and Decision of the Independent Review Board, Feb. 2, 1999.

90. *United States v. Int'l Bhd. of Teamsters*, 88 Civ. 4486, Independent Review Board's Report for the Period 1996–2001 to Honorable Loretta A. Preska, July 12, 2001, at 7.

91. *In re Anthony Antoun*, Opinion and Decision of the Independent Review Board, Sept. 21, 1999.

92. *In the Matter of Leo Connelly*, Opinion and Decision of the Independent Review Board, Sept. 21, 1999. After Connelly's release from prison, Strollo helped him get a job in Local 377.

93. *United States v. Int'l Bhd. of Teamsters*, 167 L.R.R.M. 2157 (S.D.N.Y. 2001); Steven Greenhouse, *Teamsters, Tenacious as an Old Lounge Act, Convene in Las Vegas*, NEW YORK TIMES, June 26, 2001, at A12; *Teamster Review Board Expels Top Hoffa Backers*, UNION DEMOCRACY REVIEW, Aug.–Sept. 2002, at 7.

94. *Id.*; *see also* Randy Furst & Jim West, *As Campaign Begins, Reformers Highlight Hoffa's Broken Promises*, LABOR NOTES, Aug. 2001, at 10; Alex LoCascio, *Feds Charge Hoffa Associates in Vegas Scam*, LABOR NOTES, July 2001, at 13, 16.

95. *Teamster Review Board Expels Top Hoffa Backers*, at 7.

96. *In re Dane Passo and William T. Hogan, Jr.*, Opinion and Decision of the IRB, May 29, 2002.

97. *United States v. Int'l Bhd. of Teamsters (Application 102: William T. Hogan and Dane M. Passo)*, 88 Civ. 4486, Memorandum and Order, Aug. 22, 2003.

98. TDU, *Chicago Local 714 in Trusteeship*, http://www.tdu.org/node/2053.

99. *Id.*

100. In November 1990, for instance, IA Lacey expelled Gerald Corallo, the local's president and the son of Lucchese crime family boss Anthony Corallo, for conspiring with other local officers to embezzle $835,000 from the local's retirement fund. *Investigations Officer v. Gerald Corallo*, Charge, Sept. 28. 1990.

101. National Legal and Policy Center, *New Jersey Local Placed in Trusteeship*, Dec. 29, 1999.

102. *Id.*

103. *United States v. Int'l Bhd. of Teamsters*, 88 Civ. 4486, Independent Review Board's Report for the Period 1996–2001 to Honorable Loretta A. Preska, July 12, 2001, at 16.

104. *Id.*

NOTES TO CHAPTER 9

1. Randy Furst & Jim West, *Teamsters Set the Stage for Hoffa-Leedham Rematch*, LABOR NOTES, Aug. 1, 2001, at 1.

2. *United States v. Int'l Bhd. of Teamsters*, 2000 U.S. Dist. LEXIS 8330, at *2 (S.D.N.Y. June 16, 2000); *United States v. Int'l Bhd. of Teamsters (Election Access*

Decision), 2000 U.S. Dist. LEXIS 16213, at *2–3 (S.D.N.Y. Nov. 8, 2000); David N. Herszenhorn, *David N. Edelstein, 90, Judge in Federal Court for 48 Years*, NEW YORK TIMES, Aug. 21, 2000, at B7.

3. John D. Schulz, *Hoffa-Leedham Rematch*, TRAFFIC WORLD, June 12, 2000, at 21.

4. John D. Schulz, *Hoffa Odds-On Favorite: Son of Legendary Labor Leader Seen Winning Landslide for Second Term in 2001 IBT Direct-Vote Election*, TRAFFIC WORLD, Nov. 27, 2000, at 22.

5. *Election Access Decision*, 2000 WL 1682963, at *1.

6. *United States v. Int'l Bhd. of Teamsters*, 88 Civ. 4486 (DNE) (Election Administrator, Report No. 4, July 2001).

7. Office of the Election Supervisor for the IBT, "In re: Hoffa Unity Slate," Protest Decision 2001 EAD 78, January 8, 2001, http://www.ibtvote.org/protests/2000/2001ead078.htm.

8. Convention-delegate advertisement for Local 320 (on file with author).

9. *Reformer Leedham to Oppose Hoffa in Teamster Election*, LABOR NOTES, July 2000, at 7.

10. Randy Furst & Jim West, *As Campaign Begins, Reformers Highlight Hoffa's Broken Promises*, LABOR NOTES, Aug. 2001, at 10.

11. *Reformer Leedham to Oppose Hoffa in Teamster Election*, at 7.

12. *Id.*

13. *United States v. Int'l Bhd. of Teamsters*, 88 Civ. 4486, Application 102 of the Independent Review Board, Opinion and Decision of the IRB in the Matter of the Hearing of William T. Hogan, Jr., and Dane Passo, May 29, 2002.

14. Steven Greenhouse, *More Troubles for Teamsters President*, NEW YORK TIMES, June 20, 2000, at A14.

15. Martha Gruelle, *Teamster Reformers Say They Must Battle Hoffa's Public Relations with Truth*, LABOR NOTES, Dec. 2000, at 3.

16. Richard A. Ryan, *Feds Ease Reins on Teamsters*, DETROIT NEWS, Apr. 13, 2000.

17. Barry Eidlin, *Reformers Criticize Hoffa's Anti-corruption Program*, LABOR NOTES, May 2000, at 1.

18. TEAMSTER MAGAZINE, Oct. 2001.

19. *Leedham Told Members to Ignore Picket Line*, Nov. 13, 2000.

20. *In re: Hoffa Slate, Ashley McNeely, Leedham Slate, and Danny Campbell*, 2001 EAD (Election Administrator Decision) 370, May 16, 2001, *available at* http://www.ibtvote.com/protests/2000/2001ead370.htm.

21. *Id.*

22. Randy Furst & Jim West, *News from the Teamsters Convention in Las Vegas*, LABOR NOTES, Aug. 5, 2001, *available at* http://www.laborers.com/Labornote_Teamconven_8-5-01.htm.

23. Furst & West, *Teamsters Set the Stage for Hoffa-Leedham Rematch*, at 1.

24. *Id.*

25. Peter Miller, *11K Flight Attendants Leave Teamsters*, MINNEAPOLIS STAR-TRIBUNE, June 19, 2003.

26. Furst & West, *Teamsters Set the Stage for Hoffa-Leedham Rematch*, at 10.

27. *Id.*

28. Richard A. Ryan, *Hoffa Wants Freedom from Controls: Teamsters President Says Union Is Cleanest of Any and Deserves to Be Independent*, DETROIT NEWS, Mar. 29, 2000.

29. James B. Jacobs & Ryan P. Alford, *The Teamsters' Rocky Road to Recovery: The Demise of Project RISE*, 9 TRENDS IN ORGANIZED CRIME 15 (2005).

30. Resolution on Project RISE, 2001 IBT Convention.

31. Self-Governance Resolution, 2001 IBT Convention.

32. Delegate vote at IBT convention.

33. TDU, *Fighting for Change at Teamster Conventions Past and Present*, http://www.tdu.org/node/175; TDU, *Hoffa Targets Local 624 for Trusteeship*, http://www.tdu.org/node/2068.

34. Alison Grant, *It's Leedham vs. Hoffa Again for Teamster Head*, CLEV. PLAIN DEALER, July 1, 2006, at 1C.

35. Furst & West, *Teamsters Set the Stage for Hoffa-Leedham Rematch*, at 11.

36. John D. Schulz, *Debating Time*, TRAFFIC WORLD, Aug. 20, 2001, at 11.

37. *United States v. Int'l Bhd. of Teamsters*, 88 Civ. 4486 (DNE) (Election Administrator, Report No. 6, Feb. 2002, at 20).

38. Email correspondence from Ken Paff, June 22, 2010.

39. Rules for the IBT International Union Delegate and Officer Election [hereinafter 2001 Election Rules], Article VII, Sec. 6.

40. Office of the Election Administrator, *In re: Candidate Forums, Protest Decision*, 2001 EAD 428 (Aug. 22, 2001).

41. *Id.*

42. *Id.*

43. *In re Stefan Ostrach and Jack Mandaro*, 2000 EAD 29, PR081603NA, PR082301AT, PR082501AT, and PR03102WE (Oct. 2, 2000). The Hoffagrams were entitled "Hoffa Unity Slate Petition Drive Enters Final Stage," "Hoffa Slate Campaign Wins Major Victory in Petition Challenge," and "Hoffa Unity Slate Close to Signature Goal."

44. *Id.*

45. Decision, 00 Elec. App. 007 (Oct. 2000)

46. *In re Kris Taylor & Hoffa Unity Slate*, 2000 EAD 75 (Dec. 29, 2000).

47. *Id.* (quoting 2001 Election Rules, Article XI, Section 2(e)).

48. *Id.*

49. *Id.*

50. *United States v. Int'l Bhd. of Teamsters*, 968 F.2d 1506, 1509, 1511–12 (2d Cir. 1992).

51. *In re Tom Leedham Slate and Hoffa Unity Slate*, 01 Elec. App. 082 (Sept. 25, 2001).

52. *Id.*

53. *Id.*

54. *In re Ashley McNeely*, 2001 EAD 485, PR092811MW (Oct. 2, 2001).

55. *Id.*

56. *Id.*

57. *In re Eric Jensen*, 2001 EAD 479, PR092111MW and PR092511MW (Sept. 28, 2001).

58. Article VII, Section 11(b) of the 2006 Election Rules provided that an "endorsement of a candidate may be made by a Union officer or employee, but solely in his/her individual capacity." The rules also stated that "an Executive Board of a Local Union as such may not endorse or otherwise advance a candidacy, even if all members agree on the endorsement or candidacy." *In re Eric Jensen*, 2001 EAD 479, PR092111MW and PR092511MW (Sept. 28, 2001).

59. *In re Eric Jensen*, 2001 EAD 479, PR092111MW and PR092511MW (Sept. 28, 2001).

60. *Id.*

61. Teofilo Reyes, *In Low Turnout, Hoffa Reelected Teamster Leader*, LABOR NOTES, Dec. 2001, at 8.

62. TDU, *A Message from Tom Leedham: Thank You for Working to Rebuild Teamster Power*, Dec. 5, 2006, *available at* http://www.tdu.org/node/486.

63. Nancy Cleeland, *Hoffa Leads in Balloting for Head of Teamsters*, LOS ANGELES TIMES, Nov. 16, 2001, at 3.

64. Carl Biers, *After the Teamsters Election*, UNION DEMOCRACY REVIEW, Feb.–Mar. 2002, at 8.

65. Tom Leedham election campaign, *Statement from Tom Leedham on Results of Teamster Election*, press release Nov. 16, 2001.

66. Stier, Anderson & Malone, LLC, *Report and Recommendations: Issues Concerning Chicago Organized Crime Infiltration of Teamster Entities and Attempts to Undermine IBT Anti-racketeering Reforms*, Apr. 2004 [hereinafter *Report and Recommendations*], at 16.

67. *See generally* Robert Bruno, *Reforming the Chicago Teamsters: The Story of Local 705*, DeKalb: Northern Illinois University Press, 2003.

68. *Report and Recommendations*, at 8–9.

69. *Id.* at 3–4.

70. *Id.*

71. *Id.*

72. Letter from Pat Szymanski to Edwin Stier, Apr. 16, 2004 (obtained from TDU; on file with author).

73. *Id.*

74. Carl Horowitz, *Former Ethics Watchdog Points Finger at Hoffa*, National Legal and Policy Center, May 10, 2004, *available at* http://www.nlpc.org/stories/2004/05/10/former-ethics-watchdog-points-finger-hoffa.

75. Resignation letter of Edwin Stier to Jim Hoffa, Apr. 28, 2004.

76. Steven Greenhouse, *Citing Pullback, Antigraft Team Quits Teamsters*, NEW YORK TIMES, Apr. 30, 2004, *available at* http://www.nytimes.com/2004/04/30/us/citing-pullback-antigraft-team-quits-teamsters.html?pagewanted=2.

77. *Rise Director Abandons Anti-corruption Program*, TEAMSTER MAGAZINE, July–Aug. 2004; Greenhouse, *Citing Pullback, Antigraft Team Quits Teamsters*.

78. Greenhouse, *Citing Pullback, Antigraft Team Quits Teamsters*.

79. Hoffa statement, 2004.

80. *See generally* Edward McDonald's report.

81. Edwin Stier & James Kossler, *Statement in Response to Release of IBT Report*, press release, July 2005.

82. Kelly Kennedy, *Teamsters Report Finds No Mob Influence: Findings Are Disputed by Ex-U.S. Prosecutor*, CHICAGO TRIBUNE, July 14, 2005, *available at* http://www.thelaborers.net/teamsters/teamsters_report_finds_no_mob_in.htm.

83. *United States v. Int'l Bhd. of Teamsters*, 88 Civ. 4486, Memorandum and Order, Application 113: Carlow Scalf, July 8, 2005.

84. *In re Joseph L. Bernstein*, Opinion and Decision of the Independent Review Board, Oct. 11, 2005.

85. *In re 988 Officers Chuck Crawley, Dennis Bankhead and Member Marie Espinosa*, Opinion and Decision of the Independent Review Board, Sept. 9, 2004.

86. *Id.*

87. U.S. Attorney's Office, Southern District of Texas, *Former Teamster's President Sentenced to Prison for Election Fraud and Union Embezzlement for Taking Kickbacks*, press release, May 25, 2007, *available at* http://www.justice.gov/usao/txs/releases/May2007/070525-Crawley.htm.

88. Michael Nelson, *Cleveland Local in Trusteeship: Boss Accused of Unauthorized Salary Increases*, National Legal and Policy Center, Feb. 18, 2002, http://www.nlpc.org/stories/2002/02/18/cleveland-local-trusteeship-boss-accused-unauthorized-salary-increases.

89. *Id.*

90. Nora Koch, *New Jersey Teamsters Local Placed in Trusteeship*, PHILADELPHIA INQUIRER, Oct. 1, 2002.

91. *Id.*

92. Timothy O'Connor, *Teamsters Local 456 to Remain under Union Control*, JOURNAL NEWS, June 6, 2003, *available at* http://www.teamster.net/topic/9527-teamsters-local-456-to-remain-under-union-control/.

93. *Id.*

94. *Id.*

95. *Time to End the Consent Decree in the Teamsters Union?* UNION DEMOCRACY

REVIEW, Sept.–Oct. 2003, *available at* http://www.uniondemocracy.com/UDR/49 -can%20IBT%20police%20itself.htm.

96. *United States v. Int'l Bhd. of Teamsters*, 88 Civ. 4486, Independent Review Board's Report for the Period 2001–2006 to Honorable Loretta A. Preska, Aug. 9, 2006.

97. Center for Responsive Politics, *Reelection Rates over the Years*, http://www .opensecrets.org/bigpicture/reelect.php.

98. Joe Allen & Donny Schraffenberger, *How Did Hoffa Jr. Win Again?* SOCIALISTWORKER.ORG, Nov. 30, 2001, http://socialistworker.org/2001/385/385_11_ TeamsterReform.shtml.

99. Henry Phillips, *The Year One of Hoffa Junior*, SOLIDARITY, May–June 2000, http://www.solidarity-us.org/current/node/944.

100. *United States v. Int'l Bhd. of Teamsters*, 88 Civ. 4486 (DNE) (Election Administrator, Report No. 6, Feb. 2002), at 28.

101. *Id.* at 21.

102. *International Union Files False Financial Report*, CONVOY DISPATCH (n.d.).

103. Carl Biers, lecture at NYU School of Law, Nov. 24, 2003 (discussing Stier's angry reaction when asked at a Cornell University event about TDU criticism of Project RISE); *see also* Carl Biers, *The RISE Program: Trying to Discuss the Future of Teamster Reform at a Cornell University Forum*, 150 UNION DEMOCRACY REVIEW 1.

104. Josh Margolin, *No Apologies for Quitting Teamsters Mob Probe: Former Federal Prosecutor Says Hoffa's Son Changed His Tune*, NEWARK STAR-LEDGER, May 10, 2004.

105. *Id.*

NOTES TO CHAPTER 10

1. TDU, *Fighting for Change at Teamster Conventions Past and Present*, Apr. 20, 2006, http://www.tdu.org/node/175.

2. Hoffa 2006 campaign, *Remember in November*, 5 IBT CONVENTION NEWS, June 30, 2006.

3. Consent Decree, *United States v. Int'l Bhd. of Teamsters*, No. 88 Civ. 4486 (S.D.N.Y.) (Mar. 14, 1989), at 27.

4. The parties agreed that (1) the government would not exercise its right under the consent decree to have DOL supervise the 2006 election and (2) in exchange, the IBT would comply with the election rules.

5. Both the Rail Conference (composed of BLET's 573 locals and BMWE's 635 locals) and the Graphic Communications Conference (composed of the former GCIU's 206 locals) have substantial autonomy over their constituent members' contracts, local leadership, and organizing activities. Pursuant to the merger agreements between each of these former unions and the IBT, members of the Rail and Graphic Communications Conference form their own bylaws, coordinate

their own operations, and elect their own leaders to negotiate contracts, initiate strikes, and manage assets. *See, e.g.,* Merger Agreement between the IBT and BLET ("[R]epresentatives from both unions . . . guarantee to the BLET and its members maximum autonomy within the structure of the IBT.")

6. One 2006 IBT election rule provided that Teamsters from the former BLET, BMWE, or GCIU were eligible to vote for convention-delegate candidates from their new IBT local and for international-office candidates in the general election as long as they had (1) worked for a total of two years in the jurisdiction of the new local and (2) paid dues to and worked or actively sought work in the original and/ or new local for twenty-four consecutive months before the candidate's nomination, "based on a cumulative total of months in the original and the new Local Union." 2006 Election Rules, VI(2)(f). Another election rule provided that Teamsters from the former BLET, BMWE, and GCIU could run for international IBT office in 2006 as long as they were in continuous good standing in the IBT (i.e., paid dues and either worked or actively sought work in the IBT) from January through May of 2006. 2006 Election Rules, VI(1)(d). The merger agreements between the unions prescribed the geographic subunits within the former BLW, BMWE, and GCIU from which the new Teamsters would elect delegates to the 2006 IBT convention. For election purposes, these subunits were treated as IBT locals. Members of the former GCIU elected IBT convention delegates from the "geographic regions" set out in the GCIU-IBT merger agreement; members of the former BLET elected IBT convention delegates from the "general committee of adjustment" as set out in the BLET-IBT merger agreement; and members of the former BMWE elected IBT convention delegates from their System Division or Federation as set out in the BMWE-IBT merger agreement.

7. Richard W. Mark, *Frequently Asked Questions about the Local Union Plan*, June 9, 2005, at 1, *available at* http://www.ibtvote.org/notices_advisories/LUP_FAQ.pdf.

8. *In re Yanko Fuentes and Hoffa 2006*, 2006 ESD 216, No. P-06-270-041906-NE, May 4, 2006, *available at* http://ibtvote.org/protests/2005/2006esd216.htm.

9. Thomas B. Edsall, *Two Top Unions Split from AFL-CIO: Others Are Expected to Follow Teamsters*, WASHINGTON POST, July 26, 2005, *available at* http://www.washingtonpost.com/wp-dyn/content/article/2005/07/25/AR2005072500251.html.

10. IBT, *Statement of James P. Hoffa on the Teamsters' Disaffiliation from the AFL-CIO*, July 24, 2005, http://www.teamster.org/content/statement-james-p-hoffa-teamstersamp8217-disaffiliation-afl-cio.

11. Mark, *Frequently Asked Questions about the Local Union Plan*, at 1.

12. *Members Prepare 2006 Campaign*, CONVOY DISPATCH, July 17, 2006.

13. Tom Leedham campaign materials.

14. Hoffa 2006 campaign, *Mass Hoffa Rally Kicks Off 27th Convention*, 2 IBT CONVENTION NEWS, June 27, 2006.

15. Letter from Tom Leedham to "Convention Delegates Supporting the Leed-

ham Slate": "What to Expect When You Get to the Convention" (on file with author).

16. Hoffa 2006 campaign, *Hoffa Announces Historic Card-Check Agreement with UPS: Delegates Ask Leedham to Quit*, 3 IBT CONVENTION NEWS, June 28, 2006.

17. Chris Kutalik, *Reforming the Teamsters: An Interview with Tom Leedham*, LABOR NOTES, Mar. 2006, at 8.

18. *Id.* UPS promised the IBT that its acquisition of Overnite would not affect Teamsters' jobs. According to TDU, however, UPS then took steps that could jeopardize some Teamster positions. For example, UPS added the label "UPS Freight" to many of Overnite's trucks, suggesting integration of UPS and Overnite operations. TDU, *The Road Ahead Runs through UPS Freight*, Mar. 16, 2006, http://www.tdu.org/node/153. Moreover, in January 2010, TDU reported that Teamsters in Chicago, Kansas City, Minneapolis, Memphis, and other major cities observed UPS freight "moving in and out on nonunion trailers daily." TDU, *A Loophole Big Enough to Drive a Truck Through*, Jan. 15, 2010, http://www.tdu.org/node/3600; *see also* Steven Greenhouse, *Teamsters End 3-Year Strike against Trucker without Contract*, NEW YORK TIMES, Oct. 26, 2002, *available at* http://www.nytimes.com/2002/10/26/us/teamsters-end-3-year-strike-against-trucker-without-contract.html?pagewanted=1.

19. TDU, *Hoffa Caught Using Union Funds for Campaign Poll*, July 27, 2005, http://www.tdu.org/node/82.

20. *Id.*

21. *Id.*; *In re: Certain Campaign Contributions by Officers and Employees of Local Union 78*, 2006 ESD 363 (Oct. 4, 2006).

22. *In re: Certain Campaign Contributions by Officers and Employees of Local Union 78*, 2006 ESD 363.

23. *Id.*

24. *Id.*; 2006 Election Rules, Article XI, § 1(b)(1).

25. *In re: Certain Campaign Contributions by Officers and Employees of Local Union 78*, 2006 ESD 363.

26. *In re T.C. Bundrant*, 2005 ESD 19, P-05-012-090705-SO (Oct. 25, 2005).

27. 05 Elec. App. 004 (Nov. 15 2005). Article VII, Section 11(g) of the 2006 Election Rules stated that "[r]etaliation or threat of retaliation by the International Union, any subordinate body, any member of the IBT, any employer or other person or entity against a Union member, officer or employee for exercising any right guaranteed by this or any other Article of the Rules is prohibited."

28. *In re David Thornsberry*, 2005 ESD 13, P-05-015-092905-MW (Oct. 8, 2005).

29. *Id.* Article VII, Section 11(a) of the 2006 Election Rules provides, "All Union members retain the right to engage in campaign activities. . . . This includes, but is not limited to, the right to distribute campaign literature . . . outside a meeting hall, before, during or after a Union meeting, regardless of Union policy, rule or practice."

30. 2006 Election Rules, Article VII, § 11(a).

31. 05 Elec. App. 003 (Nov. 4, 2005).

32. Barbara Harvey, *Teamster Elections: Inspiration from the Ground Up*, Union Democracy Review, Nov.–Dec. 2006, at 2.

33. Letter from Tom Leedham to "Brothers and Sisters," Nov. 21, 2006.

34. Memorandum from Charles M. Carberry to the Independent Review Board; IRB Actions from January 2005 to the Present, Apr. 1, 2010.

35. *Id.*

36. In the Matter of Robert A. Hogan before the Independent Review Board, Affidavit and Agreement, July 21, 2008.

37. *Id.*

38. *Id.*

39. Report and Recommendations Regarding Charges against Frank Incandella, Oct. 12, 2006.

40. Panel Report and Recommendations Regarding Robert Riley, hearing before a panel appointed by the general president, Apr. 3, 2006.

41. Memorandum from Charles M. Carberry to the Independent Review Board, IRB Actions from January 2005 to the Present, Apr. 1, 2010.

42. Letter from James P. Hoffa to Local 714, June 9, 2008.

43. *Id.*

44. *Id.*

45. TDU, *Still No "Justice" in Philadelphia*, Mar. 19, 2010, http://www.tdu.org/phillynepotism.

46. *United States v. Int'l Bhd. of Teamsters*, Election Agreement, 88 Civ. 4486, Nov. 18, 2009.

47. Office of the Election Supervisor for the International Brotherhood of Teamsters, *Contact Information*, http://ibtvote.org/contact_info.htm.

48. *United States v. Int'l Bhd. of Teamsters*, Election Agreement, 88 Civ. 4486, Nov. 18, 2009; *United States v. Int'l Bhd. of Teamsters*, Election Supervisor's Report #1 to the Court, 88 Civ. 4486, Aug. 16, 2010.

49. Letter from Association for Union Democracy to Chief Judge Loretta Preska, May 10, 2010.

50. 2011 Election Rules, Art. III, § 5(p).

51. Letter from Hoffa-Keegel slate to Hoffa-Keegel supporters, May 25, 2010, *available at* http://tdu.org/files/HoffaKeegelCampaignLetter.pdf.

52. Letter from Fred Gegare to Jim Hoffa, May 25, 2010, *available at* http://tdu.org/files/FredGegareCampaignLetter.pdf.

53. These include incumbent International Vice President Brad Slawson, Jr.; IBT Joint Council 94 (Kentucky, Indiana, West Virginia) President Fred Zuckerman; Decatur, Illinois IBT Local 279 Principal Officer Jerry Connor; Pennsylvania IBT Local 463 Principal Officer Robert Ryder; and Ohio Conference of Teamsters Director Tony Jones.

54. Fred Gegare election website, *Stier Quits: Why Would the Person Hoffa Hired to Fight Mob Corruption Quit in Disgust*, Aug. 7, 2010, http://fredgegare2011 .com/?zone=/unionactive/view_page.cfm&page=Stier20Quits.

55. Letter from Fred Gegare to Jim Hoffa, May 25, 2010.

56. Jane Slaughter, *Interview: Reformer Challenges Hoffa for Teamster Presidency*, LABOR NOTES, Oct. 11, 2010.

57. *Id.*

58. *In re: Fred Gegare (After Remand)*, 2011 ESD 73 (Jan. 20, 2011); *In re: Fred Gegare (After Remand)*, 10 EAM 3 (Feb. 16, 2011).

59. *In re: Fred Gegare (After Remand)*, 2011 ESD 73 (Jan. 20, 2011).

60. *Id.*

61. *Id.*

62. 11 Elec. App. 3 (KC) (April 1, 2011).

63. Seymour Martin Lipset, Martin Trow & James Coleman, *Union Democracy: What Makes Democracy Work in Labor Unions and Other Organizations?* New York: Anchor Books, 1956, at 7.

64. *Id.* at 8. In *New York State Board of Elections v. Lopez Torres*, the U.S. Supreme Court considered whether a state judicial appointment system in which appointments are made by political party delegates elected by party members violates voters' and candidates' First Amendment associational rights. The court ruled that the U.S. Constitution does not provide an individual right "to have a 'fair shot'" at winning" an election. 552 U.S. 196 (2008). Likewise, in *Arizona Free Enterprise Club's Freedom PAC v. Bennet* (July 2011), the U.S. Supreme Court (5–4) explicitly rejected Arizona's effort to "level the playing field" between statwide candidates with differential access to financial support for their political campaigns.

NOTES TO CHAPTER 11

1. David Dubinsky & A. Raskin, *A Life with Labor*, New York: Simon and Schuster, 1977, at 145.

2. Selwyn Raab, *Five Families: The Rise, Decline, and Resurgence of America's Most Powerful Mafia Empires*, New York: Thomas Dunne, 2005, at 564.

3. Nelson Lichtenstein, *Misunderstanding the Anti-union Narrative*, CHRONICLE OF HIGHER EDUCATION, Jan. 17, 2010.

4. William Serrin, *Teamsters Open Convention with Reagan Message*, NEW YORK TIMES, June 2, 1981.

5. Over the years, both the House and the Senate held shorter hearings relating to *U.S. v. IBT*. *See, e.g.*, Senate Committee on Government Affairs, Permanent Subcommittee on Investigations, *The Federal Government's Use of Trusteeships under the RICO Statute: Hearing before the Permanent Subcommittee on Investigations*, 101st Cong., 1st sess., Apr. 4, 6, and 12, 1989; House Committee on Education and the Workforce, Subcommittee on Oversight and Investigations, *The International*

Brotherhood of Teamsters One Year after the Election of James P. Hoffa: Hearing before the Subcommittee on Oversight and Investigations, 106th Cong., 2d sess., Mar. 28, 2000.

6. Gerald E. Lynch, *RICO: The Crime of Being a Criminal, Parts I & II*, 87 COLUM. L. REV. 661 (1987); Gerald E. Lynch, *RICO: The Crime of Being a Criminal, Parts III and IV*, 87 COLUM. L. REV. 920 (1987); G. Robert Blakey, *RICO: The Genesis of an Idea*, 9 TRENDS IN ORGANIZED CRIME 8 (2006); James B. Jacobs, *Mobsters, Unions, and Feds: The Mafia and the American Labor Movement*, New York: NYU Press, 2006 [hereinafter *Mobsters, Unions, and Feds*].

7. *Mobsters, Unions, and Feds*.

8. A civil RICO suit against the International Longshoremen's Association was dismissed and refiled. *See Mobsters, Unions, and Feds*.

9. For example, in 1978, Pennsylvania voters reelected Daniel Flood (D-Pa.) to the House of Representatives even though DOJ had just charged him with taking bribes from businessmen in exchange for getting federal grants or contracts for those businessmen.

10. Seymour M. Lipset, Martin Trow & James Coleman, *Union Democracy: What Makes Democracy Work in Labor Unions and Other Organizations?* New York: Anchor Books, 1956 [hereinafter *Union Democracy*], at 10; Robert Michels, *Political Parties: A Sociological Study of the Oligarchical Tendencies of Modern Democracy*, New York: Hearst's International Library, 1915 (originally published in Germany in 1911).

11. *Union Democracy*, at 1.

12. *Id.* at 6–7.

13. Clyde W. Summers, *Democracy in a One-Party State: Perspectives from Landrum-Griffin*, 43 MD. L. REV. 93 (1984), at 95.

14. *See, e.g.*, Ross Sandler & David Schoenbrod, *Democracy by Decree: What Happens When Courts Run Government*, New Haven: Yale University Press, 2003.

15. *See* James B. Jacobs & Lauryn P. Gouldin, *Cosa Nostra: The Final Chapter?* 25 CRIME & JUST. REV. RES. 129 (1999).

16. James B. Jacobs, Christopher Panarella & Jay Worthington III, *Busting the Mob: United States v. Cosa Nostra*, New York: NYU Press, 1994.

17. *See* Kenneth R. Wallentine, *A Leash upon Labor: RICO Trusteeships on Labor Unions*, 7 HOFSTRA LAB. L.J. 341 (1990); Andrew B. Dean, *An Offer the Teamsters Couldn't Refuse: The 1989 Consent Decree Establishing Federal Oversight and Ending Mechanisms*, 100 COLUM. L. REV. 2157 (2000).

18. Federal Consent Decree Fairness Act, S. 489, 109th Cong. (2005) (never took effect).

19. 129 S.Ct. 2579 (2009).

20. *Id.* at 2594–95.

Bibliography

Abrams, Douglas E. *The Law of Civil RICO*. Boston: Little, Brown, 1991.

Behar, Richard. *A Teamster Tempest*. TIME, May 15, 1995.

———. *The Trouble with the Teflon Teamster: The Feds and the Press Overlooked the Dark Side of Ron Carey*. FORTUNE, Oct. 27, 1997.

Benson, Herman. *Rebels, Reformers, and Racketeers: How Insurgents Transformed the Labor Movement*. New York: 1st Books, 2004.

Biers, Carl. *The RISE Program: Trying to Discuss the Future of Teamster Reform at a Cornell University Forum*. 150 UNION DEMOCRACY REVIEW 1 (2004).

Blakey, G. Robert. *RICO: The Genesis of an Idea*. 9 TRENDS IN ORGANIZED CRIME 8 (2006).

Brandenburg, Bert. *Brown v. Board of Education and Attacks on the Courts: Fifty Years Ago, Fifty Years Later*. 37 WTR BRIEF 66 (2008).

Brandt, Charles. *"I Heard You Paint Houses": Frank "The Irishman" Sheeran and the Inside Story of the Mafia, the Teamsters, and the Last Ride of Jimmy Hoffa*. Hanover, N.H.: Steerforth, 2004.

Brill, Steven. *The Teamsters*. New York: Simon and Schuster, 1978.

Bruno, Robert. *Reforming the Chicago Teamsters: The Story of Local 705*. DeKalb: Northern Illinois University Press, 2003.

Chin, Gabriel J., Roger Hartley, Kevin Bates, Rona Nichols, Ira Shiflett & Salmon Shomade. *Still on the Books: Jim Crow and Segregation Laws Fifty Years after Brown v. Board of Education*. 2006 MICH. ST. L. REV. 457 (2006).

Crowe, Kenneth C. *Collision: How the Rank and File Took Back the Teamsters*. New York: Scribner, 1993.

Dean, Andrew B. *An Offer the Teamsters Couldn't Refuse: The 1989 Consent Decree Establishing Federal Oversight and Ending Mechanisms*. 100 COLUM. L. REV. 2157 (2000).

Dubinsky, David, & A. Raskin. *A Life with Labor*. New York: Simon and Schuster, 1977.

Eidlin, Barry. *Is Teamster "Code of Conduct" Just Window-Dressing? Reformers Criticize Hoffa's Anti-corruption Program*. 254 LABOR NOTES 1 (2000).

Giuliani, Rudolph W. *Freeing the Economy from Organized Crime and Restoring Open, Competitive Markets*. Archives of Rudolph W. Giuliani. Oct. 23, 1997.

Goldberg, Michael J. *Cleaning Labor's House: Institutional Reform Litigation in the Labor Movement.* DUKE L.J. 903 (1989).

———. *Teamster Reformers: Their Union, Their Jobs, Their Movement.* 72 J. TRANSPORTATION LAW LOGISTICS & POLICY 13 (2005).

———. *The Teamsters Board of Monitors: An Experiment in Union Reform Litigation.* 30 LABOR HISTORY 563 (1989).

Goldstock, Ronald, Martin Marcus, Thomas D. Thacher II & James B. Jacobs. *Corruption and Racketeering in the New York City Construction Industry: Final Report to Governor Mario M. Cuomo from the New York State Organized Crime Task Force.* New York: NYU Press, 1990.

Green, Bruce A. & Fred Zacharias. *The U.S. Attorneys Scandal and the Allocation of Prosecutorial Power.* 69 OHIO ST. L.J. 187 (2008).

Holland, Michael. *The Cookbook: How the Election Officer Supervised the 1991 Teamster Election.* July 1992.

Jacobs, James B. *Individual Rights and Institutional Authority: Prisons, Mental Hospitals, Schools, and Military: Cases and Materials.* Indianapolis: Bobbs-Merrill, 1979.

———. *Mobsters, Unions, and Feds: The Mafia and the American Labor Movement.* New York: NYU Press, 2006.

Jacobs, James B. & Ryan P. Alford. *The Teamsters' Rocky Road to Recovery: The Demise of Project RISE.* 9 TRENDS IN ORGANIZED CRIME 15 (2005).

Jacobs, James B., Eileen Cunningham & Kimberly Friday. *The RICO Trusteeship after 20 Years: A Progress Report.* 19 LABOR LAWYER 419 (2004).

Jacobs, James B., Coleen Friel & Robert Radick. *Gotham Unbound: How New York City Was Liberated from the Grip of Organized Crime.* New York: NYU Press, 1999.

Jacobs, James B. & Lauryn P. Gouldin. *Cosa Nostra: The Final Chapter?* 25 CRIME & JUST. REV. RES. 129 (1999).

Jacobs, James B. & Elizabeth Mullin. *Congress' Role in the Defeat of Organized Crime.* 39 CRIMINAL LAW BULLETIN 1 (2003).

Jacobs, James B., Christopher Panarella & Jay Worthington III. *Busting the Mob: United States v. Cosa Nostra.* New York: NYU Press, 1994.

Jacobs, James B. & Ellen Peters. *Labor Racketeering: The Mafia and the Unions,* in *Crime and Justice: A Review of Research.* Chicago: University of Chicago Press, 2003.

Jacobs, James B. & Dimitri D. Portnoi. *Administrative Criminal Law and Procedure in the Teamsters Union: What Has Been Achieved after (Nearly) Twenty Years.* 28 BERKELEY J. OF EMP. AND LAB. L. 429 (2007).

———. *Combating Organized Crime with Union Democracy: A Case Study of the Electoral Reform in United States v. International Brotherhood of Teamsters.* 42 LOYOLA OF LOS ANGELES L. REV. 335 (2009).

Jacobs, James B. & David Santore. *The Liberation of IBT Local 560.* 37 CRIMINAL LAW BULLETIN 125 (2001).

Joseph, Gregory P. *Civil RICO: A Definitive Guide* (2d ed.). Chicago: ABA, 2000.

Kannar, George. *Making the Teamsters Safe for Democracy.* 102 YALE L.J. 1645 (1993).

Kennedy, Robert F. *The Enemy Within.* New York: Harper and Row, 1960.

Kruse, Kevin M. *The Paradox of Massive Resistance: Political Conformity and Chaos in the Aftermath of Brown v. Board of Education.* 48 ST. LOUIS U. L.J. 1009 (2004).

Kumar, Deepa. *Outside the Box: Corporate Media, Globalization, and the UPS Strike.* Urbana-Champaign: University of Illinois Press, 2008.

La Botz, Dan. *Rank and File Rebellion: Teamsters for a Democratic Union.* New York: Verso, 1990.

Lettow, Renee B. & Akhil R. Amar. *Fifth Amendment First Principles: The Self-Incrimination Clause.* 93 MICH. L. REV. 857 (1995).

Lipset, Seymour M., Martin Trow & James Coleman. *Union Democracy: What Makes Democracy Work in Labor Unions and Other Organizations?* New York: Anchor Books, 1956.

Lynch, Gerald E. *RICO: The Crime of Being a Criminal, Parts I & II.* 87 COLUM. L. REV. 661 (1987).

———. *RICO: The Crime of Being a Criminal, Parts III and IV.* 87 COLUM. L. REV. 920 (1987).

Marine, Frank J. & Patrice M. Mulkern. *Civil RICO: A Manual for Federal Attorneys.* Washington, D.C.: U.S. Department of Justice, 2007.

Martin, Steve J. & Sheldon Ekland-Olson. *Texas Prisons: The Walls Came Tumbling Down.* Austin: Texas Monthly Press, 1987.

Mastro, Randy M. & Steven C. Bennett. *Private Plaintiffs' Use of Equitable Remedies under the RICO Statute: A Means to Reform Corrupted Labor Unions.* 24 U. MICH. J. L. REF. 571 (1991).

McClellan, John. *Crime without Punishment.* New York: Duell, Sloan, and Pearce, 1962.

Michels, Robert. *Political Parties: A Sociological Study of the Oligarchical Tendencies of Modern Democracy.* New York: Hearst's International Library, 1915. Originally published in Germany in 1911.

Moldea, Dan E. *The Hoffa Wars: Teamsters, Rebels, Politicians, and the Mob.* New York: Paddington, 1978.

Neff, James. *Mobbed Up: Jackie Presser's High-Wire Life in the Teamsters, the Mafia, and the FBI.* New York: Atlantic Monthly Press, 1989.

O'Connor, Sandra D. *The Judiciary Act of 1789 and the American Judicial Tradition.* 59 U. OF CINCINNATI L. REV. 1 (1990).

Patterson, Eugene C. *Progress through Political Sacrifice: Southern Politicians' Response to Brown v. Board of Education.* 34 STETSON L. REV. 465 (2005).

Petro, Sylvester. *Power Unlimited: The Corruption of Union Leadership: A Report on the McClellan Committee Hearings.* New York: Ronald, 1959.

Portnoi, Dimitri D. *Resorting to Extraordinary Writs: How the All Writs Act Rises to Fill the Gaps in the Rights of Enemy Combatants.* 83 NYU L. REV. 293 (2008).

President's Commission on Organized Crime. *The Edge: Organized Crime, Business, and Labor Unions.* Washington, D.C.: U.S. Government Printing Office, 1986.

Raab, Selwyn. *Five Families: The Rise, Decline, and Resurgence of America's Most Powerful Mafia Empires.* New York: Thomas Dunne, 2005.

Reppetto, Thomas. *Bringing Down the Mob: The War against the American Mafia.* New York: Holt, 2006.

Rosenberg, Gerald N. *The Hollow Hope: Can Courts Bring about Social Change?* Chicago: University of Chicago Press, 1991.

Roth, Mitchel P. *Organized Crime.* Boston: Allyn & Bacon, 2009.

Rothman, David J. & Sheila M. Rothman. *The Willowbrook Wars: Bringing the Mentally Disabled into the Community.* New Brunswick, N.J.: Transaction, 2005.

Russell, Thaddeus. *Out of the Jungle: Jimmy Hoffa and the Remaking of the American Working Class.* New York: Knopf, 2001.

Russo, Gus. *The Outfit: The Role of Chicago's Underworld in Shaping Modern America.* New York: Bloomsbury, 2001.

———. *Supermob: How Sidney Korshak and His Criminal Associates Became America's Hidden Power Brokers.* New York: Bloomsbury, 2006.

Sandler, Ross & David Schoenbrod. *Democracy by Decree: What Happens When Courts Run Government.* New Haven: Yale University Press, 2003.

Schlanger, Margo. *Civil Rights Injunctions over Time: A Case Study of Jail and Prison Court Orders.* 81 NYU L. REV. 550 (2006).

———. *Inmate Litigation.* 116 HARV. L. REV. 1555 (2003).

Schlanger, Margo & G. Shay. *Preserving the Rule of Law in America's Jails and Prisons: The Case for Amending the Prison Litigation Reform Act.* 1 U. PA. J. CONST. L. 139 (2008).

Schlesinger, Arthur M. *Robert Kennedy and His Times.* Boston: Mariner Books, 1978.

Sheridan, Walter. *The Fall and Rise of Jimmy Hoffa.* New York: Saturday Review Press, 1972.

Sifakis, Carl. *The Mafia Encyclopedia.* New York: Facts on File, 1987.

Sloane, Arther A. *Hoffa.* Cambridge: MIT Press, 1991.

Stier, Anderson & Malone, LLC. *The Teamsters: Perception and Reality: An Investigative Study of Organized Crime Influence in the Union.* Washington, D.C.: International Brotherhood of Teamsters, 2002.

Sturm, Susan. *Resolving the Remedial Dilemma: Strategies of Judicial Intervention in Prisons.* 138 U. PA. L. REV. 805 (1990).

Summers, Clyde W. *Democracy in a One-Party State: Perspectives from Landrum-Griffin.* 43 MD. L. REV. 93, 95 (1984).

Task Force on Organized Crime. *Task Force Report: Organized Crime: Annotations and Consultants' Papers*. Washington, D.C.: U.S. Government Printing Office, 1967.

Theoharis, Athan G., ed. *The FBI: A Comprehensive Reference Guide—From J. Edgar Hoover to the X-Files*. New York: Oryx, 2000.

Toner, Gerald A. *New Ways of Thinking about Old Crimes: Prosecuting Corruption and Organized Criminal Groups Engaged in Labor Management Racketeering*. 16 J. FINANCIAL CRIME 41 (2009).

Velie, Lester. *Desperate Bargain: Why Jimmy Hoffa Had to Die*. New York: Reader's Digest Press, 1977.

Wallentine, Kenneth. *A Leash upon Labor: RICO Trusteeships on Labor Unions*. 7 HOFSTRA LAB. L.J. 341 (1990).

Witwer, David. *Corruption and Reform in the Teamsters Union*. Urbana-Champaign: University of Illinois Press, 2003.

———. *Shadow of the Racketeer: Scandal in Organized Labor*. Urbana-Champaign: University of Illinois Press, 2009.

Index

About the Authors

James B. Jacobs, legal scholar and sociologist, is Warren E. Burger Professor of Law and Director, Center for Research in Crime and Justice, NYU School of Law. Among his books are *Mobsters, Unions, and Feds: Organized Crime and the American Labor Movement*; *Gotham Unbound: How New York City Was Liberated from the Grip of Organized Crime*; *Busting the Mob: United States v. Cosa Nostra*; and *Corruption and Racketeering in the New York City Construction Industry*, all published by NYU Press.

Kerry T. Cooperman is an associate in the Litigation Department of Stroock & Stroock & Lavan LLP in Manhattan and a former fellow in the Center for Research in Crime and Justice, NYU School of Law.